Hacking
Ubuntu®

Dr. Neal Krawetz

BICENTENNIAL
1807
WILEY
2007
BICENTENNIAL

Wiley Publishing, Inc.

To my parents, for systematically crushing my dreams of becoming a cartoonist while encouraging my interest in computers.

Hacking Ubuntu®

Published by
Wiley Publishing, Inc.
10475 Crosspoint Boulevard
Indianapolis, IN 46256
www.wiley.com

Copyright © 2007 by Wiley Publishing, Inc., Indianapolis, Indiana

Published simultaneously in Canada

ISBN: 978-0-4701-0872-7

Manufactured in the United States of America

10 9 8 7 6 5 4 3 2 1

For general information on our other products and services or to obtain technical support, please contact our Customer Care Department within the U.S. at (800) 762-2974, outside the U.S. at (317) 572-3993 or fax (317) 572-4002.

Library of Congress Cataloging-in-Publication Data

Krawetz, Neal.
  Hacking Ubuntu : serious hacks, mods, and customizations / Neal Krawetz.
    p. cm.
  Includes index.
  ISBN 978-0-470-10872-7 (paper/cd-rom)
  1. Linux. 2. Operating systems (Computers) I. Title.
  QA76.76.O63K742 2007
  005.4'32--dc22
                        2007003316

Wiley also publishes its books in a variety of electronic formats. Some content that appears in print may not be available in electronic books.

Credits

Executive Editor
Chris Webb

Development Editors
John Sleeva
Ken Brown

Technical Editor
Bill Hayes

Production Editor
Angela Smith

Copy Editor
Travis Henderson

Editorial Manager
Mary Beth Wakefield

Production Manager
Tim Tate

Compositor
Kate Kaminski, Happenstance Type-O-Rama

Proofreader
Sossity Smith

Indexer
Johnna vanHoose Dinse

**Vice President and
Executive Group Publisher**
Richard Swadley

Vice President and Executive Publisher
Joseph B. Wikert

Anniversary Logo Design
Richard Pacifico

Cover Design
Anthony Bunyan

About the Author

Neal Krawetz holds a Ph.D. in Computer Science from Texas A&M University and a Bachelors degree in Computer and Information Science from the University of California, Santa Cruz. He is a computer security professional with experience in computer forensics, profiling, cryptography and cryptanalysis, artificial intelligence, and software solutions. As a hobby, Neal collects operating systems; he currently runs RedHat, Ubuntu, Mac OS X, OpenBSD, Microsoft Windows, OS/2, Solaris, and HP-UX (with dozens of other operating systems ready to go). He has been a Linux user since 1993 and has enjoyed Ubuntu since 2005 (Hoary Hedgehog). Neal has configured Ubuntu on everything from personal workstations to mission critical servers.

Neal has been active in the security community for more than 15 years and has worked with the open source community for more than 20 years. His work experience spans small startup companies, academic and university environments, and large Fortune 100 corporations. Since 2002, Neal has operated Hacker Factor, a computer security and solutions provider (www.hackerfactor.com). At Hacker Factor, he has developed novel forensic techniques for tracking people online and has identified spammers, phishers, carders, and virus writers. He actively assists many branches of law enforcement.

Contents at a Glance

Acknowledgments xiii
Introduction. xv

Part I: Optimizing Your System 1
Chapter 1: Hacking the Installation 3
Chapter 2: Making Ubuntu Usable 33
Chapter 3: Configuring Devices 65

Part II: Working with Compatibility 103
Chapter 4: Managing Software 105
Chapter 5: Communicating Online. 133
Chapter 6: Collaborating 167

Part III: Improving Performance 203
Chapter 7: Tuning Processes 205
Chapter 8: Multitasking Applications 233
Chapter 9: Getting Graphical with Video Bling 255

Part IV: Securing Your System 287
Chapter 10: Locking Down Ubuntu 289
Chapter 11: Advanced Networking. 315
Chapter 12: Enabling Services 349

Index 379

Contents

Acknowledgments xiii

Introduction xv

Part I: Optimizing Your System

Chapter 1: Hacking the Installation 3

Before You Begin 3
Selecting a Distribution 3
Installing the Server or Workstation 6
    Configuring Dual Boot. 7
    Using the Desktop CD-ROM 8
    Using the Alternate CD-ROM 10
    Using the Server CD-ROM 11
    Changing Options 13
    Installing a Minimal System 13
    Installing Over the Network 14
    Installing on a Mac 15
Using a USB Drive 17
    Formatting a USB Drive 17
    Sharing Files with a USB Drive 18
    Booting from a USB Drive 19
    Kicking Off the Network Install with a USB Drive 21
    Using the Boot Image with Files 22
    Installing a Full File System 23
    Booting Variations 27
Upgrading Ubuntu. 29
    Determining the Version 30
    Upgrading Issues with Ubuntu 30
Summary. 31

Chapter 2: Making Ubuntu Usable 33

Logging in for the First Time 33
    Changing the Startup Music 33
    Changing the Background 36
    Changing the Fonts 37
    Tuning the Shell 41

Using Ubuntu on a PC 44
    Trapping Ctrl+Alt+Delete 44
    Disabling Ctrl+Alt+Delete 45
Tuning Ubuntu on a Macintosh 46
    Using a One-Button Mouse in a Three-Button World 46
    Missing Keys and Functionality. 47
    Changing Keyboard Layouts 49
    Remapping the Command and Alt Keys 50
Tweaking GDM 51
    Adding a Prompt Button 51
    Adding Panels. 53
    Adding Menus 54
    Selecting Themes and Skins 54
Navigating Nautilus 56
    Embracing Emblems 57
    Stretching Icons. 59
    Adjusting Fonts 60
    Tuning Templates 61
    Scripting Menus. 61
Summary. 64

Chapter 3: Configuring Devices 65
Working with Device Drivers 65
Loading Modules 66
    Viewing Modules 67
    Installing and Removing Modules 67
    Optimizing Modules 69
Starting Software Devices 69
    Using Init.d 70
    Configuring Boot Options with services-admin 71
    Configuring Boot Options with sysv-rc-conf. 71
Enabling Multiple CPUs (SMP) 73
    Disabling SMP 74
    Missing SMP? 75
Adding Printers 76
    Changing Paper Size 76
    Adding a Printer 77
    Sharing Your Printer 78
Adding Drives 81
    Upgrading Drives 81
    Mounting Systems 83
    Using Simple Backups 84
    Configuring a RAID 85
Adding Other Devices. 86
    Using a Serial Mouse 88
    Supporting a Touch Pad 89

Configuring USB Devices 90
Enabling Drawing Tablets 94
Tuning TV Cards 97
Using Digital Cameras, Scanners, and Web Cameras 99
Summary 101

Part II: Working with Compatibility

Chapter 4: Managing Software 105

Understanding Package Repositories 106
Differentiating Distributions 106
Running Synaptic 108
Searching with Synaptic 109
Changing Repositories 109
Installing from a CD-ROM or Directory 110
Managing Updates 111
Living Without Synaptic 112
Modifying Sources 112
Adding CD-ROM Repositories 115
Browsing the APT Cache 116
Organizing Search Results 116
Installing with APT 117
Removing Packages with APT 117
Upgrading with APT 120
Installing Common Functions 120
Using EasyUbuntu 120
Debugging EasyUbuntu 122
Installing Common Packages by Hand 124
Installing Multimedia Support 124
Installing Web Support 125
Installing Font Packages 126
Compiling and Developing Software 127
Installing Package Source Code 128
Programming with C 129
Enabling Java 130
Summary 131

Chapter 5: Communicating Online 133

Hacking the Firefox Web Brower 133
Tuning Preferences 133
Fine-Tuning the Firefox Advanced Preferences 138
Managing Profiles 139
Extreme Firefox Tweaks with File Configurations 140
Adding Search Engines 142

Playing with Plug-ins and Extensions. 143
Helping Handlers 144
Opening Remote Browsers 145
Using Other Web Browsers 145
Securing Web Access with SSH 146
Installing the SSH Server 147
Opening Ports 149
Starting a Proxy 149
Testing the SOCKS Server 151
Establishing the Tunnel 151
Changing Ciphers for Speed 153
Managing E-mail with Evolution 153
Configuring an Account. 153
Retrieving E-mail from Gmail 154
Fetching Mail 156
Retrieving E-mail from Yahoo! 158
Retrieving E-mail with FreePOPs. 159
Addressing with LDAP 160
Crashing and Recovering Evolution. 161
Using E-mail with Thunderbird Mail 162
Instant Messaging with Gaim 163
Talking with VoIP 164
Summary 165

Chapter 6: Collaborating **167**
Synchronizing the Clock. 167
Sharing Files 170
Enabling NFS 170
Exchanging Files with SAMBA. 173
Working with Open Office. 176
Using the Word Processor 176
Making Presentations 178
Accessing Spreadsheets 180
Selecting Alternate Office Tools. 180
Collaborating Over the Network. 182
Using the VNC Viewer 184
Sharing Your Desktop 185
Securing VNC Connections. 188
Running Software in Emulators 189
Choosing an Emulator. 189
Understanding Virtual Disks 191
Differences Between VNC and VM. 192
Emulating with VNC 192
Using Qemu (Open Source). 192
Using VMware (Commercial) 196

Using Xen (Open Source) 198
Sharing Files with Emulators 200
Other Collaboration Tools 201
Summary 201

Part III: Improving Performance

Chapter 7: Tuning Processes 205

Learning the Lingo 205
Viewing Running Processes 206
Killing Processes 208
Killing All Processes 211
Identifying Resources 212
Measuring CPU 213
Measuring Disk Space 213
Measuring Disk I/O 214
Measuring Memory Usage 215
Measuring Video Memory 216
Measuring Network Throughput 217
Finding Process Startups 218
Inspecting Boot Scripts 218
Inspecting Device Startups 218
Inspecting Network Services 218
Inspecting Shell Startup Scripts 219
Inspecting Desktop Scripts 220
Inspecting Gnome Applications 221
Inspecting Schedulers: at, cron, and anacron 224
Tuning Kernel Parameters 226
Computing Swap 226
Modifying Shared Memory 227
Changing Per User Settings 228
Speeding Up Boot Time 229
Summary 232

Chapter 8: Multitasking Applications 233

Switching Applications 233
Using the Window List and Window Selector 234
Using Alt+Tab 235
Using Ctrl+Alt+Tab 236
Switching Between Firefox Tabs 236
Tweaking the Workplace Switcher 237
Switching Workspaces with Ctrl+Alt+Arrows 237
Managing Workspaces 237

Customizing Application Windows 238
    Creating X-resources 239
    Using Devil's Pie 240
Buffering Buffers 242
Automating Tasks 245
Tracking Projects 247
    Tracking Time on Projects 247
    Tracking CPU Usage 249
    Tracking Disk Usage and Quotas 250
Summary 254

Chapter 9: Getting Graphical with Video Bling **255**

Tuning Graphics 256
    Changing Screen Resolution (xrandr) 257
    Changing Video Drivers 260
    Enabling OpenGL 260
    Debugging X-Windows 263
    Adjusting with xvidtune 265
    Improving Performance 267
Switching Screensavers 269
    Adding New Screensavers 271
    Animating the Desktop Background 272
Configuring Dual Monitors 274
    Using Two Heads 274
    Using Two Computers and One Desktop 278
    Using Two Computers with Different Desktops 281
Summary 286

Part IV: Securing Your System

Chapter 10: Locking Down Ubuntu **289**

Understanding Ubuntu Security Defaults 289
Hacking with Sudo 292
    Adding Users to Sudo 293
    Tweaking other Sudo Options 294
    Becoming Root 295
Using Gnu Privacy Guard (GPG) 296
    Creating Keys 296
    Searching Keys 299
    Transferring Keys 299
    Defining Trust 300
    Encrypting Files 302
    Signing Data 303
    Integrating with e-mail 304

Encrypting File Systems 305
Installing and Configuring EncFS 305
Maintaining EncFS 307
Using EncFS 307
Knowing EncFS Limitations 309
Managing Logs and Caches 309
Clearing Temporary Files 309
Erasing Web Caches 311
Cleaning APT Cache 311
Rotating Logs 312
Summary 313

Chapter 11: Advanced Networking **315**
Configuring Network Devices 315
Configuring Wireless Networks 318
Looking for Drivers 318
Using ndiswrapper 319
Hacking with Wireless Tools 322
Enabling Wireless Security with WEP 324
Enabling Wireless Security with WPA 325
Securing the Network 326
Configuring Firewalls with Tcpwrappers 326
Configuring Firewalls with IP Tables 328
Enabling IPsec 332
Creating IPsec Keys 333
Enabling Proxies 338
Using the General System Proxy 338
Enabling Application-Specific Proxy Configurations 339
Enabling SOCKS Clients 341
Anonymizing with Tor 342
Debugging the Network 343
Using EtherApe 343
Using Ethereal 344
Using Snort and Tcpdump 346
Summary 347

Chapter 12: Enabling Services **349**
Understanding the Ubuntu Default Services 349
Using netstat 350
Running nmap 352
Recognizing Network Threats 354
Mitigating Risks Before Going Public 356
Monitoring Attacks 357
What Should You Look For? 357
What Now? After a Compromise... 357

Logging Logins 358
Enabling Intrusion Detection Systems 359
Running Services 361
Hardening SSH 361
Enabling FTP 365
Enabling Postfix 369
Enabling Apache. 372
Summary 377

Index 379

Acknowledgments

Wow, what a rush. I never would have thought that I could complete an entire book in less than five months. Between this book and my other commitments, I have had virtually no free time for friends and family. I sincerely thank them for standing by me and giving me words of encouragement (in between playful insults).

This book is intended for power users. However, I am only one type of power user: I usually turn off all the glitz and flash in lieu of speed and robustness. Fortunately, my friends are other power users: they love graphics, flash, bang, wow, and cutting edge. They provided a wealth of information that really helped cover all types of advanced Linux and Ubuntu needs. Many enlightening discussions were incorporated into parts of this text. To all of these people, I offer my sincerest thanks: Ragavan Srinivasan, Erik Lillestolen, LaMont Jones, Jer/ Eberhard, Paul Whyman, Mark Rasch, Valdis Kletnieks, Paul Ferguson, April Lorenzen, Marc Sachs and his band of Internet Storm Center handlers, the Department of Defense's Cyber Crime Center, and all of the folks who put together the Blackhat Briefings security conference. I must also thank my father, Howard Krawetz, for all of the hardware he sent my way, including the various graphic cards and network interfaces. And my mother, Sharon Krawetz, for her words of encouragement: "Why are you writing another book?"

Although I have done my best to make this book as complete, accurate, and understandable as possible, I must offer my gratitude to the people who have reviewed, tested, and helped enhance this manuscript: Bill Hayes for his thoroughness and ideas, and Michelle Mach for, well, *everything*. Their patience, feedback, and helpful comments have been an invaluable asset. Any errors in this book are strictly my own, but without them, there would be many more errors. I thank Chris Webb, John Sleeva, Ken Brown, and the staff at Wiley Publishing for this opportunity. And most importantly, I thank Neil Salkind and StudioB for infecting me with their Can-Do attitude.

Finally, nobody can use Linux without using software created by literally thousands of developers. I offer my deepest respect and thanks to the entire open source community, and to Mark Shuttleworth and Canonical Ltd. for packaging up the best of the best into one distribution: Ubuntu.

Introduction

I started seriously using Linux in 1995. Back then, Slackware 3.0 was the popular distribution, but RedHat 2.1 and Debian 1.0 were gaining a following. Ah, the good old days of the 1.2.13 kernel...

Over the last decade, I have used Linux on all types of systems and platforms—from personal computers to mission-critical servers, and from Intel's 386 to PowerPC, SGI, and Sun platforms. I view the operating system as a tool, and the right job needs the right tool. Ten years ago, the flexible Linux system filled a niche that Microsoft, Sun, and other proprietary operating systems could not fill. It had all the power and programming hooks that a developer could want, but was seriously lacking in usability and support. Custom device drivers did not exist unless you built them, and compatibility with Microsoft Windows was limited to FTP and the web.

Today, the kernel is up to version 2.6 and Ubuntu is one of the fastest growing Linux distributions available. Ubuntu combines all the desirable features—usability, security, and support—in one distribution.

This book focuses on the Dapper Drake 6.06 LTS version of Ubuntu. Although other versions of Ubuntu have an 18-month support life, Dapper is intended to have up to five years of support from its corporate sponsor, Canonical Ltd.

Note

LTS stands for Long Term Support.

Living Dangerously

The hacks that I include in this book are the ones that I have found to be the easiest to implement (even if it is a complicated hack), the simplest to maintain, and the most stable of the available options. Having said that, however, any changes you make to your operating system could result in completely screwing up the system. Unless you enjoy reinstalling the operating system or spending hours trying to undo a mistake, I strongly recommend the following precautions:

- **Make a backup!** Before editing any files or making system changes, be sure to save everything that you cannot afford to lose. Although most hacks are easy to remove, others—like upgrading the operating system—have a point of no return.

Tip See Chapter 3 for a simple system backup script.

- **Save system files!** Before you edit any system file, make a local copy of it. For example, before editing /etc/ssh/ssh_config, save a copy of the original (sudo cp /etc/ssh/ssh_config /etc/ssh/ssh_config.bak). This way, you can put back the original file quickly in case you screw something up. I also recommend commenting out undesirable configuration options rather than deleting. (It's easier to uncomment a line to restore functionality than it is to remember what it looked like before you deleted it.)

- **Don't play on mission critical systems!** If you cannot afford to have downtime, then you should not be trying new tricks on the system. Instead, tinker on a test system, make sure it works, and then apply known-stable changes to your more serious systems.

Who This Book Is For

This book is written for the power user. Power users want the most out of their system: the most speed, the most glitz, the most sounds, or the most security. This book shows how to do just that.

Although you don't have to be a programmer to get the most out of this book, you should be familiar with Linux and how to edit files. In particular, knowing how to download, install, and use the basic operating system is a must. You should be familiar enough with the Linux bash shell to create and traverse directories, search for applications, read man pages, and edit system files using whatever editor you are most familiar with. You should be familiar with commands like grep, find, and sudo.

Under Linux and Ubuntu, there are many ways to get the same results and many competing applications. There is rarely only one solution. Yet, some applications can trigger emotional responses. For example, debating the best editor (vi versus emacs) or the best desktop (e.g., Gnome, KDE, or Xfce) can quickly turn into religious wars. Although the examples in this book may use one type of editor or desktop, tasks can usually be accomplished just as easily with some other application.

Warning This is *not* an introductory book on Ubuntu. Most bookstores have a shelf dedicated to introductory books on Linux—most should be good for beginners. This book is for intermediate and advanced users. It contains hacks, tips, and techniques for power users.

This book does not completely encompass all the things you can do with Ubuntu. For most of the applications covered, there are dozens of alternate tools. And even the tools covered contain additional options and settings for doing more things than described here. The goal of this book is to show you some of the tricks, hacks, and tweaks that you can do with the system so you can better customize it to your needs. I fully expect people to build on and extend these hacks.

How This Book Is Organized

Different power users have different needs. This book is divided into four parts, depending on the type of power user.

- **Part I: Optimizing Your System**—The first part of this book focuses on usability. Chapter 1 covers the different options for installing Ubuntu. The decisions made during the installation will dramatically impact how the system functions. Chapter 2 addresses the user interface and desktop. Although the default user interface is pleasant, it can be customized into an awesome interface. Chapter 3 focuses on devices and peripherals, including installation and configuration.

- **Part II: Working with Compatibility**—In today's networked world, few people work in isolation. Part II focuses on compatibility with other systems. Chapter 4 discusses software management and how to install files for interoperability. Chapter 5 looks at networking tools like email, instant messaging, and the web. Chapter 6 covers collaboration with non-Linux systems.

- **Part III: Improving Performance**—Whereas Part I focuses on usability and Part II discusses compatibility, Part III looks at efficiency. Chapter 7 focuses on tuning the operating system's performance. Chapter 8 shows different ways to navigate the desktop, manage windows, and multitask between applications. Chapter 9 covers performance for video and graphics systems, including how to use multiple monitors to extend your desktop.

- **Part IV: Securing Your System**—It's all fun and games until someone's system gets compromised. This section shows tricks to check for vulnerabilities and prevent undesirable access. Chapter 10 provides different approaches to lock down the system and protecting your files. Chapter 11 looks at advanced networking options such as proxies and wireless networking. Chapter 12 discusses tricks for safely opening up the system with external network services.

Conventions Used in This Book

In this book, you will find occasional notes, tips, and warnings. These are used to highlight subtle issues.

Notes point out minor items related to the topic.

Tips provide small, helpful hints to make hacks work better.

Warnings alert you to possible hazards that can result from the hacks.

A `courier font` is used to indicate commands and executables, and bold text indicates interactive responses.

What You Need To Use This Book

To use this book, you will need:

- A computer for running Ubuntu's Dapper Drake. This book primarily focuses on the PC (i386) platform, but includes sections for the Macintosh (PowerPC) platform. Although the AMD64 and Sparc platforms are not explicitly discussed, most of the hacks will work on these, too.
  - For the Desktop installation, you will need at least 256 Megabytes of RAM and 3 Gigabytes of disk space.
  - For the Server installation, you will need at least 64 Megabytes of RAM and 500 Megabytes of disk space.
- Internet access for downloading ISO images and additional software packages from the online Ubuntu repositories. You will also need Internet access for the chapters that cover network services.
- For Chapter 1 (Hacking the Installation), you will need a CD-ROM burner and blank CD-R or CD-RW media. For playing with USB media, you should have one or more USB thumb drives or a USB hard drive.
- Chapter 3 (Configuring Devices) and Chapter 9 (Getting Graphical with Video Bling) cover a variety of peripherals. You will need the peripherals in order to do the hacks. For example, you cannot do a printer hack without a printer and you cannot expand your desktop across monitors if you only have one monitor.
- Chapter 6 (Collaborating) is best done with access to other operating systems. A computer running Microsoft Windows NT, 2000, XP, or ME is a good option. However, other operating systems are also acceptable. These computers should be located on the same network and have network connectivity.

What's on the Companion Website

For links and updates, please visit this book's companion website at `http://www.wiley.com/go/extremetech`.

Optimizing Your System

in this part

Chapter 1
Hacking the Installation

Chapter 2
Making Ubuntu Usable

Chapter 3
Configuring Devices

Hacking the Installation

This chapter explores options for installing and configuring devices. Where you choose to install Ubuntu, which variation you install, and what options you select will impact the system usability.

Before You Begin

Before you install the operating system, be sure to create a backup of anything you want to keep. Copy all data off of the system. You can save it to a CD-ROM, copy it to a spare computer, or physically change hard drives—the method does not matter. Do not keep sensitive data on the same system, even if it is kept on a different hard drive or in a separate partition. If you accidentally format or repartition a working hard drive that contains data you wanted to keep, then the data will be gone.

 Warning This chapter deals with drive partitioning, formatting, and installing operating systems. If you play with a working system, there is a serious risk of accidentally deleting your working configuration.

Drive device identifiers can be confusing—the label /dev/sda1 looks a lot like /dev/sda2 and /dev/hda1. Before every partition, format, and copy, be sure to *triple-check* the device identifier! When you make a mistake, there will be no going back.

Selecting a Distribution

Ubuntu is a Linux distribution based on Debian Linux. Different Linux distributions target different functional niches. The goal of Ubuntu is to bring Linux into the desktop workspace. To do this, it needs to provide a stable user interface, plenty of office tools, drivers for a myriad of peripherals, and still be user-friendly. Although different groups manage nearly every open source project, Canonical Ltd. provides a central point for development and support. Canonical, along with the Ubuntu community, can answer most of your technical (and not so technical) questions.

in this chapter

☑ Before you begin

☑ Selecting a distribution

☑ Installing the server or workstation

☑ Using a USB drive

☑ Upgrading Ubuntu

Which Distribution Is Right for You?

Different Linux distributions fill specific needs. For example, although RedHat started life as a unifying distribution, it primarily supported English applications. SuSE was a popular internationalized distribution. Many distributions were maintained by modifying other distributions. For example, Kheops is a French version of RedHat, and the Beowulf clustered computing environment is based on RedHat.

Although RedHat has seeded many different distributions, it is not alone. Debian Linux is another distribution with a significant following. As with RedHat, Debian has been used to spawn many different niche distributions. Although Ubuntu is based on Debian, it is also seeding other distributions.

Different distributions of the Linux operating system are sometimes called *flavors*. There are over 370 different supported flavors of Linux, each with a different focus. You can see the listing of official distributions at `www.linux.org`.

Ubuntu is the basis for a variety of Linux distributions—most only differ in the user interface, although some do include specific software configurations. The basic Ubuntu distribution uses the Gnome desktop and is geared toward desktop or server systems. Other distributions based on Ubuntu include:

- **Kubuntu**—a variation of Ubuntu with the K Desktop Environment (KDE).
- **Xubuntu**—a variation of Ubuntu with the Xfce Desktop Environment.
- **Edubuntu**—a modified version of Ubuntu that is loaded with educational applications.
- **nUbuntu**—a modified version of Ubuntu with a security-testing focus.

In all cases, it is possible to switch from one installed version to another. For example, you can install Ubuntu, add in KDE, and remove Gnome and you'll have an environment that looks like Kubuntu. To convert an Ubuntu installation to Kubuntu requires changing the desktop, office applications (OpenOffice to KOffice), and swapping other tools. Instead of modifying one distribution to look like another, you should just start with the right distribution.

Note Changing desktop environments is just the beginning. You will need to replace every Gnome application with its KDE equivalent.

To give you an example of the complexity, here's how to change from Gnome to KDE:

1. Install KDE.

```
sudo apt-get install kubuntu-desktop kde-core
```

This requires about 360 MB of disk space. The installation will ask if you want Gnome (gdm) or KDE (kdm) as the default desktop.

2. Log out. This gets you out of the active Gnome desktop.

3. On the login page, click Options (bottom left corner).

4. Select the Sessions menu item.

5. Select KDE from the Sessions menu and use Change Session to accept it (see Figure 1-1).

6. Log in using KDE.

7. If you no longer need Gnome, you have the option to remove it by removing every Gnome package on the system.

```
dpkg --get-selections '*gnome*' | awk '{print $1}' | \
    xargs sudo apt-get remove
```

Tip Many Gnome applications only need the Gnome libraries to run. If you keep both desktops on the same system, then you can use many of the applications under the same desktop.

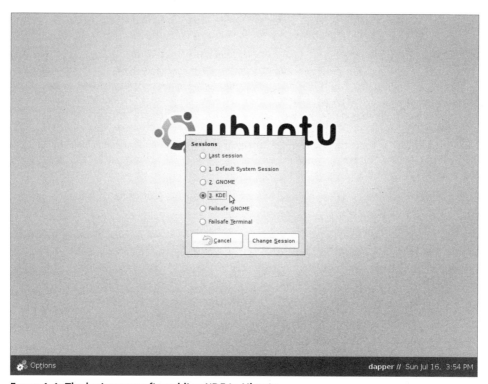

FIGURE 1-1: The login menu after adding KDE to Ubuntu

Installing the Server or Workstation

All Ubuntu versions are designed to require only one CD-ROM for installing the system. This reduces the need for swapping disks during the installation. Unfortunately, one CD-ROM cannot hold everything needed for a complete environment. To resolve this issue, Dapper Drake 6.06 LTS has three different types of initial install CD-ROMs that address different system needs.

- **Desktop**—The Desktop ISO-9660 (ISO) image provides a Live CD. This can be used to test-drive the operating system or install a desktop or workstation system. The installation includes the Gnome graphical environment and user-oriented tools, including office applications, multimedia players, and games.

- **Alternate**—Similar to the Desktop image, this image installs the desktop version of Ubuntu, but it does not use a graphical installer. This is a very desirable option when the graphics or mouse does not work correctly in the Desktop CD-ROM. This ISO is intended for use when there are additional configuration steps required beyond the default install.

- **Server**—This minimal install image has no graphical desktop. It is ideal for servers and headless (without monitor) systems. The ISO image includes server software such as a Secure Shell server, web server, and mail server, but none are installed by default (see Chapter 12).

Note The names for the CD-ROMs do not exactly match the functionality. The names were chosen to avoid confusion with previous Ubuntu releases. (If they called the Desktop CD-ROM *Install*, people might not realize it was also a live CD.) Better names might be Live CD with Desktop Install OEM and Text Desktops, and Server and Minimal System Configuration. But then again, these are pretty long names, so we'll stick with Desktop, Alternate, and Server.

In addition to these three CD-ROM images, an Ubuntu DVD image is available. The DVD ISO contains everything found on all three of the CD-ROM images, including the Live operating system.

The different CD-ROMs are used to install different types of systems. Table 1-1 lists the different options available.

Table 1-1   CD-ROM Options for Ubuntu Dapper Drake 6.06 LTS

Desktop CD-ROM	
Start or install Ubuntu	Start the Live CD and allow graphical install.
Start Ubuntu in safe graphics mode	Start the Live CD with a more standardized graphics setting.
Check CD for defects	Analyze the CD-ROM image to ensure it was created correctly.
Memory test	Test the system's RAM.
Boot from first hard disk	Allows booting the system from the hard drive.

Table 1-1 *Continued*

Alternate CD-ROM

Install in text mode	Perform a text mode installation and the installed system does not use the GUI.
Install in OEM mode	Text mode installation with the user account *oem* and includes the *GUI*.
Install a server	Minimal installation.
Check CD for defects	Analyze the CD-ROM image to ensure it was created correctly.
Rescue a broken system	Mounts the system and creates a command shell.
Memory test	Test the system's RAM.
Boot from first hard disk	Allows booting the system from the hard drive.

Server CD-ROM

Install to the hard drive	Install a minimal configuration.
Install a LAMP server	Install a server with Linux, Apache, MySQL, PHP, Perl, and Python.
Rescue a broken system	Mounts the system and creates a command shell.
Memory test	Test the system's RAM.
Boot from first-hard disk	Allows booting the system from the hard drive.

Configuring Dual Boot

Dual-boot systems were very popular during the late 1990s and early 2000. Since different operating systems are incompatible, users would boot into the appropriate system to run native applications. Today, dual-boot systems are not as common. Computers are relatively inexpensive so it is easier to have separate Windows and Linux computers, and many options exist for exchanging files and data between systems (see Chapter 6). In addition, virtual machines such as VMware, Qemu, and Xen enable you to run native applications within a window, so there is rarely a need to dual-boot.

Some users still have a need for a dual-boot system. Many games, for example, are more responsive under the native operating system and outside of a virtual machine. If you need a dual-boot system, there are a few configuration steps:

1. Partition the disk for multiple operating systems. The easiest way is to just create one partition that does not use the entire disk. If you have multiple disks, then each disk can contain a different operating system.

2. If you will be using a Windows system, install it on the allocated partition. (You can use the Windows partitioner to create the first partition.) Be sure to install Windows *first* since Windows has a bad habit of disabling boot loaders during its installation.

3. After you have installed the first operating system, use any of the Ubuntu install methods to install Ubuntu.

- Do *not* select the entire disk for installation (unless you are installing on a separate drive).

- Use the partitioner to create a new partition for Ubuntu—do not modify the existing partition.

The Ubuntu installer is smart enough to identify other operating systems and add them to the boot menu for dual-booting. This enables you to easily dual-boot between Ubuntu, Windows, BSD, and other operating systems. On PowerPC systems, you can dual-boot between Ubuntu and Mac OS 9 or Mac OS X without a problem.

 Tip   Configuring a dual-boot system is relatively easy. However, configuring a multi-boot computer with three or more operating systems can add complexity to the boot menu. I recommend installing Ubuntu last, since its boot manager installation will automatically detect other operating systems and label them properly.

Using the Desktop CD-ROM

The Desktop CD-ROM installation in Dapper Drake is different than previous versions of Ubuntu. By default, the installer starts a graphical, Live CD (see Figure 1-2). This can be used for system recovery, debugging, or browsing the Web.

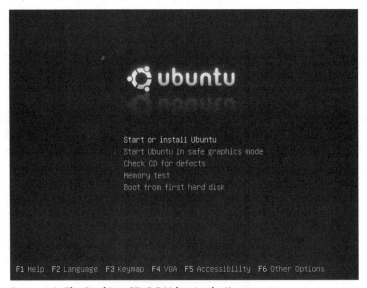

FIGURE 1-2: The Desktop CD-ROM boot selection menu

Note The Desktop CD-ROM boot selection gives you 30 seconds to make a decision before it boots the graphical Live CD. If you want to select a different option, be sure to watch it boot (don't walk away) and make a menu selection. Pressing any key while on the menu will stop the 30-second timer.

When the CD-ROM boots, you will see a graphical desktop. On the desktop is an Install icon that can be used for installing the file system (see Figure 1-3). The same option exists on the menu under System ➪ Administration ➪ Install.

FIGURE 1-3: The Desktop CD-ROM and install options

If something goes wrong during the installation, you only have a few options for debugging the problem. After the graphical desktop appears, you can press Ctrl+Alt+F1 through Ctrl+Alt+F4 to provide command line prompts. Ctrl+Alt+F7 returns to the graphical display. Otherwise, you may want to consider using the Alternate CD-ROM image for installation.

Note Pressing Ctrl+Alt with F1 through F4 keys takes you out of the graphical desktop. Once out of the graphical mode, you don't need to use Ctrl. Simply pressing Alt+F1 through Alt+F8 will switch between terminals. This is because Alt+F1 through Alt+F12 are keyboard signals used by the desktop; Ctrl with Alt is used to distinguish between desktop and console requests.

The Need for Speed

The Desktop installation CD-ROM provides a Live CD for exploring the operating system without performing an installation. It can also be used to access an existing system and perform repairs or recovery. However, the Live CD is not the fastest of systems. On a fast computer (for example, 2 GHz with a 40x CD-ROM drive) it can still take three minutes to go from boot to Live CD desktop. This can seem like an eternity if you just need to fix one text file on a critical server.

If you require a Live CD for system repairs, or for using Linux without a hard drive, consider an alternative system. Knoppix, Gnoppix, and DSL (Damn Small Linux) are designed for speed. Each is built for a fast start time when booting from a single CD-ROM.

Sometimes graphics are not even a concern. If you just need a command prompt to repair a system, consider the Ubuntu Server or Alternate CD-ROM images. Both contain a repair option that will allow you to access the local system and make quick fixes. And if you really need a prompt fast, select any of the installation options on the Server or Alternate images and press Alt+F2. This will give you a prompt where you can mount the hard drive and perform repairs quickly.

Using the Alternate CD-ROM

The Alternate CD-ROM image enables you to install a desktop image with graphics disabled, or an OEM-configurable system (see Figure 1-4). It also allows for a server install and can be used to upgrade systems that lack network access.

Text Mode Install

The text mode install and OEM installation both create user workstations, but they have very different configurations. The text mode system lacks the graphical installer, but everything else is present. This is ideal for computers with limited resources or low RAM.

OEM Installation

The OEM installation mode creates the graphical desktop, but creates the user account oem with the password oem. This account can be used to customize the system. After the install, you can run the `oem-config` script if you need to change any of the original installation responses, or `oem-config-prepare` to remove the temporary oem account and enable configuration prompting during the next boot (for end-user configuration). This is an ideal choice for installers who know that they will be customizing the system and removing the installation account before the system is passed to someone else.

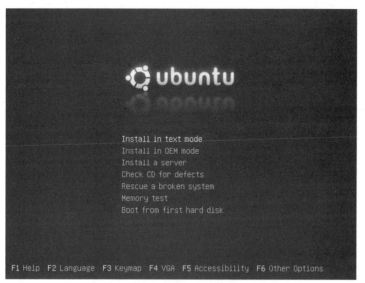

FIGURE 1-4: The Alternate CD-ROM boot selection menu

Warning During the OEM installation, the Alternate CD-ROM prompts for a password but not a user name. It is not until after the installation completes that you are told the account name for the password is `oem`. Both the account and password are removed when `oem-config-prepare` is used.

Networkless Upgrades and Repairs

The Alternate CD-ROM contains all of the necessary packages for upgrading a Breezy Badger system (Ubuntu 5.*x*) to Dapper Drake (6.06). This means that the CD-ROM can be used to perform upgrades when network access is unavailable.

Unlike the Desktop CD-ROM, the Alternate CD-ROM cannot be used to run a live graphical system. But, it does have a rescue mode for repairing a non-functioning operating system.

Using the Server CD-ROM

While the Alternate CD-ROM is focused on OEM customizations, the Server CD-ROM focuses on network services (see Figure 1-5). The two main install options are a basic server and a LAMP server. The basic server provides a minimal system image. The LAMP server adds a LAMP application stack to the server image.

Note LAMP stands for Linux, Apache, MySQL, and PHP/Perl/Python. This is a common configuration for a web server with server-side applications and database support.

Debugging problems with the Server and Alternate installations is much easier than diagnosing the Desktop CD-ROM. At any time during the installation, you can press Alt+F4 and see the current installation progress. If the system hangs, you can tell which subsystem caused the problem. Alt+F2 provides a command prompt, and Alt+F1 returns to the user-friendly installation screen.

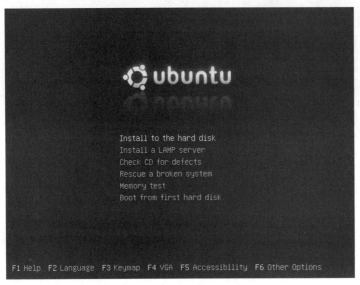

FIGURE 1-5: The Server CD-ROM boot selection menu

Using the Smart Boot Manager

One of my computers is so old that it does not support booting from the CD-ROM drive. However, all was not lost! On all the Ubuntu installation CD-ROMs is a small disk image: `install/sbm.bin`. This is the Smart Boot Manager, one of the best-kept secrets on the installation CD-ROMs. This is an image made for a floppy disk. To create the disk, use:

```
dd if=sbm.bin of=/dev/fd0
```

If you boot off of this floppy disk, then you will see a menu that includes booting from the hard drive or CD-ROM. Using this disk, you should be able to boot off any of the installation CD-ROMs. Unfortunately, SBM does not support booting off USB or Firewire devices.

The server installation can also be used to set up a system very quickly. Although the Desktop CD-ROM does allow installing a graphical desktop, the installer is very slow. In contrast, the Server CD-ROM uses a text installer and is very quick. After installing the basic text-mode operating system, you can install additional packages using `apt-get` (see Chapter 4). For example, you may want to install the Gnome desktop using `sudo apt-get install ubuntu-desktop`. This creates the same system as the Desktop CD-ROM, but is much faster than booting the Live Desktop CD and performing the graphical installation. All the necessary files are found on the Server CD-ROM.

Changing Options

The Desktop, Alternate, and Server ISO images are bootable and include a CD-ROM tester (for making sure the CD-ROM was created correctly) and a RAM tester. The System and Alternate CD-ROMs include a recovery shell for debugging an installed system, while the Desktop CD-ROM includes a Live CD system that can also be used for repairing the local host. There is also an option for specifying kernel boot parameters. Some common parameters include:

- Configure a RAM disk. The default is 1 GB for the Desktop ISO and 16 MB for the Alternate and Server ISOs. For example, the Server ISO uses:

  `ramdisk_size=16384`

- Specify an alternate root disk. The default specifies the RAM disk (`/dev/ram`) but for debugging a system, you can specify a hard drive such as `/dev/hda`.

  `root=/dev/ram`

  or

  `root=/dev/hda`

- The Advanced Configuration and Power Interface (ACPI) support on some hardware can cause the installer to fail. ACPI support can be explicitly disabled using `acpi=off`.

- Similar to ACPI, some PCMCIA chipsets (particularly on older motherboards and some Dell systems) can cause the installer's auto detection to hang. The `start_pcmcia=off` boot option disables PCMCIA, allowing you to bypass this type of problem.

At the initial installation menu, you can press F6 to see the current options and make changes. Pressing F1 shows you other kernel options that are common remedies when the system fails to install.

Installing a Minimal System

Sometimes you want to start with a minimal configuration and add packages as needed. This is usually the case for hardware that has limited disk space, little RAM, or a slow CPU. Minimal systems are also desirable for mission critical and Internet accessible servers, where unnecessary applications may consume critical resources or add security risks.

The Server CD-ROM provides the simplest minimal installation option. The basic configuration does not install any additional software packages and uses less than 300 MB of disk space. The Alternate CD-ROM does provide a basic install but does not enable many of the packages— these packages are placed on the system but not turned on. Table 1-1 (shown earlier) shows the available boot-menu options and the type of installation.

In both cases, unnecessary packages can be removed. For example, the Alsa sound driver can be uninstalled, freeing 200 KB of disk space. The command to list all installed packages is:

```
dpkg -l | more
```

If you want to see what files are included in the package, use dpkg -L packagename. For example:

```
dpkg -L alsa-base | more
```

Many packages have dependent packages, so removals are not always simple. To identify conflicts before removing a package use:

```
sudo apt-get -s remove alsa-base
```

The -s option says to simulate the removal of the alsa-base package—it does all of the safety checks and lists all dependencies and conflicts without actually doing the removal. If there are no conflicts, then you can remove the -s and perform the actual removal. You can replace alsa-base with any of the packages installed on the system. You can also list multiple packages on the apt-get command line.

Warning

The apt-get program tries to not break dependencies, so removing one package may remove a dependent package. Be careful: if you select the wrong dependent package, you can end up removing critical parts of the operating system. For example, the package perl-base cannot be removed without removing the console-data package. Removing perl-base and console-data will also automatically select and remove cron, debconf, LVM support, python, wget, and dozens of other system packages. Even if you have no plans to program in Perl, removing it will cripple your system. Use the -s option before doing the removal to check if there will be undesirable consequences.

Installing Over the Network

Although installing from a CD-ROM can be convenient, it does not scale well when you need to manage dozens or hundreds of systems. In addition, systems without CD-ROM drives need an option for installing the operating system. Ubuntu provides a bare-minimum boot image for installing Ubuntu over the network. There are different versions of the mini image based on the desired architecture. For example:

```
http://archive.ubuntu.com/ubuntu/dists/dapper/main/installer-i386/
current/images/netboot/
```

This directory contains the Dapper Drake mini image for the i386. There are similar directories for the AMD64 (install-amd64), PowerPC (install-powerpc), and Sparc (install-sparc) platforms. Similarly, there are directories for Breezy, Hoary, and other Ubuntu releases. Each of the directories contains similar pre-configured boot images.

- **boot.img.gz**—A compressed, 8 MB image of a bootable installer.
- **mini.iso**—The boot.img file ready for burning to a CD-ROM.
- **netboot.tar.gz**—The boot.img contents, ready for installing over the network.
- **pxelinux.0**—The Pre-boot eXecution Environment (PXE) for network installation. This requires a DHCP and TFTP server.
- **pxelinux.cfg**—A directory required for PXE installations.
- **ubuntu-installer**—A directory required for PXE and TFTP installations.

 Note If you only have a few systems or are installing on a home system, then you do not need the PXE option—use the `boot.img` or `mini.iso` instead. If you plan to update more than a few dozen systems or are already using DHCP to configure operating systems, then PXE is a good option.

To use the mini images, simply copy the image onto a device. For example, to use an external hard drive for installing Ubuntu, use:

```
zcat boot.img.gz | dd of=/dev/hdb
```

This command uncompresses the image and copies it to the external drive (/dev/hdb). This works for most external media.

To boot the network installer from the CD-ROM, just burn the `mini.iso` image to the CD-ROM. This can either be done two ways. From the Ubuntu desktop, you can right-click the ISO and select Write to Disc from the menu (see Figure 1-6), or you can burn it from the command-line using the `cdrecord` command.

```
cdrecord dev=/dev/hdc blank=fast mini.iso
```

The result from all of these different boot options is a disk (or CD-ROM or PXE configuration) that can install Ubuntu over the network.

Installing on a Mac

In general, installing Dapper Drake on a Macintosh, like an iMac or PowerBook, is no more complicated than installing on a PC. In fact, the menus and display look identical. However, there are a few caveats.

With respect to the installation ISO images, don't use the PowerPC Desktop CD-ROM. For the Dapper Drake 6.06 LTS release, the PowerPC Desktop CD-ROM is larger than a CD-ROM. Most CD-ROMs hold 650 MB or 700 MB, but the PowerPC image requires 701 MB. Unless you have a DVD writer or uncommon media such as an 800 MB CD-R, you will not be able to burn this CD-ROM. The 6.06.1 version of the PowerPC Desktop CD-ROM corrected this problem by reducing the ISO to just less than 700 MB. However, I have not been able to boot *any* of my PowerPC systems with this ISO.

FIGURE 1-6: The Write to Disc menu option for ISO images

When installing Ubuntu on a Mac, consider using the Alternate or Server CD-ROM images, or perform a network install (see Installing Over the Network). The PowerPC version of the Alternate, Server, and mini.iso CD-ROM images are all bootable and functional. To boot off of any of these installation disks:

1. Burn the selected ISO to a CD-ROM. You can do this on a Mac, Windows, or Linux system.

2. Insert the CD-ROM into the Mac.

3. As you power-on the Mac, hold down the C key. This will boot the CD-ROM. Alternately, you can power-on while holding down the Option key. This enables you to select the boot drive, including the CD-ROM.

Although you can install Ubuntu to most hard drives, you cannot install it to a USB drive. Although most of the installation process will work, the installation of the Yaboot boot loader will fail since it does not support booting from USB devices.

Using a USB Drive

The ubiquitous USB flash memory drives (also called *thumb drives*) have effectively replaced floppy disks. They are smaller, less fragile, and store much more data. Because they are convenient, they can be used to kick off an installation, repair a damaged system, run a stand-alone operating system, or simply share files.

Formatting a USB Drive

USB drives support two basic formats: floppy drive and hard drive. A USB floppy drive consists of one large formatted drive. In contrast USB hard drives contain partition tables and one or more formatted partitions. If you purchased a thumb drive and never formatted it, then it is most likely configured as a USB hard drive with one large partition.

Warning Before formatting or partitioning any device, be sure the device is not mounted! Use the `mount` command (without any parameters) to see if it is mounted, and then use `umount` to unmount any partitions. For example, to unmount `/dev/sdc1` mounted at `/media/usbdrive`, you can use `sudo umount /dev/sdc1` or `sudo umount /media/usbdrive`.

Thumb drives are usually partitioned just like a regular hard drive. Commands such as `fdisk` and `cfdisk` can easily modify the drive partitions, and `mkfs` can be used to format a partition. Besides capacity, speed is a significant difference between thumb drives and hard drives. When you change the partition table on a flash drive or format a partition, wait a few seconds before removing the drive; otherwise, some data may be buffered and not yet transferred.

Tip When writing to a thumb drive, I usually run the `sync` command (`sudo sync`). This flushes all cached data to the disk. When the command returns, it is safe to remove the drive.

When you use the `fdisk` or `cfdisk` command on a thumb drive, you configure it as a USB hard drive. However, you can also configure it as a USB floppy drive. This requires formatting the device *without* partitioning it. For example, to make an ext2-formatted USB floppy drive on my 64 MB USB thumb drive (`/dev/sdc`), I can use:

```
$ sudo mkfs /dev/sdc
mke2fs 1.38 (30-Jun-2005)
/dev/sdc is entire device, not just one partition!
Proceed anyway? (y,n) y
Filesystem label=
OS type: Linux
Block size=1024 (log=0)
Fragment size=1024 (log=0)
16128 inodes, 64512 blocks
3225 blocks (5.00%) reserved for the super user
First data block=1
8 block groups
```

```
8192 blocks per group, 8192 fragments per group
2016 inodes per group
Superblock backups stored on blocks:
        8193, 24577, 40961, 57345

Writing inode tables: done
Writing superblocks and filesystem accounting information: done

This filesystem will be automatically checked every 22 mounts or
180 days, whichever comes first.  Use tune2fs -c or -i to override.
$ sudo sync
```

Warning   When you first plug in a USB hard drive, all the partitions will appear and automatically mount. However, to create a USB floppy drive, be sure to unmount all partitions and then format the main device (for example, /dev/sda or /dev/sdc) and not a partition (for example, /dev/sda2 or /dev/sdc1). You will need to disconnect and reconnect the device after you format it in order to remove any stale device partition identifiers.

Sharing Files with a USB Drive

The simplest and most common use for a USB drive is to share files between systems. Dapper supports most USB drives. Simply plugging the drive into the USB port will automatically mount the drive. From there, you can access it as you would access any mounted partition.

Tip   Many thumb drives have a light to indicate that the drive is being accessed. Even if the drive is not mounted, do not unplug the drive until the light indicates all activity has stopped.

Linux, Windows, Mac, and most other systems support FAT file systems. In order to share files with other users, consider formatting the drive with mkdosfs. For example:

1. Install the dosfstools package if mkdosfs is not already installed.

   ```
   sudo apt-get install dosfstools
   ```

2. Unmount the drive (for example, /dev/sda1) if it is currently mounted.
   ```
   sudo umount /dev/sda1
   ```

3. Format the drive using either FAT16 or FAT32.

   ```
   mkdosfs -F 16 /dev/sda1  # format FAT16
   mkdosfs -F 32 /dev/sda1  # format FAT32
   ```

Tip   If you want to create a FAT-formatted USB floppy drive, then use the -I option. For example: sudo mkdosfs -I -F 32 /dev/sda.

If you do not mind restricting file sharing to Linux-only systems, then you can format the drive using an ext2 or ext3 file system using any of the following commands:

```
mkfs /dev/sda1          # default format is ext2
mkfs -t ext2 /dev/sda1  # explicitly format type as ext2
mkfs -t ext3 /dev/sda1  # explicitly format type as ext3
mkfs.ext2 /dev/sda1     # directly call format ext2
mkfs.ext3 /dev/sda1     # directly call format ext3
```

Booting from a USB Drive

Beyond file sharing, USB drives can be used as bootable devices. If your computer supports booting from a USB drive, then this is a great option for developing a portable operating system, emergency recovery disk, or installing the OS on other computers.

Although most systems today support USB drives, the ability to boot from a USB thumb drive is not consistent. Even if you create a bootable USB drive, your BIOS may still prevent you from booting from it. It seems like every computer has a different way to change BIOS settings. Generally, you power on the computer and press a key before the operating system boots. The key may be F1, F2, F10, Del, Esc, or some other key or combination of keys. It all depends on your computer's BIOS. When you get into the BIOS, there is usually a set of menus, including one for the boot order. If you can boot from a USB device, this is where you will set it. However, every computer is different, and you may need to have the USB drive plugged in when you power-on before seeing any options for booting from it.

 Warning   Making changes to your BIOS can seriously screw up your computer. Be careful!

Different USB Devices

Even if your computer supports booting from a USB device, it may not support all of the different USB configurations. In general, thumb drives can be configured one of three ways:

- **Small USB floppy drives**—Thumb drives configured as USB floppy devices (that is,, no partitions) with a capacity of 256 MB or less are widely supported. If your computer cannot boot this configuration, then the chance of your computer booting any configuration is very slim.

- **Large USB floppy drives**—These are USB floppy devices with capacities greater than 256 MB. My own tests used two different 1 GB thumb drives and a 250 GB USB hard drive.

- **USB hard drives**—In my experience, this is the least-supported bootable configuration. I only have one computer that was able to boot from a partitioned USB hard drive.

Changing between a USB hard drive or USB floppy drive is as simple as formatting the base device or using `fdisk` and formatting a partition. However, converting a large USB floppy device into a small USB floppy device is not direct.

1. Use `dd` to create a file that is as big as the drive you want to create. For example, to create a 32 MB USB drive, start with a 32 MB file:

```
dd if=/dev/zero of=usbfloppy.img bs=32M count=1
```

2. Treat this file as the base device. For example, you can format it and mount it.

```
mkfs usbfloppy.img
sudo mkdir /mnt/usb
sudo mount -o loop usbfloppy.img /mnt/usb
```

3. When you are all done configuring the USB floppy drive image, unmount it and copy it to the real USB device (for example, `/dev/sda`). This will make the real USB device appear as a smaller USB floppy device.

```
sudo umount /mnt/usb
dd if=usbfloppy.img of=/dev/sda
```

The 10-Step Boot Configuration

Creating a bootable USB thumb drive requires 10 basic steps:

1. Unmount the drive. When you plug a USB drive into the computer, Ubuntu immediately mounts it. You need to unmount it before you can partition or format it.

   a. Use the `mount` command to list the current mount points and identify the USB thumb drive. Be aware that the device name will likely be different for you. In this example, the device is `/dev/sda1` and the drive label is NEAL.

```
$ mount
/dev/hda1 on / type ext3 (rw,errors=remount-ro)
proc on /proc type proc (rw)
/sys on /sys type sysfs (rw)
varrun on /var/run type tmpfs (rw)
varlock on /var/lock type tmpfs (rw)
procbususb on /proc/bus/usb type usbfs (rw)
udev on /dev type tmpfs (rw)
devpts on /dev/pts type devpts (rw,gid=5,mode=620)
devshm on /dev/shm type tmpfs (rw)
lrm on /lib/modules/2.6.15-26-686/volatile type tmpfs (rw)
/dev/sda1 on /media/NEAL type vfat (rw,nodev,quiet,umask=077)
```

   b. Use the `unmount` command to free the device:

```
sudo umount /dev/sda1
```

2. Blank, or zero, the USB device. This is needed because previous configurations could leave residues that will interfere with future configurations. The simplest way to zero a device is to use dd. Keep in mind, large drives (even 1 GB thumb drives) may take a long time to zero. Fortunately, you usually only need to zero the first few sectors.

```
dd if=/dev/zero of=/dev/sda              # format all of /dev/sda
dd if=/dev/zero of=/dev/sda count=2048 # format the first 2048 sectors
```

Use the sync command (sudo sync) to make sure all data is written. After zeroing the device, unplug it and plug it back in. This will remove any stale device partitions. Ubuntu will not mount a blank device, but it will create a device handle for it.

3. If you are making a USB hard drive, then partition the device.

4. Format the partitions. If you are making a USB floppy drive, then format the base device. For USB hard drives, format each of the partitions.

5. Mount the partition.

6. Copy files to the partition.

7. Place the kernel and boot files on the partition.

8. Configure the boot menus and options.

9. Use the sync command (sudo sync) to make sure all data is written and then unmount the partition.

10. Install the boot manager.

Now the device should be bootable. The next few sections show different ways to do these 10 steps.

Kicking Off the Network Install with a USB Drive

USB drives can be used to simplify system installs. For example, if the computer can boot from a USB drive then you can use it to kick off a network install.

 Note The preconfigured network boot image, boot.img, is very small—only 8 MB. It should work on all USB drives.

Configuring the thumb drive for use as a network installation system requires some simple steps:

1. Plug in the USB drive. If it mounts, unmount it.

2. Download the boot image. There is a different boot image for every platform. Be sure to retrieve the correct one.

```
wget http://archive.ubuntu.com/ubuntu/dists/\
dapper/main/installer-i386/current/images/netboot/boot.img.gz
```

3. The boot image is pre-configured as a USB floppy drive. Copy the image onto the thumb drive. Be sure to specify the base device (for example, `/dev/sda`) and not any existing partitions (for example, `/dev/sda1`).

```
zcat boot.img.gz > /dev/sda
```

Now you are ready to boot off the thumb drive and the operating system will be installed over the network.

Every PC that I tested with Boot from USB support was able to run the default network installer: `boot.img.gz`. However, since USB support is not consistent, this may not necessarily work on your hardware. If you cannot get it to boot, then make sure your BIOS is configured to boot from the USB drive, that it boots from the USB before booting from other devices, and that the USB drive is connected to the system. If you have multiple USB devices connected, remove all but the bootable thumb drive.

Using the Boot Image with Files

The `boot.img.gz` image is a self-contained file system and only uses 8 MB of disk space. If you have a bigger thumb drive (for example, 64 MB or 512 MB), then you can copy diagnostic tools or other stuff onto the drive.

In order to create a bootable USB drive, you will need a boot loader. The choices are GRUB or SYSLINUX. There are significant tradeoffs here. GRUB is the default boot loader used when Ubuntu is installed. However, GRUB requires knowing the drive identifier (for example, `/dev/sda1`). Since you may plug-in and remove USB devices, the identifier may change, breaking the boot loader's configuration. SYSLINUX does not use a static drive identifier, but is limited to supporting FAT12 or FAT16 drives. Since USB devices are expected to be portable, use SYSLINUX:

```
sudo apt-get install syslinux mtools
```

The main steps require you to format the drive as FAT16 and use `syslinux` to make it bootable.

1. Become root.

```
sudo bash
```

2. Unmount the USB drive, if it is already mounted.

3. Format the drive as a FAT16 USB floppy drive (in this example, `/dev/sdc`) and mount it.

```
mkdosfs -I -F 16 /dev/sdc
sync
mkdir /mnt/usb
mount -o loop /dev/sdc /mnt/usb
```

4. Mount the `boot.img` file. You will use this to provide the boot files.

```
zcat boot.img.gz > boot.img
mkdir /mnt/img
mount -o loop boot.img /mnt/img
```

5. Copy the files over to the USB drive. This can take a few minutes.

```
sudo bash  # become root, run these commands as root
(cd /mnt/img ; tar -cf - *) | (cd /mnt/usb ; tar -xvf -)
sync
```

6. Set up the files for a bootable disk. This is done by copying over the SYSLINUX configuration files for an ISO image (isolinux.cfg) to a configuration file for a FAT16 system (syslinux.cfg).

```
mv /mnt/usb/isolinux.cfg /mnt/usb/syslinux.cfg
rm /mnt/usb/isolinux.bin
sync
```

7. Unmount the drive and make it bootable by installing the boot loader.

```
umount /mnt/usb
syslinux /dev/sdc
sync
eject /dev/sdc
exit  # leave the root shell
```

Now you can boot from the USB drive in order to install the operating system.

Installing a Full File System

The Holy Grail for USB hacking is the ability to boot a standalone operating system from a
thumb drive. It is not fast, it may not have much space, but it sure is cool. Given a large enough
USB drive and a computer that can boot from the USB port, you can configure a thumb drive
as a standalone operating system.

Warning

There are many different methods discussed in online forums for configuring a USB drive as a
bootable system. Unfortunately, most of the instructions are either incomplete or very complicated. Even if you follow these steps exactly, you may still be unable to boot from the USB device.
The instructions listed here worked consistently for me, but I spent days trying to make it work.

There are two configurations for making a bootable file system: a huge USB floppy drive or a
large USB hard drive. In both of these examples, I will use the Ubuntu Desktop Live CD as
the bootable device.

Using the Live CD from a USB Floppy Drive

Converting the Live CD to a bootable USB floppy drive requires at least a 1 GB thumb drive.

1. Become root. This is done for convenience since nearly every command must be done as
root.

```
sudo bash
```

2. Unmount and blank the thumb drive. (See the section "The 10-Step Boot Configuration"
for directions.)

3. Format the disk as one big FAT16 drive. The `-I` parameter to `mkdosfs` says to format the entire device. In this example, the USB drive is `/dev/sdc`.

```
mkdosfs -I -F 16 /dev/sdc
sync
```

Tip FAT16 only supports drives up to 2 GB. If you have a larger USB drive, then you will need to use the hack found in the Different USB Devices section to convert a large USB drive into a smaller one.

4. Mount the Live CD and the USB drive.

```
mkdir /mnt/usb
mkdir /mnt/img
mount -o loop ubuntu-6.06-desktop-i386.iso /mnt/img/
mount /dev/sdc /mnt/usb
```

5. Copy over the files. This can take 20 minutes or longer. Go watch TV or have lunch. Also, ignore the errors about symbolic links since FAT16 does not support them.

```
(cd /mnt/img ; tar -cf - *) | (cd /mnt/usb ; tar -xvf -)
sync
```

6. Set up the files for a bootable disk. Since SYSLINUX does not support subdirectories for kernel files, you need to move these to the top directory on the USB drive.

```
# move the kernel files and memory tester
mv /mnt/usb/casper/vmlinuz /mnt/usb/vmlinuz
mv /mnt/usb/casper/initrd.gz /mnt/usb/initrd.gz
mv /mnt/usb/install/mt86plus /mnt/usb/mt86plus
# move boot files to top of the drive
mv /mnt/usb/isolinux/* /mnt/usb/
mv /mnt/usb/isolinux.cfg /mnt/usb/syslinux.cfg
rm /mnt/usb/isolinux.bin
# Optional: Delete Windows tools and ISO files to free space
rm -rf /mnt/usb/start.* /mnt/usb/autorun.inf
rm /mnt/usb/bin /mnt/usb/programs
rm -rf /mnt/usb/isolinux
# All done
sync
```

7. Edit the `/mnt/usb/syslinux.cfg` file and correct the kernel paths. Remove the paths `/casper/` and `/install/` wherever you see them. This is because Step 6 moved the files to the root of the USB drive. There should be eight occurrences of `/casper/` and one for `/install/`. After you write your changes, run `sync`.

8. Unmount the drive and make it bootable.

```
umount /mnt/usb
syslinux /dev/sdc
sync
eject /dev/sdc
exit  # leave the root shell
```

This USB thumb drive should now be bootable! You can run the Ubuntu Live operating system or install from this USB thumb drive.

For customization, you can change the boot menu by editing the /mnt/usb/syslinux.cfg file and modify the kernels.

Using the Live CD from a USB Hard Drive

Converting the Live CD to a USB hard drive is much more complicated. First, many computers that support booting from USB devices do not support this configuration. Even if the basic configuration is supported, there may be BIOS restrictions on the disk's layout. Second, the boot loader needs to support partitions. Finally, the USB drive's identifier cannot change after installation. This final issue is the main reason that I do not use GRUB or LILO as the boot loader.

Hard drives are defined by a combination of heads, sectors, and cylinders. Although heads and cylinders used to match physical drive heads and platters, this is no longer the case. In general, each sector contains 512 bytes of data, and each cylinder contains one set of heads × sectors. However, when booting from a USB hard drive, many BIOS manufacturers assume 64 heads and 32 sectors per cylinder. This is the configuration used by USB ZIP drives. If you use a different configuration, it may not boot. In addition, the first partition must not be larger than 1023 cylinders.

Although the syslinux command only supports FAT12 and FAT16 file systems, the syslinux package includes extlinux, which support ext2 and ext3 file systems. For this example, we will use extlinux as the boot loader with an ext2 file system on the bootable partition.

There are 10 steps to configure a bootable operating system on the USB drive:

1. Become root.

```
sudo bash
```

2. Unmount the drive.

3. Use fdisk of cfdisk to partition the drive (for example, /dev/sdc). Be sure to specify 64 heads and 32 sectors. The last cylinder of the first partition must not be larger than 1023. If you have additional disk space after allocating the first partition, then you can allocate additional partitions.

```
# fdisk -H 64 -S 32 /dev/sdc
Command (m for help): d
No partition is defined yet!

Command (m for help): n
Command action
   e   extended
   p   primary partition (1-4)
p
Partition number (1-4): 1
First cylinder (1-983, default 1): 1
Last cylinder or +size or +sizeM or +sizeK (1-983, default 983): 983

Command (m for help): a
```

```
Partition number (1-4): 1

Command (m for help): p

Disk /dev/sdc: 1030 MB, 1030750208 bytes
64 heads, 32 sectors/track, 983 cylinders
Units = cylinders of 2048 * 512 = 1048576 bytes

   Device Boot       Start        End     Blocks   Id  System
/dev/sdc1    *           1        983    1006576   83  Linux

Command (m for help): w
The partition table has been altered!
```

Warning The partition must be marked as "active," otherwise you will not be able to boot from it.

4. Format the partition as an ext2 file system.

```
mkfs /dev/sdc1
```

5. Mount the Live CD and the USB drive.

```
mkdir /mnt/usb
mkdir /mnt/img
mount -o loop ubuntu-6.06-desktop-i386.iso /mnt/img/
mount /dev/sdc /mnt/usb
```

6. Copy over the files. As mentioned in the previous section, this can take 20 minutes or longer.

```
(cd /mnt/img ; tar -cf - *) | (cd /mnt/usb ; tar -xvf -)
sync
```

7. Create the boot files. Unlike `syslinux`, the boot files for `extlinux` can be located in a directory. In this case, we will reuse the casper directory since it already contains the kernel files.

```
cp /mnt/usb/isolinux/* /mnt/usb/casper/
rm /mnt/usb/casper/isolinux.bin
mv /mnt/usb/casper/isolinux.cfg /mnt/usb/casper/extlinux.conf
sync
```

Note The extension for the boot configuration file is `.conf`, and not `.cfg`.

8. *Do not unmount* the drive yet! Making it bootable with `extlinux` requires the mounted directory containing the `extlinux.conf` file.

```
extlinux -z /mnt/usb/casper
sync
```

9. Copy over the boot loader. There is a file missing from the `syslinux` binary package but available in the source package. This file is called `mbr.bin` and is a master boot record containing the boot loader. Download the source package:

```
apt-get source syslinux
```

This creates a directory, such as `syslinux-3.11/`. In this directory is the missing file. Install it on the drive using:

```
cat mbr.bin > /dev/sdc
sync
```

 Warning If you are configuring a file image instead of the actual drive, then this `cat` command will truncate your file. Instead, use `dd if=mbr.bin of=usbdrive.img bs=1 notrunc` to install the master boot record to your USB drive image file (in this case, `usbdrive.img`).

10. Now, unmount the drive and boot from it.

If all goes well, you should have a working, bootable USB thumb drive. This drive can also be used as a bare-bones recovery and repair system.

As an alternative configuration, you can format the drive with FAT16 and use `syslinux` to make the partition bootable. In this case, you will also need to copy the boot files to the top of the partition and edit the `syslinux.cfg` file as described in the previous section.

Booting Variations

I used a variety of computers for testing the USB boot process. Every computer acted differently to different boot configurations.

- Every computer with Boot from USB support was able to boot the original boot.img file.

- Most computers were able to boot the Ubuntu Live operating system when my 1 GB thumb drive was formatted as a USB floppy drive. However, one computer gave a generic boot error message.

- Only one computer could boot the USB hard drive with the ext2 file system. Using a real USB hard drive or thumb drive did not make any difference. In addition, specifying the USB ZIP configuration was the only way to make the hard drive configuration work.

Depending on the configuration variation and hardware that you use, you may see some well-known errors.

- **Blank screen**—If all you see is a blank screen with a blinking cursor, then something definitely did not work. This happens when the boot loader fails. It could be due to failing to install the boot loader properly, or it could be a BIOS problem. Try rebuilding the USB drive in case you missed a step. Also, try booting the USB drive on a different computer. If it works on one computer and not on another, then it is a BIOS problem. But if it fails everywhere, then it is probably the boot loader.

- **"PCI: Cannot allocate resource region..."**—This indicates a BIOS problem. You may be able to boot using additional kernel parameters to bypass the PCI errors, for example:

  `live noapic nolapic pci=noacpi acpi=off`

  However, you may not be able to get past this. Check if there is a BIOS upgrade available for your computer.

- **"cdrom: open failed"**—This error is generated by the `initrd.gz` file because Ubuntu's installer wants to run from a CD-ROM. You can either choose a different installer image, or edit this `initrd.gz` file to disable the failure. To edit `initrd.gz`:

  1. Extract the file. The `initrd.gz` file is actually a compressed archive containing all of the executables, libraries, and configuration files needed during boot.

  ```
  mkdir extract
  cd extract
  zcat /mnt/usb/casper/initrd.gz | cpio -i
  ```

Note If you have ever pressed Alt+F2 from the installation menu and noticed that there was a very minimal operating system with few commands available, this is it. The minimal operating system files are stored in the `initrd.gz` archive.

  2. Edit the file `scripts/casper`. In the `mountroot()` function, comment out the following lines:

  ```
  # for i in 0 1 2 3 4 5 6 7 8 9 a b c d e f 10 11 12 13; do
  #      live_image=$(find_cd)
  #      if [ "${live_image}" ]; then
  #          break
  #      fi
  #      sleep 1
  # done
  # if [ "$?" -gt 0 ]; then
  #    panic "Unable to find a CD-ROM containing a live file system"
  # fi
  ```

  3. Right below the section you commented out, insert these lines:

  ```
  mount -t vfat -o ro /dev/sda $mountpoint
  live_image=$mountpoint/casper/filesystem.squashfs
  ```

  This example assumes that you are using a USB floppy drive configuration (/dev/sda). If you are using a USB hard drive configuration, then replace /dev/sda with /dev/sda1.

Warning The device identifier must match the identifier found by the booted thumb drive. This is not necessarily the same device identifier that you are currently using to configure the thumb drive.

4. Repackage the `initrd.gz` file and put it on the USB drive:

```
find . | cpio -o --format='newc' | \
   gzip -9 > /mnt/usb/casper/initrd.gz
```

- **Root not found**—There are a variety of errors to indicate that the root partition was not available during boot. This is usually caused when the USB drive is still initializing or transferring data and is not ready for the root partition to be mounted. You can fix this by extracting the `initrd.gz` file and editing the `conf/initramfs.conf` file. Add in a `WAIT` line to delay mounting by 15 seconds, giving the USB time to initialize, configure, and transfer data.

  ```
  WAIT=15
  ```

  Now you can repackage the `initrd.gz` file and boot with it.

The hack for editing the `initrd.gz` file can also be used to add commands to the basic boot image. For example, you can add an editor or diagnostic tools to the `/bin` directory. However, be sure that the commands that you add do not use shared libraries. For example, `file /usr/bin/vim.basic` shows a dynamically linked executable, so you cannot use it unless you also include all of the dependent libraries. In contrast, any executable identified as statically linked is good to go! If you are compiling programs (see Chapter 4 for installing the compilation environment), then you can use `gcc -static` to generate statically linked executables.

Upgrading Ubuntu

People who already use Ubuntu have the option to upgrade rather than reinstall. Ubuntu follows a strict upgrade path between major revisions; you should not just upgrade straight from Hoary to Dapper. The upgrade path follows the major Ubuntu releases:

- Warty Warthog (Warty, version 4) ⇨ Hoary Hedgehog (Hoary, version 5.04)
- Hoary ⇨ Breezy Badger (Breezy, 5.10)
- Breezy ⇨ Dapper Drake (Dapper, 6.06 LTS)
- Dapper ⇨ Edgy Eft (Edgy, 6.10)

Note   Although you could upgrade directly from Warty or Hoary to Dapper, this is likely to cause problems. Each upgrade assumes you are upgrading from the previous version. Skipping a version may break this assumption and cause upgrade problems.

To perform the upgrade:

1. Make sure all packages are currently up-to-date:

```
sudo apt-get update
sudo apt-get upgrade
```

2. Edit the file /etc/apt/source.list. This file tells the apt-get command where to retrieve the software (see Chapter 4). Replace all instances of the current version with the new version. For example, when upgrading from Breezy to Dapper, change lines such as:

```
deb http://us.archive.ubuntu.com/ubuntu breezy main restricted
deb-src http://us.archive.ubuntu.com/ubuntu breezy main restricted
```

to

```
deb http://us.archive.ubuntu.com/ubuntu dapper main restricted
deb-src http://us.archive.ubuntu.com/ubuntu dapper main restricted
```

3. Perform the upgrade:

```
sudo apt-get dist-upgrade
```

Warning When you start the upgrade, there is no going back. Attempting to stop the upgrade will likely screw up the system, and a power outage during the upgrade can be disastrous. Be sure to make a backup before beginning the upgrade.

Determining the Version

Upgrading gets complicated when Ubuntu users refer to the operating system by names while the operating system reports numeric versions. The question becomes: How can you tell which version of Ubuntu is in use?

One approach is to use the graphical desktop. On the menu bar, System ➪ About Ubuntu displays the version number and common name. Unfortunately, this is not an option for text-only systems such as the Ubuntu Server. This is also not practical for automated systems.

Another approach is to look at the current /etc/apt/source.list file. Assuming nobody has drastically modified the file, the common name for the operating system should be listed on the deb installation lines.

A better option is the lsb_release command. This command displays distribution specific information from the Linux Standard Base.

```
$ lsb_release -a
No LSB modules are available.
Distributor ID: Ubuntu
Description:    Ubuntu 6.06 LTS
Release:        6.06
Codename:       dapper
```

Upgrading Issues with Ubuntu

Ubuntu upgrades are not always painless. (I have not yet had a simple upgrade.) Although upgrading from a new Hoary install (with no additions) to Breezy to Dapper works well, you are unlikely to be running a new installation of Hoary or Breezy. Customizations lead to upgrade complications. For example:

- **Custom system files**—Customizing files, such as `/etc/gdm/gdb.conf` (see Chapter 9), will prompt you to resolve installation conflicts. You can either overwrite or keep the old file, but you cannot merge changes.

- **Proprietary drivers**—Binary and custom drivers, ranging from the Macromedia Flash player to wireless network support, may break. You will need to uninstall and reinstall the software.

- **Shared Libraries**—Different versions of Ubuntu use different linked libraries. For example, Dapper uses newer libraries than Breezy. Code that is compiled for one set of libraries may break under the new system; be prepared to recompile as needed.

The time required to do an upgrade can be another significant issue. An upgrade usually takes at least three times longer than a clean install. This is because the upgrade checks files before modifying the system. While a 2 GHz computer may install in 15 minutes and upgrade in under an hour, a slower computer can take many hours. My 550 MHz iMac upgraded over the network from Breezy to Dapper in just less than 4 hours. The same computer did a network install of Dapper in less than 30 minutes.

Warning Be prepared to devote time to upgrading. Because you may be prompted occasionally to resolve conflicts, you cannot walk away and expect the upgrade to finish without your intervention. If the upgrade takes two hours, you should be near the computer for two hours. After the upgrade has been completed, you may need to spend additional time fixing broken drivers and recompiling software. (Be sure to stock up on coffee and order in for lunch.)

Even though Hoary, Breezy, and Dapper are all versions of Ubuntu, they are all major releases. They should be treated as different operating systems. Just as the upgrade path from Windows 2000 to Windows XP is not recommended, I don't recommend the upgrade path between major Ubuntu revisions. Instead, back up your files, inventory the software you need, and perform a clean install. After the install, restore your personal files and add in your software. This is faster and less painful than debugging Ubuntu after an upgrade failure.

Summary

The initial Ubuntu configuration will determine the ease and flexibility available when modifying the operating system. A right decision at the beginning can make everything else easier. The questions addressed in this chapter include:

- Do you upgrade or reinstall?

- Do you want a desktop, server, or custom installation?

- Should you install from a floppy disk, CD-ROM, USB, or across the network?

- If you upgrade, what are some problems you may run into?

Chapter 2 covers the post-installation environment and discusses things that you might want to change after you first log in. In Chapter 3, you'll learn how to configure the different types of devices and peripherals that you may want to use with your system.

Making Ubuntu Usable

in this chapter

☑ Logging in for the first time

☑ Using Ubuntu on a PC

☑ Using Ubuntu on a Macintosh

☑ Tweaking GDM

☑ Navigating Nautilus

The basic install of Ubuntu provides a usable system. But *usable* is not the same as *optimal*. When you first log into the system, there are some things that you will definitely want to change, like the colors (nobody likes brown—seriously, what can brown do for you?). This chapter discusses options for making the desktop and workspace environment more usable.

Logging in for the First Time

When you first log into Ubuntu, a few things will get your attention, like the login music. It's this increasing tone with twinkles that sound like an orchestra tuning up. And the desktop color scheme: brown. Before you can call the system usable, you will need to change these and other things.

Changing the Startup Music

The startup music is one of the easiest items to change. From the menu at the top, select System ➪ Preferences ➪ Sound. This brings up the Sound Preferences applet (see Figure 2-1). From here, you can assign sounds to system events. For example, I have a blood-curdling scream for error messages, and a telephone ringing for question dialog boxes.

 Warning | New sound selections are not always used immediately. If you find that your new sounds are not immediately used, log out and log back in. This seems to be a bug in the Gnome Sound Preferences applet.

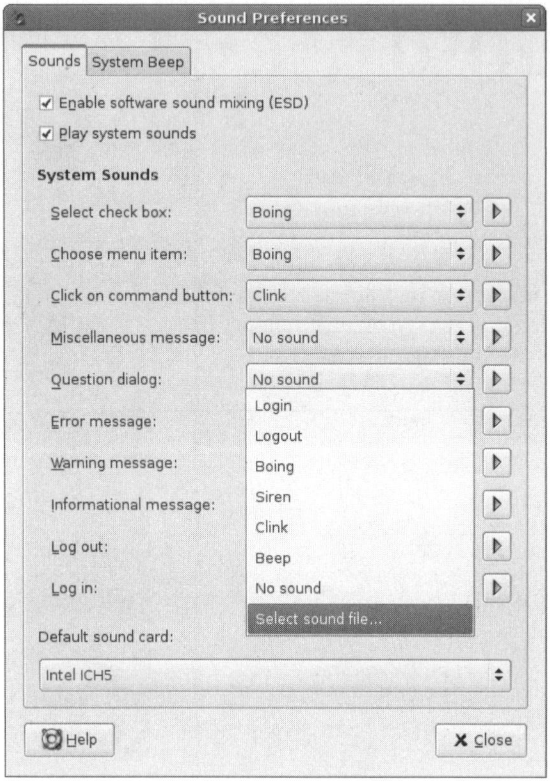

FIGURE 2-1: The Sound Preferences applet

Converting Audio Files

You may select any WAV audio file for any of the audio events. If you want to use a different audio format, such as MP3 or OGG, you will need to convert it to a WAV file. The easiest way to convert audio files is with sox—the universal sound exchanger.

1. The sox package comes from the universe repository, but this repository is not enabled by default. As root, you will need to edit /etc/apt/sources.list and uncomment the two universe lines. These should be near the top of the file and look similar to:

```
deb http://us.archive.ubuntu.com/ubuntu/ dapper universe
deb-src http://us.archive.ubuntu.com/ubuntu/ dapper universe
```

You will also need to update the repository cache:

```
sudo apt-get update
```

Note The `/etc/apt/sources.list` file and the `apt-get` process are detailed in Chapter 4.

2. Install `sox` if it is not already installed.

   ```
   sudo apt-get install sox
   ```

3. Use `sox` to convert the audio file. By default, `sox` determines file types by the file extension.

   ```
   sox fileIN.mp3 fileOUT.wav
   ```

4. Test the sound file using the `play` command.

   ```
   play fileOUT.wav
   ```

5. From the Sound Preferences applet, select the pull-down menu for the desired system sound, for example, Log in and click Select sounds file...

6. Select the WAV file you just created.

Note Although `sox` comes from the universe repository, `lame` comes from the multiverse repository. You will need to uncomment the multiverse lines in `/etc/apt/sources.list` and run `sudo apt-get update` before you can install it. See Chapter 4 for more details.

SOX Ain't LAME

The `sox` application is a great tool for converting and modifying sound files, but it does not support all formats for all functions. In particular, even though it can read MP3 files, it cannot be used to create MP3 files without additional libraries. To resolve this constraint, you can use `lame` package to encode MP3 files from WAV files.

Just as GNU is a recursive acronym "**G**NU is **N**ot **U**nix", LAME uses a recursive name: LAME **A**in't an **M**P3 **E**ncoder. Ignoring the name, `lame` is a powerful tool for creating MP3 files. First, make sure the package is installed: `sudo apt-get install lame`. Then, convert your WAV file to an MP3 file: `lame fileIN.wav fileOUT.mp3`.

The MP3 file from LAME cannot be used for system sounds (because system sounds do not support MP3 files) but can be used by other audio applications and portable music devices.

Modifying Audio Files

Most WAV files are larger than a few seconds, and you probably do not want a three-minute song playing every time you click a button. The sox program can be used to trim audio files, but you will need to know the starting time for the sound you want and the length. For example, to start 3 seconds into the file and keep a 2.31 second duration, use:

```
sox fileIN.mp3 fileOUT.wav trim 3 2.31
```

Trim times can be written in a variety of formats. You can specify seconds (and fractions of a second) or actual time values. The value 125.6 can be written as 2:05.6 or 0:2:5.6. The notations indicate seconds (with fractions), minutes, and hours. Also, if you do not specify the duration, then it goes to the end of the file.

The sox command can also add effects such as echos, high-pass and low-pass filtering, stretching, and reversing. For a full list of functions, refer to the sox man page (man sox).

Changing the Background

The default background for Ubuntu Dapper Drake is a brown screen with a bright highlight. As my fashionable coworker tells me, "Nobody likes brown." So the background must be changed. The System ⇨ Preferences ⇨ Desktop Background menu item brings up the Desktop Background Preferences applet.

Tip   You can also bring up the Desktop Background Preferences applet by right-clicking the desktop background and selecting Change Desktop Background from the popup menu.

Although Ubuntu does include some very colorful backgrounds, you can always add your own. Unlike the Sound Preferences, where you are limited to one type of audio file format, the desktop supports many graphic formats. GIF, JPEG, BMP, PCX, TIF, and PNG are all acceptable formats. Besides selecting an alternate image, you can also select whether the image should be tiled, stretched, or centered, or have a border color . In Figure 2-2, I selected my Safe Computing logo, centered, with a vertical gradient background. Since my image is a GIF with a transparent background, the desktop's color scheme blends well with the picture.

Note   Even though the desktop supports many different graphical formats, there are some graphics that it does not support. In particular, the desktop background displays static pictures. Animated GIFs are not animated, MPEG videos do not work as backgrounds, nor do Adobe Flash movies. In Chapter 9, you'll see how to create animated backgrounds.

Tip   If you need to crop or modify your picture, the Dapper Desktop installation automatically includes Gimp, a powerful graphics editor.

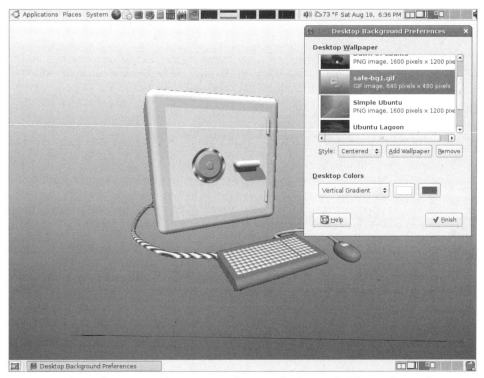

FIGURE 2-2: The Hacker Factor Safe-Computing logo as a background with a gradient color

Changing the Background As-Needed

The picture and color on the desktop does not need to be static. You can write a simple program to change the picture (or color) as needed. The basic commands are:

```
gconftool-2 -t str --set /desktop/gnome/background/picture_filename \
    /path/picture.gif
gconftool-2 -t str --set /desktop/gnome/background/primary_color "#AABBCC"
gconftool-2 -t str --set /desktop/gnome/background/secondary_color "#112233"
```

The Gnome Desktop Manager (GDM) keeps a set of configuration parameters, similar to the Microsoft Windows registry. Although the `gconf-editor` command enables you to interactively view and edit the values (similar to the Windows `regedit` command), and the `gconftool-2` command enables you to edit values from the command line. Within the registry, the `picture_filename` field stores the name of the background image (in this example, `/path/picture.gif`). Be sure to specify the *full path* to the image. As soon as you change the image in the registry, the image on the background changes.

Similar to `picture_filename`, the `primary_color` and `secondary_color` fields are used to control the background color. If you only have a solid background, then the color is defined by `primary_color`. The `secondary_color` is only used with a color gradient. Colors are represented by three hex bytes that denote red, green, and blue. Black is #000000, white is #FFFFFF, and a nice light blue is #2255FF. As with the background image, as soon as you change the color in the registry, the color on the background changes.

Using Informative Colors

The background color does not need to be a static color. You can create a script to change the color based on system events. For example, you can monitor a log file and change the background to red when something serious happens. To give you an example, Listing 2-1 is a simple Perl script that changes the background color to represent the system load.

Note The results from the script in Listing 2-1 will only be visible if you have some portion of the desktop background displaying the primary background color. If you have a graphic that covers the whole desktop, then you will not see anything.

Listing 2-1: Script to Change Background Color with Load

```perl
#!/usr/bin/perl
# Color the background based on system load
my $Key = "/desktop/gnome/background/primary_color";
my $Load; # system load
my $R, $G, $B; # Red, Green, Blue colors
while ( 1 )
  {
  $Load=`uptime`; # get the current load
  # format is "time duration, users, load average: 0.00, 0.00, 0.00"
  # remove everything except the first load value
  $Load =~ s/.*: //;
  # load values: 1 minute, 5 minute, 15 minute averages
  # these are colored: 1=Red, 5=Green, 15=Blue
  ($R,$G,$B) = split(', ',$Load);

  # scale up to the range 0-255, but cap it at 255
  $R = $R * 255; if ($R > 255) { $R = 255; }
  $G = $G * 255; if ($G > 255) { $G = 255; }
  $B = $B * 255; if ($B > 255) { $B = 255; }
  # convert to hex
  $Load = sprintf "%02X%02X%02X",$R,$G,$B;

  # set the color
  system("gconftool-2 -t str --set $Key '#$Load'");
  sleep 15; # Update 4 times per minute
  }
done
```

This script will change the background color every 15 seconds based on the system load. A reddish color indicates that the system is very active. Yellow indicates an active process that has been running at least 5 minutes; white means at least 15 minutes. If no processes are raising the system load, then the colors will cycle from green to blue to black. If you want to know when the system is busy, a sudden change in the background color should get your attention.

Changing the Fonts

The default font for the Ubuntu desktop is Sans at 10pt. You can change the font used by the desktop through the System ➪ Preferences ➪ Font applet. Changing the fonts immediately changes what is displayed on the desktop.

Changing the DPI

Different output devices render the fonts at different resolutions. Increasing the font size will make it appear larger on all devices including the screen and printer. On the other hand, if you change the rendering resolution for a single device, then the same font size appears different.

The default desktop fonts are rendered at 96 dots per inch (dpi). You can change the dpi value by opening the System ➪ Preferences ➪ Font applet and clicking the Details button.

Although the Font applet is good for one-time changes, it cannot be easily automated. The dpi value can also be set through the `gconf-edit` registry under `/desktop/gnome/font_rendering/dpi`. This value can be adjusted to match your screen. For example, a monitor that is 14 inches across at 1024×768 has approximately 73 horizontal pixels per inch, while a 20-inch wide screen at the same resolution has 51 pixels per inch. The default desktop assumes 1024×768, with 10 inches across. If you change the screen resolution or use a different size monitor, then fonts may appear larger or smaller.

To change the dpi value, use:

```
gconftool-2 -t float --set /desktop/gnome/font_rendering/dpi 96
```

Values larger than 96 will make the fonts appear larger (but not change the actual font size), whereas a smaller number decreases the rendered size. In general, changing the dpi setting only changes how fonts are rendered on the screen. It does not change the size of the application windows nor impact how documents will print.

Helping with Big Fonts

I have a couple of co-workers who wear reading glasses when sitting at the computer. More than once, they have come over to my work area and had to run back to get their glasses. To help them (and tease them), I created a *Grandpa Mode* macro that increases the screen font size—just for them. Permanently setting up the ability to use Grandpa Mode as desired requires four commands. The first two define custom commands that change the dpi value. The second two bind the commands to key sequences.

```
gconftool-2 -t str --set /apps/metacity/keybinding_commands/command_7 \
  'gconftool-2 -t float --set /desktop/gnome/font_rendering/dpi 200'
gconftool-2 -t str --set /apps/metacity/keybinding_commands/command_8 \
```

```
'gconftool-2 -t float --set /desktop/gnome/font_rendering/dpi 96'

gconftool-2 -t str --set /apps/metacity/global_keybindings/run_command_7 \
    '<Control>F7'
gconftool-2 -t str --set /apps/metacity/global_keybindings/run_command_8 \
    '<Control>F8'
```

Now pressing Ctrl+F7 changes the resolution to 200 dpi and make the fonts appear large (and coworkers can read it without glasses). Ctrl+F8 returns the screen to the system default of 96 dpi (see Figure 2-3).

Note   Changing the rendering resolution only alters fonts rendered by the desktop. For example, the Gnome terminal (Applications ⇨ Accessories ⇨ Terminal) changes size, but an `xterm` window will not. Also, some applications, such as `xchat`, use hard-coded window heights, so the tops or bottoms of large fonts may get cut off.

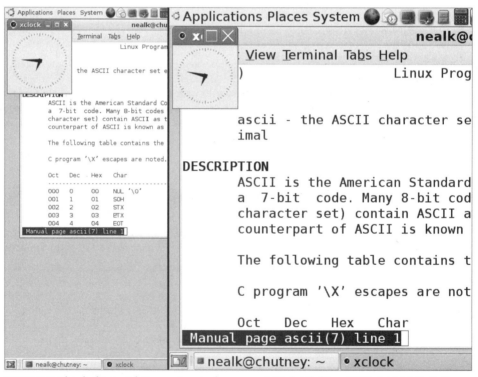

FIGURE 2-3: The desktop and Gnome terminal as seen at 96 dpi (left) and 200 dpi (right). Both are taken on the same 1280×1024 monitor.

If you want to remove Grandpa Mode, you can use the `gconftool-2 --unset` option:

```
# reset default dpi
gconftool-2 -t float --set /desktop/gnome/font_rendering/dpi 96
# unset key mappings
gconftool-2 --unset /apps/metacity/keybinding_commands/command_7
gconftool-2 --unset /apps/metacity/keybinding_commands/command_8
gconftool-2 --unset /apps/metacity/global_keybindings/run_command_7
gconftool-2 --unset /apps/metacity/global_keybindings/run_command_8
```

Tuning the Shell

Most of these Ubuntu hacks require you to use the command line and that means using the GNU Bourne-Again Shell (`bash`). Bash has replaced shells such as `sh`, `csh`, and `tcsh` on most Linux distributions. When you open up a command prompt or terminal window, the default shell is `bash`. Bash uses the same syntax as the original Bourne Shell (`sh`) but has many more features for usability. For example, the up and down arrows can be used to scroll through the shell history.

Bash also enables you to edit command lines in either `vi` or `emacs` mode.

```
set -o vi    # enable vi-mode
set -o emacs # enable emacs-mode
```

The default edit mode under Ubuntu is `emacs`. If you want to specify the mode (rather than inherit default settings), then add the appropriate `set` command to the end of your `.bashrc` file. This way, it will be set whenever you log in or open a new terminal window.

Tip You can tell if Bash is using vi or emacs mode by running `set -o` (with no other options) or with `echo $SHELLOPTS`.

You may also want to change the default editor for applications by adding one of these lines to your $HOME/.bashrc file:

```
export EDITOR=vi    # enable vi-mode
export EDITOR=emacs # enable emacs-mode
```

After modifying your `$HOME/.bashrc` file, you can reload it using: `. $HOME/.bashrc`. This is called *dotting in* because the command you are running is a single dot.

Completing Completion

Bash includes file completion so you don't need to type in very long file names. Pressing the Tab key fills out a partial file name with the available files. Pressing Tab twice lists the available files. For example, `ls a<TAB>` will complete the file name if there is only one file beginning with the letter a. And `ls a<TAB><TAB>` lists all files beginning with a. In these examples, if you do both <TAB> and <TAB><TAB> and see no file completion, then you have no file names that start with a.

Shell Games

There are a few topics in the computer field that can start passionate arguments on the scale of religious wars. The first topic is "Windows or Unix". Both sides have zealots who are willing to argue this topic to the death. (And anyone who is thinking "What about Macs?" knows the depth of this debate.) Even among Unix users, "Linux versus BSD" can spark heated debates. One of the most violent topics comes from the choice of editors. "Emacs vs. vi" can lead to real bloody battles.

When you need to help someone else at his terminal, it is a common courtesy to ask before switching modes. A vi user who finds himself in emacs mode can become very miffed. Instead, consider creating a subshell while you work. Running bash -o vi or bash -o emacs will open a shell in your favorite mode. Now you can change directories, set aliases, or edit the command line without interfering with the system's owner. When you're done, just exit and the shell closes. This leaves the owner's terminal unchanged.

Under Dapper Drake, the default .bashrc loads the file /etc/bash_completion. This file contains many other completion settings. For example, there is a special completion sequence for the command apt-get. Typing apt-get up<TAB><TAB> displays update and upgrade since those are the available options. This default file (/etc/bash_completion) contains options for many widely used commands.

Note Older versions of Ubuntu, such as Hoary and Breezy, have the file /etc/bash_completion on the system, but it is not loaded by default. The default .bashrc contains some commented-out lines for loading the completion file.

Awesome Aliases

Aliases are simple shortcuts for commonly typed commands. Usually people add aliases for the ls command to their .bashrc file. For example:

```
alias l.='ls -d .[a-zA-Z]*'  # list all system files
alias ll='ls -l --color=tty' # list using "ls -l"
alias llf='ls -l --full-time' # list using the full timestamp
alias ls='ls -F' # make ls display the file type
```

Tip If you don't want to use the command alias then preface the command with a backslash. For example ls uses the ls -F alias, but \ls will just run the regular command.

There are a couple of other aliases that I find useful. The first is telco. The telco alias
enables me to quickly look up phone numbers. Simply give it the area code and prefix for a
phone number in North America and it will provide you with the city, state, and rate center.
This is a useful command when you begin to wonder, "What city has phone numbers that
begin with 781-202?" (Burlington, Massachusetts).

```
$ alias telco='whois -h whois.telcodata.us'
$ telco 781-202
Telcodata.US Whois Server
-=-=-=-=-=-=-=-=-=-=-=-=-=-=-=-=-=-=-=-=-=-=-=-=-=-=
Your command was: 781-202
Data for 781 - 202 follows:
Area-code:      781
Exchange:       202
State:          MA
Company:        ACC NATIONAL TELECOM CORPORATION - MA
Type:           CLEC
Ratecenter:     BURLINGTON
Switchtype:     WECO 5ESS Host (Digital)
CLLI:           BSTNMACODS2
```

The telco alias logs your IP address. If you use it too often, then you will receive a warning
about too much usage. The kind people who run whois.telcodata.us do not want you to
abuse their service.

Another alias that I use often is pinger. This alias simply displays a number every five seconds. Many firewalls assume that no traffic after a while indicates a closed connection. If I
know I will be walking away from a live connection, I run the pinger alias just to generate
traffic and keep the connection alive.

```
alias pinger='(i=0; while [ 1 ] ; do sleep 5 ; echo $i; ((i=$i+1)); done)'
```

Fun Functions

Besides storing aliases, the .bashrc file can store shell functions that can be used in place of
commands. For example, pinger can also be written in the .bashrc file as:

```
function pinger() { i=0; while [ 1 ] ; do sleep 5 ; echo $i; ((i=$i+1)); done }
```

Another function that I use is ccd:

```
function ccd()
{
  if [ "$1" == "" ] ; then
    echo "Usage: ccd location"
  elif [ -d "$1" ] ; then
    # if it is a directory, go there
```

```
    cd "$1"
  else # must not be a directory
    # Cut off filename and cd to containing directory
    cd "${1%/*}"
  fi
}
```

The `ccd` function works similar to the `cd` command, except that it does not mind when you paste a line containing a file name. For example, `cd ~/public_html/logo.gif` will fail because the target must be a directory. But `ccd ~/public_html/logo.gif` will see that `logo.gif` is a file and place you in the same directory as the file.

Cool Commands

There are two other lesser-known features of Bash. Ctrl+T transposes the last two characters at the cursor. This way, the common typing error `sl` can be quickly corrected to `ls`. For other lesser-known Bash commands, see the Bash man page (`man bash`).

The other is the CDPATH environment variable. The PATH environment variable specifies where to look for commands. This usually looks something like:

```
export set PATH=/usr/local/bin:/usr/bin:/bin:/usr/bin/X11:/usr/games
```

When you run a command, the shell first checks if the program exists in `/usr/local/bin`, then in `/usr/sbin`, and then `/usr/bin`, and so on until it is found. The CDPATH variable tells `cd` where to look when the directory is not in your current directory. For example:

```
export set CDPATH=.:~:/usr:/etc
```

If you type `cd bin`, then the shell will first check for `./bin`. If that does not exist, then it will try `~/bin` followed by `/usr/bin` and `/etc/bin`. This can come in really handy if you find yourself frequently trying to type `cd public_html` (or some other directory) when you're in the wrong location.

Using Ubuntu on a PC

The default installation of Ubuntu is optimized for a PC system, so there is not too much that requires modification. Most things that need tuning are physical devices, which are covered in Chapter 3. The only real PC-only functionality that may need tweaking is the use of Ctrl+Alt+Delete.

Trapping Ctrl+Alt+Delete

Different versions of Linux either have the Ctrl+Alt+Delete (CAD) key sequence enabled or disabled. In Ubuntu Dapper Drake, this key sequence is enabled, allowing a quick shutdown and reboot. However, the Gnome desktop intercepts CAD. To reboot, you need to switch to a text window (Ctrl+Alt+F1) and then press CAD.

Since the Gnome desktop intercepts CAD, you can remap this key sequence to run a different command. For example, to bring up the Gnome System Monitor, you can use:

```
gconftool-2 -t str -set /apps/metacity/global_keybindings/run_command_10 \
  '<Control><Alt>Delete'
gconftool-2 -t str --set /apps/metacity/keybinding_commands/command_10 \
  "gnome-system-monitor"
```

The system monitor enables you to see the running processes and selectively kill applications. This is similar to using CAD under Microsoft Windows to bring up the System Monitor.

Unfortunately, the reboot command runs as root, so you cannot make CAD run /sbin/reboot. However, you can use gksudo (a graphical front-end to sudo) to prompt you for your password and then run reboot as root:

```
gconftool-2 -t str --set /apps/metacity/keybinding_commands/command_10 \
  "gksudo reboot"
```

Disabling Ctrl+Alt+Delete

Sometimes you may want to prevent CAD from rebooting the system. For example, a critical server may have CAD disabled to prevent someone from playing with the keyboard and cycling the system.

1. Edit the /etc/inittab file.

   ```
   sudo vi /etc/inittab
   ```

2. Find the line that says:

   ```
   ca:12345:ctrlaltdel:/sbin/shutdown -t1 -a -r now
   ```

   This line says, for all init levels (1, 2, ... 5), run the shutdown command and reboot now.

3. To disable CAD, comment out the line by inserting # at the beginning of the line.

   ```
   #ca:12345:ctrlaltdel:/sbin/shutdown -t1 -a -r now
   ```

4. To alter the CAD action, change the /sbin/shutdown command to run your own program. For example, you may want to send an alert to an administrator or play some Disco music to let the user know that CAD is outdated.

   ```
   ca:12345:ctrlaltdel:/usr/bin/play /home/nealk/disco.mp3 > /dev/null
   ```

   Only one application can use the audio driver at a time, so this will only play music if nothing else is playing at the same time.

5. After changing the inittab file, reload it using: sudo telinit q.

Warning Unmapped keyboard signals can be lost. If you disable CAD, then you may find that you cannot re-enable it without rebooting the system. But if you change the functionality (without disabling the command) then you do not need to reboot. The same is true for power level signals and Alt-UpArrow.

Tell Init

The init process is the parent of all processes. It manages different run levels and kicks off processes to start and stop at different run levels. For example, run-level 1 is a single-user mode. It contains a minimal number of running processes and is usually used to fix a broken system. Usually Ubuntu operates at run-level 2, supporting multiple users and graphics. To view the current and previous run level, use the runlevel command. (If there was no previous run-level, then N is displayed.)

If you want to tell init to change run levels, use the telinit command. For example, to switch from the current run level to single-user mode, change to a text window (Ctrl+Alt+F1) and use sudo telinit 1 or sudo telinit s.

Running the shutdown command is similar to running sudo telinit 0. Run-level 0 is the shutdown mode.

The file /etc/inittab tells init what to do at each run level, what processes to spawn, and how to handle hardware signals such as Ctrl+Alt+Delete, Alt+UpArrow, and power modes such as low battery. After modifying the inittab, you will need to tell init to re-examine (query) the file. This is done using telinit q.

Tuning Ubuntu on a Macintosh

Many versions of Linux have been ported to the Macintosh, but were not initially developed for the Mac. Ubuntu falls into this category. There are some PC features that do not exist on the Mac, and some Mac features that lack support under Ubuntu.

Using a One-Button Mouse in a Three-Button World

The biggest issue with using Ubuntu on a Mac is the lack of a three-button mouse. Under Ubuntu, the left mouse button performs actions, such as selecting icons and moving windows. The right button brings up menus, and the middle button is used for pasting from the clipboard.

Tip   There are many different types of PC mice. Some only have two-buttons. The middle button can be emulated by clicking both the right and left buttons at the same time. Others have a scroll wheel that can be pushed in for use as the third button.

Most Macs include a one-button mouse. If you swap the one-button mouse for a three-button model, it will work fine with Ubuntu, but if you do not want to swap hardware then how do you use the other buttons?

By default, Ubuntu on the Mac (PowerPC platform) maps the F11 and F12 keys to the middle and right mouse buttons. This is configured in the /etc/sysctl.conf file. On the PowerPC installation, this file contains the following additional lines:

```
# Emulate the middle mouse button with F11 and the right with F12.
dev/mac_hid/mouse_button_emulation = 1
dev/mac_hid/mouse_button2_keycode = 87
dev/mac_hid/mouse_button3_keycode = 88
```

On a Mac, keycode 87 is F11 and keycode 88 is F12. One easy way to see the keycodes is to use the X Event Tester (xev). This tool opens a window and displays all X-Windows events. If you type in the window, it displays the keycodes (see Figure 2-4).

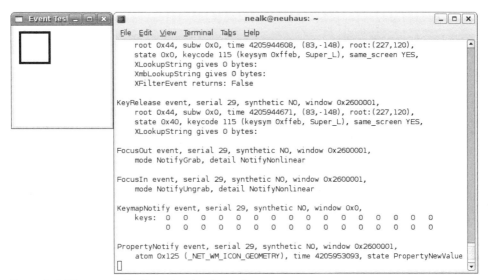

FIGURE 2-4: The xev application, showing keycodes

Missing Keys and Functionality

PC keyboards usually do not look like Mac keyboards. The standard 104-key PC keyboard contains many extra keys that are not found on a Mac. Some of the missing keys include:

- **Two Alt keys**—Every Mac keyboard has a left Alt key (Alt_L), but the right Alt key (Alt_R) is not always present.

- **Two Ctrl keys**—While Control_L always exists, Control_R may be missing on some Mac keyboards.

- **System keys**—The Print Screen, System Request, Scroll Lock, Pause, and Break keys are missing. With Ubuntu on a PC, the Print Screen button is mapped to the screen capture application. Without this button, you will need to remap the functionality to another key combination.

- **Edit keys**—Most PC keyboards have a set of keys for Insert, Delete, Home, End, Page Up, and Page Down. Although Mac keyboards do have Page Up and Page Down, they are not in the same location as a PC keyboard. Different Mac keyboards can have very different keys. For example, the Mac iBook G4 has Home/End while the older iMac G3 keyboard has Home and Help (where Help generates the same keycode as Insert).

- **Windows keys**—The Windows keys do not exist on the Mac keyboard (for obvious reasons). Similarly, the Menu key does not exist.

- **Numeric keyboard**—Although they are usually not labeled on the Mac, the numeric keyboard does have the same arrows (KP_Up, KP_Down, KP_Left, and KP_Right) and navigation keys as a standard PC keyboard.

Keys Please

Under X-Windows, there are two types of keyboard values: keycodes and keysyms. Keycodes are the actual numeric representation sent by the keyboard when a key or button is pressed. Keysyms are the values assigned to the keycodes. For example, when you press the A key on the keyboard, it generates keycode 73. Keycode 73 is mapped to the keyboard symbol 0x61 (the letter a). The command xmodmap -pk prints the key table, showing the keycode to keysym mapping. For example, here's a section of output from the key table:

```
55          0xff6a (Help)      0xff6a (Help)
56          0x0030 (0)         0x0029 (parenright)
57          0x0031 (1)         0x0021 (exclam)
58          0x0032 (2)         0x0040 (at)
59          0x0033 (3)         0x0023 (numbersign)
```

This key table shows that keycode 56 is mapped to the number zero, and when shifted, maps to a right parenthesis.

It is important to realize that not every keyboard can generate every keycode, and not every keycode is mapped to a keysym. Other input devices also generate keycodes. For example, the mouse buttons are keycodes 1, 2, and 3 (for left, middle, and right). Using xmodmap, you can change the key table, swapping keyboard keys or mouse buttons. For example, the command xmodmap -e "pointer = 3 2 1" flips the mouse buttons for a left-handed mouse.

Warning Many Mac keyboards do not have an indicator light to show when NumLock is enabled, so switching between keypad navigation and numeric entry can be confusing.

There are also some keys that exist on the Mac but not on the PC. By default, these are not mapped to anything but can be mapped to other keys.

- **Command keys**—On a Macintosh keyboard, there is at least one and possibly two Command keys. These are located on either side of the spacebar and are labeled with a flower pattern. Mac users call this the Apple or Command key. Under Linux, it is called the Super key. The left one (Super_L) is mapped to keycode 115 and the right key (Super_R) is keycode 116.

- **Keypad Equal (=)**—On a standard PC keyboard, there is no equal sign on the numeric keypad, but there is one on the Mac. This key is mapped to keycode 157 but is not mapped to any keyboard value.

Note Specialized keyboards may have additional keys, such as volume up/down, power, and even buttons labeled for e-mail or the Web. Each generates a distinct keycode. Use `xev` to see the codes. This way, you can map the keys to functions.

Changing Keyboard Layouts

By default, Ubuntu configures itself for a generic 104 key PC keyboard. This is not the same layout as a Macintosh. You can change the configuration to match your keyboard by choosing System ⇨ Preferences ⇨ Keyboard. This brings up the keyboard configuration applet. From here, you can change the keyboard model to match your Mac keyboard (see Figure 2-5). Changing the keyboard layout changes the keycode to keysym map.

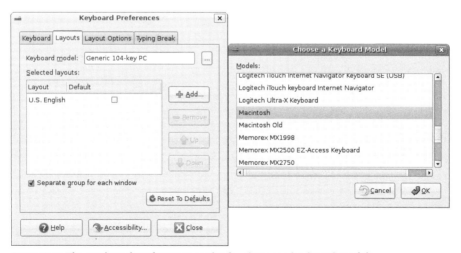

FIGURE 2-5: The Keyboard Preferences applet for changing keyboard models.

Remapping the Command and Alt Keys

One of the biggest distinctions for Mac users is the use of the Command key. Under Mac OS, this key modifier is used for most shortcuts. For example, Command+W closes the window and Command+Q quits an application. Under Ubuntu and on most PC operating systems, the Ctrl key has the same usage (for example, Ctrl+W instead of Command+W). Adding to the confusion, a PC keyboard has Alt next to the spacebar whereas a Mac has the Command keys in that location. What this means is that a Mac user running Ubuntu will need to relearn how to use the Alt key instead of the Command key, or you can just remap the keys.

To remap the Command keys to act as Alt keys, use the xmodmap program. This program maintains a list of keycode mappings (xmodmap -pke) and special key modifiers such as Shift and Control (xmodmap -pm). The easiest way to remap the Command keys is to simply change the modifiers. First, remove the control and command keys, then add the Ctrl keys again.

```
xmodmap -e "remove control = Control_L Control_R" # unmap control
xmodmap -e "remove mod4 = Super_L Super_R"        # unmap old Super keys
xmodmap -e "add control = Super_L Super_R"        # map Super to Ctrl
```

Alternately, you could actually re-map the Command and Ctrl keys.

```
xmodmap -e "remove control = Control_L Control_R" # unmap Ctrl
xmodmap -e "remove mod4 = Super_L Super_R"        # unmap super
xmodmap -e "keycode 115 = Control_L Control_L"    # map Command to Alt
xmodmap -e "keycode 116 = Control_R Control_R"    # map Command to Alt
xmodmap -e "keycode 64 = Super_L Super_L"         # map Alt to Command
xmodmap -e "keycode 113 = Super_R Super_R"        # map Alt to Command
xmodmap -e "add control = Control_L Control_R"    # map new Ctrl to Ctrl
```

Mapping the keyboard using xmodmap only creates a temporary change. If you reboot the computer or restart the X-server, the changes will be lost. To make the changes permanent, you can put the changes in ~/.Xmodmap or /usr/X11/xinit/Xmodmap—depending on whether you want the changes to be per user or system wide:

```
remove control = Control_L Control_R
keycode 115 = Super_L Super_L
keycode 116 = Super_R Super_R
remove mod4 = Super_L
add control = Super_L Super_R
```

Tip   After creating .xmodmap, you can test it using the command xmodmap .xmodmap. Be sure to correct any errors, otherwise the configuration will not load.

Note   Under the default Dapper installation, Super_R is not defined, so you will need to map it to keycode 116 before using it. Also, Super_L is part of the mod4 modifiers. Use xmodmap -pm to display the modifier list.

Instead of adding the mappings to the `.xmodmap` file, you can add the `xmodmap` commands to `~/.xinitrc` or `/etc/X11/xinit/xinirrc`. You might want to do this anyway since Gnome will prompt you about using a new `.xmodmap` file each time you log in.

Shas't Nos Funny!

There's an old practical joke where people pry the keys off a keyboard and replace them out of order. A user who is not a touch typist can get really confused when they look for the right letters. The `xmodmap` command can be used for an excellent alternative to this prank. For example, you can add the following commands into the victim's `.bashrc` file:

```
xmodmap -e 'keycode 91 = t T'
xmodmap -e 'keycode 92 = s S'
```

This prank swaps the s and t keys on the keyboard without requiring any physical keyboard modifications. Alternately, if you can pry up and replace the keys on the keyboard, follow it up by remapping the keyboard so it actually works correctly! Your coworkers should get a big laugh out of it!

Tweaking GDM

After you configure the color scheme, fonts, and sound, you'll want to modify the Gnome Desktop Manager (GDM). This means adding buttons and menus for frequently used functions. You may also want to change the overall widget theme and application skins.

Adding a Prompt Button

The toolbars at the top and bottom of the screen are convenient locations for buttons. Buttons give you a quick way to run commands. I usually add buttons for X-terminals since I regularly use the command- line. I also add a button for my favorite games and other applications that I regularly run.

Adding a new button is pretty straightforward: just right-click an empty part of either the top or bottom toolbar and select Add to Panel. The default applet shows you common applications, like Weather Report and Workspace Switcher, that you can drag and drop onto the toolbar. But when the application you want does not exist, you'll need to select the Custom Application Launcher (see Figure 2-6).

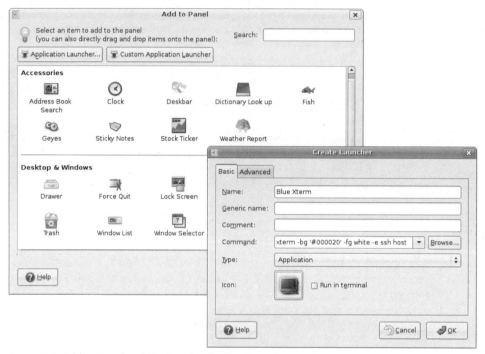

FIGURE 2-6: Add to Panel and Custom Application Launcher.

The Custom Application Launcher prompts you for the button's name. This is the text that will appear when you hover the mouse over the button. The command is the active element—this is any line that you can enter on a command line. In Figure 2-6, I created an xterm with a dark blue (#000020) background and white text. Rather than opening a terminal on the local system, I use Secure Shell (ssh) to connect to a remote host. This way, I can color-code my terminal windows to specific hosts. You should also choose an icon for your button. Clicking the empty icon button shows you a large system of ready-to-go icons. Alternately, you can create your own; PNG is the best format for this.

Note   The command can be any valid command line. If you want to use pipes or redirection, consider using the bash command. For example: bash -c 'ls | more'. And be sure to select the Run in Terminal check box. This way, the command will run and you can see the output. Otherwise, it will never open a window (which could be desirable if you don't want to see any text results).

After you create your button, it will appear on the toolbar. You can always right-click the button to change its properties (name, command, icon, and so on). This menu also enables you to move the button along the toolbar, to another toolbar (for example, from the top to the bottom), or to lock the icon so it won't move.

Tip Laptop computers can either use their own screen or an external monitor. These screens are commonly at different resolutions. If you find yourself switching resolutions often, you might want to enable the Lock To Panel property for each toolbar icon. Otherwise, they can move around and get bunched up in the middle of the toolbar.

Buttons are not restricted to the toolbars. They can also be created on the desktop.

1. On the desktop, right-click to bring up the desktop menu.

2. Select Create Launcher. The applet looks just like the menu from the panels.

3. Enter a name and command line for the button, then click OK.

The new button appears on your desktop. Double-clicking the button starts the application.

Adding Panels

The default Dapper user interface has two panels (toolbars): one at the top and one at the bottom. Each panel has a limited amount of screen real estate for placing menus and buttons; you might run out of room. To resolve this, you can add more panels.

1. Right-click any empty space on any panel. This brings up the panel menu.

2. Select New Panel from the menu. A new panel appears.

To move the panel, grab it with the mouse (left button) and move it. It can reside along any screen edge or along another panel. For example, you can easily stack multiple panels along the top edge for adding lots of buttons.

Panels can also have sub-panels, called drawers. A drawer is a pop-out panel where you can store more buttons. To create a drawer:

1. Right-click any empty portion of the panel to bring up the panel menu.

2. Select the Add to Panel option. This brings up the list of available applets.

3. Drag the drawer icon from the Add to Panel window to the panel.

4. Left-click the drawer icon in order to open the drawer.

Clicking the drawer icon once opens it. Clicking it a second time closes it. The open drawer acts as another panel and you can add panel icons to it. The opened drawer is normally three icons tall. However, if you add more icons to add then it will automatically widen.

Adding Menus

The default Dapper desktop contains one text-based top-level menu with three items in it: Applications, Places, and System. In Gnome2, the developers removed the ability to add custom menus. The implementation was reportedly unstable, so it was disabled. Hopefully this will be added to a later version of Ubuntu. In the meantime, you can add custom menus under the existing top-level menu items (Applications and System) by right-clicking the menu and selecting Edit Menus.

Note Other menu items were also disabled in Dapper. For example, earlier Ubuntu versions had an Applications ⇨ System Tools menu for running the Configuration Editor (`gconf-edit`) and other tools. That menu option is gone under a Dapper clean install, but present if you performed an upgrade to Dapper.

The Gnome Menu items contain can contain two different types of items. First, they can contain additional menus. For example, Applications contains Games (Applications ⇨ Games). There is no limit to the depth of the menus; you can have a menu in a menu in a menu.

Second, the Gnome Menu can contain entries. An entry is just like a button but uses text (with an optional graphic) to denote the functionality; buttons only have graphics. Like buttons, entries can run any command on the system.

Warning Only menu items that contain items are displayed, and only empty menus can be deleted.

Although adding menu items is easy, deleting them can be a little confusing (the Gnome interface is not exactly production quality in this regard).

1. Open the Alacarte Menu Editor by right-clicking the menu and selecting Edit Menu.

2. Delete all menu entries by right-clicking each item and selecting Delete. You can delete menus that started off empty, but you cannot delete a menu that you just emptied. The next steps (Steps 3–5) are for deleting an empty menu.

3. Close the Alacarte Menu Editor. (That's right! Close it so you can open it again to delete it!) The menu editor does not update and realize that the menu is empty until you close it.

4. Re-open the Alacarte Menu Editor.

5. Now delete the empty menu by right-clicking and selecting Delete.

Selecting Themes and Skins

The default widgets—window borders, scrollbars, and buttons—that ship with Ubuntu are nice, but they can be made nicer. You can change the desktop theme by selecting System ⇨ Preferences ⇨ Theme. From this menu you can select from a wide range of themes, color schemes, and control widgets (see Figure 2-7). Besides the existing theme selections, you can choose Theme Details, and modify the controls, window borders, and icons. Your choices here will impact every application you run.

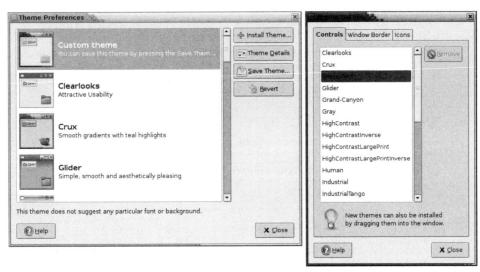

FIGURE 2-7: The Theme Preferences and Theme Details applets

Unfortunately, the theme selection applet does not give as many options as other operating systems. (Yes, Windows and even OS/2 both have more options than Gnome.) But there are ways to tweak aspects that are not available from the Theme Preferences applet.

1. Become root. Open a terminal and type:

```
sudo bash
```

Warning This starts a command prompt as root. You have the ability to delete and destroy the entire operating system. Be careful and have fun.

2. Go to the directory /usr/share/themes.

```
cd /usr/share/themes
```

3. Copy your favorite theme to a new directory. This uses the existing theme as a template. For example, if you like the AgingGorilla theme, then use:

```
cp -R AgingGorilla MyTheme
```

4. In the MyTheme/metacity-1 directory is a file called metacity-theme-1.xml (/usr/share/themes/MyTheme/metacity-1/metacity-theme-1.xml). Edit this file.

The theme file contains XML that describes the theme's name and attributes. By editing this file, you can change colors, border sizes, icons, and more. And this gives you much more editing power for creating a custom theme than other operating systems. As an example, I can set the title bar to have a couple of bars that grow by editing the "title_tile" section and specifying:

```
<draw_ops name="title_tile">
  <line color="#0000ff" x1="0" y1="0" x2="width" y2="0"/>
  <line color="#3030f0" x1="0" y1="1" x2="width" y2="1"/>
</draw_ops>
```

This sets two alternating horizontal stripes. One is blue (#0000ff) and the other is a grayish blue (#3030f0). If you want to change the icons for close, maximize, minimize, and so on, then you just need to edit the appropriate PNG file in the /usr/share/themes/MyTheme/metacity-1/ directory.

Changes to the active theme take effect immediately. If you change the theme using the System ⇨ Preferences ⇨ Theme applet, you can re-select your customizations by clicking the Theme Details button and choosing the MyTheme selection.

Navigating Nautilus

Nautilus is the graphical file browser that is incorporated into the GDM. It enables you to graphically view files, navigate directories, and start applications when you double-click icons. Besides appearing as a window with files in it, Nautilus also manages the desktop—the desktop is just another file folder that is open all the way.

You can create a button to quickly start Nautilus.

1. On the top panel, right-click to bring up the menu.

2. Select Add to Panel. This brings up the applet.

3. Click the Custom Application Launcher button.

4. Type **Nautilus** for the Name field of the button and **nautilus** (lowercase) as the Command field.

5. Choose an appropriate icon. I like /usr/share/icons/gnome/48x48/apps/ file-manager.tif.

6. Click OK to create the button.

Nautilus has many configurable items that are similar to other operating systems. For example, you can set the background in the Nautilus window to be a color or an image. There is also a side pane (View ⇨ Side Pane) that can list information about the directory or show the directory tree.

Beyond these common features, Nautilus offers a few uncommon features, such as emblems, scalable icons, and customized context-sensitive menus.

Configuring Nautilus

Even though Gnome uses Nautilus for directory navigation, Nautilus is not the same as Gnome. This distinction becomes very apparent when customizing the system. Gnome uses `gconf-edit` to manage all configuration options. Any changes to this registry take effect immediately.

In contrast to Gnome, Nautilus uses a variety of configuration methods, and few take place immediately. To tell Nautilus about changes, your best option is to restart it. The command `nautilus -q` tells Nautilus to quit. Gnome will immediately restart Nautilus and new configuration changes will be loaded.

Embracing Emblems

Emblems are small accents that you can add to a file or directory icon. For example, critical files can all be tagged with an urgent emblem, and finance files can have a dollar sign on them. Emblems appear at the corner of the icons, so you can easily enable four emblems per file. There are many different ways to enable emblems:

- **Properties**—You can right-click an icon and select the properties option. In the properties menu, select the Emblem tab. This enables you to put a check box next to the desired emblem. If you select multiple files, then you can view the preferences and enable all of their emblems at once.

- **Backgrounds and Emblems**—Under the Nautilus menu you can select Edit ⇨ Background and Emblems. A dialog box appears that enables you to drag over a different background (patterns or colors) for the Nautilus window. There are also icon emblems. Just drag the emblem onto the file icon and it will be set (or if it is already set, then it will be removed).

- **Side Pane**—The Nautilus side pane has a pull-down menu that displays the emblems. As with Backgrounds and Emblems, you can drag the emblem onto an icon in order to enable or disable it.

Emblems provide visual cues about a file's purpose, but they have little use beyond human interpretation right now. You cannot automatically select files or sort them by emblem, enable emblems on subdirectories, or programmatically change them (without some serious programming efforts).

Practical Uses for Emblems

Although emblems have no functionality beyond human interpretation, they can be very usable. For example, I have a friend who is a freelance writer. She uses emblems to denote the status of different articles. One emblem denotes a submission, a different emblem marks a sale, and a third indicates work in progress.

Technical Details

Emblems are stored in a set of XML files found in $HOME/.nautilus/metafiles/. There is one XML file per directory, and only customized directories are present. You can edit these XML files to make system changes, but you'll need to restart Nautilus for the change to take effect.

Listing 2-2 shows a simple script for changing emblems. In this case, every icon with the "special" emblem is changed to have an "important" emblem. More complicated scripts can be created to add emblems to specific files, manipulate files according to their emblems, or to set an emblem based on an event. For example, if an "important" icon is more than 48 hours old, then it can be set to "urgent" or an e-mail notification can be generated.

Listing 2-2: Script to Change "Special" Emblems to "Important"

```sh
#!/bin/sh

# for each of the meta files...
for i in ~/.nautilus/metafiles/* ; do
  # convert any "important" emblems to "special"
  # save the result to a temporary file
  cat $i | sed -e 's/name="special"/name="important"/g' > $i.new
  # move the temporary file into place
  mv $i.new $i
done
# restart Nautilus so the changes take effect
nautilus -q
```

Stretching Icons

One of the coolest features in Nautilus is the ability to stretch icons. You can take any icon on the desktop and scale it—making it very tiny or extremely large. If the icon denotes a text document, then it can be scaled large enough to read the text. To scale an image:

1. For desktop icons, right-click the icon to bring up the icon's menu and select the Stretch Icon menu option. For icons within a Nautilus directory window, select the icon and choose Edit ⇨ Stretch Icon from the Nautilus menu bar.

2. When you select Stretch Icon, four blue dots appear on the corners of the icon.

3. Grab one of the blue dots (left mouse button) and drag it. This will stretch or shrink the icon.

One great use for stretching icons is to uncluttered desktops. When I'm working on a project, I may end up having dozens of files on my desktop. Before going to lunch, I can stretch the current file to a larger size—this way, I can find it quickly when I get back. Figure 2-8 shows a couple of stretched icons.

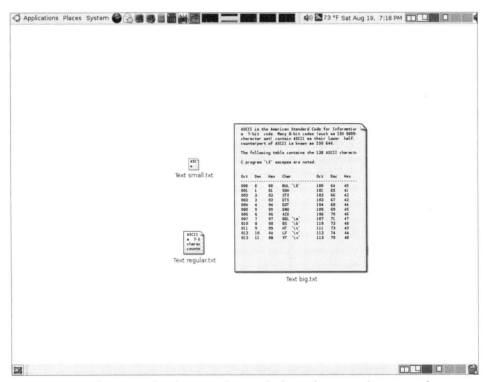

FIGURE 2-8: A regular icon, a shrunk icon, and a stretched icon that is very large. Icons for text files show the file contents.

To un-stretch the icon, bring up the icon's menu and select Restore Icon's Original Size.

Note   Under the previous section on emblems, I mentioned that you can have up to four emblems per icon. That isn't exactly true. Emblems are placed along the sides of the icon. If the icon is stretched to a very large size, then you can have lots of emblems without any overlap.

Stretching Exercises

Stretching icons is still a work in progress for Nautilus. As a result, not all options are available all the time. For example, when an icon is on the desktop, there is a menu option to stretch the icon's size. But the stretch option is not on the icon menu when an icon is selected from inside a Nautilus window. Instead, you need to use Edit ⇨ Stretch Icon.

Nautilus enables you to drag and drop a stretched icon into a folder—and it will retain the stretched dimensions. Unfortunately, dragging an icon will lose the Restore Icon's Original Size menu entry. In order to restore the icon's size, you will need to first stretch the icon. This reactivates the Restore menu option.

Technical Details

As with emblems, the stretched value is saved in the $HOME/.nautilus/metafiles/ XML files. Scripts can be created to manipulate the size of the icons. This way, important files can be suddenly made larger. A great use, for example, would be to increase an icon in size right before an online meeting. This way, you can quickly find the files you need. As with emblems, any automated changes to the stretched value require you to restart Nautilus before they take effect.

Adjusting Fonts

The System ⇨ Preferences ⇨ Font applet enables you to set font types, but not font colors. The default font uses white lettering with a dark shadow. Although this font is nice when you have a dark (or brown) background, it can appear hard to read with a light colored background. Changing the font color under Nautilus requires a $HOME/.gtkrc-2.0 file. In your favorite editor, create (or edit) this file. Add or modify a section for desktop icons:

```
style "desktop-icon"
{
NautilusIconContainer::frame_text = 1
NautilusIconContainer::normal_alpha = 0
text[NORMAL] = "#000000"
}
class "GtkWidget" style "desktop-icon"
```

In this example, the font color is set to black (#000000). The `frame_text` value indicates that you are specifying the text format, and the `normal_alpha` field controls the transparency of the font (0 is not transparent). After editing the file, you can save your changes and restart Nautilus (`nautilus -q`). The text color matches your setting and (hopefully) offers a higher contrast than the default colors.

Tuning Templates

On the Nautilus menu (including the desktop menu) is an option called Create Document. The Create Document option enables you to make a new file that is based on a template file. By default, there is only one template file—empty file. This creates a zero-sized file just as if you ran the `touch` command. You can create your own templates by placing files in a Templates directory.

1. Create a directory called Templates in your home directory.

   ```
   mkdir $HOME/Templates
   ```

2. Place any template file in this directory. The template file name (without extension) appears in the Create Document menu.

For example, you can start up Open Office (Applications ➪ Office ➪ OpenOffice.org Word Processor) and save an empty file called `WordProcessor.doc` in the Templates directory. As soon as you save it, you will have the WordProcessor option listed in the Create Document menu. Selecting this menu option creates a file called `WordProcessor.doc`, with the name WordProcessor highlighted for renaming.

Scripting Menus

The single most powerful feature of Nautilus is the ability to create context-sensitive menu items. For example, you can create a special menu item that only appears when you select an MP3 file. You can control the types of files, directories, or both where the menu item appears, and whether it appears for one selected item or multiple selections.

To do this, you will first need to install Nautilus Actions:

```
sudo apt-get install nautilus-actions
```

Now you can create custom menus. For example, here's a menu for securely deleting files (see Figure 2-9).

1. Run `nautilus-actions-config`. This brings up the configuration menu.

Tip   You can also find this tool on the top menu under System ➪ Preferences ➪ Nautilus Actions Configuration.

2. Click Add to create a new menu script. A new window opens.

3. For the label, enter `Secure Delete`. This is the text that will appear on the menu.

4. You can add a tooltip, such as `Safely delete files`. This appears when the mouse hovers over the menu item.

5. Optionally select an icon for this menu item. The icon appears in the menu.

6. Path is the name of the command that is called. Any command that can be used on the command line can be entered here. For this command, use `find` (or `/usr/bin/find`) as the Path.

7. The Parameters will be passed to the Path command. An example of the command line is displayed below the Parameter field as you type. The %M parameter becomes the list of selected files. If you click the Legend button, you will see other variables that can be used. For this action, use `%M -type f -exec shred -u -f '{}' \;`. This parameter tells `find` to identify all files and run the command `shred`, forcefully unlinking (deleting) each file.

Note The `shred` command does not securely delete directories. The result is a bunch of empty directories. See the Shred Everything entry in Table 2-1 for a solution to this problem.

8. Under the Conditions tab, you can select when the menu item appears. You can make the selections based on any combination of file name, Meta type, file or directory, and single or multiple selections. In this case, you should select both files and directories (even through directories are not deleted), and allow multiple file selections.

9. Click OK to add the action to the menu.

10. Click Close to end the Nautilus action application.

11. Restart Nautilus so it loads the new menu item.

    ```
    nautilus -q
    ```

You can test the new menu item by bringing up Nautilus and deleting something. Right-clicking an icon should show the Secure Delete menu item. Selecting the delete item should remove all of the files selected.

Warning Shred overwrites files with garbage before deleting. There is no prompt to check if this is what you really want to do, and anything deleted will be gone forever.

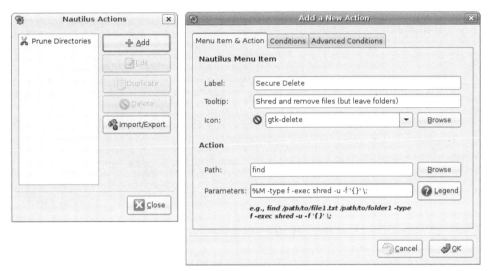

FIGURE 2-9: Adding the Secure Delete menu item

Action scripts can be used to convert files (for example, for any GIF, make it a PNG), e-mail a file (such as a Mail To command), or view a file under the web browser. Actions are limited to one command line, but you can specify a shell script for performing multiple-step commands. Some useful custom menu items are included in Table 2-1.

Note Only one command can be specified. You cannot use &, |, or ; to join multiple commands.

Table 2-1 Examples of Useful Custom Menu Commands

Name	Path	Parameters	Condition	Notes
Command Prompt	gnome-terminal	g--working-directory ='%M'	Folders only, no multiple selection.	Opens a terminal window.
Open in Firefox	firefox	'%M'	Both files and folders, no multiple selection	Keep in mind, Firefox must be opened first; otherwise, nothing may happen.

Continued

Table 2-1   *Continued*

Name	Path	Parameters	Condition	Notes
Shred Everything	. bash	-c 'find %M -type f -exec shred -u -f "{}" \; ; rm -rf %M'	Files or folders with multiple selection.	Although we can only run one command, this only runs the bash command. The bash argument translates as two commands.
Convert WAV to MP3	. bash	-c "lame %M %d/`basename %M .wav`.mp3"	Only for files ending in .wav, no multiple selections.	This converts file.wav to file.mp3 in the same directory. Instead of running lame directly, bash is used to create the subshell basename (used to rename the file). Without the basename program, you would end up with a file named file.wav.mp3.

Warning   Some commands, such as shred and lame, may take minutes (or longer) to process very large files. During this time, result files (for example, Convert WAV to MP3 files) may be created even though they are incomplete. Requesting the same task multiple times may result in many running processes, that all interfere with each other. The net result may not be what you want. Instead, wait for the task to finish. See Chapter 7 for different ways to monitor processes.

Summary

Just as a home isn't a home until you add furniture, the default installation of Ubuntu is fine for short-term use, but to really be usable over the longer term, it needs to be customized. Changing the background, sounds, fonts, buttons, and themes enables you to configure the desktop for whatever is best for you. For some users, static environments are best, but the user interface supports scripts that can dynamically change the desktop based on the current environment. Informative backgrounds, changing icons, smart menus, and adjustable fonts can really add to the system's usability and your own productivity.

Configuring Devices

Linux is a powerful operating system, and much of that power comes from its ability to support different hardware configurations and peripheral devices. Everything from multiple CPUs and video cards to printers and scanners require device drivers and kernel modifications. In this chapter, we'll look at getting some common devices configured properly.

Working with Device Drivers

in this chapter

☑ Loading modules

☑ Starting software devices

☑ Enabling multiple CPUs (SMP)

☑ Adding printers

☑ Adding drives

☑ Adding other devices

Under Linux, there are a couple of required elements for working with devices. First, you need a kernel driver that can recognize the device. These are usually low-level drivers, such as *support a parallel port* (for example, for use with a parallel printer) or *provide USB support* (regardless of the USB device).

The second element depends on the type of hardware—some devices need software support for managing the device. The kernel driver only knows how to address the device; the software driver actually speaks the right language. This means that different versions of the same device may speak different languages but communicate over the same kernel driver. Printers are one such example. A printer may use PostScript, HP PCL, oki182, or some other format to communicate data. The kernel driver knows how to send data to the printer, but the software driver knows what data to send. The same is true for most scanners, cameras, pointer devices, and even keyboards.

The final element is the user-level application that accesses the device. This is the program that says "print" or the audio system that says "play."

There are four steps needed before using any device:

1. Install a device driver, if one is not already installed.
2. Create a device handle if one is not created automatically.
3. Load any required software drivers and configuration parameters.
4. Configure applications as necessary for using the device.

In some cases, some or all of these steps are automated. In other cases, devices will need manual configuration.

Useful Programs

Many computer peripherals and add-ons are either pointer or video devices. There are two very useful programs when trying to test these devices. The first is the GNU Image Manipulation Program or `gimp` (`http://www.gimp.org/`), an open source version of Adobe Illustrator. This is a very powerful drawing tool that supports most types of pointer devices and can also capture input from video devices such as cameras, scanners, and TV cards.

The second useful program is the Scanner Access Now Easy or `sane` (`http://www.sane-project.org/`) program. This is strictly used for capturing images from a video device such as a scanner, digital still camera, digital video camera, or TV card. The `xsane` program provides an X-Windows front end for sane. As with `gimp`, `xsane` can capture images from a variety of input devices.

The `sane`, `xsane`, and `gimp` programs are installed by the default Ubuntu desktop configuration.

Loading Modules

Very early versions of Linux had all the necessary kernel drivers compiled into the kernel. This meant that the kernel knew exactly what was supported. If you needed to add a new device, you would need to compile a new kernel.

Unfortunately, including every driver in the kernel led to a big problem: the kernel became too large. Back in the days of floppy disks, it would take two 1.44 MB disks to boot Linux—one for the kernel and the other for the rest of the operating system. The kernel developers introduced compressed kernels, but even those became too large for floppy disks.

Fortunately, the barbaric days of compiling all desired modules into the kernel are long gone. Today Linux uses loadable kernel modules (LKMs). Each LKM can be placed in the kernel as needed. This keeps the kernel small and fast. Some LKMs can even perform a check and see if they are required. If you don't have a SCSI card on your computer, then the SCSI LKM driver won't bother to load and won't consume kernel resources. Usually hardware is found through device identifiers, but sometimes you need to tell the operating system to enable the device.

Ubuntu includes a healthy selection of common and uncommon kernel modules. If the device has any type of stable Linux support, then it is very likely that Ubuntu has the LKM on the system.

Viewing Modules

The basic command to see what modules are currently loaded is `lsmod`. Running `lsmod` displays the LKM's common name, size of the LKM, and any other LKMs that depend on it. For example:

```
$ lsmod | head
Module                  Size   Used by
floppy                 64676   0
rfcomm                 43604   0
l2cap                  28192   5 rfcomm
bluetooth              54084   4 rfcomm,l2cap
ppdev                   9668   0
speedstep_lib           4580   0
cpufreq_userspace       6496   0
cpufreq_stats           6688   0
freq_table              4928   1 cpufreq_stats
```

This shows that the bluetooth module is loaded and is in use by the rfcomm and l2cap modules. A second command, `modprobe`, can be used to show the actual LKM files.

```
$ modprobe -l bluetooth
/lib/modules/2.6.15-26-686/kernel/net/bluetooth/bluetooth.ko
```

The `modprobe` command can also list available modules—not just ones that are loaded. For example, to see all the asynchronous transfer mode (ATM) network drivers, you can use:

```
$ modprobe -l -t atm
/lib/modules/2.6.15-26-686/kernel/net/atm/pppoatm.ko
/lib/modules/2.6.15-26-686/kernel/net/atm/mpoa.ko
/lib/modules/2.6.15-26-686/kernel/net/atm/lec.ko
/lib/modules/2.6.15-26-686/kernel/net/atm/br2684.ko
/lib/modules/2.6.15-26-686/kernel/drivers/usb/atm/xusbatm.ko
/lib/modules/2.6.15-26-686/kernel/drivers/usb/atm/usbatm.ko
/lib/modules/2.6.15-26-686/kernel/drivers/usb/atm/speedtch.ko
/lib/modules/2.6.15-26-686/kernel/drivers/usb/atm/cxacru.ko
/lib/modules/2.6.15-26-686/kernel/drivers/atm/zatm.ko
/lib/modules/2.6.15-26-686/kernel/drivers/atm/uPD98402.ko
/lib/modules/2.6.15-26-686/kernel/drivers/atm/suni.ko
...
```

The `-t atm` parameter shows all modules with the ATM tag. LKMs are stored in an organized directory, so the tag indicates the directory name. This is different than using `modprobe -l '*atm*'` since that will only show modules containing "atm" in the LKM file name.

Installing and Removing Modules

Modules are relatively easy to install. The `insmod` command loads modules, and `rmmod` removes modules. The `modprobe` command actually uses `insmod` and `rmmod`, but adds a little more intelligence. The `modprobe` command can resolve dependencies and search for modules.

As an example, let's look at the suni.ko ATM driver (you probably do not have it installed and you probably don't need it). Listing 3-1 shows different queries for the driver, installing the driver, and removing it.

Note   Asynchronous Transfer Mode (ATM) network cards are uncommon on home PCs, so this is a good type of device driver to play with when learning how to load and unload LKMs. If we used a common driver for this example, then you could end up disabling your floppy drive, printer, or other device. If you do happen to have a Saturn User Network Interface (SUNI) ATM card, then consider using a different driver for this example, such as pppoatm.

Listing 3-1: Sample LKM Queries and Management

```
$ lsmod | grep suni
[none found]
$ modprobe -l -t atm   # show all ATM modules
/lib/modules/2.6.15-26-686/kernel/net/atm/pppoatm.ko
/lib/modules/2.6.15-26-686/kernel/net/atm/mpoa.ko
/lib/modules/2.6.15-26-686/kernel/net/atm/lec.ko
/lib/modules/2.6.15-26-686/kernel/net/atm/br2684.ko
/lib/modules/2.6.15-26-686/kernel/drivers/usb/atm/xusbatm.ko
/lib/modules/2.6.15-26-686/kernel/drivers/usb/atm/usbatm.ko
/lib/modules/2.6.15-26-686/kernel/drivers/usb/atm/speedtch.ko
/lib/modules/2.6.15-26-686/kernel/drivers/usb/atm/cxacru.ko
/lib/modules/2.6.15-26-686/kernel/drivers/atm/zatm.ko
/lib/modules/2.6.15-26-686/kernel/drivers/atm/uPD98402.ko
/lib/modules/2.6.15-26-686/kernel/drivers/atm/suni.ko
. . .
$ modprobe -l '*suni*'   # Show only the suni.ko module
/lib/modules/2.6.15-26-686/kernel/drivers/atm/suni.ko
$ modprobe -l -a 'suni'  # Show all suni modules
/lib/modules/2.6.15-26-686/kernel/drivers/atm/suni.ko
$ sudo modprobe -a suni   # install all suni modules
$ lsmod | grep suni   # show it is installed
suni                    7580  0
$ sudo modprobe -r suni   # remove it
$ lsmod | grep suni   # show it is removed
[none found]
```

Note   Using modprobe -l without any other parameters will list every module on the system.

The installation step could also be accomplished using

```
sudo insmod /lib/modules/2.6.15-26-686/kernel/drivers/atm/suni.ko
```

Similarly removal could also use any of the following commands:

```
sudo rmmod /lib/modules/2.6.15-26-686/kernel/drivers/atm/suni.ko
sudo rmmod suni.ko
sudo rmmod suni
```

To make the installation permanent, you can either add the module name to /etc/modules or /etc/modprobe.d/. (See the man pages for modules and modprobe.conf.) In general, /etc/modules is simpler for adding a new module, but the /etc/modprobe.d/ configuration files provide more control.

Optimizing Modules

If you're trying to streamline your system, you may not want to have all of the various modules installed or accessible. Although unused modules take virtually no resources (even if they are loaded into memory), systems with limited capacity or that are hardened for security may not want unnecessary LKMs. Between the lsmod and modprobe -l commands, you can identify which modules are unnecessary and either remove them from the system or just not load them.

For example, if you do not have a printer on your parallel port, then you probably do not need the lp module loaded. Similarly, if you want to disable the floppy disk, you can remove that driver, too.

```
sudo modprobe -r lp
sudo modprobe -r floppy
```

You can make these changes permanent by removing lp from /etc/modules and adding both lp and floppy to /etc/modprobe.d/blacklist, or if you need the disk space then you can just delete the drivers from the system (use modprobe -l lp and modprobe -l floppy to find the files).

Starting Software Devices

After the device driver is loaded into the kernel, it usually needs to be configured. Each device driver has it's own set of tools for doing the configuration. For example, the network uses ifconfig to configure addresses, and PCMCIA support uses cardmgr to notify the operating system when a new card is added or removed. Each driver is different. Some software drivers are only needed once to configure the system (for example, network, audio, and system clock), others are needed continually while the device is in use (for example, high resolution graphics and mouse). A few KLM drivers require no additional assistance—keyboard, hard drives, and USB fall into this category.

In addition to configuring and managing kernel drivers, some software drivers are software-only (no KLM needed). These services include virtual file systems, schedulers, and network services like SSH and the Web.

Using Init.d

As the system boots, kernel drivers are loaded into memory and the init process begins setting the run level. At each run level, different software drivers and services are started. Which ones are started and the order that they are started in is determined by /etc/init.d/ and the rc script. There are eight rc directories: /etc/rc0.d, /etc/rc1.d, ... /etc/rc6.d, and /etc/rcS.d. These correspond with the different run levels (0 through 6, and S for single user mode). In each of these directories are symbolic links to files in /etc/init.d. The name of the symbolic link determines whether the script is called when starting (S) or leaving (K for kill) the run level (see Listing 3-2). Each name also has a number, used to order when the service is started. This way, dependent processes can be started in the right order. For example, S13gdm is started before S99rmnologin since the Gnome Display Manager (gdm) should be started before the user login prompt.

The directory /etc/init.d/ contains the actual control scripts (without the S/K and number). Each script has a start, stop, and restart option. So, for example, if you want to restart the network and stop the cron server, you can run:

```
sudo /etc/init.d/networking restart
sudo /etc/init.d/cron stop
```

To make system changes happen after the next reboot, add the appropriate S or K script to the appropriate run-level directory.

Listing 3-2: Directory Contents of /etc/rc6.d

```
$ ls /etc/rc6.d
K01gdm            K20NVidia-kernel   K88pcmciautils
K01usplash        K20postfix         K89klogd
K11anacron        K20powernowd       K90sysklogd
K11atd            K20rsync           K99timidity
K11cron           K20ssh             S01linux-restricted-modules-common
K15fetchmail      K20tor             S20sendsigs
K19cupsys         K20vsftpd          S30urandom
K20acpi-support   K21acpid           S31umountnfs.sh
K20apmd           K21hplip           S35networking
K20bittorrent     K25hwclock.sh      S40umountfs
K20dbus           K25mdadm           S49evms
K20festival       K50alsa-utils      S50lvm
K20hotkey-setup   K74bluez-utils     S50mdadm-raid
K20laptop-mode    K86ppp             S60umountroot
K20makedev        K88pcmcia          S90reboot
```

Running Ragged

Ubuntu includes seven different run levels: 0-6 and S. Many of the run levels provide very specific services. For example, level 0 is a system halt, 6 reboots the system, and S provides the single-user mode. Under Ubuntu, level 1 provides an alternate single-user mode environment.

The remaining run levels provide different types of multi-user support. Usually the system uses level 2. This provides a graphical user interface (when available) and network support. The default level 3 provides support for accessibility devices, such as a Braille TTY display. Finally, levels 4 and 5 usually look like level 2, however, you can modify them if you need customized run-time environments.

Configuring Boot Options with services-admin

Managing services by hand can be time consuming. Ubuntu offers an easy applet for enabling and disabling some system services: services-admin. You can run this from the command line, or select it from System ⇨ Administration ⇨ Services (see Figure 3-1). Enabling or disabling services only requires changing a check box.

 Tip   Checking or unchecking a service will immediately change the service's current running status. It will also alter the service's boot status. This way, if you uncheck a service, you don't need to manually stop any running processes and it will not start at the next boot. Checking a service makes it start immediately and it will start with the next boot.

Although this tool does identify some of the better-known services, it does not list custom services and does not identify different run levels. Since Ubuntu normally runs at run-level 2, you are only modifying whether services will start during run level 2. In order to control more of the boot options, you either need to modify the files in the /etc/init.d and /etc/rc*.d directories, or you need a better tool, like sysv-rc-conf.

Configuring Boot Options with sysv-rc-conf

The services-admin applet does not list all services but is more convenient than manually editing services. The sysv-rc-conf tool offers a middle ground by allowing easy access to the boot services without requiring manual modification of the different startup files found in /etc/init.d and /etc/rc*.d/.

```
sudo apt-get install sysv-rc-conf
```

FIGURE 3-1: The Services settings applet

Running this tool (sudo sysv-rc-conf) brings up a text list of all services and run-levels (see Figure 3-2). Using this tool, you can immediately start or stop services by pressing + or -, and spacebar enables or disables the service in specific run levels. The tool also supports the mouse; clicking a check box enables or disables the service.

Tip

As with the services-admin application, selecting or clearing a service will immediately change the service's running status and alter the service's boot-up configuration.

```
                    nealk@chutney: ~                          _ □ X
File  Edit  View  Terminal  Tabs  Help

 SysV Runlevel Config   -: stop service  =/+: start service  h: help  q: quit

 service     1     2     3     4     5     0     6     S

 acpi-supp$ [ ]   [X]   [X]   [X]   [X]   [ ]   [ ]   [ ]
 acpid      [ ]   [X]   [X]   [X]   [X]   [ ]   [ ]   [ ]
 alsa-utils [ ]   [ ]   [ ]   [ ]   [ ]   [ ]   [ ]   [ ]
 anacron    [ ]   [X]   [X]   [X]   [X]   [ ]   [ ]   [ ]
 apmd       [ ]   [X]   [X]   [X]   [X]   [ ]   [ ]   [ ]
 atd        [ ]   [X]   [X]   [X]   [X]   [ ]   [ ]   [ ]
 aumix      [X]   [X]   [X]   [X]   [X]   [ ]   [ ]   [ ]
 bittorrent [ ]   [ ]   [ ]   [ ]   [ ]   [ ]   [ ]   [ ]
 bluez-uti$ [ ]   [X]   [X]   [X]   [X]   [ ]   [ ]   [ ]
 bootlogd   [ ]   [ ]   [ ]   [ ]   [ ]   [ ]   [ ]   [ ]
 brltty     [ ]   [ ]   [X]   [ ]   [ ]   [ ]   [ ]   [X]
 cron       [ ]   [X]   [X]   [X]   [X]   [ ]   [ ]   [ ]
 cupsys     [ ]   [X]   [X]   [X]   [X]   [ ]   [ ]   [ ]

 Use the arrow keys or mouse to move around.     ^n: next pg    ^p: prev pg
                   space: toggle service on / off
```

FIGURE 3-2: The sysv-rc-conf tool

The `sysv-rc-conf` tool has one other huge benefit over the `services-admin` program: it is text based. Although usually graphical applications are easier to use, most system services only need modification when the system is not working properly, and that means using the command line. Furthermore, if you installed the Ubuntu server instead of the desktop (see Chapter 1), then there is no graphical display available. The `sysv-rc-conf` tool works without needing the entire overhead and installation of a graphical interface.

Enabling Multiple CPUs (SMP)

Many of today's computers have multiple CPUs. Some are physically distinct, and others are virtual, such as hyper-threading and dual-core. In any case, these processors support symmetric multiprocessing (SMP) and can dramatically speed up Linux.

 Note The kernel supports multiple CPUs and hyper-threading. If your computer has two CPUs that both support hyper-threading, then the system will appear to have a total of four CPUs.

Older versions of Ubuntu, such as Hoary and Breezy, had different kernels available for SMP. To take advantage of multiple processors, you would need to install the appropriate kernel.

```
sudo apt-get install kernel-image-2.4.27-2-686-smp
```

Without installing an SMP kernel, you would only use one CPU on an SMP system.

Dapper changed this requirement. Under Dapper, all of the default kernels have SMP support enabled. The developers found that there was no significant speed impact from using an SMP kernel on a non-SMP system, and this simplified the number of kernels they needed to maintain.

There are a couple of ways to tell if your SMP processors are enabled in both the system hardware and kernel.

- `/proc/cpuinfo`—This file contains a list of all CPUs on the system.

- `top`—The `top` command shows what processes are running. If you run `top` and press 1, the header provides a list of all CPUs individually and their individual CPU loads. (This is really fun when running on a system with 32 CPUs. Make sure the terminal window is tall enough to prevent scrolling!)

- System Monitor—The System Monitor applet can be added to the Gnome panels. When you click it, it shows the different CPU loads (see Figure 3-3).

In each of these cases, if only one CPU is listed, then you are not running SMP. Multiple CPUs in the listings indicate SMP mode.

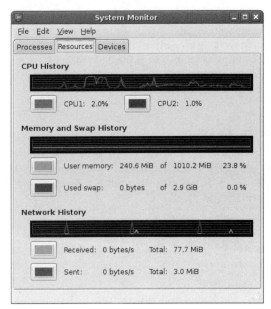

FIGURE 3-3: The System Monitor applet showing multiple CPUs

Disabling SMP

In some situations, such as application benchmarking or hardware debugging, you may want to disable SMP support. This can be done with the kernel parameters `nosmp` or `maxcpus=1`. If this is a temporary need, you can just boot the system, catch Grub at the menu by pressing ESC, and typing `boot nosmp maxcpus=1` at the prompt. If you have multiple boot options, then you may need to edit the kernel line and add `nosmp maxcpus=1` to the kernel boot line.

Warning Some kernels do not work with `nosmp`, but in my experience `maxcpus=1` always works.

Note The default Grub boot loader gives you three (3) seconds to press the escape key before it boots the operating system.

For a longer-term solution, consider adding these boot parameters to the Grub configuration.

1. As root, edit `/boot/grub/menu.lst`.

2. Scroll down to your kernel.

3. Add a kernel option for disabling SMP. For example:

```
kernel /boot/vmlinuz-2.6.15-26-686 root=/dev/hda1 ro splash maxcpus=1
```

4. Save your changes.

The next reboot will use your new changes.

If you modify `/boot/grub/menu.lst`, be aware that the contents could be overwritten the next time you upgrade the kernel or run `update-grub`.

Missing SMP?

If you find that you only have one active CPU on a multiple CPU system, try installing the explicit SMP kernel: `sudo apt-get install linux-686-smp`. Beyond that, there are few generic debugging options and the problem is unlikely related to Ubuntu—it is probably a general Linux kernel problem.

- Check with the motherboard manufacturer and see if Linux supports their chipset. For example, I have an old dual-CPU motherboard that is not supported by Linux.

- Check the Linux Hardware FAQ for the motherboard or chipset. This will tell you if other people managed to get it to work. Web sites such as `https://wiki.ubuntu.com/HardwareSupport` and `/www.faqs.org/docs/Linux-HOWTO/SMP-HOWTO.html` are good places to start.

- If all else fails, post a query to any of the Linux or Ubuntu hardware forums. Maybe someone else knows a workaround. Some good forums include `http://www.ubuntuforums.org/`, `http://www.linuxhardware.org/`, and `http://www.linuxforums.org/forum/`. Be sure to include details such as the make and model of the motherboard, Ubuntu version, and other peripherals. It is generally better to provide too much information when asking for help, rather than providing too little.

Unfortunately, if SMP is not enabled after installing the linux-686-smp kernel, then it probably will not work. But you might get lucky—if someone has a patch then you will probably need to recompile the kernel.

Compiling the kernel is not for the weak-of-heart. Many aspects of Linux have become automated or given easy-to-use graphical interfaces, but compiling the kernel is not one of them. There are plenty of help pages and FAQs for people daring enough to compile their own kernel.

Adding Printers

Printers are one of the most common types of external device. Today, many computer manufactures bundle printers with new computers—it's hard *not* to have a printer. Printers used to come with one of two types of connectors: serial or parallel. Today, USB printers are very common. In corporate and small-office/home-office (SOHO) environments, networked printers are common. Ubuntu supports an amazing number of printers; making Ubuntu work with most printers is relatively easy.

Changing Paper Size

Before you install your first printer, be sure to set the system's default paper size. This is found in the file /etc/papersize. The default paper size probably says A4 or letter—this depends on the geographical location you selected during the installation. If the default paper size is not set right, then every printer you add to the system will be configured with the wrong default paper size. Changing /etc/papersize *after* you create a printer will not alter any already existing printers.

To change the default paper size, edit the /etc/papersize file and change the value. Common values are A4, letter, and legal. A4 is a commonly used standard paper in Europe. Letter and legal refer to the 8.5" × 11" and 8.5" × 14" paper sizes common in the United States. Less common paper sizes that I have come across include A5, B2, C2, ledger, and 10 × 14.

Tip   If you have multiple printers that take different paper sizes, set the value in /etc/papersize before adding each printer.

Papers Please

Paper sizes, such as A0, A1, A2, B3, C4, and D4, refer to ratios from a larger piece of paper. For example, A0 has a total area of one square meter. The A0 dimensions are 841 × 1189 mm. A1 is half of A0's longest direction: 594 × 841mm. A2 is half of A1 (420 × 594), and so on. As a result, 16 sheets of A4 cover a surface area of $1m^2$. Other paper types follow the same ratios—four sheets of B2 can fit in one B0 sheet. B0 is 1000 × 1414 mm and C0 is 917 × 1297 mm.

Specific fields use different paper sizes. For example, A is common in publishing and C is used in construction for building plans. If you have a large printer or plotter, be sure to set up /etc/papersize with the right default before adding the printer.

Adding a Printer

Adding a printer under Ubuntu is straightforward. Go to System ⇨ Administration ⇨ Printing to open the printer applet. From there, you can double-click New Printer to configure the device.

The first step in adding a printer requires specifying which kernel device communicates with the printer (see Figure 3-4). The default choices are a local printer using a USB or parallel port, or a network printer. Although the local printer configuration is easy (simply select the detected USB printer or parallel port), networked printers require additional information.

- **CUPS Printer (IPP)**—The Common Unix Printing System allows the sharing of printers between different Unix computers. You will need to provide a URL for the printer, such as `ipp://server/printer_name`.

- **Windows Printer (SMB)**—More common than CUPS are Windows printers. In small offices, a user with a printer directly connected to their Windows host can share the printer with the network. You will need to provide the Windows host name, printer name, and any user name and password needed to access the device.

- **Unix Printer (LPD)**—The Line Printer Daemon protocol is one of the oldest and most reliable network printing options. Most stand-alone network printers support LPD. For this option, you will need to provide the host name and the name of the LPD print queue.

- **HP JetDirect**—This is another common protocol for stand-alone printers. You only need to provide the host name (and port number if it's not the default 9100).

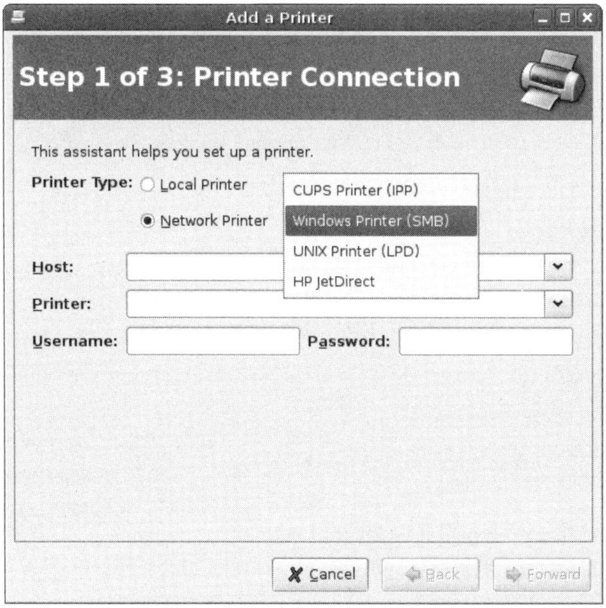

FIGURE 3-4: The applet for adding a new printer

The second step for adding a printer enables you to specify the type of printer. If your exact printer model is not listed, chances are good that there is a model that is close enough. In the worst case, you can always select one of the generic printer options.

Finally, you should name the printer. Give it something descriptive so you can recognize it later.

Sharing Your Printer

After you have added your printer, you can share it with other people on the network. Sharing the printer requires knowing who will use it: other system using CUPS, other devices using LPD, or other computers running Windows.

Sharing With CUPS

To share the printer with CUPS, you will need to configure both the printer server and the client.

On the print server:

1. Edit `/etc/cups/cups.d/ports.conf` and change the line that reads `Listen localhost:631` to `Port 631`. This tells CUPS to allow printing from any remote system.

2. (Optional) Edit `/etc/cups/cups.d/browse.conf` and change `Browsing off` to `Browsing on`. This allows the server to announce the printer's availability to other hosts on the network. The default is an announcement every 30 seconds.

3. Restart the CUPS subsystem on the print server.

   `sudo /etc/init.d/cupsys restart`

On the print client:

1. Go to System ➪ Administration ➪ Printing to open the printer applet.

2. Double-click New Printer to configure the device.

3. Select a Network Printer and the CUPS Printer (IPP) protocol.

4. Enter the printer host name and printer name as a URL. For example, if the server is named *printer.example.com* and the printer is called *Okidata127*, then you would use `ipp://printer.example.com/printers/Okidata127`.

5. Click the Forward button and select the printer model.

6. Create a description for the printer

7. Click on the Apply button to create the printer.

Tip

If you enabled browsing in Step 2 of the server configuration, then Ubuntu clients can use the Global Settings ➪ Detect LAN Printers option on the Printing applet. This will automatically discover and configure the remote printer.

CUPS Runneth Over

CUPS provides many configuration options, but it has a long history of being a security risk. The CUPS installation includes a web-based administration interface. By default, it is not accessible remotely. (But if you followed the steps under Sharing With CUPS, then it *is* remotely accessible.) The URL for this interface is `http://localhost:631/`.

Although you can use the CUPS web interface to view and manage the print queue, the default administration interface does not permit adding new printers or changing configurations. This functionality is disabled in Ubuntu primarily due to security risks. Enabling this interface is not recommended. Instead, if you need to modify printer configurations, use the System ⇨ Preferences ⇨ Printing applet.

Sharing With LPD

Enabling LPD support is a little more complex since Ubuntu does not normally include servers.

On the print server:

1. Install `xinetd` on the print server. This is the extended Internet daemon for running processes.

   ```
   sudo apt-get install xinetd
   ```

2. Create a configuration file for the printer service. This requires creating a file called `/etc/xinetd.d/printer`. The contents should look like this:

   ```
   service printer
   {
     socket_type = stream
     protocol = tcp
     wait = no
     user = lp
     group = sys
     server = /usr/lib/cups/daemon/cups-lpd
     server_args = -o document-format=application/octet/stream
   }
   ```

3. Restart the `xinetd` server.

   ```
   sudo /etc/init.d/xinetd restart
   ```

On the printer client:

1. Go to System ⇨ Administration ⇨ Printing to open the printer applet.

2. Double-click New Printer to configure the device.

3. Select a Network Printer and the Unix Printer (lpd) protocol.

4. Enter the print server host name (or IP address) in the Host field and the CUPS printer name under the Queue field.

5. Continue through the remaining screens to select the printer type and configuration. On the final screen, click the Apply button to create the printer.

Sharing with Windows

It is usually best to use a native printing protocol. For Ubuntu, LPD and CUPS are native. Most versions of Windows support network printing to LPD servers, so sharing with LPD should be enough, but it requires user to configure their printers.

Native Windows environments can share printers using the Server Message Block (SMB) protocol. This allows Windows users to browse the Network Neighborhood and add any shared printers—very little manual configuration is required. For Ubuntu to share a printer with Windows users requires installing SAMBA, an open source SMB server.

On the print server:

1. Install SAMBA on the print server. This provides Windows SMB support.

   ```
   sudo apt-get install samba
   ```

2. Create a directory for the print spool.

   ```
   sudo mkdir /var/spool/smbprint
   ```

3. Edit the SAMBA configuration file: /etc/samba/smb.conf.

4. Change workgroup = to match your Windows Workgroup.

5. Under the [global] section is an area for printer configuration. Uncomment (remove the leading ;) the load printers = yes and CUPS printing lines.

6. Set the [printers] section to look like this:

   ```
   [printers]
       comment = All Printers
       browseable = no
       security = share
       use client driver = yes
       guest ok = yes
       path = /var/spool/smbprint
       printable = yes
       public = yes
       writable = yes
       create mode = 0700
   ```

This setting allows any Windows client to access the printers without a password.

7. (Optional) Under the [printers] section, set browseable = yes. This allows Windows systems to see the printers through the Network Neighborhood.

8. Restart the SAMBA server.

```
sudo /etc/init.d/samba restart
```

On the Windows client, you can add the printer as if it were a Windows printer. For example, if the server's name is *printer.example.com* and the printer is *Okidata127*, then the shared printer resource would be \\printer.example.com\Okidata127. Windows clients will need to install their own print drivers.

Adding Drives

Back in the good old days, people would buy computer components separately. After gathering the necessary components, such as a motherboard, case, memory, video card, and monitor, they would slap together a working computer. Today it is usually cheaper to get a pre-built system. Few people (except power users like yourself) upgrade the video card or memory after buying the computer; most people will just upgrade the entire system. Even though most of the hardware stays the same, there is one thing that is usually upgraded: the hard drive. This could be because you need more disk space, or maybe you want a second drive for backups or additional storage.

Upgrading Drives

When you upgrade your hard drive, you want to make sure you transfer over all of your personal files. This could be as simple as transferring the contents of /home from one system to another. But if you have installed any custom applications (very likely) or tuned any configurations, then you will probably need to transfer system files too. Here's an easy way for doing it.

1. Shut down the system, remove the old drive, and install the new drive. Do not leave the old drive in the system since you do not want to accidentally reformat the wrong drive.

2. Install Ubuntu on the system (see Chapter 1). Be sure to use the same base install. Don't bother customizing this new install—it is only needed for making the drive bootable.

3. Shut down the system and install the old hard drive as the second drive. Do not boot from the old hard drive.

4. Start up the computer and boot from the new drive.

5. Log in when the computer has rebooted, then run the System ⇨ Administration ⇨ Disks. This brings up the Disks Manager applet. All of the drives on the system are listed, including their disk size. The new drive should be listed first, and the old one listed second. (See Figure 3-5.)

6. Select the old drive and click on the Partitions tab.

7. Mount the old drive partition(s).

- If you only have one partition, then select the partition name, enter a temporary mount point, such as /mnt/disk, and click the Enable button. You may need to make the mount point first (for example, sudo mkdir -p /mnt/disk).

- If you have multiple partitions, such as /usr and /home, mount the root partition first, and then mount the other partitions in place. For example, the old / would be mounted at /mnt/disk and /usr would be at /mnt/disk/usr.

Tip   If you don't know what is on a particular partition then mount it to a temporary location and click on the Browse button. This allows you to see the partition's contents.

8. As root, copy over all of the files to the new system.

```
$ cd /mnt/disk
$ ls
bin    dev    initrd         lib         mnt    root  sys  var
boot   etc    initrd.img     lost+found  opt    sbin  tmp  vmlinuz
cdrom  home   initrd.img.old media       proc   srv   usr  vmlinuz.old
$ sudo tar -cf - * | ( cd / ; tar -xvf - )
```

Note   You may want to remove temporary and device directories first, such as /mnt/disk/mnt, cdrom, tmp, dev, and proc. Alternately, you could only list the directories to keep in the tar -cf command.

9. Since the copy may have brought over a newer kernel, you will want to reset the boot loader.

```
sudo update-grub
```

10. Now that everything is copied over, you can reboot the system immediately. You don't want to use the shutdown applet since that can save desktop settings over your new settings. To force an immediate reboot, use the -f parameter.

```
sudo reboot -f
```

When the system comes back up, you should have all of your old files right where you left them, and a minimal amount of residue (undesirable files) that you did not originally want. This method is great for switching partition layouts since it only copies files, but it should not be used when upgrading operating systems.

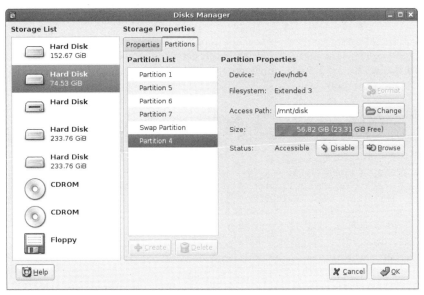

FIGURE 3-5: The Disk Manager applet

Mounting Systems

In Chapter 1, we covered how to partition and format a drive. Now, since you have a second drive in the system, you can make it mount each time you boot the system.

1. Unmount the drive, partition, and format it. For this example, we will assume you have configured it with one partition: `/dev/hb1`.

2. Create a place to mount the drive. For example: `sudo mkdir /mnt/backup`.

3. Add the drive (`/dev/hdb1`) to the `/etc/fstab` file so it is mounted automatically.

```
# /etc/fstab: static file system information.
#
# <file system> <mount point>    <type>  <options>          <dump>
<pass>
proc            /proc            proc    defaults          0         0
/dev/hda1       /                ext3    defaults,errors=remount-ro 0
1
/dev/hda5       none             swap    sw                0         0
/dev/hdc        /media/cdrom0    udf,iso9660 user,noauto     0         0
/dev/hdb1       /mnt/backup      ext3    defaults          0         0
```

4. Mount the new file system using either `sudo mount -a` or `sudo mount /mnt/backup`.

With these changes in place, the new drive will be mounted every time you boot.

Using Simple Backups

Back in the old days, I would make backups using floppy disks. As drives increased in size, I switched over to magnetic tapes. Today, home systems can be cheaply backed up using a second hard drive. Listing 3-3 is a simple script that I use to backup my Ubuntu system onto a second hard drive.

Listing 3-3: Very Simple Backup Script: /usr/local/bin/backup2disk-full

```
#!/bin/sh
# backup files to disk
# (Be sure to make this executable! chmod a+rx backup2disk)
for i in bin boot etc home lib opt root sbin sys usr var ; do
  tar --one-file-system -cf - "/$i"  2>/dev/null | \
    gzip -9 > /mnt/backup/backup-$i-full.tgz
done
```

This simple script creates a bunch of compressed TAR files containing all of my data. For example, `/mnt/backup/backup-home-full.tgz` contains the contents of my `/home` partition. You can also create a version that does incremental backup by replacing the `tar` command in Listing 3-3 with:

```
tar  -newer /mnt/backup/backup-$i-full.tgz \
  --one-file-system -cf - "/$i" 2>/dev/null | \
  gzip -9 > /mnt/backup/backup-$i-inc.tgz
```

For my system, I added the full backup script to my root crontab and configured it to run once a week. The incremental runs nightly.

1. Edit the root crontab. This allows files to run at specific times.

   ```
   sudo crontab -e
   ```

2. Add a line to make the full backup run weekly and the incremental run daily. (See Chapter 7 for details on Cron.)

   ```
   # minute hour day-of-month month day-of-week    command
   5 0 * * 0 /usr/local/bin/backup2disk-full
   5 0 * * 1-6 /usr/local/bin/backup2disk-inc
   ```

Using this script, I can restore any file or directory using `tar`. For example, to restore the `/home/nealk/book2` directory, I can use:

```
cd /
sudo tar -xzvf /mnt/backup/backup-home-full.tgz home/nealk/book2
sudo tar -xzvf /mnt/backup/backup-home-inc.tgz home/nealk/book2
```

Warning This backup script is very simple and can still lead to data loss. It does not keep historical backups and can lose everything if a crash happens during the backup. Although this script is a hack that is better than having no backups, it should not be depended on for critical backup needs. For long-term or critical data recovery, consider using a professional backup system.

Configuring a RAID

A Redundant Array of Inexpensive Disks (RAID) is a simple solution to surviving a disk crash. Ubuntu supports hardware RAIDs as well as software RAIDs. A hardware RAID needs no extra configuration for use with Ubuntu. The entire RAID just appears as a single disk. On the other hand, software RAIDs require some configuration.

A software RAID requires multiple hard drives. The simplest RAID uses two identical hard drives. I recommend buying the same make and model at the same time because they are certain to be identical. Other people recommend buying similar—but not identical—drives in case the drives have an unknown common problem. The choice really depends on your level of paranoia. I have had identical drives die within months of each other, but never both at the same time.

After installing the drives (for example, sda and sdb), partition them with the same size partitions (sda1 and sdb1). Now comes the fun part, turning them into a RAID.

 Note This example assumes that you have added two additional hard drives to your systems and they are already partitioned. The software RAID works by combining multiple real partitions into one virtual partition. Usually the partitions are on different hard drives, since having a RAID hosted on a single hard drive does not protect against hardware failure.

 Warning Creating a RAID requires modifying disk partitions and format. If you accidentally specify the wrong partition, you may end up destroying some or all of your system.

1. Use the `mdadm` tool to create the RAID. The man page for `mdadm` contains many additional options for striping, setting the RAID level, and so on. In this example, we will create a simple RAID1, or mirrored disks, configuration using the two partitions. The result is one RAID drive called `/dev/md0`.

   ```
   sudo mdadm --create /dev/md0 --level=1 \
               --raid-devices=2 /dev/sda1 /dev/sdb1
   ```

2. Creating the RAID happens in the background and can take hours to complete. Do not continue until it finishes. To watch the progress, use:

   ```
   nice watch cat /proc/mdstat
   ```

3. Now you can create the file system for the RAID. You can use any file system on the RAID. For example, to create an Ext2 file system, you can use:

   ```
   sudo mkfs /dev/md0
   ```

When you're done, you can view the RAID details using `sudo mdadm -Q --detail /dev/md0`. You can also mount the partition (`sudo mount /dev/md0 /mnt/disk`) and add it to your `/etc/fstab`.

 Note Under earlier versions of Ubuntu, such as Hoary, you could not easily add a RAID to `/etc/fstab` since the drivers started up in the wrong order. Dapper has fixed that problem and you can now boot the system with a RAID listed in `/etc/fstab`.

Between a Rock and a Hard Disk

In 2004 I had a hard disk crash that hurt. Years worth of research was on that drive and it had a head crash. Although I did have simple backups, that's not the same thing as having the entire working system. Although 98 percent of the data was recovered (thank you Reynolds Data Recovery in Longmont, Colorado!) and the lost 2 percent was easily recreated, I quickly learned my lesson: don't store critical data on one hard drive.

Today, my main research computer has four hard drives. One is the main operating system, one is configured as a removable backup, and two are identical drives used in a software RAID for storing all research. A single drive failure will not cause me any data loss, and a massive electrical surge should only cost me a day of work and some hardware. I also use daily backups and off-site, out-of-state storage. A massive file system corruption might take a day or two to recover and result in a few hours of lost work, but the majority of my data is safe.

Although this type of configuration may sound like overkill for most home and SOHO environments, you need to ask yourself: which costs less? Configuring a software RAID and a simple backup script, or rebuilding everything after a total loss? Even the hourly costs for recovery time are less when maintaining a minimal backup system.

Adding Other Devices

Printers, keyboards, and hard drives are just the start of the list of device that people use with their computers. Mice, touch pads, and video capture devices are also common. Unfortunately, hardware support within the open source community is hit-and-miss. Some devices have plenty of support, some have drivers that almost work, and some have no support at all. Adding to this problem, Ubuntu natively supports a much smaller set of hardware options than Linux in general. As a result, some drivers may need to be downloaded and compiled from scratch.

There is a basic rule of thumb when looking for Linux and Ubuntu support. If the device is standard and has been around for a while then it is likely to have support. Proprietary devices and closed technologies are unlikely to have drivers. Similarly, most peripherals that are new and cool either lack support or are supported by standard drivers.

Almost Compatible

Some vendors provide drivers for Linux in binary format only. Although these will work for a specific platform, they may not work with all platforms.

When choosing new hardware that requires Linux drivers, make sure that they support *your* version of Linux. A kernel driver for RedHat Enterprise Linux 4.2 may not work with Ubuntu's Dapper Drake, and a device driver for Dapper Drake may not work with Edgy Eft.

In general, the best hardware vendors use standard protocols and do not require specialized kernel drivers. This means that drivers will be around for a long time. Your second choice should be vendors that provide source code. This enables you to recompile the code for use with other kernels and operating system versions. In the worst case, you may need to tweak the driver to work, but at least you will have the source code for tweaking. Finally, if you have no other option, then choose a vendor that has a long track record of Linux support. Hardware that does not support Linux today should not be expected to support Linux tomorrow.

For example, Timex offers a set of watches with USB ports. This enables you to synchronize the alarms with your computer's calendar program. (This is a huge cool factor in geek terms.) Unfortunately, the watches use a non-standard USB protocol. As of August 2006, drivers are only available for Windows. Even though a few open source groups are trying to create drivers for other operating systems, Mac OSX and Linux users are currently out of luck.

NVIDIA is another example of a vendor with proprietary protocols. But instead of USB watches, NVIDIA manufacturers video cards. In contrast to the Timex non-existent drivers, NVIDIA supports Linux by providing proprietary video drivers, including versions that work with Ubuntu (see Chapters 4 and 9). Although source code is not available, NVIDIA has a long history of providing drivers for Linux.

Under Linux, it is generally easier to find drivers for legacy hardware. Few devices have ever been completely dropped. (The notable exceptions are the original 80386 and older CPU architectures due to their lack of a math coprocessor.) Although Windows XP may not have drivers for the Colorado Memory Systems' QIC-80 tape backup system, the Linux `ftape` driver's source code should be available for decades (although you may need to download, compile, and install them manually).

Using a Serial Mouse

One of the first problems I encountered when installing Ubuntu was the mouse. By default, Ubuntu only supports a USB mouse, but my mouse uses the serial port. This problem can be quickly resolved by editing the `/etc/X11/xorg.conf` file, which describes the displays and input devices that should be used with the graphical display.

1. As root, make a backup of /etc/X11/xorg.conf.

   ```
   $ sudo cp /etc/X11/xorg.conf /etc/X11/xorg.conf.original
   ```

2. Edit the file. You may want to make the window wide enough so lines do not wrap.

   ```
   $ sudo gedit /etc/X11/xorg.conf
   ```

3. Search for the sections titled "InputDevice". One will refer to the keyboard with the title "Generic Keyboard" and the other refers to the mouse ("Configured Mouse").

4. Add a new section after "Configured Mouse" for the serial mouse. In this example, the mouse is on `/dev/ttyS0` (first serial port). Other port options include `/dev/psaux` (for a PS/2 mouse) and `/dev/ttyS1` for the second serial port. The sample configuration also supports three-button emulation, where pressing the left and right mouse buttons acts the same as pressing the middle mouse button. If you have a three-button mouse, then you can choose to leave this line out of the configuration. Other options include specifying the mouse protocol, such as "Microsoft" or "Logitech" for most serial mice, and "PS/2" for a PS/2 mouse.

   ```
   Section "InputDevice"
           Identifier          "Serial Mouse"
           Driver              "mouse"
           Option              "CorePointer"
           Option              "Device"                "/dev/ttyS0"
           Option              "Emulate3Buttons"       "true"
   #       Option              "Protocol"      "Microsoft"
   #       Option              "Protocol"      "Logitech"
   #       Option              "Protocol"      "PS/2"EndSection
   ```

5. Go down to the "ServerLayout" section. You should comment out the `Configured Mouse` line (for a USB mouse) and add a line for the serial mouse.

   ```
   Section "ServerLayout"
           Identifier          "Default Layout"
           Screen              "Default Screen"
           InputDevice         "Generic Keyboard"
           InputDevice         "Configured Mouse"
           InputDevice         "Serial Mouse" "SendCoreEvents"
           InputDevice         "stylus" "SendCoreEvents"
           InputDevice         "cursor" "SendCoreEvents"
           InputDevice         "eraser" "SendCoreEvents"
   EndSection
   ```

6. Save your changes.

Now you can restart the X-server by pressing Ctrl+Alt+Backspace. This immediately logs you out and closes all running processes. When the system comes back (after a few seconds) you will be at the login screen. Moving the serial mouse should work.

Debugging Xorg.conf

There are a few things that could go wrong here. First, you could have entered the wrong information for your mouse (for example, specifying `/dev/ttyS0 instead of /dev/ttyS1`) or the wrong protocol (for example, Microsoft instead of Logitech). This appears as a mouse pointer that does not move. You can press Ctrl+Alt+F1 to get to a command prompt and re-edit your `/etc/X11/xorg.conf` file. Pressing Alt+F7 returns you to the graphical window and you can reset the server again using Ctrl+Alt+Backspace.

Note   At the text command prompt, you will need to use a text editor such as `vi` or `emacs`. For example, `sudo vi /etc/X11/xorg.conf`.

The other bad result is a black screen (maybe with a cursor blinking). This means that you did something wrong and the server failed to start. Use Alt+F1 (or Ctrl+Alt+F1—both key combinations work) to get to a command prompt where you can edit the `/etc/X11/xorg.conf` file. Look in the `/var/log/Xorg.0.log` file for error messages. Common things that can go wrong include:

- **Typo**—A mistake when entering the configuration file can stop the server from booting.
- **Driver conflict**—If you forgot to disable the USB mouse, then there is a driver conflict with the serial mouse. That will block the server.

Unfortunately, if the server crashed, you will be unable to restart it with Ctrl+Alt+Backspace. Instead, run `startx` to bring up the X server. If the server fails, it will display a lot of debugging information that you can use to resolve the problem. In the worst case, copy the backup back (`sudo cp /etc/X11/xorg.conf.backup /etc/X11/xorg.conf`) and try again. When you finally have a working X-server, you can reboot the system to restart the login screen.

Supporting a Touch Pad

The other type of pointer device that you will likely come across is a touch pad. Touch pads are very common with laptops. Normally, these are identified by the mouse driver and used without any additional configuration.

The default mouse driver does not support special features such as double tapping the pad in place of double clicking, or hot corners in place of shortcuts. These features can be added through the Synaptics mouse driver.

```
sudo apt-get install xserver-xorg-input-synaptics
```

The full list of configuration options and requirements can be found at `http://web.telia`
`.com/~u89404340/touchpad/index.html`. As with other devices, you will need to install
the devices driver, configure /etc/X11/xorg.conf, and restart the X-server. The basic "InputDevice"
section will look something like this:

```
Section "InputDevice"
  Identifier "Synaptics Touchpad"
  Driver "synaptics"
  Option "SendCoreEvents" "true"
  Option "Device" "/dev/psaux"
  Option "Protocol" "auto-dev"
  Option "HorizScrollDelta" "0"
  Option "SHMConfig" "on"
EndSection
```

You will also need to add `InputDevice "Synaptics Touchpad"` to the "ServerLayout"
section of `/etc/X11/xorg.conf` and restart the X-server.

After installing the device, you can install `qsynaptic`. This application enables you to graphically configure the touch pad.

```
sudo apt-get install qsynaptics
qsynaptics
```

Configuring USB Devices

Ubuntu supports many types of USB devices. Some devices are recognized instantly and are
very usable, but others need additional drivers and some configuration. The first step for configuring a USB device is simple enough: plug it in. The core USB kernel driver should
immediately recognize that a USB device has been connected. You can check this with the
`lsusb` command.

```
$ lsusb
Bus 005 Device 003: ID 0781:5406 SanDisk Corp.
Bus 005 Device 001: ID 0000:0000
Bus 003 Device 001: ID 0000:0000
Bus 001 Device 001: ID 0000:0000
Bus 004 Device 003: ID 056a:0014 Wacom Co., Ltd
Bus 004 Device 001: ID 0000:0000
Bus 002 Device 002: ID 05ac:0301 Apple Computer, Inc. iMac Mouse
Bus 002 Device 001: ID 0000:0000
```

You should also see the device listed at the end of /var/log/messages.

```
$ dmesg | grep usb
[17183135.308000] usb-storage: device found at 3
[17183135.308000] usb-storage: waiting for device to settle before scanning
[17183135.308000] usbcore: registered new driver usb-storage
[17183140.348000] usb-storage: device scan complete
[17183277.088000] usb 4-1: USB disconnect, address 2
[17183279.400000] usb 4-1: new low speed USB device using uhci_hcd and
address 3
```

```
[17183279.644000] usbcore: registered new driver wacom
[17183279.644000] drivers/usb/input/wacom.c: v1.44:USB Wacom Graphire and
Wacom Intuos tablet driver
```

Making Static USB Devices

USB supports hot-plug devices. This means that USB devices can be disconnected and reconnected without advanced notice for the operating system. The operating system will not crash or become unstable just because a USB device is suddenly unplugged.

Warning

Although the core USB subsystem permits disconnects at any time, other systems can have problems. Disconnecting a USB thumb drive while it is being written to can corrupt the thumb drive's partition, and disconnecting an X-Windows input device can crash the computer.

Every device on the system needs a device handle in the /dev directory. This can lead to problems with hot-plug devices: each time a device is connected, it may be assigned a different device handle. One time the tablet may be on /dev/input/event0 and the next time it could be /dev/input/event3. The maintenance of these devices is handled by udev, the dynamic device management system. The udev daemon (udevd) is actually a process started by init. You can configure udev to assign a static name to a device. For example, if you have a Wacom USB drawing tablet, you can have it automatically assigned to /dev/wacom rather than using the dynamic device driver handle.

Tip

The same approach for assigning the tablet to /dev/wacom can be used for assigning a mouse, scanner, or other USB device.

Note

The Wacom graphic tablet is used throughout this example because it requires each of the configuration steps. Other USB devices may need some or all of these items.

1. Determine the event driver(s) assigned to the device by looking in /proc/bus/ input/devices. In this example, the device is a Wacom Graphire3 6x8 tablet and it uses the device handlers /dev/input/mouse0, /dev/input/event2, and /dev/input/ts0 for the mouse, stylus, and touch screen, respectively.

```
$ more /proc/bus/input/devices
. . .
I: Bus=0003 Vendor=056a Product=0014 Version=0314
N: Name="Wacom Graphire3 6x8"
P: Phys=
S: Sysfs=/class/input/input3
H: Handlers=mouse0 event2 ts0
B: EV=f
B: KEY=1c43 0 70000 0 0 0 0 0 0 0 0
B: REL=100
B: ABS=3000003
. . .
```

2. Determine the driver attributes using the event driver (event2 in this example) identified in /proc/bus/input/devices. The udevinfo command will traverse the chain of USB device drivers, printing information about each element. (There will be similar entries for /dev/input/mouse0 and /dev/input/ts0.)

```
$ sudo udevinfo -a -p `udevinfo -q path -n /dev/input/event2`
...
device '/sys/class/input/input3/event2' has major:minor 13:66
  looking at class device '/sys/class/input/input3/event2':
    KERNEL=="event2"
    SUBSYSTEM=="input"
    SYSFS{dev}=="13:66"

follow the "device"-link to the physical device: looking at the
device chain at '/sys/devices/pci0000:00/0000:00:1d.3/usb4/4-1/
4-1:1.0':
    BUS=="usb"
    ID=="4-1:1.0"
    DRIVER=="wacom"
    SYSFS{bAlternateSetting}==" 0"
    SYSFS{bInterfaceClass}=="03"
    SYSFS{bInterfaceNumber}=="00"
    SYSFS{bInterfaceProtocol}=="02"
    SYSFS{bInterfaceSubClass}=="01"
    SYSFS{bNumEndpoints}=="01"
    SYSFS{modalias}=="usb:v056Ap0014d0314dc00dsc00dp00ic03isc01ip02"
...
```

3. As root, create (or edit) the /etc/udev/rules.d/10-local.rules file. This is where udev will look when determining how to handle the device. Rules can consist of comparisons (for example, == or !=) and assignments. Rules can use any of the fields displayed by udevinfo. There are other rules files in the same directory if you need additional examples. The manual for udev (man udev) is also very informative.

4. Add the following line to the /etc/udev/rules.d/10-local.rules file. Be sure to use the name found in /proc/bus/input/devices and the driver name and fields found from the udevinfo command.

```
BUS=="usb", DRIVER=="wacom", KERNEL=="event[0-9]*", SYMLINK="wacom"
```

This says to match any device where the bus is usb, the driver is wacom, and the kernel is the string event followed by some digits. Any match will be assigned to the link /dev/wacom.

Note   Try to make the rule as specific as possible, but be aware that fields like ID and SYSFS{dev} can change each time the device is plugged in. For example, if we don't specify the KERNEL, pattern, then the mouse0 and ts0 devices will also match the rule. But, if we add in SYSFS{dev}=="13:66", then it may not match if we plug the device into a different USB port.

5. Restart the udev system.

```
sudo /etc/init.d/udev restart
```

If your tablet is already plugged in, you may also need to unplug the tabled from the USB socket and then plug it in again; otherwise, its device driver may not be recognized.

6. Check to see if the device appears.

```
$ ls -l /dev/wacom
lrwxrwxrwx 1 root root 12 2006-08-16 21:45 /dev/wacom -> input/event2
```

With these changes, every time the tablet is plugged in, it may still be assigned a dynamic device handle, but the well-known symbolic link will always point to the correct place. When the tablet is disconnected the symbolic link will be removed.

Associating Applications with USB

By default, all new device handles created by udev are only accessible by root. You can change the default ownership and permissions by including an OWNER, GROUP, or MODE assignment in your udev rule. For example:

```
SYSFS{idVendor}=="e2e3", SYSFS{idProduct}=="0222", MODE="664", GROUP="floppy"
```

The udev rules can also run commands. For example, /etc/udev/rules.d/85-hal.rules contains a command to unmount any mounted USB drives when they are disconnected.

```
SUBSYSTEM=="block",ACTION="remove", RUN+="/usr/lib/hal/hal-unmount.sh"
```

A similar rule could be added to start a specific program when a specific USB device is connected. For example, when you connect a scanner, you may want the drawing program gimp to start automatically. This way, you can immediately use Gimp to scan in images.

All commands executed by udev are run as root. This can be a security risk for multi-user systems and a problem for interactive applications. For example, if you start the gimp drawing program whenever a scanner is connected, then it will try to run as root; it will also try to connect to the X display and fail. To resolve both of these problems, we can create a /usr/bin/run_gimp command to always run the program as the user who owns the display (see Listing 3-4). We can then add this script to the scanner's run line in /etc/udev/rules.d/45-libsane.rules. For example, to run Gimp when an HP ScanJet 4100C scanner (USB vendor 03f0, product 0101) is plugged in, you çan use:

```
SYSFS{idVendor}=="03f0", SYSFS{idProduct}=="0101", MODE="664", \
    GROUP="scanner",  RUN="/usr/bin/run_gimp"
```

Note   Don't forget to make the script executable by using chmod a+x /usr/bin/run_gimp.

Now, every time the scanner with the USB identifier 03f0:0101 (as seen by `lsusb`) is connected, the driver will be added to group "scanner" and `gimp` will be started with the right permissions.

Listing 3-4: /usr/bin/run_gimp

```
#!/bin/sh
# Get the username of the person running the X-window on tty :0
NAME=`/usr/bin/who | /bin/grep " :0 " | /usr/bin/awk '{print $1}'`
# Udev runs as root but this needs to run as the user
# Run as the user and set the display
/bin/su - "$NAME" "/usr/bin/gimp --display :0"
```

When Programs Run...

There are many different places where a program can be told to run automatically. Some are easy to find, but others can be more difficult to hunt down. More importantly, there is no single right place to install a program. For example, if you want to start a program when a scanner is plugged in, you can either modify /etc/udev/rules.d/45-libsane.rules, or you can run `gnome-volume properties` (System ➪ Preferences ➪ Removable Drives and Media) and change the program that Gnome runs when a scanner is detected.

The main difference between these different options is flexibility. Although Gnome knows about scanners and cameras, only udev knows about other types of devices. In contrast, Gnome is generally easier to configure since udev has no graphical interface. Chapter 7 covers other ways for programs to start automatically.

Enabling Drawing Tablets

Ubuntu supports the many types of drawing pads, but the Wacom drawing pad has drivers installed by default. Even though the drivers are installed, they are not completely configured. To complete the configuration, you will need to follow a few steps.

1. Follow the steps mentioned in the "Making Static USB Devices" section to create the /dev/wacom driver handle.

2. By default, the `/etc/X11/xorg.conf` contains three "InputDevice" sections for the Wacom driver. It also has these input devices listed in the "ServerLayout" section.

3. Plug the Wacom drawing pad into the USB port and restart the X-server by pressing Control-Alt-Backspace.

The mouse cursor on the screen should now be controllable by the mouse or drawing pad.

Note Tablets and drawing pads may not be common, but installing them requires all of the device configuration steps. This is a fairly long example, but if you have troubles with any new device then you can use this example to help debug the problem.

Debugging the Wacom Tablet

If the tablet does not work, start with the xorg.conf debugging instructions for configuring a serial mouse. This will resolve any problems with the graphical display not starting.

You can also install the wacom-tools. These are a set of diagnostic applications.

```
sudo apt-get install wacom-tools
```

After installing these tools, you can see the list of supported tablets as well as run the diagnostics program (see Figure 3-6). As you move the tablet's mouse or stylus, the diagnostics program should register movement and any tablet button presses.

```
$ wacdump -1
art      wacom    serial   "ArtPad"
art2     wacom    serial   "ArtPadII"
dig      wacom    serial   "Digitizer"
dig2     wacom    serial   "Digitizer II"
pp       wacom    serial   "PenPartner"
gr       wacom    serial   "Graphire"
pl       wacom    serial   "Cintiq (PL)"
int      wacom    serial   "Intuos"
int2     wacom    serial   "Intuos2"
c100     acer     serial   "C100"
pp       wacom    usb      "PenPartner"
gr       wacom    usb      "Graphire"
gr2      wacom    usb      "Graphire2"
gr3      wacom    usb      "Graphire3"
gr4      wacom    usb      "Graphire4"
int      wacom    usb      "Intuos"
int2     wacom    usb      "Intuos2"
int3     wacom    usb      "Intuos3"
ctq      wacom    usb      "Cintiq (V5)"
pl       wacom    usb      "Cintiq (PL)"
ptu      wacom    usb      "Cintiq Partner (PTU)"
vol      wacom    usb      "Volito"
vol2     wacom    usb      "Volito2"
$ sudo wacdump -c usb /dev/wacom
```

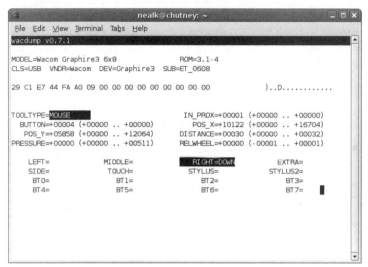

FIGURE 3-6: The text-based wacdump diagnostics program

Warning

Disconnecting a USB device that is used by the X-server can crash the computer.

Not all removable devices can be removed safely. Removing a USB device that is in use by the X-server can only create problems. In the best case, the device will not function until you restart the X-server. In the worst case, the X-server can hang or the entire computer may crash. If you want to disconnect the Wacom graphics tablet, first log out, then disconnect it, and then *immediately* restart the X-server by pressing Ctrl+ Alt+Backspace.

Tuning the Tablet

Depending on the tablet model, the coordinates on the tablet may not match your screen resolution. You can resolve this by adding the following options to each of the Wacom "InputDevice" sections in the xorg.conf file.

To automatically set the coordinates on your tablet to match your screen resolution, you can use:

```
Option "KeepShape" "on"
```

The KeepShape option scales the active area of the tablet so it matches the screen. For example, the tablet likely has a 4:3 aspect ratio. If your screen is 16:9, then the active area on your tablet will start at the top left corner and scale to match a 16:9 region. The bottom of the active area on the tablet will not be usable since it is outside of the 16:9 ratio.

To manually set the coordinates on your tablet, you can use:

```
Option "TopX" "0"
Option "TopY" "0"
Option "BottomX" "16704" # match wacdump resolution
Option "BottomY" "12064" # set to match wacdump resolution
```

The Wacom tablets have very high resolutions. For example, the Wacom Graphire3 (6 × 8) has a maximum resolution of 16,704 × 12,064. The Wacom driver scales the tablet's range to match the screen resolution. If you set the bottom coordinates to something small, like 1024 × 768, then only a very tiny area of the tablet will be active.

Using Other Tablets

Although support for the Wacom tablet is included by default, other tablets have available drivers. Use `apt-cache search tablet` to display the list of available drivers. In addition, some tablets may be compatible with other drivers or have drivers available for download from other sources. Your best bet is to research the tablet first and select one that has Linux, and preferably Ubuntu, support.

Each different tablet model will likely have different configuration requirements. Some of the requirements may be automated, while others may require manual modifications. Regardless of the specific requirements, they will all have the same basic steps:

1. Install a device driver, if one is not already installed.

2. Create device handle if one is not created automatically.

3. Load any required software drivers and configuration parameters.

4. Configure `/etc/X11/xorg.conf`.

5. Restart the X-server using Ctrl+ Alt+Backspace.

Tuning TV Cards

TV capture cards are a must-have for any power user. These add-on cards allow you to watch TV through your computer and configure a video recorder such as MythTV (an open source version of the TiVo™ video recorder system). The driver for video devices is called video4linux (v4l). The v4l driver supports bt848 and bt878 TV cards.

Note Most TV cards use the bt848 or bt878. If you look at the card, you should see a quarter-sized chip with "848" or "878" printed on it.

Configuring TV cards is relatively easy.

1. Install the video card and hook up the TV cable to it. Most TV cards support both broadcast and cable TV signals.

2. Install the v4l driver.

   ```
   sudo apt-get install xserver-xorg-driver-v4l
   ```

3. Edit `/etc/X11/xorg.conf` and add v4l to the "Modules" section so X-Windows knows about the video driver.

   ```
   Section "Module"
           Load    "i2c"
   ```

```
        Load    "bitmap"
        Load    "ddc"
        Load    "dri"
        Load    "extmod"
        Load    "freetype"
        Load    "glx"
        Load    "int10"
        Load    "type1"
        Load    "vbe"
        Load    "v4l"
EndSection
```

4. Restart the X-server using Ctrl+ Alt+Backspace.

5. Test the video configuration. The xsane program has a scan option and menu for selecting the TV as input (Figure 3-7). If you see a picture (or static) then the v4l driver is working properly.

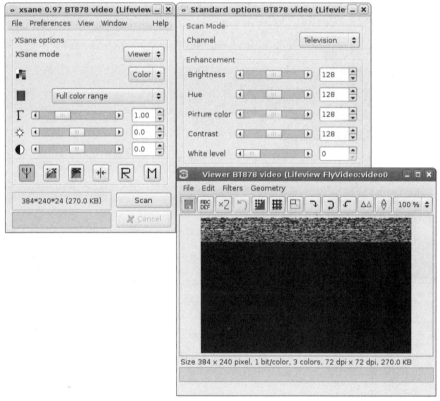

FIGURE 3-7: Using xsane to test the v4l driver. Since the channels are not configured, only static is captured.

Now that the v4l driver is working, you can install capture, recording, and viewing programs that can configure and use the video card. My favorite is xawtv. This is a simple program for tuning the TV, watching channels, capturing images, and recording shows.

```
sudo apt-get install xawtv xawtv-plugin-qt tv-fonts xawtv-tools
```

When you first start xawtv it will display the TV screen but may need a little configuration. Right-clicking the TV window will bring up the configuration menu. Be sure to set the norm (PAL, NTSC, and so on), type of signal (for example, us-cable), and the input source (Television). Use the up and down arrows to change channels. When you find a configuration that works for you, save it using E. This option is actually used to set channel names, but saves the entire configuration in $HOME/.xawtv. Listing 3-5 shows a sample configuration. At this point, xawtv should be working for you and the TV card is fully configured (see Figure 3-8).

FIGURE 3-8: The xawtv program showing the TV in a window

With a working TV card you can also configure your screen saver to grab pictures from the TV.

Tip

If you change the screensaver from the default gnome-screensaver to xscreensaver (see Chapter 9), then you can configure some of the screensavers to use the TV card. You will find this option in xscreensaver's preferences as Grab Video Frames under the Advanced tab settings. Screensavers such as Distort and Flipscreen3D will manipulate TV captures.

Using Digital Cameras, Scanners, and Web Cameras

Although TV cards are cool, they are not as common as digital cameras, scanners, and webcams. Unfortunately, this is where hardware support really becomes hit-and-miss. My eight-year-old SCSI scanner is supported, whereas my newer USB scanner is not. And although both of my digital cameras can work as webcams under Windows, neither can work as webcams under Linux.

Note Not every camera provides the same compatibility. If your camera does not support a capture mode, then you cannot use the computer to take pictures with it and you cannot use it as a high-resolution webcam.

A tool that you may want to consider installing is gphoto2. This program provides support for over 700 different camera models. It enables you to scan for compatibility with the camera and query supported functionality.

1. Install gphoto2 as well as the graphical front end (gtkam) and the gimp plug-in to allow captures from cameras.

    ```
    sudo apt-get install gphoto2 gtkam gtkam-gimp
    ```

2. Plug your camera into the USB port. There is no need to restart the X-server in order to load the drivers. If any windows, such as the camera import applet, pop up with prompts to import images or show the camera's contents, just close them.

3. Determine if the camera is supported. If the gphoto2 command does not auto-detect your camera, then the camera is not supported. You may need to use a different driver if one is available. If the camera is mounted as a disk, then it will not be listed as a camera device.

    ```
    $ gphoto2 --auto-detect
    Model                                   Port
    ----------------------------------------------------------------
    HP PhotoSmart 618                       usb:
    ```

Note Depending on your camera model and capabilities, you may see multiple lines of output from the gphoto2 --auto-detect command.

4. List the camera's capabilities. Most digital cameras have two PC-connect modes. The first mode is usually called something like *digital device* and makes the camera appear as an actual USB camera. The second mode makes the camera appear as a USB drive. The different camera modes provide different attributes. For example, here are the attributes for the HP PhotoSmart 618 in digital device mode.

Note The ability to switch PC-connect modes depends on the camera. You will need to hunt through the camera's configuration menu to see if mode selection is supported and to change modes.

```
$ gphoto2 --abilities
Abilities for camera            : HP PhotoSmart 618
Serial port support             : yes
USB support                     : yes
Transfer speeds supported       :
                                : 9600
                                : 19200
                                : 38400
```

```
                                            : 57600
                                            : 115200
Capture choices                             :
                                            : Capture not supported by
the driver
Configuration support                       : no
Delete files on camera support              : yes
File preview (thumbnail) support            : yes
File upload support                         : no
```

For a comparison, here are the attributes for the same camera in USB disk drive mode.

```
$ gphoto2 --abilities
Abilities for camera                        : USB PTP Class Camera
Serial port support                         : no
USB support                                 : yes
Capture choices                             :
                                            : Capture not supported by
the driver
Configuration support                       : yes
Delete files on camera support              : yes
File preview (thumbnail) support            : yes
File upload support                         : yes
```

Depending on your supported capture modes, you may be able to use the camera with scanner software such as Gimp and xsane, or with VoIP and teleconference software like WengoPhone (see Chapter 5). Even if the camera does not support captures or webcam mode, you can still access the device as a USB drive and copy (or move) off images. In USB disk drive mode, the camera appears no different than a USB thumb drive. You can transfer files by opening the drive via Nautilus and copying off the files. In digital device mode, use gtkam to view the photos and copy them to the desktop.

Summary

Hardware support for Linux, and Ubuntu in particular, varies greatly. Although printers, hard drives, and TV cards have excellent support, other devices have more spotty support options. In many cases, installing the driver is not the last step; you will also need to configure the driver and dependent applications. Fortunately, once Linux supports a device, it is effectively supported for life. You can still find drivers for ancient MFM hard drives and ten-year-old scanners.

The best resources for hardware support are the Linux and Ubuntu forums, and sites that specialize in specific hardware types.

- https://wiki.ubuntu.com/HardwareSupport lists hardware that is supported by Ubuntu, as well as any particular quirks and issues.

- www.linux.org/hardware provides a very complete list of hardware that has known support for the Linux kernel.

- www.gphoto.org/ lists more than 700 supported digital camera models.

Loading the device and making it work is one thing, but making it work well can be something entirely different. In Chapter 4, you'll see how to get the most out of video and audio devices by installing different codecs. Chapter 6 covers hardware emulation. In Chapter 9 you will start playing with screen resolutions and multiple monitors, and in Chapter 12 you will dive into advanced networking.

Working with Compatibility

in this part

Chapter 4
Managing Software

Chapter 5
Communicating Online

Chapter 6
Collaborating

Managing Software

Operating systems evolve. There is a constant flow of patches and updates that needs to be reviewed and installed. And then there is custom software—packages that are not included in a standard distribution but can be very valuable anyway. How do you even begin to browse for these packages?

As part of the Linux open source family, Ubuntu can use most open source packages. Large repositories such as SourceForge (`sourceforge.net`) and FreshMeat (`freshmeat.net`) store hundreds of thousands of projects. Unfortunately for some projects, downloading, compiling, and installing can be overwhelming. In addition, dead projects, unchanged in years with no active maintainers, are available for download.

Fortunately, the Ubuntu community maintains many different repositories of precompiled packages that are ready to install and use. All you need to do is specify the ones you want and they are installed—no manual compilation required. Programs such as the Advanced Package Tool (APT) and its graphical front end, Synaptic, simplify the search and install process.

Each package contains several items:

- Precompiled applications
- Dependency information for other packages needed by this package
- Install scripts
- Package information and description
- License information

You can obtain packages from the Ubuntu CD-ROM, DVD, or over the network.

Not every package works after a successful installation. Some packages require additional configurations before working properly. Scripts such as EasyUbuntu have automated a few of the common, complex installations. In the worst cases, you will still need to download sources and compile code. For these situations, you will need to install a programming environment.

in this chapter

- ☑ Understanding repositories
- ☑ Running Synaptic
- ☑ Living without Synaptic
- ☑ Installing common functions
- ☑ Installing common packages by hand
- ☑ Compiling and developing software

Understanding Package Repositories

Packages (precompiled executables) come from a variety of locations. Ubuntu maintains four main repository types (called *components*) where most software can be retrieved.

- **main**—This component contains all officially supported open source projects without restrictive licensing. Gnome, GDM, and the Linux kernel are all found in main.

- **restricted**—These packages are officially supported, but have restrictive licenses. This component primarily contains third-party video and network drivers.

- **universe**—These packages are not officially supported by Ubuntu, but are provided and maintained by the Ubuntu community. As with main, the universe component only contains open source projects without restrictive licensing. Games, compilers, and a wide variety of tools are found here.

- **multiverse**—This is the catchall component that contains community-supported packages with restrictive licensing. Example packages include Adobe's Acrobat PDF reader, some fonts, and MP3-related tools.

Packages from the main and restricted components are included on the Ubuntu installation CD-ROMs (see the /pool directory). Although Ubuntu officially supports these two components, the community provides the other two: universe and multiverse. This means that their contents may not be as thoroughly tested or updated as the official repositories.

By dividing software based on licensing and support, software developers and corporations can make intelligent decisions based on their own needs. For example, a company that develops custom software may want to stay away from the restricted and multiverse repositories in order to reduce the risk of licensing contamination. A small office looking for reliable support may stick to fully supported packages from the main and restricted repositories.

Differentiating Distributions

Along with the four components (main, restricted, universe, and multiverse) are a variety of Ubuntu repositories. For Ubuntu, each repository contains the name of the Ubuntu version. For Dapper Drake, all distributions contain "dapper".

- **dapper**—This indicates the primary distribution for the operating system.

- **dapper-updates**—This repository holds updates to the main dapper distribution. Updates are kept separate from the main distribution so an installation baseline is maintained.

- **dapper-security**—This is a special repository specifically used for security updates.

- **dapper-backports**—This repository contains software that has been backported—compiled from a newer version of Ubuntu to work with Dapper. For example, Edgy Eft will use a newer version of Gnome than Dapper. Edgy's Gnome version may be backported to work with Dapper. Because these versions are not thoroughly tested under Dapper, the backport distributions are disabled by default.

Debs, RPMs, and Repositories

Most large Linux distributions provide some form of precompiled code. RedHat and SUSE Linux, for example, use the RedHat Package Manager (RPM). Although the `rpm` package exists for Ubuntu, it is not commonly used. Each RPM contains licensing information. A single RPM repository may contain packages with both restricted and unrestricted licenses.

Debian Linux uses the Debian Package Manager (`dpkg`) to install `deb` packages. Since Ubuntu is based on Debian, it too uses `dpkg` and `debs`. Other package management tools, such as APT and Synaptic, are actually wrappers around `dpkg`. As with Ubuntu, Debian divides packages based on licensing, but Debian uses slightly different divisions.

- **Debian main**—This is similar to the Ubuntu main component. All code is supported, open source, and provided with unrestrictive licensing.

- **Contrib**—This component contains open source with unrestrictive licensing, but may be dependent on code that has restrictive licensing.

- **Non-Free**—As with the Ubuntu restricted component, these packages contain licenses that restrict use or distribution.

- **Non-US/Main**—These packages do not have restrictive licensing, but may not be exported outside of the United States. This usually means the packages contain cryptography.

- **Non-US/Non-Free**—This component is the counterpart to Non-US/Main. Most of these packages use proprietary cryptography or are restricted by patents.

Although you can install Debian deb packages under Ubuntu, most of these packages have been ported to the Ubuntu repositories.

Compatibility leads to the biggest problems when using binaries from other platforms. Depending on the software and how it was compiled, some packages may not work under your version of Ubuntu. Different kernel and shared library versions can break executables. If you can, consider sticking with Ubuntu binaries. If you can't find Ubuntu binaries, then be careful. Don't try binary kernel modules without knowing how to remove them first; incompatible modules can crash your system. For regular user applications, incompatible binaries may not run or may complain about missing libraries. Sometimes you can fix dependencies by installing older libraries, but you are probably better off looking for source code. If the binaries are proprietary, then you are out of luck unless you can use them in a virtual machine (see Chapter 6).

Each distribution contains main, restricted, universe, and multiverse repositories. Different servers may host some or all of the different distributions and repositories.

Note   Not all Ubuntu servers provide the same software. Even though the official repositories are supposed to be mirrors, sometimes they contain different packages. Similarly, a mirror may only carry the main component for Dapper, whereas the original server may provide all components for Dapper and other Ubuntu versions.

Running Synaptic

Synaptic is the graphical interface for selecting packages for installation. To open it, choose the System ⇨ Administration ⇨ Synaptic Package Manager menu (see Figure 4-1). The Synaptic Package Manager displays the available sections on the left, and the available packages on the right. At any time, you can select a package for installation or deselect an already installed package. If you select a package that has dependencies, then all dependencies are automatically selected (or deselected). The bottom status line of the window displays a summary of the selections.

When you are ready to make the system changes, select the Apply button. Although there are a few confirmation and status screens, the installations usually require no manual efforts.

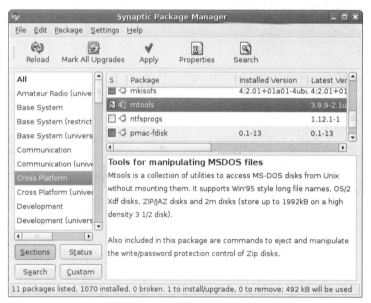

FIGURE 4-1: The Synaptic Package Manager

Searching with Synaptic

The most powerful part of Synaptic is its search capabilities. You can search for packages by name, description, version, dependencies, and more. Searches are listed as a category on the left side, with search results showing the packages on the right.

To switch back to the repository list, click the Sections button. You can always return to your search history by clicking on the lower Search button.

Synaptic Gaps

As powerful as Synaptic is, it has a couple of usability issues. First, there isn't a Stop button available when you do a search. If you have a slow computer (or slow network connection) and you search for a common term, such as the word *the*, you should be prepared to wait until the search completes.

A second limitation concerns the search button itself: there are two of them. One is at the top and the other is at the bottom. The top Search button allows you to conduct a new search. The bottom Search button shows you the search history and previous search results.

Finally, the search history is limited to the current session. When you close Synaptic, you will lose your search history.

Changing Repositories

The default Ubuntu installation only has the officially supported dapper, dapper-updates, and dapper-security distributions enabled. You may want to also enable the universe and multiverse repositories. You can do this while in Synaptic through the Settings ➪ Repositories menu. A list of standard distributions is provided—you can simply check the appropriate entries to enable them.

Besides enabling distributions, you can select specific repositories from the distributions using the Add button (see Figure 4-2). After modifying the repositories, you will need to click Reload to rescan the list of packages.

Warning Synaptic does little to prevent you from adding invalid repository-component combinations, or from adding the same distribution twice. Bad choices may result in error messages later, but you will get no warning when you make the selection.

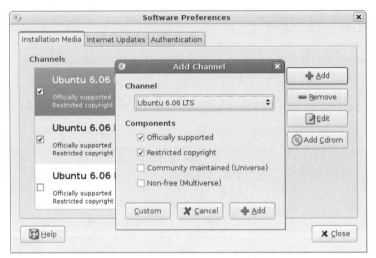

FIGURE 4-2: Adding to the repository list

Installing from a CD-ROM or Directory

Besides installing over the network, Synaptic supports installations from a CD-ROM drive or fixed directory. This can come in really handy when working without a network connection or in a close network environment such as a mission critical server room. Installing from a CD-ROM is very easy—simply put the CD-ROM in the drive. Ubuntu will recognize the disk as being a repository and will prompt you to add it to the repository list. At this point, the CD-ROM will act like any other repository.

Note
If the CD-ROM is not automatically recognized, you can use Settings ➪ Repositories to get to the Add Cdrom button.

In closed environments, it is usually more convenient to install from a shared or local directory. You can configure this using Settings ➪ Repositories. Rather than selecting a pre-set value, click on the Add button and then select Custom to add your own repository. For example, the following enables package installation from a downloaded ISO file:

1. Download one of the Ubuntu installation CD-ROMs. Let's call it `ubuntu.iso`.

2. Mount the disk image.

```
sudo mkdir -p /mnt/iso
sudo mount -o loop ubuntu.iso /mnt/iso
```

3. Using the custom add button under Synaptic (Settings ➪ Repositories ➪ Add ➪ Custom), add the following repository:

```
deb file:/mnt/iso dapper main restricted
```

Note When using Synaptic to add repositories, each repository will appear at the end of `/etc/apt/source.list` file. However, when searching for a package, the repositories are scanned from the top of the file to the bottom. If you want your new repository to be used first, you will need to edit `/etc/apt/sources.list` and change the order of the repositories.

Synaptic will look for the dapper distribution's main repository in the `/mnt/iso/dists/dapper/main` and `/mnt/iso/pool/dapper/main` directories. The `dists` directory contains the indexes for packages, whereas the `pool` directory contains the actual packages.

Turning Off Repositories

Using a repository from a CD-ROM or local directory can improve install speeds since you are not dependent on the network. Local repositories also give you the ability to customize the software your system can access.

However, as useful as it is to use a CD-ROM or local directory as a repository, you may want to disable them after you do an installation. Without turning them off, Synaptic will complain that the repository is no longer accessible after you remove the CD-ROM or disable the directory.

To turn off repositories, select System ⇨ Repositories. You can clear the CD-ROMs and custom directories to turn them off. If you do not think you will need them again, you can also click on the Remove button.

Managing Updates

The default Synaptic installation periodically checks for new revisions. If there are updates or patches for packages that you already have installed, then Synaptic can flag these or automatically install them. When new updates are available, you will see a star icon on the top panel. Hovering the mouse over this icon will show you the number of pending updates (see Figure 4-3), and clicking on the icon will allow you to apply updates.

FIGURE 4-3: The indicator showing that updates are available

You can change the update settings by using Software Preferences applet. Either select it from the System ⇨ Administration ⇨ Software Properties menu, or by right-clicking the update indicator. The Internet Updates tab shows the settings. You can tell Ubuntu to periodically check for updates (or never check), download updates (but not install), or automatically install security updates.

Some updates require a special confirmation before installing. These include kernel updates and critical libraries. Upgrading these usually requires a reboot and could break some applications. As a result, these packages require additional confirmation and are not automatically installed.

By default, Dapper checks for updates daily and automatically installs all security updates. For critical systems and controlled environments, you may want to completely disable automatic updates. This enables you to apply updates during a scheduled period rather than when updates they are available. In contrast, regular home users should keep the defaults: check for updates daily and automatic installation of security updates. If you are on a slow network connection, you may want to change the check for update frequency, but it should be at least every two weeks.

 Completely disabling updates is usually a bad decision. While many updates apply security patches, others address stability issues. The only time you may want to disable auto-updates is when you have some other plan for maintaining the system.

Living Without Synaptic

Despite its quirks, Synaptic is a very useful utility for keeping up-to-date on patches and installing new software. Unfortunately, Synaptic requires human interaction and a graphical interface. If you installed the Ubuntu server or are remotely logged into the system, then you probably do not have the graphical interface. And when managing dozens (or hundreds) of systems, depending on a graphical interface becomes an impediment.

Fortunately, Synaptic is a graphical front end to the Advanced Package Tool environment; every basic Synaptic function comes from APT. Using the APT commands, you can search for software, install packages, and perform upgrades from the command line.

Modifying Sources

APT uses a configuration file to tell it where repositories are located. The file /etc/apt/sources.list contains a list of servers, distributions, and repositories. Listing 4-1 shows some sample repositories. If you want to add or change repositories, simply edit the file (as root) and make your additions or modifications. There is no need to restart any services or processes.

Note The /etc/apt/sources.list file is used by dpkg, APT, and Synaptic. Technically, APT is a wrapper around dpkg, and Synaptic is a graphical front-end to APT. Changes to this file affect all of these tools.

Each line within this file contains four key elements:

- **Type of data**—The available data is either precompiled binaries (deb) or source code for compiling binaries (deb-src).

- **Location**—A URL says how to get the data. This is usually an HTTP, HTTPS, or FTP server, but it can also be a local CD-ROM or a directory.

- **Distribution**—The name of the distribution is provided. Example names include dapper, dapper-updates, and dapper-security.

- **Component**—One or more components are specified, such as main, restricted, universe, or multiverse.

When All Else Fails...

Knowing how Synaptic works under the hood, and how to use APT from the command line can be critical for system recovery. On August 21, 2006, the maintainers of Ubuntu accidentally released a bad update. This update disabled X-Windows, leaving users at a command line prompt. Graphical tools, such as Synaptic, suddenly became unavailable. The only mitigation option was to use apt-get to reinstall the X-server from the command line after Ubuntu fixed the error in the X-Windows packages.

Not all failures are due to bad updates. On Saturday, July 22, 2006, many of the servers hosting Ubuntu repositories went offline—and some stayed offline the entire weekend. Refreshing the Synaptic repository list generated a cryptic error message (and sometimes crashed Synaptic). Knowing how to manually change the servers from one region to another was the only way to apply patches and install essential software. And changing the servers is a task easier done without using Synaptic. (The downtime was later attributed to a series of server upgrades.)

Accidents happen, but without knowing how to identify errors or recover from them, you can end up with an unusable system. The command line apt-get and apt-cache tools generate informative errors that can be used to diagnose these problems. In the case of a bad server or network connection, editing the /etc/apt/sources.list file can provide a quick solution.

Listing 4-1: Sample Entries from an /etc/apt/source.list

```
# The server "uk.archive.ubuntu.com" contains source code for the "dapper"
# distribution. The distribution contains "main" and "restricted" repositories.
deb-src http://uk.archive.ubuntu.com/ubuntu/ dapper main restricted

# The same server contains binary for the updates distribution.
deb http://uk.archive.ubuntu.com/ubuntu/ dapper-updates main restricted

# The CD-ROM with label "Ubuntu 6.06 _Dapper Drake_ - Release i386 (20060531)"
# also contains dapper main.
deb cdrom:[Ubuntu 6.06 _Dapper Drake_ - Release i386 (20060531)]/ dapper main

# A local directory -- this can be a mounted directory such as a CD-ROM or a
# networked file system (NFS)
deb file:/mnt/iso dapper main

# My full list of sources
deb http://us.archive.ubuntu.com/ubuntu/ dapper main restricted
deb-src http://us.archive.ubuntu.com/ubuntu/ dapper main restricted
deb http://us.archive.ubuntu.com/ubuntu/ dapper-updates main restricted
deb-src http://us.archive.ubuntu.com/ubuntu/ dapper-updates main restricted
deb http://security.ubuntu.com/ubuntu dapper-security main restricted
deb-src http://security.ubuntu.com/ubuntu dapper-security main restricted
deb http://security.ubuntu.com/ubuntu dapper-security universe
deb-src http://security.ubuntu.com/ubuntu dapper-security universe
```

Tip If you want to exclude a specific repository, then make sure the `/etc/apt/sources.list` file does not include it on any of the repository lines. For example, to exclude multiverse, make sure all multiverse lines are commented out (with a # character) or removed from the uncommented line.

After you make any changes to `/etc/apt/sources.list`, you will need to refresh the APT cache of available packages: `sudo apt-get update`. This updates the cache of available software. Without this command, you won't search the list of available software. When you enable the automatic check for patches, the system actually runs the `apt-get update` command.

Note If you make changes to `/etc/apt/sources.list` and you use Synaptic, then you can click the Reload button to refresh the cache. Otherwise you need to run `sudo apt-get update`.

The list of servers should match your region. For example, us.archive.ubuntu.com is intended for users in the United States. The uk.archive.ubuntu.com server is for the United Kingdom, and ca.archive.ubuntu.com supports Canada. A few two-character country codes (for example, uk and us) are currently defined; undefined country codes are redirected to the United Kingdom because that is where Canonical is located. If you find that a particular region is temporarily unavailable, then try changing regions by modifying each of the server's names in /etc/apt/source.list. It is rare for all of the servers to be unavailable at the same time.

Adding CD-ROM Repositories

Besides using Synaptic, there are two ways to add a CD-ROM to /etc/apt/source.list. The first way requires you to manually identify the CD-ROM label and then add it. The apt-cdrom command can list the disk's label. Let's assume that the Ubuntu installation CD-ROM is mounted at /mnt/iso:

```
$ apt-cdrom -m -d /mnt/iso ident
Using CD-ROM mount point /mnt/iso/
Mounting CD-ROM
Identifying.. [d9f91a1075ce140463bf88837cc07be6-2]
Stored label: Ubuntu 6.06 _Dapper Drake_ - Release i386 (20060531)
```

Tip   The -m parameter for apt-cdrom says to not mount the disk, otherwise the CD-ROM sitting in the drive will be used. The -d parameter specifies the mount point for acquiring the label and ident directs the command to identify the CD-ROM label.

After finding the CD-ROM name, you can add it to the /etc/apt/sources.list file with a cdrom: resource. For example, to install the main component, I would use:

```
deb cdrom:[Ubuntu 6.06 _Dapper Drake_ - Release i386 (20060531)]/ dapper main
```

Although you can add a disk manually, the easiest way to add a CD-ROM is to let apt-cdrom do it.

1. Insert the CD-ROM into the drive.

2. Run the command.

```
sudo apt-cdrom add
```

The CD-ROM is automatically added to the /etc/apt/source.list file.

Note   After adding a CD-ROM to the /etc/apt/sources.list file, be sure to run apt-get update. This adds the packages on the CD-ROM to the cache of known packages.

Browsing the APT Cache

Another command, `apt-cache`, enables you to search the repositories for a particular subject or file name. The search word will match any package's name or description. For example, if you are searching for a calculator, you could use:

```
$ apt-cache search calculator
bc - The GNU bc arbitrary precision calculator language
gcalctool - A GTK2 desktop calculator
dc - The GNU dc arbitrary precision reverse-polish calculator
bison - A parser generator that is compatible with YACC
```

Tip

Searches are case-insensitive and look for sub-strings. You can search for multiple words in sequence using quotes like `apt-cache search "gnu bc"`. You can also list multiple terms (without quotes) that will be matched in any order. For example: `apt-cache search calculator calctool`.

It may seem odd that Bison (Yet Another Compiler-Compiler) is listed as a calculator, but another `apt-cache` command shows the entire package's description and lets us understand why it was listed. (Bison's description contains the word *calculator*.)

```
$ apt-cache show bison
Package: bison
Status: install ok installed
Priority: standard
Section: devel
Installed-Size: 1264
Maintainer: Chuan-kai Lin <cklin@debian.org>
Architecture: i386
Version: 1:2.1-0.2ubuntu1
Depends: m4, libc6 (>= 2.3.4-1)
Recommends: bison-doc
Description: A parser generator that is compatible with YACC
 Bison is a general-purpose parser generator that converts a
 grammar description for an LALR(1) context-free grammar into a C
 program to parse that grammar.  Once you are proficient with Bison, you
 may use it to develop a wide range of language parsers, from those used
 in simple desk calculators to complex programming languages.
...
```

Other options for `apt-cache` can show dependencies, requirements, and contents. The man page for `apt-cache` details other options (`man apt-cache`).

Organizing Search Results

The results from `apt-get search` are not sorted by package name. Instead, they are sorted by server repository. In the case of the calculator search, `bison` is listed after `dc` because it came from a different repository. If you want the results sorted by package name, then you will need to sort them yourself:

```
apt-cache search calculator | sort
```

Similarly, if you are searching for a specific package name or description, then you will need to apply a filter:

```
apt-cache search calculator | grep gcalctool
```

Tip

You can use `grep` to restrict results to the displayed text. This is different than using multiple terms with `apt-cache search` since the matched results may not be in the displayed text.

Installing with APT

After you know what to install, you can use the `apt-get install` command to perform the installation. You can list one or more packages after the `install` instruction. If you want to see what will happen without actually doing the install, use the `-s` option to simulate the installation. You will see every warning and message without actually doing the install.

```
sudo apt-get -s install gcalctool    # check the install
sudo apt-get install gcalctool       # perform the install
```

Although the `gcalctool` application is installed by default, when you install the Ubuntu desktop, its source code is not. Source code is available for all packages in main and universe. However, source may not be available for packages found in restricted or multiverse.

Tip

While Synaptic gives cryptic error messages (or crashes) when `/etc/apt/sources.list` contains bad entries or is misconfigured, the `apt-cache` and `apt-get` commands will display plenty of errors and warnings.

Removing Packages with APT

Package removal is nearly as painless as installation.

1. First, find the package name you want to remove. You can use `apt-cache search` or `apt-cache pkgnames` to list all packages, but the easiest way is to use `dpkg`.

   ```
   dpkg -l | more
   ```

   Alternately, if you know a file that is in the package, then you can use `dpkg -S` to list all packages containing that file. For example, to remove whatever package provides the program `bc`, you can use:

   ```
   dpkg -S `which bc`
   ```

2. Use `apt-get` to check what will be removed. Some package dependencies will force the removal of other packages. For example, to check the removal of the `bc` package, use:

   ```
   sudo apt-get -s remove bc
   ```

3. If the removal looks safe, then use `apt-get` to remove the package. For example, to remove the `bc` package, use:

   ```
   sudo apt-get remove bc
   ```

The bc package is installed as part of the default desktop. Removing bc removes a dependency from a trivial package called ubuntu-desktop. This isn't the actual desktop, but it is used as a flag to indicate that the full desktop is installed. To see everything in the ubuntu-desktop package, use dpkg -L ubuntu-desktop.

Removing Residues

Most software removals are clean—everything that went in is taken out. Unfortunately, some removals leave residues, such as configuration and data files. Removing or reinstalling a package because it is misconfigured may not replace critical configuration files. This can result in the package remaining misconfigured after being installed. A few examples:

- Removing and reinstalling a Web browser will not clear user-caches or replace user settings. This is not a solution for fixing privacy issues from cached Web pages.

- Removing and reinstalling Gnome will not remove $HOME/.gnome, $HOME/.gnome2, and other Gnome-related files in user directories.

- Many packages check for modified configuration files. If you modify a configuration file, such as /etc/X11/xorg.conf or /etc/gdm/gdm.conf, then it may not be removed when these packages are removed.

If you are reinstalling software because of a configuration problem, be aware that this may not fix the problem.

Leftover files and other residues may need to be manually cleaned up (or deleted) before you decide to reinstall the package. In the case of a misconfiguration, reinstalling the system usually will not resolve problems—especially if the configuration problem is due to files stored in a user's directory or created after the installation.

Tracking Removals

As mentioned earlier, one of the biggest problems with removals comes from dependent packages. Removing one package may automatically select other packages and remove them too. Although using apt-get -s remove can be useful, always remember to use the -s to check first. If you forget the -s then you will need some way to see everything that was removed (so you can put back critical packages). Fortunately, you have two options (besides restoring from a system backup). First, the /var/log/dpkg.log file contains a list of every addition and removal (see Listing 4-2). This log file is updated every time Synaptic, ATP, or dpkg installs or removes packages. Using this list, you can see what was removed and undo an accidental removal.

Listing 4-2: Sample Contents from /var/log/dpkg.log

```
2006-08-25 18:37:17 install dpkg-dev <none> 1.13.11ubuntu6
2006-08-25 18:37:17 status half-installed dpkg-dev 1.13.11ubuntu6
2006-08-25 18:37:18 status unpacked dpkg-dev 1.13.11ubuntu6
2006-08-25 18:37:18 status unpacked dpkg-dev 1.13.11ubuntu6
2006-08-25 18:37:18 status unpacked dpkg-dev 1.13.11ubuntu6
2006-08-25 18:37:18 status unpacked dpkg-dev 1.13.11ubuntu6
2006-08-25 18:37:18 status unpacked dpkg-dev 1.13.11ubuntu6
2006-08-25 18:37:18 status half-configured dpkg-dev 1.13.11ubuntu6
2006-08-25 18:37:18 status installed dpkg-dev 1.13.11ubuntu6
2006-08-26 08:06:01 status installed dpkg-dev 1.13.11ubuntu6
2006-08-26 08:06:02 remove dpkg-dev 1.13.11ubuntu6 1.13.11ubuntu6
2006-08-26 08:06:02 status half-configured dpkg-dev 1.13.11ubuntu6
2006-08-26 08:06:02 status half-installed dpkg-dev 1.13.11ubuntu6
2006-08-26 08:06:02 status config-files dpkg-dev 1.13.11ubuntu6
```

The second option is to use the `script` command. This command logs all command line output to a file:

```
$ script -c "sudo apt-get remove dpkg-dev" apt-get.log
Script started, file is apt-get.log
Reading package lists... Done
Building dependency tree... Done
The following packages will be REMOVED:
  dpkg-dev
0 upgraded, 0 newly installed, 1 to remove and 2 not upgraded.
Need to get 0B of archives.
After unpacking 541kB disk space will be freed.
Do you want to continue [Y/n]? y
(Reading database ... 106427 files and directories currently installed.)
Removing dpkg-dev ...
Script done, file is apt-get.log
```

From the `script` command, you will get a file called `apt-get.log` containing the entire removal session. This command can even be turned into a simple script that you can use instead of using the actual `apt-get` command (see Listing 4-3).

Listing 4-3: Replacement /usr/local/bin/apt-get for Logging Results

```
#!/bin/sh
# Run the apt-get command and append (-a) results to ./apt-get.log
script -a -c "sudo /usr/bin/apt-get $*" apt-get.log
```

Upgrading with APT

Applying upgrades is a two-step process. First, use `apt-get update` to retrieve the list of available software packages and upgrades based on your `/etc/apt/sources.list`. If there are any updates, then the update indicator will appear on the top panel. After getting the list of updates, use `apt-get upgrade` to perform the upgrade.

```
$ sudo apt-get update
Get:1 http://archive.ubuntu.com dapper Release.gpg [189B]
Get:2 http://archive.ubuntu.com dapper Release [34.8kB]
Get:3 http://archive.ubuntu.com dapper/universe Packages [2458kB]
Hit http://us.archive.ubuntu.com dapper Release
Hit http://us.archive.ubuntu.com dapper-updates Release
Hit http://us.archive.ubuntu.com dapper/main Sources
...
Fetched 3117kB in 7s (416kB/s)
Reading package lists... Done
$ sudo apt-get upgrade
```

Installing Common Functions

When setting up an Ubuntu desktop system, there are some packages that most people want to install. Many of these center around multimedia functionality: playing MP3 files, DVD movie media, and multimedia streams with RealNetwork RealPlayer. Although downloading with `apt-get` is relatively easy, many of these packages still require configuration before they can be used. At this point, you have two options: use an automated installer that will perform any required configurations, or install and configure packages by hand.

Using EasyUbuntu

EasyUbuntu is a script designed to download and automatically configure common packages. It only supports about 40 widely used packages (not every available package) and it does not install any source code packages. This software has one other limitation: EasyUbuntu is not found in any of the main, restricted, universe, or multiverse repositories. Instead, you will need to visit the EasyUbuntu homepage (`http://easyubuntu.freecontrib.org/`) and follow the installation instructions. The installation itself is straightforward:

1. Apply all updates. EasyUbuntu can have problems if the system is not up to date. Fortunately, problems simply means that components are not installed; problems do not cause system instability.

   ```
   sudo apt-get update
   sudo apt-get upgrade
   ```

2. Go to the EasyUbuntu home page and follow the installation instructions. These are usually a few lines of code for installing and running EasyUbuntu. Be sure to choose the current release. For EasyUbuntu 3.022, the installation instructions are:

   ```
   wget http://easyubuntu.freecontrib.org/files/easyubuntu-3.022.tar.gz
   tar -zxf easyubuntu-3.022.tar.gz
   ```

```
cd easyubuntu
sudo python easyubuntu.in
```

Note If you use these commands as is, you will use EasyUbuntu version 3.022. Newer versions are periodically released as packages are updated. You should use the current version (whatever version number that may be). Newer versions may also include different installation steps. See the EasyUbuntu homepage for the latest installation instructions.

3. Open a terminal window (Applications ⇨ Accessories ⇨ Terminal) and paste the installation instructions into the terminal.

4. The final `sudo` command will prompt you for your password. After that, the graphical interface will start up.

Easy Does It

EasyUbuntu cannot be installed using `apt-get` because it does not exist in any of the repositories. The reason is mainly based on legal issues. EasyUbuntu can help you install drivers that may not be legal in your country. For example the `w32codecs` enables you to play proprietary Windows multimedia files, and `libdvdcss2` enables you to play DVD movies by cracking the DVD encryption. In some countries, these packages are illegal.

EasyUbuntu also supports packages from the Penguin Liberation Front (PLF) repository. As with main, restricted, universe, and multiverse, PLF is a specialized repository. It can be added to `/etc/apt/sources.list` and used to install software. The line to add is:

```
deb http://medibuntu.sos-sts.com/repo/ dapper free non-free
```

However, PLF has an interesting history: it distributes software that cannot be included in the standard repositories due to copyright, patents, or other legal restrictions. Installing software from this repository may also be *illegal* depending on your country's laws.

The user interface for EasyUbuntu displays four tabs showing the different package categories, and each tab displays the available packages. Since some packages are not available on every platform, only the available software is displayed (see Figure 4-4). For example, since the binary audio packages gstreamer0.10-pitfdll and w32codecs, and the NVIDIA video drivers do not exist for the PowerPC, EasyUbuntu on a PowerPC does not display the Binary Codecs option.

FIGURE 4-4: The EasyUbuntu user interface as seen on a PC (i386) and Macintosh (PowerPC). Some options are not available on all platforms.

EasyUbuntu uses dpkg to check which software has already been installed. If a package already exists on the system, then the check box is grayed out. This prevents you from trying to reinstall software. After making your selections, you can click OK to perform the installation. Depending on your choices and network speed, this may take a while.

Note EasyUbuntu is used only to install and configure packages. You cannot use it to remove software.

Software sometimes changes faster than EasyUbuntu—the EasyUbuntu developers are constantly playing catch-up with other package developers. If an installation fails, EasyUbuntu will not corrupt your system. Instead, it will create a variety of popup windows that display errors and warnings. These are similar to the messages given by APT. You will need to manually install any failed packages.

Debugging EasyUbuntu

Errors during EasyUbuntu installation are usually due to invalid entries in /etc/apt/source.list, missing repositories, new package locations, or bad package dependencies. Unfortunately, EasyUbuntu will not tell you what failed or why. The /var/log/dpkg.log file will show you specific package failures, but not missing repositories. In other words, if the installation cannot find a required package, EasyUbuntu will not tell you about the failure.

If EasyUbuntu fails, try installing each checked item individually. This enables you to identify which packages fail. In the EasyUbuntu directory is the file packagelist-dapper.xml. This shows every package that is installed for each selection. For example, when I select Video from the Web tab, EasyUbuntu 3.022 installs the package totem-gstreamer-firefox-plugin. Unfortunately, on the PowerPC platform, this package depends on a specific version of totem-gstreamer, and the dependency was outdated. Although the failure was due to the repository,

EasyUbuntu does not identify what caused the installation failure. Instead, I narrowed down this problem by installing each item, one at a time, until I found that Video would not install. Then I looked in `packagelist-dapper.xml` and saw that it included `totem-gstreamer-firefox-plugin`. Finally, I performed the installation by hand using `apt-get` and saw the cause of the failure.

```
$ sudo apt-get -s install totem-gstreamer-firefox-plugin
Reading package lists... Done
Building dependency tree... Done
The following packages have unmet dependencies:
  totem-gstreamer-firefox-plugin: Depends: totem-gstreamer (= 1.4.1-0ubuntu4)
but 1.4.3-0ubuntu1 is to be installed
E: Broken packages
```

My solution to this problem is to download the source code to the plug-in (`apt-get source totem-gstreamer-firefox-plugin`) and compile it manually.

Ain't So Easy

There is an alternative to EasyUbuntu: Automatix. This tool is similar to EasyUbuntu in many ways. Automatix automates software installation and is not found in any of the standard repositories. Visit the Automatix home page (`http://www.getautomatix.com/`) for installation instructions.

Automatix supports more packages than EasyUbuntu, but has other limitations. The biggest concern with Automatix is its automatic installation of potentially harmful packages. It is very possible to trash your system if you select incompatible packages. It also requires modification to `/etc/apt/sources.list` for installation, and it requires a high technical level to understand all of the options.

In my opinion, community recommendations carry weight. Most forums that compare Automatix with EasyUbuntu recommend EasyUbuntu because of the low technical requirements, safe installations, and simpler download instructions. Two evaluations of these tools are available at `https://lists.ubuntu.com/archives/ubuntu-users/2006-March/071696.html` and `http://nalioth.hostdestroyer.com/comparison.html`.

If you just want to click-and-run, then EasyUbuntu is the simpler option. If you're looking for more detailed configurations, consider the *Easy Linux Ubuntu Guide*, available at `http://easylinux.info/wiki/Ubuntu_dapper` and `http://ubuntuguide.org/wiki/Dapper`. Although this guide is not automated, it is very complete—covering more options than either EasyUbuntu or Automatix—and has relatively easy to follow step-by-step instructions.

Installing Common Packages by Hand

Because automated installation systems, such as EasyUbuntu and Automatix, use graphical interfaces, they cannot be used from the default Ubuntu server installation. In addition, remote logins may not support the required graphic interface. If you want to install additional multimedia support without using graphics, then you will need to install the packages by hand.

Installing Multimedia Support

Different multimedia formats need different libraries to encode and decode the formats. A variety of coder-decoder (codec) libraries are available for Ubuntu. Each of these packages is installed using apt-get install package_name. Some of these packages are located on the universe, multiverse, or plf repositories. No additional configuration steps are required.

- **MP3**—MP3 is one of the most common and popular audio formats. As mentioned in Chapter 2, the sox and lame packages provide MP3 encoding and decoding support. While these tools do provide command-line support, they do not provide audio libraries. For libraries that will work with most audio players, you will need to install the ffmpeg package from the universe repository.

- **Ogg**—Ogg Vorbis is an alternate audio format that is free from MP3's licensing restrictions. To support Ogg Vorbis files, you will need to install the vorbis-tools package from the restricted repository.

- **MPEG and Video**—For MPEG and other video file formats, you will want to install the mjpegtools package. This multiverse package provides codecs for MPEG, AVI, QuickTime, and other video formats.

- **MPEG4**—The libxvidcore4 and faad packages provide video and audio support for this file format. Both packages are found in the multiverse repository.

- **Windows Codecs**—The w32codecs package provides binary support for proprietary Microsoft codecs such as WMA and WMV. This package is found in the plf repository.

- **DVD**—Commercial DVD movies are encoded using a system called CSS. The libdvdcss2 permits unlicensed DVD players to view these movies. This package is found in the plf repository.

Warning   Packages such as libdvdcss2 and w32codecs could cause legal headaches—particularly in corporate and government environments. If you have any questions here, you might want to consult legal council before installing these packages.

After you load the codecs onto the system, you will need to add plug-ins to your multimedia players so that they know the codecs exist.

- **Gstreamer**—The Gstreamer interface provides multimedia support for most Gnome applications. Although there are generic plug-ins, their package naming convention is less than descriptive.

    - gstreamer0.10-ffmpeg: This package provides support for the ffmpeg package.

- `gstreamer0.10-pitfdll`: Adds support for the controversial `w32codecs` package.

- `gstreamer0.10-plugins-bad`: Support for codecs, such as WAV audio codecs, that are not as refined as other codecs. The naming convention bad denotes codecs that are still under development. They are close to production quality, but are not there yet.

- `gstreamer0.10-plugins-bad-multiverse`: Support for multiverse codecs that are not as refined as other codecs. This includes `faad` and `libxvidcore4`.

- `gstreamer0.10-plugins-ugly`: This package provides support for MPEG formats. While the "bad" codecs are just not refined, the "ugly" codecs may have distribution issues due to licensing restrictions or patents.

- `gstreamer0.10-plugins-ugly-multiverse`: Similar to `gstreamer0.10-plugins-ugly`, this supports packages from the multiverse repository.

- **Xine**—Xine is an alternative audio and video player to Gnome's totem player. As with the Gstreamer interface, Xine supports plug-ins. The `gxine` package installs the `gxine` base player. The `libxine-main1` and `libxine-extracodecs` packages provide codecs.

Installing Web Support

Some multimedia formats are primarily found on the Web. This includes Macromedia Flash movies and RealNetworks audio and video streams.

Getting Flashy

Macromedia provides a Flash player for Ubuntu. Installing the `flashplugin-nonfree` package from the multiverse repository will actually download and install the Linux Flash player from the Adobe web site. After installing the package, you will need to run the `update-flashplugin` command to configure your browser.

```
sudo apt-get install flashplugin-nonfree
sudo update-flashplugin
```

Unfortunately, the `flashplugin-nonfree` package is only available for PCs. As an alternative, the `swf-player` package provides basic SWF (Flash file) support for all Ubuntu platforms.

Note   The `swf-player` package does not support all SWF versions. Newer versions of Flash animations may not play using `swf-player`.

Getting Real

In contrast to Flash, there are two different RealPlayer packages for Ubuntu. The `realplayer` package in the multiverse repository provides support for RealPlayer 8, while the PLF repository has a `realplay` (not `realplayer`) package that provides support for RealPlayer 10.

These packages configure the Firefox browser so they are automatically recognized and available for use.

Note

RealPlayer support is only provided on the x86 architecture. If you are using a PowerPC or AMD64 system, then there is no native driver available.

Finally, you may want to have a multimedia player like Totem integrated into your web browser. Normally multimedia files are saved to disk. Having the player integrated in the browser can create a seamless user experience by automatically running the player when you click on a link. You can enable the integration by installing the `totem-gstreamer-firefox-plugin` package. For using Xine in Firefox, use `totem-xine-firefox-plugin`.

Installing Font Packages

There are a few desktop packages that you will probably want to install. The first set of packages provides different desktop fonts. These are used by everything from text menus to PDF and Postscript viewers. If an application cannot find a particular font, then it will attempt to substitute it with a different font, and the results can be ugly.

Ubuntu supports three main types of fonts: xfonts, gsfonts, and ttf. Xfonts are used by X-Windows. These bitmapped fonts are designed for specific resolutions (dpi) and can appear blocky when scaled. For example, the `xfonts-100dpi` package provides fonts that render best at 100dpi.

Ghostscript fonts (gsfonts) are vector-based rather than bitmapped. These may take longer to render than bitmapped fonts, but they will look smoother and scale well. These are usually used for displaying documents, word processing, and printing, but not for regular screen fonts.

The final group consists of TrueType fonts (ttf). These are also vector-based and are commonly used on Windows systems. If you receive a document in PDF or Word that has ugly or missing fonts, then you probably need to install a ttf font package.

Font definitions are relatively small and consume no system resources if they are not used. For best results, consider installing all of the available fonts for languages that you expect to encounter. This way, you won't end up rendering with poor substitutions.

Note

The default font in most cases is called *misc-fixed* and is a monospaced San Serif font. When converting between graphic formats, like Postscript and PDF, missing system fonts may be replaced with bitmapped fonts, resulting in very rough text that is readable but not pretty. The technical term for drawing text with bitmapped fonts is *ugly* rendering.

- **Ghostscript fonts**—Ghostscript is the open source Postscript rendering and viewing system. The fonts used by Ghostscript can be used by any available X-Windows application. The `gv` package provides the Ghostscript Ghostview program for viewing Postscript files. The `gsfonts` package provides Ghostscript fonts, and `gsfonts-x11` makes the fonts available for X11.

```
sudo apt-get install gv gsfonts gsfonts-x11
```

- **International fonts**—There are many different packages for providing international language support. All of the most common languages are supported, as well as some lesser-known languages. Example font packages include:

    - `xfonts-intl-european` provides support for most European and Latin-based languages. This includes Spanish, German, and French.

    - `gsfonts-wadalab-common`, `gsfonts-wadalab-gothic`, `gsfonts-wadalab-mincho`, `konfont`, and `ttf-sazanami-mincho` each provide support for Japanese.

    - Chinese is supported through a variety of font packages including `ttf2pt1-chinese`, `ttf-arphic-ukai`, `ttf-arphic-uming`, `xfonts-cmex-big5p`, `xfonts-intl-chinese`, and `xfonts-intl-chinese-big`.

    - `ttf-farsiweb` and `ttf-paktype` supplies Farsi and Urdu fonts.

    - `ttf-khmeros` supplies fonts for the Khmer language of Cambodia.

    - There are dozens of xfont packages (`apt-cache search xfonts`) for supporting most European, Asian, and Middle-Eastern languages.

- **Windows fonts**—The `msttcorefonts` package provides the core TrueType fonts found on Microsoft systems. While this does provide true compatibility with Windows systems, there may be licensing issues.

After installing the fonts, you will need to inform applications that they exist. Fortunately, all standard applications look at the same cache directories. The command `sudo fc-cache -f -v` will scan and list the font directories, and update the shared font information.

Note   If the fonts do not appear after you install them, you may have forgotten to run `fc-cache`.

Compiling and Developing Software

The packages found in the Ubuntu repositories do not include all open source software (far from it!). The main and restricted repositories only include software explicitly supported by Ubuntu and its managing company, Canonical. The universe and multiverse repositories only include Ubuntu packages that are (or were) supported by someone in the community. There are hundreds of thousands of open source projects that are not in these repositories, and many only require you to download the source and compile them.

There are many reasons why you might want to download source code. Some of the common reasons include:

- **Cutting edge**—Software found in the Ubuntu repositories may be outdated. If you want the most recent version, you will probably need to visit the project's home page and download source code.

- **Tweaking**—If you don't like how some piece of software functions, you can download the source code and change it.

- **Fixing**—Some packages do not work. This may be due to broken dependencies or out-dated software components. In any case, you can retrieve the code, patch it as necessary, and install it on your system. You are not limited to precompiled software.

- **Educating**—If you want to understand how something works, you can download the source and look at the code. Code from open source projects can be used as excellent examples and templates.

- **Extending**—Many projects are extensible. By downloading the source code, you can see how to interface new software into a project.

- **Leveraging**—Why reinvent the wheel? If some source code does a function that you need, you can download the code and adapt it to your needs. Be sure to pay attention to the original author's licensing requirements; some source code cannot be freely used without restrictions.

- **Sharing**—Every package in the universe and multiverse repositories was compiled and tested by someone. Perhaps you would like to add your favorite projects so the community can benefit?

- **Uniqueness**—Many open source projects not found in the Ubuntu repositories provide very unique and useful functions. If you cannot download the functionality in binary form, then you will need to acquire the source.

Regardless of the reason, you will need some way to retrieve the source code and compile it. Some open source code is built for specific platforms and operating systems. For example, the mail reader elm and the graphic program xv were both designed for very old versions of Linux and have not been maintained. Downloading the source to these projects is not enough. You will likely need to edit the files before you can build these executables. To compile any incompatible projects, you may need a full development environment.

Installing Package Source Code

Many packages are available as pre-compiled executables and as source code. If you plan to install any source code then you'll need to install the dpkg-dev package. This brings in one required executable: /usr/bin/dpkg-source. This is used to unpack source code packages.

Many packages include developer installs. For example, the linux-kernel-devel package places source code on the system for people doing kernel development. Most major subsystems, including audio, USB, and X-Windows, provide developer packages.

 Note Some packages do not actually install code. For example, linux-kernel-devel is a package that is only used to install some specific dependencies. The code actually comes from its dependencies.

The other way to retrieve source code from the Ubuntu repositories is to actually download the source, and not an installation package. Source code is downloaded using apt-get source package_name. Every package in the main and universe repositories should include source code, but source code may be missing from the restricted and multiverse repositories.

Note Not every package includes source code. Although source code is expected for packages in the main and universe repositories, it may not exist for software found in the restricted and multiverse repositories.

The installation of binary files requires you to run apt-get as root. This is because files are placed in privileged directories and the catalog of installed packages must be updated. In contrast, source files are deposited in the current directory, so root permission is not required. This also means that there is no automatic removal. For example, to download the source code to gcalctool and unpack it, use:

```
mkdir src
cd src
apt-get source gcalctool
```

If you also want to automatically compile it, add the --compile flag to the apt-get line.

```
apt-get --compile source gcalctool
```

Warning While apt-get install downloads dependencies, the apt-get source command does not. You may be required to download and install different developer packages and additional source code. Do not expect automatic compilation to work perfectly every time.

If you are done with the source code, you can remove it without using apt-get.

```
rm -rf gcalctool*
```

Programming with C

Most open source projects are written in C, C++, Java, Perl, Python, or Shell Script. Perl, Python, and Bash (for Shell Scripts) are installed by default. Although basic C and C++ compilers are installed, these are not the full development environments. You should consider installing full environments.

There are many components to the full C and C++ environment. The key ones to install are:

- The Gnu C Compiler (gcc) and Gnu C++ (g++). These packages also install the manuals and documentation in case you need to look up any standard library calls.

  ```
  sudo apt-get install gcc g++
  sudo apt-get install gcc-doc manpages-dev
  ```

- The make command is commonly used for building executables. Other build-environment tools include autoconf, automake, and libtool.

  ```
  sudo apt-get install make autoconf automake libtool
  ```

- If the code uses any complicated state machines or lexical analyzers, then you will proba-bly need `flex` and `bison`.

  ```
  sudo apt-get install flex bison bison-doc
  ```

- The `zlib` library is very common. Most tools that perform compression use it. Some well-known examples include `gzip`, `bz2`, and `unzip`, but other tools like JPEG render-ing systems and MP3 players also use `zlib`.

  ```
  sudo apt-get install zlib1g zlib1g-dev
  ```

- Most graphic systems use the X11 graphic library. You will probably need the develop-ment environment since it provides the application programming interface (API) to X-Windows.

  ```
  sudo apt-get install xlibs-dev
  ```

- If you plan to do any hard-core development, you might want an integrated development environment (IDE). Under Ubuntu, you have a couple of options.

    - Anjuta is a fully functional IDE with a graphical interface. To install it, use `sudo apt-get install anjuta`.

    - Eclipse is a very popular IDE for Java, but it does have an extension for C pro-gramming. Use `sudo apt-get install eclipse-cdt` to install the C Developer Tool.

Note Anjuta is designed for C and C++ software development. In contrast, Eclipse is an extension of a Java IDE. As a result, Eclipse requires include a lot of additional packages that Anjuta does not need. The list of requirements for Eclipse includes Ant (a Java build system that is comparable to `make`), Java (the full environment), and even the Mozilla web browser (Uh, I don't know why, but it *is* a prerequisite).

Enabling Java

Java is a programming language that is used by some developers as an alternative to C and C++. Its strength is in portability: a program created in Java does not need to be recompiled on every platform. Because of its portability, some web sites use Java instead of static HTML or dynamic HTML with JavaScript.

Note Despite the naming similarity, Java and JavaScript are very different languages. The JavaScript name was more of a marketing blitz than a functional expression. At the time the language was created, Java was popular and *scripts* implied *simple*. Unfortunately, many non-programmers still think that JavaScript uses Java.

In previous versions of Ubuntu, there were many options for installing Java, and all required multiple steps. The problem was the licensing: Sun Microsystems used a restrictive license that was not appropriate for the restrictive or multiverse repositories. When Ubuntu Dapper was released, Sun changed the licensing, allowing the package to be placed in the multiverse reposi-tory. To install Java:

1. Enable the multiverse repository by editing `/etc/apt/source.list` and removing the commented line for the multiverse repository.

```
deb http://us.archive.ubuntu.com/ubuntu/ dapper-backports main \
restricted universe multiverse
```

2. Install the Java Runtime Environment (JRE).

```
sudo apt-get install sun-java5-jre
```

3. If you would like to use Java with the Mozilla Firefox web browser, you will need to install the Java plugin and configure it as the default JRE.

```
sudo apt-get install sun-java5-plugin
sudo update-alternatives --config java
```

4. For build environments, Ant is the tool of choice (few Java environments use `make`).

```
sudo apt-get install ant ant-doc
```

5. If you need a full IDE for Java, consider using Eclipse.

```
sudo apt-get install eclipse
```

The Sun Java 5.0 runtime environment requires you to agree to the Sun licensing. In some environments, this may not be desirable. In addition, this version of Java is not available for all platforms. For example, as of August 2006, `sun-java5-jre` did not install on the PowerPC because the `sun-java5-bin` package was unavailable. Fortunately, there are some alternatives to Sun's Java implementation.

- The `free-java-sdk` package provides an open source Java development and runtime environment.

```
sudo apt-get install free-java-sdk
```

- The GNU compiler for Java is an alternate open source Java implementation. A basic GCJ compiler is installed by the default, but you may want to install the entire JRE and the web browser plug-in.

```
sudo apt-get install gcj gij
sudo apt-get install gcjwebplugin
```

Summary

Ubuntu provides many different ways to search for software, install packages, and manage updates. Some of the methods require a graphic display—these are very easy to use but may limit remote administration. If the graphic display is unavailable (or inconvenient), you can always fall back to the command line software management system. Although most of the common software that you might want is available from one of the four standard repositories, you should be pre-pared to download source code and compile software by hand since some cool projects are not readily available for Ubuntu.

Communicating Online

chapter

5

The default Ubuntu desktop installation includes a web browser, e-mail reader, instant messaging and chat-room client, and even a VoIP system. Although anyone can use them as is, you can get much more out of them by performing a few tweaks and tuning a couple of parameters. Whether you want speed, security, or fancier graphics and cooler features, you are going to want to modify the default applications. In this chapter, you will see how to adjust the web browser settings, secure your web traffic using Secure Shell, access your mail on a variety of systems, and chat online.

in this chapter

☑ **Hacking the Firefox web browser**

☑ **Securing web access with SSH**

☑ **Managing E-mail with Evolution**

☑ **Using E-mail with Thunderbird Mail**

☑ **Instant messaging with Gaim**

☑ **Talking with VoIP**

Hacking the Firefox Web Brower

The default web browser for Ubuntu is Mozilla Firefox. This browser is fast and supports HTTP 1.0 and 1.1 protocols, as well as HTML and DHTML (dynamic HTML). Although you can immediately use the browser for accessing web sites, some of the default settings could use a little modification.

Tuning Preferences

Firefox has a set of common preferences that can be adjusted to fit your needs. Open the main preferences menu by starting the browser and choosing Edit ➪ Preferences from the Firefox menu. The preferences menu is divided in to categories, denoted by icons on the top of the window (see Figure 5-1). I change my preferences for security, speed, and convenience. Whenever I use a new browser, I immediately change the home page, Java and JavaScript settings, and cache options. If I plan to repeatedly use the browser (instead of a one-time install on a temporary system), then I also adjust the connection and privacy settings.

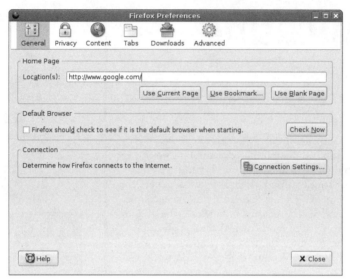

FIGURE 5-1: The Firefox Preferences window

Tuning the General Preferences

The General category provides basic settings for the browser.

- **Change the default location.** I usually use a search engine or a blank page. If there is a particular site you usually go to first, put the URL here. But specifying a blank page gives you a faster startup time since the browser isn't busy accessing the network.

- **Make sure the default browser check box is not set.** If you only have one browser, this is not an issue. Ubuntu is not like Windows, where various Windows applications can (and frequently do) hijack the default browser settings.

- **If you use a proxy instead of directly connecting to the Internet, Ubuntu gives you two choices.** You can configure a system-wide proxy that will work for all network services (see Chapter 12), or you can give Firefox a special proxy setting through the Connection Settings button.

Tuning the Privacy Preferences

The Privacy category provides settings for managing cached information.

- **I usually reduce the history from the default nine days to one day.** If I need to visit a site often, then I bookmark the URL. Keeping nine days of history just clutters the list of sites I have visited. But there are some reasons to keep a large history. For example, if you use the browser for researching a project, then a large history can allow you to quickly find places you visited days or weeks ago. Consider changing this value to match your needs.

Tip

Anyone using your browser can see the sites you have visited. If you have privacy concerns, consider lowering the history or disabling it completely by setting the number of days to zero and then clearing the history once.

- **I usually disable saved forms and saved passwords.** This is mainly for privacy. On the other hand, enabling these options can really speed up some web access. If you don't have privacy concerns and frequently visit the same sites that require forms or passwords, then you can enable these options.

- **Firefox keeps a history of downloaded files**. The default setting enables you to manually clean up the list of files. I usually enable automatic removal of entries after downloads. This way, my list only shows failed downloads and ones in progress.

- **As much as privacy advocates complain about tracking people, cookies have become a way of life on the web.** Yet, there are some safer ways to handle cookies. I suggest enabling cookies for only the originating site and blocking cookies that I have intentionally removed (see Figure 5-2). Unless you have a need for maintaining cookies long after you close the browser, I suggest the Keeping cookies: Until I close Firefox setting. When you close the browser, all cookies are removed.

Note Firefox uses shared memory. You must close *all* Firefox browsers and windows to clear out the cookies. Closing one browser does not do it since the shared memory is not released.

- **Cache files are stored on your hard drive for quick access to sites you commonly visit.** The default is 50 MB of cache. I usually reduce it to 20 MB. Most sites that I visit have dynamic content that changes hourly (active web forums, news sites, and so on). Despite what advertisers may think, I usually don't *need* to cache 50 MB of banner ads on my system.

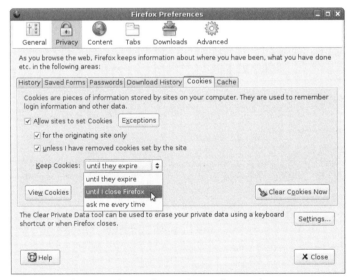

FIGURE 5-2: Changing the Firefox cookie preferences

Tip If a web page does not show current information, then it is likely cached. Hold down the Ctrl key when you click on the Reload icon in order to forcefully refresh the page. You can also use Ctrl+F5 or Ctrl+Shift+R.

Cache and Privacy

The browser cache can lead to privacy concerns. Everything from web pages of online bank accounts to porn that you accidentally stumbled across gets stored in the cache. If your system is compromised or accessed by someone else, then everything in your cache becomes fair game.

Keeping a small cache does remove the data from a typical user, but it won't stop the professionals. Even through a file is deleted, it can still be recovered through tools such as e2undel and recover (for ext2 file systems), or more complicated tools such as The Coroner's Toolkit (tct), Sleuthkit, and Autopsy. Although these are not easy-to-use programs, they can recover most deleted files.

The best way to stay very safe is to completely disable caching, but that will lead to slow web pages. Every icon—regardless how small—must be downloaded from the network every single time. In general, adjusting the cache size is done more for speed and disk space than for privacy since anything saved to disk could potentially be recovered.

Tuning the Content Preferences

The Content category provides settings for handling HTML content.

- **I always enable popup blocking.** If a specific site wants to create a popup, Firefox will inform me with a bar at the top of the page. Then I can explicitly permit popups for that page.

Note Blocking popups does not stop all popups. JavaScript can also be used to spawn popup windows without being caught by this setting. However, enabling popup blocking does stop a lot of the annoyances.

- **Enable warnings about new extensions and themes.** Although this does not stop a web page from trying to install something cool, it does give you the option to stop it. This is really essential when you consider that the same auto-install mechanism for loading extensions can also be used to load a virus.

- **Disable Java.** There are very few web sites that require it and there are security risks. I used to recommend that people disable JavaScript, but today there are too many web sites using JavaScript for making active web pages. If you do leave it enabled, be sure to look at the Advanced settings for JavaScript. Turn off anything you do not require. (And if you don't know, turn it off until you do know—usually you will not notice a difference.)

Tuning the Tabs Preferences

Tabs enable you to open new pages in the same window rather than opening a new browser. I find this to be the most useful feature of Firefox. I always have tabs shown (disable the Hide the tab bar option). This way, if I want to open a new tab, I can either press Ctrl+T or double-click on an empty part of the tab bar. Also, always having tabs displayed means the screen will not resize when I open a new tab bar.

Tuning the Downloads Preferences

The Downloads category determines how and where files are saved.

- For downloaded files, I make a directory on my desktop called Downloads and set it as the default download directory. This way, I can easily find things I just downloaded. If you stick with the default, then files are saved to your desktop. If you have a cluttered desktop, then finding a new item could take some hunting.

- Personally, I like to see the Download Manager, but I also like it to close when it finishes (the Close the Download Manager when all downloads are complete option). If you don't like seeing the download manager when a download finishes, this is where you can disable showing it. At any time you can always go to Tools ➪ Downloads to see the Download Manager.

Tuning the Advanced Preferences

The Advanced category is a catchall for other Firefox options. The available options under Ubuntu are different than the Firefox settings under Windows. For example, you do not have the option to check for Firefox updates. This is because the Synaptic's update manager will tell you if new updates are available. You could choose to disable update checks for Installed Extensions and Themes and for Search Engines—neither of these change often enough to require periodic update checks, but leaving the options enabled does not hurt either.

The Advanced category contains three tabs: General, Update, and Security. The General tab covers accessibility and language support; the Update tab manages automatic software updates; and the Security tab manages SSL certificates. Unless you have special needs, you probably do not need to change anything under these tabs.

Fine-Tuning the Firefox Advanced Preferences

The Firefox Preferences menu shows you the most common things to tune, but those are not the only configurable items. There is a hidden configuration screen that you can access by entering **about:config** in the address bar (see Figure 5-3).

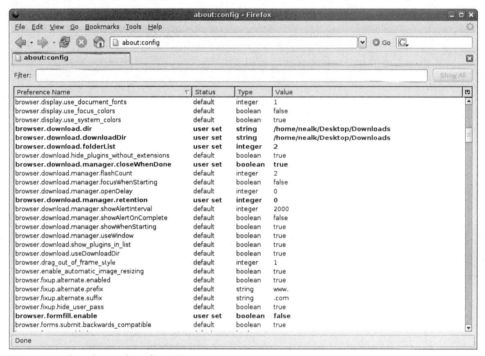

FIGURE 5-3: The advanced configuration menu

This configuration menu shows all of the configuration settings and their values. Default values are shown in regular text, whereas bold text denotes modified settings. In this case, you can see that when I changed my default download directory on the Preferences menu, it changed the settings in the advanced configuration. All items from the Preferences menu can also be modified here. To change a preference, double-click the item to change and enter a new value. Alternately, you can right-click the line to bring up a small menu. Selecting the Modify menu option is the same as double-clicking. For example, to completely disable saving files web pages and images to the disk cache, set the `browser.cache.disk.enable` option to `false`.

Beyond the common preferences, `about:config` gives you access to other configurable items. Some configuration items affect how the browser looks or how it displays items. For example, `browser.blink_allowed` controls whether the HTML `<blink>...</blink>` tags will make text flash. Setting this to `false` turns off blinking text.

Note Modifying how HTML is displayed, such as turning off blinking text, only affects new web pages. You will need to reload pages that are currently being displayed in other browser windows or tabs.

Other items manage performance. For example, the Hypertext Transport Protocol (HTTP) uses TCP for transferring data. TCP is not the fastest protocol and takes time to create and tear down network connections. To speed things up, HTTP allows you to make multiple requests over an established TCP connection. This way, when you need to request multiple pages or images from one server, you don't have the added delay from managing new connections. After a connection sits idle for a while, it is disconnected. You can adjust this timeout value using the `network.http.keep-alive.timeout` setting. The default value is 300 seconds (five minutes). If you use a home firewall (you have a home firewall, right?) then the timeout value on the firewall may be less than five minutes. For best performance, consider adjusting the Firefox timeout to match your firewall. Mine is set to 120 seconds (two minutes).

Since one TCP connection can transfer one piece of data at a time, the browser uses multiple connections for parallel downloads. You can also control the number of simultaneous connections by adjusting the `network.http.max-connections` and `network.http.max-connections-per-server` settings. The default settings, 24 total connections and 8 per server, are good for a cable modem or DSL users. But, if you have a faster network connection, you might want to increase these values (for example, 32 and 10) and if you are using a slow connection, such as a dialup modem or 802.11b wireless network, then you might want to lower these values to 8 and 4 for dialup, and 12 and 4 for wireless. The reason is based on bottlenecks: if you try to download too much data at once, it will all arrive at the same time. The resulting traffic will be interlaced and the network protocol may send flow-control packets back to the server, or the server may resend unacknowledged packets. As a result, lots of parallel downloads will be slower than if you download the data one file at a time.

Tip If you can see the browser slowly loading many images, and frequently get broken or partially loaded images, then you probably have a slow connection. Lower the number of simultaneous connections and see if performance improves. In general, the total number of concurrent connections should be two to three times larger than the number of connections per server.

Fortunately, there is nothing in this advanced configuration menu that is dangerous—changing a setting will not corrupt anything (but may slow down performance) and can always be reset to the default value but right clicking on the item and selecting Reset from the item's menu.

Managing Profiles

Firefox stores all settings in a profile. You don't need to use the same Firefox settings every time; you can create different profiles. For example, I use Ubuntu on a laptop that I carry between home and work. I have one profile configured to use a proxy for work, and another to connect directly to the Internet for home.

Note You can also use profiles if you are using a shared machine. Ideally, everyone should have different user accounts on the system. This gives all users independent profiles. But sometimes it is easier for family members to just use the same account. You can easily give everyone (including your dog) different profiles.

To bring up the profile manager, you will need to run Firefox at a command prompt:

```
firefox -ProfileManager
```

This brings up the Profile Manager, where you can add, edit, or remove profiles (see Figure 5-4). The main profile is called *default*—don't delete this unless you want to lose all of your settings. After you create your new profile, you can select it and click the Start Firefox button. All preferences that you change now will only impact your new profile. Later, you can start Firefox with your new profile by specifying it on the command line. For example, in Figure 5-4, I created a profile called *SOCKS Proxy*. I can use this proxy by running: `firefox -P "SOCKS Proxy"`. Alternately, I can specify the default proxy by using `-P default`, or I can just use `-ProxyManager` to see the menu again.

FIGURE 5-4: The Profile Manager window

Extreme Firefox Tweaks with File Configurations

The settings from the Edit ⇨ Preferences menu are minimalist, and the `about:config` menu allows you to control a lot of functionality, but not everything. If you really want to tweak Firefox, you'll need to edit some configuration files.

Firefox stores all files in the `$HOME/.mozilla/firefox/` directory. In this directory are subdirectories for each profile you created. These directories have a random eight-character string followed by the profile's name. In each profile directory are all of the configuration files. For example, the file `prefs.js` contains all of your modified configuration settings from the `about:config` menu.

Another cool directory is the chrome subdirectory (for example, `~/.mozilla/firefox/*.default/chrome/`). This is where you can define what Firefox should actually *look* like. There are two example files in this directory: `userChrome` and `userContent`. The former controls the display of Firefox and the latter controls the default rendering options.

1. At a command prompt, go into the chrome directory. In this example, you'll use the default profile, but you can really choose any profile.

   ```
   cd ~/.mozilla/firefox/*.default/chrome
   ```

2. If you have not already created customized files, then copy over the examples.

   ```
   cp userChrome-example.css userChrome.css
   cp userContent-example.css userContent.css
   ```

3. Edit `userChrome.css`. This allows you to alter what the browser looks like. The other file, `userContent.css`, is for customizing the default web page settings.

4. After modifying these files, save your changes. You will need to close all open browsers and then open Firefox to see the changes.

Here are some examples of cool things you can do with these configuration files:

- Stop scrolling text! While scrolling marquee text at the bottom of the browser's window can be informative, most web sites are just annoying. Besides, I like to see the URL when I hold the mouse over a link. To disable marquee text, add the following to the `userContent.css` file:

  ```
  marquee {
    -moz-binding : none !important;
    display : block;
    height : auto !important;
  }
  ```

- While you can turn off blinking text in the `about:config` menu and pref.js file (set `browser.blink_allowed` to `false`), you can also set it in the `userContent.css` file.

  ```
  blink {
    text-decoration: none ! important;
  }
  ```

- By default, all tabs have a dull gray background color. If you use lots of tabs then you might find it convenient to highlight the active tab. In this case, I modified the `userChrome.css` file to change the active tab to a light green and the inactive tabs are set to dark red.

  ```
  /* Change tab colors */
  tab{
    -moz-appearance: none !important;
  }
  ```

```
tab[selected="true"] {
  background-color: lightgreen !important;
  color: black !important;
}
/* Change color of normal tabs */
tab:not([selected="true"]) {
  background-color: darkred !important;
  color: white !important;
}
```

- You can specify any web color by name (for example, lightgreen or white) or by specifying the RGB values. For example, rgb(128,255,128) is a puke green color.

You will need to close all open browsers and then re-open Firefox to see the changes made to the userChrome.css and userContent.css files.

Tip   The sample userChrome and userContent files contain few examples. They are mainly used to show formatting and offer a few simple examples. You can find larger lists of tunable items at www.mozilla.org/unix/customizing.html and www.mozilla.org/support/firefox/tips.

Adding Search Engines

When Firefox first starts, the top left corner has a text entry field for doing searches on Google, Yahoo!, eBay, and a few other sites. There is no reason why you cannot add your own search engine. For example, if you work for a large corporation, then your company probably has its own search engine for the internal network. You can create your own search entry for performing these searches. As another example, you might want to add the search engines for SourceForge (http://sourceforge.net) or Google Linux (www.google.com/linux) to the menu so you can quickly look for open source software.

1. Open a command prompt and go to the /usr/lib/firefox/searchplugins directory. This is where the search engine plug-ins are defined.

2. Create a new search engine.

   ```
   sudo gedit sourceforge.src
   ```

Tip   The /usr/lib/firefox directory contains all of the system-wide default settings. All changes you make here will impact all users on the system. You can create a search engine that is only accessible to your default profile by using the $HOME/.mozilla/firefox/*.default/searchplugins/ directory instead. Initially you will need to create this directory, but you do not need root access to create any files in your home directory.

3. Edit the src file for your needs. For example, I created an engine to search SourceForge for open source projects. I found the query values by typing **anything** into the search bar. What I saw was a search URL that said:

   ```
   http://sourceforge.net/search/?type_of_search=soft&words=anything
   ```

This has a URL with two query fields (listed after the "?"). The first field is static and defined by SourceForge for software searches: type_of_search=soft. The second field is the user field and it holds the query. So, my sourceforge.src file becomes:

```
<search
  name="SourceForge"
  description="SourceForge Search"
  method="GET"
  action="http://sourceforge.net/search/"
  queryCharset="utf-8"
>
<input name="type_of_search" value="soft">
<input name="words" user>
</search>
```

4. (Optional) Create an icon for your search engine. This can be a 16x16 GIF or PNG file. Give it the same name as your engine (sourceforge.gif or sourceforge.tif). If you do not create an icon, then it will be assigned the default spyglass icon.

5. Save the file, close all browsers, and restart Firefox. You should see your plug-in (for example, SourceForge Search) added to the list of search engines.

There are other options for the search plug-in file, but most are not needed. If your search engine uses a POST instead of a GET (you'll know because the search term will not appear in the URL), then you will need to find out the parameters. You can do this by viewing the source of the search engine's web page and seeing what fields get sent with the form (or jump to Chapter 11 and learn how to capture packets and see what is really being sent).

Playing with Plug-ins and Extensions

Plug-ins and extensions are small programs for Firefox that provide additional functionality. For example, the default Firefox installation cannot play SWF (Macromedia Flash) files. By adding in the Flash plug-in (see Chapter 4), you can add in an SWF player. To see the list of installed plug-ins, enter **about:plugins** in the address bar. While you cannot add, edit, or remove plug-ins from here, you can see what is installed.

Adding Plug-ins

When Firefox does not know how to handle a particular file type, it gives you a couple of options. First, it can save the file to disk. Although this doesn't run any programs, at least it can save it for you.

Another option is to search for an available plug-in. Firefox searches for plug-ins at https://addons.mozilla.org/plugins/. You can also proactively go to this URL and browse the list of available plug-ins. Another site that hosts plug-ins for Linux is at http://plugindoc.mozdev.org/linux.html, but Firefox does not normally search this site.

A final option requires you to know the plug-in's name and install it using apt-get. Some plug-in packages include mozilla-helix-player, totem-gstreamer-firefox-plugin, and totem-xine-firefox-plugin.

Removing Plug-ins

In the event that you add in a plug-in and it turns out not to be what you wanted, you need some way to remove it. Unfortunately, the Firefox menus offer no solution here. If you installed the plug-in using `apt-get`, then you can remove it (for example, `sudo apt-get remove totem-xine-firefox-plugin`). But if Firefox installed the plug-in, then you need to delete it by hand.

Plug-ins are stored in one of two directories. The `$HOME/.mozilla/plugins/` directory stores plug-ins owned by you and that are only available to you; it is created when you install a plug-in without being root. The other directory, `/usr/lib/firefox/plugins/`, stores system-wide plug-ins. Deleting files from these directories removes unwanted plug-ins from FireFox.

Note   Some plug-ins create multiple files in the plug-in directory. For example, the Helix plug-in creates `nphelix.so` and `nphelix.xpt`. Be sure to delete all the files associated with the plug-in.

Helping Handlers

When a file is downloaded, it can be displayed in the browser window, saved to disk, or passed to another application. Web browsers have two ways to determine how to handle a downloaded file. The first method uses MIME types. For example, HTML pages are text/html, plain text is text/plain, and an image could be image/gif or image/jpeg. Each MIME type contains a general category (for example, text or image) and a specific format identifier (for example, gif or jpeg). The second method uses file name extensions. For example, a file named `ch05.doc` is a word processor document file, and `05-03.tif` is a PNG image.

Note   Many Unix and Linux applications use a third method to determine file content. Called a *magic number file*, this method looks at the file's contents for identifying features. The file `/usr/share/file/magic` under Ubuntu lists the common magic values. Firefox uses this method when no mime-type is available, but not to identify unknown mime-types.

When you access data on a web site, the information is returned with a mime-type. The file name may be specified in the HTTP header, but is usually taken from the end of the URL. If the browser sees something it knows, such as text/html or image/gif, then it renders the file. However, if the browser does not recognize the MIME type (for example, application/binary-octet or video/x-ogm+ogg), then the options are limited: save the file or search for a plug-in. Although other web browsers allow you to associate helper applications to MIME types or file extensions, Firefox does not allow you to create your own helpers.

The solution to this limitation is a plug-in called `mozplugger`.

```
sudo apt-get install mozplugger
```

This plug-in creates a configuration file called /etc/mozpluggerrc that allows you to associate a MIME type or file extension with a program on the computer. For example, if you want PostScript (`ps` and `eps`) files to open using Ghostview (`gv`), follow these steps:

1. Install the Ghostview Postscript viewer (if you have not already installed it).

```
sudo apt-get install gv
```

2. As root, add the following lines to `/etc/mozpluggerrc`:

```
application/postscript:ps,eps:Postscript
  : gv $file
```

The first line specifies the MIME type, extensions, and a description. Multiple extensions can be placed in a comma-separated list. The second line identifies the handler. The documentation for `mozplugger` (`man mozplugger`) explains many more options for this control file, including conditionals and special handling.

3. Remove the cached plug-in list generated by Firefox. Without this step, new handlers will not be recognized.

```
rm $HOME/.mozilla/firefox/pluginreg.dat
```

4. Enter **about:plugins** in the address bar. Your new handler will be listed in the mozplugger section.

When using `mozplugger`, you do not need to close your browser for changes to take effect.

Opening Remote Browsers

Firefox is an intelligent program. It knows how to communicate with other running instances in order to save memory. If you open two browsers and look at the process list for Firefox (`ps -ef | grep firefox`) you will see only one running process. This is because the second process detected the first and told it to open a new window rather than actually running a new, independent browser.

While reusing code is great for reducing memory requirements, it does have one undesirable side effect: you cannot run a browser remotely if you have one open locally. This situation happens often to system administrators. For example, you will log in to a remote host with X-Windows enabled, and want to run Firefox *on* that remote host, but want the browser's display shown on your local system. This is different than running the browser on your system because all web-network requests will originate from the remote system. Unfortunately, just running `firefox` on the remote host will tell your local browser to spawn a new window. Instead, use `firefox --no-xshm`. This tells Firefox *not* to communicate through the X-Windows system in order to identify any running browsers. The result is that the remote browser will not see your local browser, it will start running on the remote system, and it will send its display over to your system.

Using Other Web Browsers

Although Firefox is the default web browser, it is not the only one available. Many other browser packages can be installed, including `mozilla`, `epiphany-browser`, `amaya`, `konqueror`, and `lynx`.

- **Mozilla**—The Mozilla browser is similar to the Mozilla Firefox browser because they stem from the same source. But Mozilla provides slightly different options compared to Firefox.

- **Konquerer**—Konquerer is the default browser for the KDE environment. If you choose to install Konquerer, you will need to install the entire KDE run-time environment.

- **Lynx**—Although Lynx is a text-based browser, I strongly recommend installing it and knowing how to use it. When you crash X-Windows, lose the graphical display, or are simply using an Ubuntu server installation, you cannot use Firefox to search the web for help—*no graphics* means *no Firefox*. As primitive as Lynx may appear, it will allow you to search for help and download patches.

Why Use Different Browsers?

Although some web browsers are suited to different purposes, others just provide alternatives. Many web developers install an assortment of browsers in order to test their web pages. A page you design may look nice under one browser, but have serious problems with a different browser.

I sometimes use different web browsers in place of different Firefox profiles. Even if I give each profile a distinct color scheme, they can still look too familiar. For example, I use one browser for direct Internet use and a different browser for connections through a public proxy. The last thing I want to do is use the direct browser for things that should be done via proxy. If I use two different Firefox profiles at the same time, then I risk mistaking the two windows. But, if I use Firefox for direct access and Mozilla for proxy access, then the browsers look completely different—I won't mistakenly use Firefox thinking it is using the proxy. (See the next section, "Securing Web Access with SSH," to understand why I'd want to use a proxy.)

Mitigating Crashes

Firefox is a pretty stable browser, but it has crashed on me during rare instances. When it crashes, all Firefox windows vanish. Even if you connect with multiple profiles and one window crashes, all Firefox windows close—regardless of the profile. This can seriously impact productivity if you're like me and you heavily depend on web access for your work. A browser crash at an inopportune moment can cost me hours of searching that will need to be redone.

If you're going to access sites that occasionally crash your browsers (in 2006, www.cnn.com comes to mind), you can limit the risk from a crash by running a different type of browser. For example, one browser can be used to look at news and entertainment sites and another can be used for work-related web access. Besides making a distinction between work and play, this also prevents a crash due to a fun web site from impacting the work browser. (This is something your boss may care about, even if you don't.)

Securing Web Access with SSH

When you use the network from the comfort of your own home or small office, there is a degree of security because you are not sharing the Internet connection. You can access your favorite web sites or manage your bank account with relatively little risk of someone watching you. Although an evil hacker on the network between you and your bank can see your connection, the odds are very slim that someone is actually on the exact network route between you and your bank.

Unfortunately, the same sense of security cannot be said for remote locations. Coffee shops, airports, bookstores, libraries, hotels, and other places that offer network access for free (or a fee) not only cannot protect you from eavesdropping, but they will happily offer the same free (or fee) connection to anyone—even an attacker. I've been in enough crowded coffee shops to realize that the chances of someone eavesdropping could be as high as 25 percent (and that's assuming that *I'm* not in the coffee shop with *my* laptop). Some people do it for fun or curiosity, but other people can be malicious—playing with connections or stealing passwords and accounts. Even using SSL and HTTPS cannot offer you much protection against an active attacker.

Since you don't know who might be listening, it is best to play it safe. If you want to access the network securely *and* want the freedom of browsing from anywhere, then consider using a Secure Shell (SSH) tunnel. SSH provides an encrypted connection between two computers, and can forward network traffic across the tunnel. To do this, you will need:

- **Two computers.** One will be your server at home (or at your trusted location), and the other will be your laptop that you will take with you to the coffee shop.

- **A SOCKS server proxy running on the server.** This is how you will relay your traffic from the coffee shop, over the SSH connection to your home, and proxy out to the network.

The goal is to use SSH to create a secure tunnel from your laptop at the coffee shop to your home. You will send all web traffic through the tunnel and relay the web requests through your own SOCKS server. This way, all your web traffic is encrypted as it passes through the coffee shop.

Although this approach is not foolproof, it is about as safe as accessing the network from your home. The basic steps are:

1. Install a SSH server at your home.

2. Open your home SSH server to the Internet. This way, you can access it from the coffee shop, library, or any other public location.

3. Install and configure a SOCKS server that can be accessed only from your home.

4. Test the configuration before going to the public location.

5. Establish the full end-to-end tunnel and start relaying your web traffic.

6. Configure your SSH connection based on your speed requirements.

Installing the SSH Server

The first thing you will need to do is install the SSH server. The Ubuntu installation gives you an SSH client, but not a server. To get the server, install the `openssh-server` package.

```
sudo apt-get install openssh-server
```

Besides installing the server, this package will also generate cryptographic keys, add itself to `/etc/init.d` for automatically starting at boot, and starts the daemon. I usually check the default server's configuration found in `/etc/ssh/sshd_config`:

- **Make sure X11 forwarding is enabled** (`X11Forwarding yes`). This way, if your laptop supports X-Windows, then you can run graphical applications from the remote system. For the SSH client (`/etc/ssh/ssh_config`), you will also want to enable `X11Forwarding`. If either the client or server does not support this option, then you cannot run graphical applications across the tunnel.

- **Check to make sure** `KeepAlive yes` **is set.** This prevents an idle SSH connection from being disconnected by an overzealous firewall.

- **I like to enable a banner message** (`Banner /etc/issue.net`). This way, people see a friendly greeting when they connect to the SSH server. This message is displayed before the user is prompted for a password. You will also want to edit the `/etc/issue.net` file. The default banner gives the operating system version and that could be a security risk. I changed mine so it displays this happy message (see Figure 5.5):

  ```
  All connections and packets are being recorded.
  Unauthorized access attempts can and will be viewed as a network
  attack. Where unauthorized access is enforceable by law, it will
  be prosecuted.
  ```

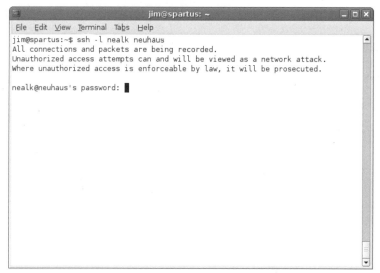

FIGURE 5-5: A SSH connection showing the /etc/issue.net message

After making any changes to the server's configuration, you will need to restart the daemon.

```
sudo /etc/init.d/ssh restart
```

Opening Ports

Since you will be accessing the SSH server from the Internet, you will need to open the SSH port to the world. If you have a firewall, it will need to allow traffic to enter on TCP port 22.

Tip

For the cautious user, consider changing the SSH server to a different port (/etc/ssh/sshd_ config, Port option). This way, worms and kiddies scanning for active SSH servers will be unlikely to find your server. Although this is security-by-obscurity, it is very effective against automated attacks.

Every firewall is different, so you will need to check how to open a port. If you are using a small home firewall and NAT system, then look for a setting for incoming connections. At minimum, you will need to supply the port (22) and the SSH server's IP address. Depending on your firewall, you may also need to supply the protocol (TCP).

After you have the port opened, test it. Using the ssh command, connect to the server using your laptop. This will do two things: first, it will validate that the port is open and the SSH server is running properly. Second, it will transfer over the server's key to the laptop. This way, when you go to the coffee shop nobody will be able to hijack your SSH connection.

Starting a Proxy

The second key component for creating a secured relay system is to install the proxy on your home system. There are two packages that provide this functionality: socks4-server and dante-server. Both servers provide SOCKS proxies and both are basically equivalent, although socks4-server does require a little more configuration. In any case, you will only need to install one SOCKS server—do not install both. Since both servers use the same port (1080/tcp), only one can run at a time.

Using Socks4-Server

The socks4-server package provides a basic SOCKS version 4 proxy that is intended for use through inetd. To use this, you will need an inetd agent, such as xinetd. You will also need to edit /etc/sockd.conf to allow network traffic.

1. Install both server packages:

   ```
   sudo apt-get install xinetd socks4-server
   ```

2. As root, create a socks service for xinetd. The contents of /etc/xinetd.d/socks should look like:

   ```
   service socks
   {
     disable = no
     socket_type = stream
     protocol = tcp
     wait = no
     user = daemon
     group = sys
     server = /usr/sbin/sockd
   }
   ```

3. Restart `xinetd`: `sudo /etc/init.d/xinetd restart`. At this point, the SOCKS server is accessible from the network, but not configured.

4. Configure the SOCKS server to allow traffic relaying. The default configuration file, `/etc/sockd.conf`, forbids all connections. At bare minimum, you will want to remove the "deny all" command and replace it with permissions for the local host. If you want other systems to use this proxy, then you will need to permit additional hosts or subnets.

```
# deny   ALL  0.0.0.0    .my.domain  0.0.0.0
  permit  localhost 255.255.255.255    ALL  0.0.0.0
```

Warning Permitting *all* network traffic to relay through your box is a huge security risk for machines accessible from the Internet. If this computer is directly connected to the Internet, then spammers will likely use your open SOCKS server to relay e-mail. The time between making a public SOCKS server and relaying spam could be as little as a few hours. For this secure tunnel, we only allow the local host to use the SOCKS server, and the SOCKS server is not accessible from outside the firewall. As long as you only permit access to the SOCKS server from the local host (and not the entire Internet), you should be secure enough.

In case the SOCKS server does not appear to work right, look in the `/var/log/syslog` file for error messages. Both `sockd` and `xinetd` log their status to this file.

Using Dante-Server

The Dante server supports both SOCKS version 4 and version 5. Although Dante can run from `xinetd`, it is usually used as a standalone server.

1. Install the Dante server. When you install this, it will try to start the server and it will immediately fail since it is not configured:

```
sudo apt-get install dante-server
```

2. Configure the server by editing the `/etc/dante.conf` file. You will need to enable a port as well as connection rules. For example:

```
# log results to /var/log/syslog (for debugging)
logoutput: syslog stderr
# use 'ifconfig -a' to determine your network interface (e.g. eth0)
# in this case, lo is the loopback port so it only allows localhost
internal: lo port = 1080  # where to listen
external: eth0            # where to relay
# enable SOCKS connection methods
method: username none #rfc931
clientmethod: none
# configure which clients to relay; this only allows localhost
client pass {
   from: 127.0.0.1/32 to: 0.0.0.0/0
}
pass {
```

```
      from: 127.0.0.1/32 to: 0.0.0.0/0
      protocol: tcp udp
      log: connect error
}
# log all failed connections
block {
      from: 0.0.0.0/0 to: 0.0.0.0/0
      log: connect error
}
```

3. Restart the Dante server. Look at /var/log/syslog for any error messages:

```
sudo /etc/init.d/dante start
```

Testing the SOCKS Server

Regardless of which SOCKS server you installed, you will need to test it before you head to the coffee shop.

1. Open Firefox on the same host that has the SOCKS server.

2. Open the connection preferences: Edit ⇨ Preferences ⇨ General ⇨ Connection Settings.

Tip If you do not want to modify your default Firefox settings, then create a new profile for this test.

3. Enable the SOCKS server. The server should be running on localhost port 1080 (see Figure 5-6). If you are using socks4-server, then specify SOCKS v4 as the protocol. If you are using Dante, then either SOCKS v4 or SOCKS v5 will work.

4. Use the browser to connect to a web site, for example, www.google.com.

If the connection works, you should see log entries in /var/log/syslog and the web page should be displayed. If the connection fails, look in /var/log/syslog for error messages or the reason for the failure.

Establishing the Tunnel

Now that you have working SSH and SOCKS servers, you can create a secure tunnel.

1. Find out your server's IP address. If you are doing this from home, then your ISP assigned you an IP address. If you have a stand-alone firewall, then connect to it and find out what its external (WAN) IP address is. On the other hand, if your computer is directly connected to the Internet, then you can run ifconfig -a to list your IP address (it is probably in the eth0 record). Without knowing your IP address, you will be unable to connect from the outside.

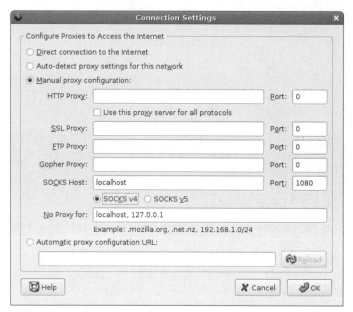

FIGURE 5-6: Configuring Firefox to use the proxy

Tip   If the IP address starts with 10., 192.168., 172.16. to 172.31. or 169.254., then you are looking at a private network address. You will need to identify the public address before you can access the server from outside your local network.

2. On your laptop, use SSH to create a tunnel to the server. The tunnel should forward the local port 8080 to port 1080 on the server. For example, if your IP address is 1.2.3.4, then you would use:

```
ssh 1.2.3.4 -L 8080:localhost:1080
```

This command says to relay local connections to port 8080 to the host and port localhost:1080 on the server. The host name localhost will be resolved by the server.

3. On your laptop, configure your browser to use a proxy. In this case, you want to use localhost and port 8080 (not port 1080).

4. Test the connection by accessing a website.

If all goes well, you should see a web page. This means that all web connections go from your laptop to your local port 8080, where SSH securely tunnels all requests to the server, and the server sends it to the local SOCKS server, which in turn sends the request to the Internet.

Although this path does not remove the risk from someone sniffing the network connection between your home and the Internet, it does prevent anyone at the coffee shop from spying on your bank accounts.

Changing Ciphers for Speed

SSH uses cryptographic ciphers for protecting data, but not all ciphers are equal. By default, SSH uses AES. While AES is a very strong algorithm, it is not as fast as others. If you plan to use the Web over a secure tunnel, consider using a different algorithm, such as Blowfish. This cipher is strong enough for everyday use and is much faster. As a result, you will see a speed enhancement for requests sent over this secure tunnel:

```
ssh -c blowfish 1.2.3.4 -L 8080:localhost:1080
```

Note   As cryptography goes, AES is considered to be a very strong algorithm. However, it isn't the fastest cryptographic algorithm. The Blowfish algorithm isn't necessarily as strong, but it is much faster.

Depending on the type of network traffic, you may always want to enable or disable compression. For example, X-Windows traffic can be heavily compressed, while images (for example, GIF and JPEG) and multimedia files such as MP3 and MOV cannot. If you are browsing the Web or streaming audio, then do not use compression—this is the default setting. But, if you are doing remote administration over X-Windows, then enable compression with the -C parameter:

```
ssh -C -c blowfish 1.2.3.4 -L 8080:localhost:1080
```

Managing E-mail with Evolution

The default e-mail reader for Dapper Drake is called Evolution. This program is an open source clone of Microsoft Outlook. Besides viewing and composing e- mail, it also manages your calendar, task list, and contacts (see Figure 5-7). Evolution also enables you to manage multiple e-mail accounts. While it natively supports many different mail server configurations, it does have a couple of quirks.

Configuring an Account

The most powerful part of Evolution is its list of supported mail protocols. It natively supports the Post Office Protocol (POP, also called POP3) and Instant Message Access Protocol (IMAP), as well as Microsoft Exchange and Novell GroupWise. This means that you should be able to use Evolution at home and in most corporate and small office environments.

When you first run Evolution (by clicking the mail icon in the default top panel or by selecting Applications ➪ Internet ➪ Evolution Mail), it asks you to set up an account. You can later add or edit accounts by running Evolution and selecting Edit ➪ Preferences ➪ Mail Accounts. You will be asked to provide three main types of information.

- **Identity**—This specifies the e-mail address and the name of the person on the address.

- **Receiving options**—This identifies how you retrieve your e-mail. For example, if you use a POP mail server, then you will specify the server's address and your account name.

- **Sending options**—The way you receive mail is not necessarily the same as the way you send mail. For example, you may receive mail using POP, but send using SMTP.

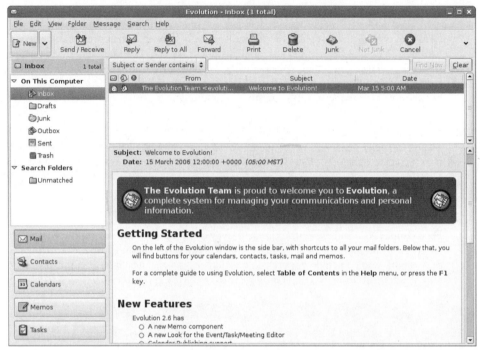

FIGURE 5-7: Evolution mailer

Note   Your specific configuration will depend on your mail server. Most ISPs provide some type of mail server and instructions for configuring mail readers. Although they are unlikely to specify the configuration for Evolution, they should list the server's host name, protocol (for example, POP3 or IMAP), and any required security steps such as using SSL (or TLS) for encryption.

There are other options you can configure after creating a new account (select the Edit option under Mail Accounts). For example, you can specify how often to check for new mail and whether to save a copy of every out-going e-mail message.

Besides using e-mail from your local ISP, you will probably want to manage your free e-mail accounts. Some of the most common free e-mail accounts are Google Gmail, Yahoo! Mail, and Microsoft MSN Hotmail. Knowing how to configure e-mail for these free mail services will help you configure mail for most other mail services.

Retrieving E-mail from Gmail

Of all the free e-mail account systems, Google's Gmail is the simplest to configure. Gmail offers a standard POP3 server that uses SSL for security. Google provides a detailed list of supported POP3 configurations at `http://mail.google.com/support/bin/topic.py?topic=1555`. The mail configuration, including server, protocol, and security, is detailed at `http://mail.google.com/support/bin/answer.py?answer=13287`.

Getting a Gmail Account

Gmail is an invitation-only mail system. To get an account, you need an invitation sent to you by someone who already has a Gmail account. There used to be web sites where you could donate invites and use donated invites, but most of those services have been disabled or replaced by spam sites. If you need a Gmail account, ask a friend (but please don't ask me).

In August 2005, Gmail added an option to request an invite by sending a text message from your cell phone. Details are available at www.gmail.com. If you have a cell phone, then you don't need a friend (ironic, isn't it?).

Preparing Your Gmail Account

After you have your account, you will need to configure it for use with POP.

1. Open a web browser and connect to www.gmail.com. Log in using your Gmail account.

2. Select the Settings option in the top left corner.

3. Select the Forwarding and POP tab.

4. Enable POP support (see Figure 5-8). You can either turn it on for all e-mail, or only for future e-mail.

5. Save your settings.

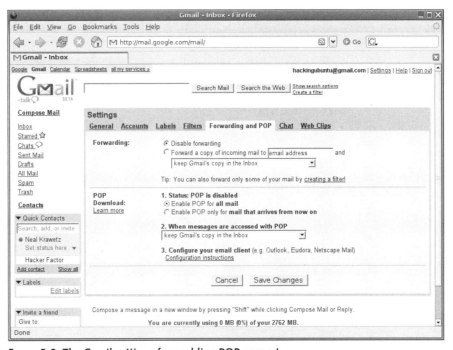

FIGURE 5-8: The Gmail settings for enabling POP support

Adding a Gmail Account

To add your Gmail account to Evolution:

1. Open the account manager by selecting Edit ⇨ Preferences ⇨ Mail Accounts and click on the Add button. This brings up the Mail Configuration helper.

2. The first information requested is your identity. Put in your name and Gmail e-mail address (*your_login*@gmail.com).

3. The second required information is for receiving e-mail. Gmail uses the POP protocol. The mail server is `pop.gmail.com` on port 995, so you should enter `pop.gmail.com:995`. It also uses SSL. Figure 5-9 shows an example configuration. Although a password is needed to access the account, you will be prompted for the password when you first try to send or receive e-mail. Selecting the Remember password option will save the password for you.

4. On the Receiving Options page, I usually choose to leave messages on the server. This way, I always have a backup.

5. For the sending options, Gmail uses SMTP and server is `smtp.gmail.com`. You need to specify a security protocol. Gmail supports SSL on port 465 (`smtp.gmail.com:465`) and TLS on port 587 (`smtp.gmail.com:587`).

6. Set the account name for Evolution. It defaults to the e-mail address.

7. Apply the new account. This completes the account creation.

8. Click the Send/Receive button. You will see a prompt for your password and a notice about the Gmail SSL/TLS certificate.

   ▪ You must approve the certificate. If you don't, then you cannot access your Gmail account. You will only see this prompt once.

   ▪ If you select the Remember password option, then you will not be prompted for your password again.

9. After entering your password, you should see the system checking your e-mail and retrieving any messages.

Fetching Mail

The command-line program `fetchmail` (`sudo apt-get install fetchmail`) is a standard component of most Unix mail systems. This program enables you to retrieve e-mail from a remote mail server using POP2, POP3, or IMAP. While `fetchmail` cannot be used to send e-mail, it can be used to collect e-mail from multiple accounts.

Note
To use `fetchmail`, you will also need to install a local mail delivery system. Chapter 12 shows how to install the Postfix mail system. The default Postifx installation (`sudo apt-get install postfix` and select any of the default configuration settings) is enough for `fetchmail` to work.

FIGURE 5-9: Configuring Evolution for receiving e-mail from Gmail

The `fetchmail` program looks for the configuration file `$HOME/.fetchmailrc`. Each line in this file specifies a different account. For example, to retrieve e-mail from `account@gmail.com`, you would have a line that says:

```
poll pop.gmail.com port 995 protocol POP3 username account password password ssl
```

Running `fetchmail` retrieves the e-mail and sends it to your local mail system. This should place it in your mail spool. If you configure Evolution to retrieve e-mail from a mail spool, you can read your e-mail from the `/var/mail/` directory.

Tip

The mail spool stores e-mail under your account name. If your account on the Ubuntu system is billh, e-mail will be stored in `/var/mail/billh`. The file is first created when you receive mail.

Harvesting e-mail with `fetchmail` can come in very handy if you are not always running Evolution. I have `fetchmail` configured to check for new mail every 10 minutes. This way, if Evolution is not running, new e-mail will be retrieved. Even though Evolution has an account setting to periodically check for new e-mail, this only happens after you start Evolution. If you reboot your computer then new e-mail will not be checked until you start the mail reader.

Retrieving E-mail from Yahoo!

Unlike Gmail, Yahoo! Mail only provides POP access for paid accounts; free accounts do not have POP access. If you want to use Evolution with your free Yahoo! Mail account then you have two options: harvest or proxy.

Harvesting E-mail from Yahoo! Mail

Although `fetchmail` does not support Yahoo! Mail, there is a script that does. The `fetchyahoo` program (`sudo apt-get install fetchyahoo`) is designed to access e-mail from a Yahoo! Mail account and store it in a mail folder. You will need to create a `$HOME/.fetchyahoo` configuration file. An example file can be obtained with the following command:

```
zcat /usr/share/doc/fetchyahoo/examples/fetchyahoorc.gz > $HOME/.fetchyahoorc
```

Before you can use the example file, you will need to edit it. You will need to replace the `yahoo-user-name`, `yahoo-password`, and `local-user-name` variables to match your configuration. The rest of the options are well documented and should work for most environments. When you are all done, you can run `fetchyahoo` to retrieve your e-mail.

Warning Yahoo! periodically changes their login process. This can make `fetchyahoo` incompatible with them. You may need to download and install a newer version of `fetchyahoo` from `http://fetchyahoo.twizzler.org/` if the version found in the Ubuntu repository is not up to date. If you see errors from `fetchyahoo`, check what version is installed using **fetchyahoo -v**, and compare it with the latest version available from the web site.

Relaying Yahoo! Mail

While harvesting mail with `fetchyahoo` is good for retrieval, it does not allow you to send and it won't work with Evolution's Send/Receive button. For a more complete interface, consider YPOPs (`www.ypopsemail.com`). This program creates a POP3 interface for Yahoo! Mail.

1. Go to `www.ypopsemail.com` and download the latest code. The source code is available in a ZIP file. I recommend downloading the source code instead of the Linux executable since the pre-compiled executable may not include the latest source.

Note YPOPs is not in the Ubuntu repositories. You will need to download, compile, and install it without using APT.

2. Unzip the source code. This should create a `ypops/src` directory containing all of the source.

3. Follow the steps in `README.unix-linux` to compile and install YPOPs.

4. Create a `ypopsrc` file as described in the README. There should be a sample file (`ypops_samplerc`) containing configuration options.

When YPOPs is running, it creates a POP3 server on the local system and translates POP3 requests into commands for Yahoo! Mail. The default YPOPs port is 110 (POP3), but you might want to change this if you are already running a POP3 server. This is not the fastest server, but it gets the job done. Using YPOPs, you can send and receive Yahoo! Mail using Evolution, `fetchmail`, and other mail programs.

Tip

If you like using YPOPs, consider adding it to `/etc/init.d/` and the `/etc/rc*.d/` directories. This way, it will run whenever the computer boots.

To use YPOPs with Evolution, configure the Evolution e-mail account to use the POP3 server on `localhost:110`. Evolution should use your Yahoo! Mail address and password for accessing the YPOPs POP3 server. You do not need any encryption since the POP3 traffic never leaves the local computer. Instead, YPOPs translates the requests into HTTPS for accessing Yahoo! Mail.

Retrieving E-mail with FreePOPs

Many providers use the Web for accessing e-mail. Although some providers, such as Yahoo! Mail and Microsoft MSN Hotmail provide POP3 access for paid accounts, free accounts can only use the Web. Also, although YPOPs is available for Yahoo! Mail, it does not work with MSN Hotmail, AOL, Juno, Lycos, or even free web mail systems such as SquirrelMail.

Fortunately, there is a solution for web mail users. FreePOPs provides a generic POP3 system for accessing MSN Hotmail, AOL, Yahoo! Mail, and many other web-based mail systems. Just as YPOPs creates a translation between Yahoo! Mail and POP3, FreePOPs provides a POP3 translation system. It works by using screen scrapings to read e-mail from the web pages.

The really neat thing about FreePOPs is that it comes with a bunch of already configured files for screen scraping different mail systems. Each of these configuration files are found in `/usr/share/freepops/lua/`.

To use FreePOPs with Evolution:

1. Install FreePOPs. This will install the server (`freepopsd`) and create `/etc/init.d/freepops`:

   ```
   sudo apt-get install freepops
   ```

2. Start the FreePOPs service:

   ```
   sudo /etc/init.d/freepops start
   ```

3. Configure your Evolution e-mail settings: Edit ➪ Preferences ➪ Mail Accounts. The important values you will need are:

   - **Server**—The POP server is on `localhost:2000`. This is used for sending and receiving e-mail. No SSL or TLS is needed since the POP3 server is local.

- **Account name**—Your account name must include your full domain. For example, `account@yahoo.com` or `account@hotmail.com`. FreePOPs uses the domain name (e.g., @yahoo.com or @hotmail.com) to identify to correct configuration script.

- **Password**—This will be the password that matches your e-mail account.

A Cheap Hack

POP3 and IMAP are two of the most supported mail protocols. If your server supports either protocol, then retrieving e-mail is simple. Unfortunately, some mail systems only provide web interfaces, or charge for POP3 or IMAP support. Although tools like YPOPs and FreePOPs allow you to access web-only e-mail sites, there is another option.

Most mail servers allow you to forward e-mail to another address. You can forward your web-only e-mail to a service like Gmail, where free accounts have POP3 access. By forwarding your AOL, Yahoo! Mail, and MSN Hotmail accounts to you Gmail account, you can retrieve all e-mail using POP3. Gmail also allows you to invite other people to join Gmail. You can send these invitations to yourself and open one Gmail account for your AOL mail, one for Yahoo! Mail, and so on. This way, the e-mail does not get all mixed up in one mailbox, and you can download the entire e-mail (headers and all) without resorting to screen scrapings.

The downside of this cheap hack (for people too cheap to pay for POP3 access) is that all of your e-mail gets relayed one more time and stored at Gmail. This might be a problem for some business needs, but then again, if you have security concerns about e-mail storage then you probably should not be using a free mail account.

Addressing with LDAP

One of Evolution's biggest strengths is its integration with Lightweight Directory Access Protocol (LDAP) systems. In many large office environments, LDAP provides directory support, listing employee names, e-mail addresses, and other contact information. To enable LDAP support, simply add a new address book, File ➪ New ➪ Address Book, and change the type to On LDAP Servers (see Figure 5-10). After you enter your LDAP server's information, you can access the directory when composing an e-mail.

FIGURE 5-10: Adding an LDAP server

Crashing and Recovering Evolution

Although Evolution has the makings of a very nice mail system, it still has some stability and usability problems. For example, when configuring an account you can test the SSL/TLS connection. Unfortunately, if you select the wrong security protocol (for example, SSL instead of TLS, or TLS instead of none) then it will sit indefinitely—until you click Cancel.

Evolution has other minor annoyances. For example, pop-ups that alert you to an upcoming appointment may appear behind windows. This may not seem critical until you realize that you forgot to pick up flowers for your anniversary. Evolution also has trouble importing meeting invitations from some Microsoft Outlook clients. For example, it may forget to apply any time zone differences—so that 11:00 meeting was actually at 9:00. In some cases, Evolution will just refuse to add meetings to your calendar.

Evolution can also crash. I usually see this happen with using LDAP for looking up name or modifying recipient e-mail addresses while composing an e-mail. (Even though it crashes, the default version of Evolution under Dapper is still a huge improvement over previous versions.)

Unfortunately, when Evolution crashes or closes, it does not kill all running processes. Instead, you will need to kill any running processes that became detached. To do this, use:

```
killall -r 'evolution*'
```

This command will kill every running process from Evolution.

If you forget to kill all the old processes and just restart Evolution, you can expect to miss appointments, not retrieve e-mail, and to crash more often. This is because the dependent processes, such as GNOME_Evolution_Calendar_AlarmNotify_Factory are no longer connected to the main Evolution process.

With each new release, Evolution lives up to its name—evolving to become better. Unfortunately, at times it can still appear prehistoric.

Note At the time of this writing, many of these problems were fixed by the next version of Evolution and included in Edgy Eft. However, the fixes had not been back-ported to Dapper Drake. Edgy contains many fixes, but also many experimental and bleeding edge components. Edgy is also not an LTS, so its support will expire before Dapper's. It is unclear when or if Dapper will receive the fixed version of Evolution.

Using E-mail with Thunderbird Mail

The Evolution mailer provides a full set of office services including e-mail management, calendar scheduling, and task lists. While it does each of these tasks, it still has some stability and usability problems. If you only need e-mail access, you might want to consider Mozilla Thunderbird:

```
sudo apt-get install mozilla-thunderbird
```

This installation enables you to run mozilla-thunderbird from the command line or select it from the menu: Applications ➪ Internet ➪ Thunderbird Mail. Unlike Evolution, this only runs one application and starts up a little faster.

In my opinion, Thunderbird is much more refined than Evolution, but not as full featured. Table 5-1 shows a functionality comparison. Generally speaking, both systems are nearly equivalent when it comes to e-mail-only requirements. Although Evolution does support more protocols and non–e-mail features, Thunderbird currently offers more stability.

Table 5-1	Comparison of Evolution and Thunderbird	
Feature	*Evolution 2.6*	*Thunderbird 1.5.0.5*
Protocols	POP, IMAP, Exchange, Hula, Files	POP, IMAP, Files
Security	SSL and TLS	SSL and TLS; only available by Edit ➪ Acccount Settings ➪ Security Settings after creating account
LDAP	Yes	Yes

Table 5-1   *Continued*

Feature	Evolution 2.6	Thunderbird 1.5.0.5
E-mail Security Options		
Load Images	Can be disabled, enabled for all, or enabled for known contacts; default: enabled	Can be disabled, enabled for all, or enabled for known contacts; default: enabled
JavaScript	No	No
E-mail Scam Detection	No	Yes
Antivirus Support	No	Yes; default: disabled
Additional Functionality		
Address Book	Yes	Yes
Calendar	Yes	No; available as plug-in
Task List	Yes	No
Memos	Yes	No

Instant Messaging with Gaim

The Web is great for one-way communications: someone posts a web page and someone else views it. Even in online forums, discussions may span days. E-mail is a faster communication method, and is bi-directional, but is not instant. Instant messaging (IM) systems allow real-time communications with groups of people.

Internet Relay Chat (IRC) was one of the first IM protocols. (IRC predates most IM protocols by more than a decade.) There are plenty of IRC clients for Dapper, including the graphical xchat and text-based irssi. But IRC is only one type of IM protocol available today. Yahoo!, AOL, MSN, and Napster all have their own IM protocols. Beyond proprietary systems, the open-source Jabber protocol is growing in popularity; Jabber is essentially IRC over an encrypted channel.

Although you could download a specific IM client for every protocol, it is much more convenient to have one client that supports them all. Gaim in an IM client that ships with Ubuntu and supports eight of the most common IM protocols. To run Gaim, go to Applications ➪ Internet ➪ Gaim Instant Messanger. When Gaim first starts, you will need to add an account. Accounts specify IM servers and your identities on each server (see Figure 5-11). Each server protocol has different requirements that you will need to specify.

After creating an account, you can log in to the account—this connects to the server. From there, you can join chat rooms and communicate in real-time. Although Gaim does not allow you to bridge between IM connections, it does allow you to connect to many different servers at the same time.

FIGURE 5-11: Adding an IM account to Gaim

| Tip | Gaim uses many different windows and there is no central text menu for opening a specific window. To see the list of windows, right-click on the yellow Gaim icon that appears in the top panel. This will pull up the main menu and allow you to see accounts, chat windows, and even exit the application. |

Talking with VoIP

Ubuntu users are not restricted to the world of text and graphics. There are three different VoIP packages available for Dapper. The default Dapper desktop includes Ekiga—formerly called *GnomeMeeting*. This is an open source VoIP system that supports SIP and H.323 protocols. This means you can use Ekiga to talk to other Ekiga users, as well as Microsoft NetMeeting, Skype, and WengoPhone users. Skype and WengoPhone are also available for

Ubuntu (see Figure 5-12). Unlike Ekiga, Skype and WengoPhone provide VoIP to landline services. For a small fee, you can use your computer to dial a real telephone number.

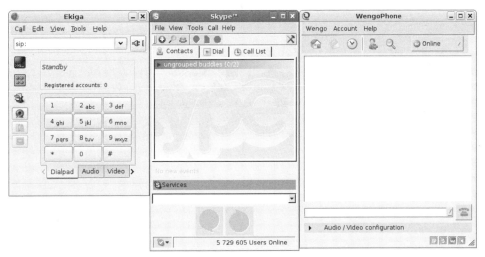

FIGURE 5-12: The Ekiga, Skype, and WengoPhone VoIP systems

Each of these VoIP choices offers similar functionality. Each supports audio, video, and text messaging, each can call directly or use a centralize registration and directory system, and each can handle multiple calls at once. The main differences are in licensing and landline access: Ekiga and WengoPhone are open source, whereas Skype is not, and only Skype and WengoPhone allow you to call a real telephone number (for a nominal fee). Although each of these systems can chat with a Microsoft NetMeeting user, none of them can view a shared NetMeeting desktop.

Note   As I mentioned in Chapter 3, Ubuntu does not support all video devices. But if Ubuntu supports the device, then Ekiga and WengoPhone can probably use it for video conferencing. Unfortunately, Skype (for Linux) does not support video conferencing.

Summary

Ubuntu supports a variety of configurations. Although Ubuntu server is ideal for a standalone server, Ubuntu desktop enables you to reach out and communicate with other people. There are plenty of options for accessing the Web, e-mail, IM and VoIP networks. While the default tools (Firefox, Evolution, Gaim, and Ekiga) are very powerful, there are plenty of readily available alternatives such as Mozilla, Lynx, Thunderbird, xchat, irssi, WengoPhone, and Skype. In the case of e-mail, there are even options for extending support to non-standard and web-based mail systems.

With online communications come risks related to network security. There are options for securing web browsers, e-mail, and even off-site communications, but the topics listed in this chapter, such as tuning applications and using SSH tunnels, are just the tip of the iceberg. If you are interested in more information about network security, consider some of these other resources:

- *Steal This Computer Book*, by Wallace Wang, discusses threats from online forums.

- *Hacking Exposed: Network Security Secrets & Solutions*, by Stuart McCluer, Joel Scambray, and George Kurtz, covers many different network threats. Although this resource focuses on Windows, many of the threats are similar for Linux users.

- *Introduction to Network Security*, by Neal Krawetz, delves into many of the threats from online communications, regardless of the operating system.

Collaborating

In today's always connected world, few people work in isolation. In office environments, files and folders are shared with coworkers. In research groups, documents are passed back and forth. Even the hard-core hacker working along in a dark basement isn't really alone—he's sharing files and projects with other people online. Teams of people collaborate on projects in real time while members can be physically located around the world. Incompatible operating systems do not work. Collaboration includes working with people who don't run Ubuntu (let's call them "Windows users"). The default install of the Ubuntu desktop includes a wide variety of collaboration tools, and additional tools available in the standard repositories offer many more options.

Collaboration begins with sharing and compatibility. If you cannot share documents, then you cannot collaborate. And if your system and software cannot handle the files you need, then you won't be able to work with other people.

Unfortunately, some file formats lack strong support, and many applications demand specific operating systems. In order to work with others, you may need to share desktops or actually run a different operating system. Fortunately, Ubuntu has many options for supporting both of these needs.

Synchronizing the Clock

With the need to share files, file systems, desktops, and tools, where do you begin? You begin with the system clock. This may sound like a trivial piece of information, but if your clock is off by more than a little, then it can actually hamper collaboration efforts. e-mails won't be sorted in the right order, files won't have consistent timestamps, and some applications are time sensitive. For developers, timestamps are used to determine what files to compile—if your clock is way off, then source code may not compile correctly.

When you first installed Ubuntu (see Chapter 1), it asked you to set your time zone and to choose whether the hardware clock should be in UTC. Everything else about the clock has been silently done behind the scenes.

in this chapter

☑ Synchronizing the clock

☑ Working with Open Office

☑ Collaborating over the network

☑ Running software in emulators

☑ Other collaboration tools

Ubuntu sets the clock automatically each time the network interface is brought up. This happens in the script /etc/network/if-up.d/ntpdate. Ubuntu checks to see if the file /etc/default/ntpdate exists. This file should contain one line—the host name of the network time protocol (NTP) server. By default, this file does not exist and the operating system falls back to using the server ntp.ubuntu.com. Here are some tips to make sure your clock is set correctly:

- If you cannot access the default server (ntp.ubuntu.com) from your network, then your clock will not be set at boot time and will likely drift. Use /etc/default/ntpdate to specify an alternate NTP server.

Warning NTP uses UDP packets. If you use a proxy or outbound firewall that blocks UDP, then you will need to change the default NTP server, or configure an alternate network route.

- If your computer never reboots (and uptimes of over 100 days is common), then your clock can drift—usually by a few seconds per month. Consider adding ntpdate to your root's Cron entry so it runs weekly.

  ```
  sudo crontab -e
  ```

  And add this line to run ntpdate every Sunday at two minutes after midnight. (Cron is detailed in Chapter 7.)

  ```
  2 0 * * 0 /etc/network/if-up.d/ntpdate
  ```

- For Ubuntu systems that operate as network router, tying the clock to a network interface can be a problem—particularly if the network connection continually bounces up and down. (Do you really need to synchronize the clock a few times each hour?) In these situations, you might consider removing /etc/network/if-up.d/ntpdate and creating an /etc/init.d/ntpdate command.

Note The boot scripts found in /etc/init.d/ are discussed in Chapter 3. Actual sample scripts are in Chapters 10 and 11.

NTP is just one protocol for setting the date. Another option is to use rdate (sudo apt-get install rdate). By default, rdate uses TCP to query the network daytime service (port 13/tcp) of the timeserver. You will still need to create /etc/init.d/rdate, /etc/network/if-up.d/rdate, and Cron entries, but this command will work through a proxy.

Tip The server ntp.ubuntu.com only supports the NTP protocol; rdate won't work with this server. If you want to use rdate and need a time server, consider one of the official atomic clock sites like time.nist.gov.

Plays Well With Others

There is always a small, fanatical group who thinks *collaboration* means everyone should run the same operating system. Whether this is Linux people criticizing Windows users, BSD users criticizing Linux users, or Windows users trying to convert the world, the fringe groups are always shouting to be heard. In real life, a homogeneous network is neither realistic nor desirable. Although one operating system for everyone will ease collaboration, it can lead to many other issues.

Some of the issues involve security. If everyone runs the same operating system, then everyone is vulnerable to the same weaknesses. Whether the risk comes from viruses, overflows, or unstable software, all computers running the same configuration are vulnerable. (Windows may have more viruses today, but if everyone used Ubuntu then the virus writers would focus on Ubuntu instead. The lack of viruses for Linux is not due to a lack of opportunity, but rather the lack of effort from virus writers.) Darwin called this "survival of the fittest"; there is safety in diversity.

Usability is another issue. Many programs create log files and time-tracked reports. If your clock is off, then these files can be really difficult to map to real time. For example, was that spike in web traffic really at 2:00 A.M.? Or did it happen after 9:00 A.M. when you released a new document on the Web? Clocks usually appear off by a few minutes (or an hour for daylight savings time). Each time you reboot, it may drift a few more minutes. If you don't occasionally reset the system's time, then the drift can become hours or longer.

Other issues concern use models. An operating system is a tool—and nothing more. You should select the right tool for the right job. Windows offers excellent hardware support and many high-quality applications, but lacks collaboration support for non-Windows systems. BSD offers security from the ground up and a proven track record for stability, but has minimal support from the community (compared to Windows and Linux). Linux has a wide variety of software (although quality varies dramatically) and excellent collaboration efforts. If you need an operating system that plays well with an assortment of other systems, then Linux is a terrific option and Ubuntu's long-term support commitments make it an ideal choice.

Sharing Files

When you collaborate on a project, you need some way to pass files between group members. The direct approach is to send the file as an e-mail attachment. Although this does give them a copy, it does not provide updates—people may pass around very old copies of files. This approach also does not incorporate changes. In most cases, there will need to be an owner whose responsibility is to collect changes and incorporate them into a single document. This may work well with a few people, but it does not scale well to a dozen people working concurrently.

Note Other downsides to using e-mail for sharing files concerns disk space and convenience. Most corporations and service providers limit the mail queue size. If the queue fills, then no more e-mail can be received. Also, transferring large attachments can be time consuming and searching for a specific attachment is usually inconvenient.

Another option is to place files on an FTP or web server. This gives a central source for distribution, allowing people to view recent changes to files, but web servers don't readily allow feedback and active collaboration, and FTP servers are not known for security.

The best option is to share a file system's directory among computers. This way, everyone can see all files in one common location. Everyone can also see all changes and everyone can make changes as needed. For Unix and Linux systems, there is NFS for file sharing, but for compatibility with Windows users, you'll probably want SAMBA.

Enabling NFS

Under Linux and most Unix operating systems, the network file system (NFS) is the common way to share directories. With other Unix and Linux operating systems, NFS is part of the core installation. But with Ubuntu, you need to install it as a package. There are three main components required by NFS:

- `portmap`—This package provides support for remote procedure calls (RPC) and is used by NFS. You don't need to install `portmap` by itself—the `apt-get` commands for the other two components will install `portmap` as a requirement.

- `nfs-common`—Although portmap provides *support* for RPC function, this package actually *provides* the RPC functions for NFS. This package is required for NFS clients and servers. It provides basic RPC functions like file locking and status. If you only need to install an NFS client (meaning you will mount a directory exported by some other server), then you can use: `sudo apt-get install nfs-common`.

Note Installing `nfs-common` will generate an error message, "Not starting NFS kernel daemon: No exports." This is expected since it is not configured. To configure it, see the section titled "Acting as an NFS Server."

- `nfs-kernel-server`—This package adds kernel modules so you can actually export a directory for use by a remote host; with this package, you get a server. You can install it using: `sudo apt-get install nfs-kernel-server`. This brings in `portmap` and `nfs-common` as required packages.

NFS is a great collaboration tool because entire file systems can be shared transparently. Everyone sees the same files and file changes are immediately accessible by everyone. The main limitation is operating system support. Although NFS exists for Linux, BSD, HP-UX, AIX, Solaris, BeOS, Mac OS X, and even OS/2, Windows does not natively include it. If you need to share files with Windows users, skip to the next section on SAMBA.

Tip

If you want to use NFS with Windows, consider installing the Windows Services for UNIX (`www.microsoft.com/technet/interopmigration/unix/sfu/`). This free product from Microsoft includes NFS server and client support.

Acting as an NFS Client

Mounting a remote file system with NFS is really easy. Just as the `mount` command can be used to access a hard drive, CD-ROM, or other block device, it can be used to mount a remote file system. You just need three items: the server's name, the directory name on the server that is being exported, and the mount point on your local system (a directory) for the connection. For example, to mount the directory /home/project from the server sysprj1 and place it at `/mnt/project` on your local computer, you would use:

```
sudo mkdir /mnt/project # to make sure it exists
sudo mount -t nfs sysprj1:/home/project /mnt/project
```

Now, all the files under `/home/project` on the host sysprj1 are accessible from the local directory `/mnt/project`. The access is completely transparent—anything you can do on your local file system can be done over this NFS mount.

Tip

Access restrictions are set by the NFS server and follow the Unix permissions. If you find that you cannot access the directory after mounting it, check the permissions with `ls -l`. If you do not have permission, then talk to the administrator for the NFS server.

If you don't know the name of the exported directory, NFS enables you to browse the list of exported partitions using the `showmount -e` command. This lists the directories and list of clients that can access it. The client list returned from the server can be an entire domain (for example, `*.local.net`) or a list of clients.

```
$ showmount -e sysprj1
/home/projects *.local.net
/media/cdrom *.local.net
```

When you are done with the mounted partition, you can remove it using `sudo umount /mnt/project`.

For short-term access, you will probably want to use `mount` and `umount` to access the directory as needed. For long-term collaboration, you can add the entry in `/etc/fstab`. For example:

```
sysprj1:/home/project   /mnt/project   nfs   defaults   0   0
```

Having the entry in `/etc/fstab` will make sure the directory is mounted every time you reboot. You can also use `sudo mount /mnt/project` (specifying only the mount point) as a shortcut since mount consults `/etc/fstab` when determining devices.

Warning NFS has one huge limitation. If the server goes down then all file accesses to the network partition will hang—up to hours—before failing. The hang-up is due to network timeouts and retries. If your connection to the server is unstable, then don't use NFS.

Acting as an NFS Server

NFS servers export directories for use by NFS clients. This is a two-step process. First, you need to create a file called `/etc/exports`. This file contains a list of directories to export and clients that are permitted to access the directories. Special access permissions can also be specified such as `ro` for read-only, `rw` for read-write, and `sync` for synchronous writes. An example `/etc/exports` file is given in Listing 6-1.

Tip There are many more options besides ro, rw, and sync. See the man page for exports (`man 5 exports`) for the full list of options.

Listing 6-1: Example of a /etc/exports File

```
/home/project          *.local.net(rw,sync)
/home/solo_project     host.local.net(rw,sync)
/media/cdrom           *.local.net(ro,async)
```

Note The NFS server will not start if `/etc/exports` is missing or contains no exported directories. The default file contains only a few comments, so the server will not start. After you create your first entries, you will need to start the server. The easy way to start it is with the command `sudo /etc/init.d/nfs-kernel-server start`.

After modifying the `/etc/exports` file, you need to tell the NFS server to actually export the entries.

```
sudo exportfs -r  # re-export all entries in /etc/exports
```

The `exportfs` command can also be used for other tasks:

- **List the current export table**—Run `exportfs` without any parameters.
- **Export a specific directory once**—This is useful if the export is not intended to be permanent (`/etc/exports` is really for permanent mounts). You will need to specify options, and the list of clients is specified before the directory. For example:

  ```
  sudo exportfs -o ro,async '*.local.net:/media/cdrom'
  ```

- **Un-export directory**—If the entry is still listed in `/etc/exports`, then the removal is temporary; the mount will be re-exported the next time you reboot or restart the NFS server.

  ```
  sudo exportfs -u '*.local.net:/media/cdrom'
  ```

Tip Add -v to any of the `exportfs` commands (for example, `exportfs -v -r`) to verbosely list additional information.

You can export anything that is mounted. This includes CD-ROM drives, USB thumb drives, and even mounted NFS partitions from other servers! Although you cannot export single files or block devices, you can export the entire /dev directory (not that you would want to).

Warning NFS offers no security, encryption, or authentication. Furthermore, established NFS connections can be easily hijacked. NFS is fine for most internal, corporate networks and for use within your home, but don't use it to share files across the Internet.

Exchanging Files with SAMBA

Although NFS is useful for collaborating with Unix and Linux systems, it is not ideal for sharing directories with Windows users. As mentioned in Chapter 3, SAMBA allows Linux to use the SMB protocol and communicate with Windows systems. Chapter 3 showed how to share printers, but SAMBA can also be used to share directories. First, if you have not done it already, install the SAMBA server: `sudo apt-get install samba`. You will need to edit /etc/samba/smb.conf and configure your workgroup. This configuration file contains many other options that you will probably want to review. For example, you can bind the SAMBA server to a specific network interface, control client logging, and configure alternate login credentials—these are documented with comments found in the file. After configuring the server, you should restart it: `sudo /etc/init.d/samba restart`.

There are two ways to use SAMBA for collaboration. It can be a server that shares directories with Windows users, or a client that receives directories exported from Windows servers.

Sharing a Directory with Windows

The /etc/samba/smb.conf file comes with an entry that allows you to share every user's home directory. Search the configuration file for the "[homes]" section and uncomment it (remove the ; before each line). The section should look like:

```
[homes]
    comment = Home Directories
    browseable = no
```

This defines a Windows service (called a *share*) that can be accessed using \\server\username, where `server` is the name of your Ubuntu system and `username` is an account found under /home/username. There are other options that can be uncommented in order to restrict access (`valid users = %S` and `writable = no`) and set file permissions.

If you want to export a specific directory then you will need to create your own section in /etc/samba/smb.conf. Listing 6-2 gives an example for exporting the CD-ROM and a projects directory.

Listing 6-2: Sample Export Directories for /etc/samba/smb.conf

```
# Export the CD-ROM.
# The Windows system will use \\server\cdrom\ to access it.
[cdrom]
  comment = CD-ROM drive
  path = /media/cdrom

# Export a group project directory.
# The Windows system will use \\server\groupproject\ to access it.
[groupproject]
  comment = Group Project directory
  path = /home/project
  read only = no
  valid users = nealk, @team # nealk and group "team" have access
```

Tip

Although the default Windows installation cannot access NFS partitions, SAMBA can export a mounted NFS partition to Windows users.

Learning to SAMBA

Although SAMBA is very powerful, it is not very easy to manage if you are new to it. If SAMBA does not immediately share partitions, then be prepared to devote an hour or more to debugging. Common problems that I usually check (in order) before going into "Search the web for solutions" mode:

- Is the `smb.conf` file correct? Use the `testparms` program to check for problems. Not all problems are critical, but big problems will be identified. (Some warnings come from default settings in the configuration file.)

- Is the share name spelled correctly? I have spent hours chasing down problems only to find typos in the `smb.conf` share name or on the Windows side.

- If you are using a "valid user" option for the share, you may need to use `smbpasswd` to create a user account. SAMBA does not consult `/etc/passwd`. Instead, it uses its own password database found in `/var/lib/samba`. The command `sudo smbpasswd -a username` adds a new user to the database, and `smbpasswd` (as the user) changes the password.

Learning to SAMBA *Continued*

- Older versions of Windows (for example, Windows 95, 98, and NT) use plain-text passwords. Later versions use encrypted passwords. Check the "encrypted password" value in `smb.conf` and make sure it matches the system you are supporting. Unfortunately, SAMBA cannot support old and new systems at the same time unless they all use the same encrypted (or unencrypted) password system.

- If the Windows system can read the partition but not write, then check the permissions on the directory. The SAMBA account may not have write-access.

If all else fails, refer to the FAQ list HOWTO guides at `www.samba.org` and the Ubuntu Guide at `http://ubuntuguide.org/`.

Accessing a Windows Directory

There are many different ways for SAMBA to access a Windows directory. The main things you need are the Windows system name and the share. The command `smbclient -L` can be used to list the public shares on a system:

```
$ smbclient -L wserver
Password: [hit enter with no password]
Domain=[WSERVER] OS=[Windows 5.1] Server=[Windows 2000 LAN Manager]

        Sharename       Type        Comment
        ---------       ----        -------
        IPC$            IPC         Remote IPC
        print$          Disk        Printer Drivers
        Big             Disk
        Printer         Printer     Brother HL-1850/70N BR-Script3
        ADMIN$          Disk        Remote Admin
```

The `smbclient` command can be used as an FTP-like client for accessing the Windows share. In this example, `smblcient //wserver/big` will open an FTP client for accessing the Big share.

For remote backups, I prefer to use `smbtar`. This command enables you to use remotely archive (or restore) files in a share. The backup is saved to a TAR file. For example, to back up the Big share from host Wserver, you can use either:

```
smbtar -t archive.tar -s wserver -x big              # regular archive
smbtar -t - -s wserver -x big | gzip -9 > archive.tgz # compressed archive
```

For restores, add in the `-r` parameter:

```
smbtar -r -t archive.tar -s wserver -x big          # regular archive
zcat archive.tgz | smbtar -r -t - -s wserver -x big  # compressed archive
```

Warning

This is good for backing up user files, but it is not necessarily a full system backup. For example, Windows XP and Me will not allow SMB access to the system directory or registry.

Although `smbclient` and `smbtar` enable you to access files, they do not allow you to actually mount the share. For this, the `smbfs` package is needed.

```
sudo apt-get install smbfs
```

The `smbfs` package provides an SMB file system driver and the `smbmount` command. This allows you to transparently mount a share and use files concurrently with other people.

```
sudo mkdir /mnt/smb
sudo smbmount //wserver/big /mnt/smb
```

Tip

The `smbmount` command is actually a wrapper around the `mount` command. You can also use `sudo mount -t smb`.

As with other mounted directories, `sudo umount /mnt/smb` will remove the mount.

Working with Open Office

In nearly every corporate environment, you will need to read and write Microsoft Word, PowerPoint, and Excel files. Although only Microsoft Office can handle all of these formats perfectly, Ubuntu includes OpenOffice.org 2.0—a set of open source tools that can read, write, and modify Microsoft Office documents. The OpenOffice.org main tools consist of a word processor, presentation system, and spreadsheet application. Each of these are available under the Applications ➪ Office menu.

Using the Word Processor

The OpenOffice.org word processor (`oowriter`) is an open source alternative to Microsoft Word (see Figure 6-1). Using this program, you can access most DOC files. This word processor has a number of benefits over Microsoft Word.

- **PDF**—Under Microsoft Word, an additional plug-in is required to save documents as PDF files. Normally this wouldn't be too big of a hassle, but the official PDF plug-in from Adobe is a resource-intensive application that can take a while to start up and frequently checks for updates. In contrast, every document in OpenOffice.org can be immediately exported to PDF by selecting File ➪ Export as PDF from the menu. This same menu option is available under all OpenOffice.org tools.

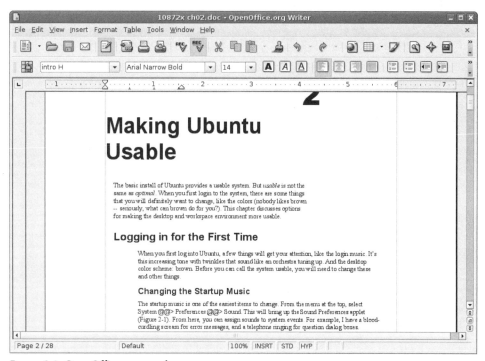

FIGURE 6-1: OpenOffice.org word processor

- **Security**—Microsoft Word embeds lots of unnecessary information in documents. This includes information about the author as well as deleted or edited text. The simple act of adding a character, deleting the character, and resaving the document can make the file larger. OpenOffice.org enables you to remove personal information and deleted text from saved documents. You can configure this option under the Tools ➪ Options ➪ OpenOffice.org ➪ Security settings (see Figure 6-2). The option is labeled Remove personal information on saving.

Note   With Microsoft Office 2003 and later, you do have the option to exclude personal information— on a file-by-file basis. Under OpenOffice.org, this option is a default configuration that impacts all documents.

- **OpenDocument Standard**—Microsoft uses a proprietary format for storing documents. In contrast, OpenOffice.org defaults to the OpenDocument standard. On the one hand, OpenDocument is much more portable. On the other hand, it is not supported by most versions of Microsoft Office. For compatibility, you will need to explicitly export the document for Microsoft Office. Alternatively, you can go to Tools ➪ Options ➪ Load/Save ➪ General and change the default file format.

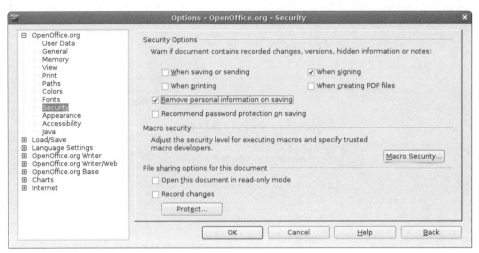

FIGURE 6-2: OpenOffice.org Options for security

As powerful as OpenOffice.org's word processor is, there are still some limitations.

- **Formatting**—Although it can view most Microsoft Office documents, the proprietary file format was reverse-engineered. As a result, complex formatting may look odd and may not save correctly. If the document has extremely complex formatting, it can actually crash the word processor.

- **Bullets, Numbers, and Headings**—This is a weakness in OpenOffice.org. If you just want a bulleted list, numbered list, or section heading, it can do it. If you want special formatting or characters, then you are better off initially creating the formats in Microsoft Office. OpenOffice.org can use formats included in a document, but cannot be easily used to create them. Although I expect this to change in later revisions, this is what you have to use today.

- **Macros**—As with formatting, OpenOffice.org does not handle Microsoft Word macros very well.

- **Annoying Pop-ups**—Whenever you go to save a document in the Microsoft Word format, OpenOffice.org may generate a pop-up warning you about the potential to lose formatting information. This would not be so bad if it did not appear every fifteen minutes due to the auto-save setting.

Making Presentations

Either you love Microsoft Office PowerPoint or you hate it. Personally, it is one of my favorite presentation tools. The OpenOffice.org equivalent is called Impress (ooimpress). This presentation tool can read and write PowerPoint (PPT) documents. While the general look and feel of Impress is similar to PowerPoint (see Figure 6-3), there are some distinct differences.

- **Complexity**—As with the OpenOffice.org word processor, Impress may not display formatting correctly and can even crash if the PPT file is too complicated.

- **Animation**—Animated graphics, slides, and slide transitions do not always display properly.

- **Connectors**—These are my favorite drawing items; they consists of a line with anchors that can attach to objects so they move as you move objects. If you reflow a connector (by moving the red square that appears in the middle of the line), Impress will forget the reflowed direction.

- **Compatibility**—Some PPT files exported from Impress do not load under PowerPoint. I have not seen this happen consistently, but it always happens when you need it most.

My general rule of thumb when working on presentations is to not change presentation tools. If the talk will be given using PowerPoint, then stick with real PowerPoint. If the talk will use Impress, then stick with Impress. Although Impress from OpenOffice.org 2.0 is useful for viewing PPT files, the compatibility with PowerPoint is not complete enough for real collaboration.

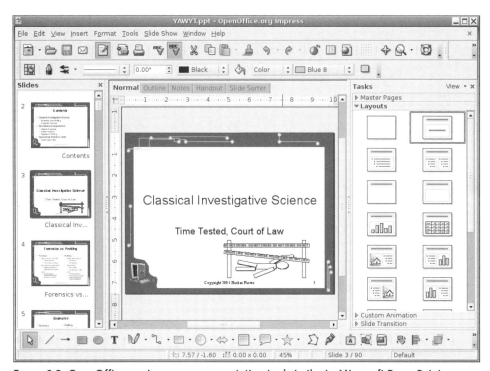

FIGURE 6-3: OpenOffice.org Impress—a presentation tool similar to Microsoft PowerPoint

Accessing Spreadsheets

Although ooimpress is an acceptable presentation tool and oowriter is a good word processor, Calc (oocalc) is an excellent spreadsheet application. Calc has a very similar look to Microsoft Excel and supports all of the standard functions and layouts (see Figure 6-4). There is virtually no learning curve between Excel and Calc. The only limitation I could find was in macro support; Calc won't run most Excel macros and does not support programmed shortcuts. For example, I have a large Excel spreadsheet where I mapped Ctrl+G to a specific macro. Under Calc, Ctrl+G does nothing and running the macro (Tools ⇨ Macros ⇨ Run Macros) generates errors about a missing parenthesis that is not missing.

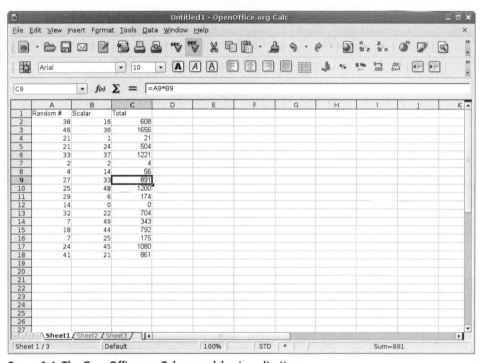

FIGURE 6-4: The OpenOffice.org Calc spreadsheet application

Selecting Alternate Office Tools

OpenOffice.org 2.0 includes many other useful tools. For example, oobase is the Open Office version of Microsoft Access, oomath is a powerful equation editor and oodraw is a very simple drawing tool for when you do not need the complexities of Gimp. OpenOffice.org even includes a database connection application for managing remote databases. These tools will help you be productive, even if they are not fully compatible with Microsoft equivalent applications. Unlike word processors, spreadsheets, and presentation tools, lacking perfect compatibility between database interface front-ends, equation editors, and drawing tools usually does not impact collaboration efforts.

Although OpenOffice.org provides the flagship office tools for Ubuntu, they are not the only office tools available to Ubuntu. I believe that the best tool should be used for the task at hand, and that does not mean always using a word processor for viewing a Word document.

Alternate Document Viewers

One tool that I frequently use is `antiword` (`sudo apt-get install antiword`). This program converts a Microsoft Word document to plain text. This is so much easier than loading up a document and using File ➪ Save As to convert the format. It also comes in handy when you don't have a graphical login—you can use `antiword` to quickly see the text inside a Word file, even if fonts and graphics are excluded.

There is one other useful feature in `antiword`. As mentioned earlier, Microsoft Word documents can include hidden comments. Using `antiword -s`, you can see the hidden text. If you ever wondered what information you were leaking, or what might be hidden inside a document, this tool will show you. To see what text was hidden in a document (for example, file.doc), I use these commands:

```
antiword file.doc > plain.text
antiword -s file.doc > hidden.text
sdiff plain.text hidden.text
```

The `sdiff` command shows the line-by-line, side-by-side differences between two files. Every line with a difference is flagged so you can immediately see where changes occur.

Another powerful tool is `wv` (formerly called WordView—`sudo apt-get install wv`). This program includes a suite of conversion tools like `wvPDF` to convert Word documents to PDF and `wvRTF` to convert to RTF. This suite also contains forensic tools like `wvVersion` and `wvMime` for displaying a document's version and metadata information.

Other alternatives, such as `catdoc`, are also available for converting Word documents to text. In general, if you want to convert a Word document to any other format—especially text—you do not need the overhead of a full word processor.

If you need a full word processor and not a file converter, consider Abiword (`sudo apt-get install abiword`). This program can read and write Microsoft Word documents including style formats and embedded images. It does have a few limitations, including display problems with embedded math equations, custom bullet formats, and no support for Word macros. However, Abiword offers similar functionality to OpenOffice without the massive overhead and slow startup time of `oowriter`.

Alternate Presentation Viewers

Although there are not many alternatives for presentation tools, there is `ppthtml` (`sudo apt-get install ppthtml`). This is a primitive program for extracting text from PPT slides and displaying them as HTML.

Alternate Spreadsheet Viewers

Besides OpenOffice.org's Calc, there is Gnumeric (`sudo apt-get install gnumeric`). At first glance, Gnumeric looks just like Calc and Excel. The difference is in the functionality: Gnumeric has many numerical analysis settings under the Tools ➪ Statistical Analysis menu (see Figure 6-5). If you need a spreadsheet that makes numerical analysis easy, Gnumeric is a good choice. It is not that Gnumeric has functionality that is missing from Calc and Excel, but rather Gnumeric makes it easy to access. Gnumeric also has a much faster startup time—Calc and Excel usually takes seconds to start up, and large spreadsheets can take a noticeably long time; Gnumeric usually starts up instantly, and large XLS files only take a few seconds.

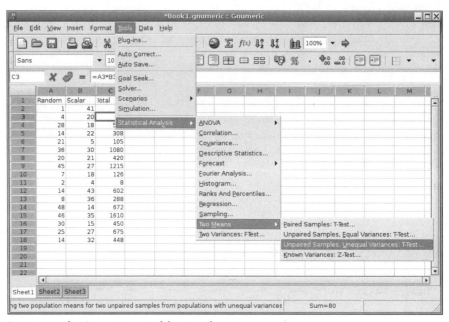

FIGURE 6-5: The Gnumeric spreadsheet application

Gnumeric is not perfect—it completely lacks programmable macro support, and cannot display images and diagrams. But for spreadsheets that don't require these features, I find Gnumeric a better option than Calc or Excel.

Collaborating Over the Network

While sharing files allows people to work on different parts of large projects concurrently, everyone still works on independent pieces. For real productivity, nothing beats an occasional meeting. This allows people to identify problems, understand issues, and address details. Meetings can also be used as a teaching forum and used to spread knowledge.

Note   Too many meetings can impede productivity. Lots of companies (and projects) get into situations where they spend more time talking than actually doing work.

In today's online world, physically getting people together is not always practical. Some people work at home, some are in other countries, and some people are too lazy to walk across the hallway. VoIP and IM can provide real-time communication, but they don't let you see what is really going on. This is where sharing desktops comes in. It's one thing to describe a problem in an e-mail or over the phone; it's another to actually show it. When working together, a shared desktop allows everyone to actually see what is going on. Under Ubuntu, Virtual Network Computing (VNC) is the best option for sharing desktops.

VNC is supported on Unix, Linux, Mac OS X, and Windows operating systems. Rather than struggling with almost-compatible software, VNC provides access to remote desktops where you can use software on its native platform. For example, I frequently find myself in phone conferences where Microsoft NetMeeting or LiveMeeting is used to shares slides. This is convenient for Windows users, but not for Linux users. To get around this problem, VNC is started on one of the Windows clients. This way, Linux users can use VNC to watch the shared presentation.

VNC consists of two parts: a server and one or more clients (called *viewers*). The server shares the desktop, while the client creates a window to display the server's desktop.

Warning Under Microsoft NetMeeting, the server can choose which windows to share. Under VNC it is all or nothing; either the entire desktop is shared or nothing is shared. If you are sharing your desktop, don't forget that everyone can see you checking your e-mail.

Remote Desktops

There are a couple of different ways to share desktops between Windows and other systems. Although VNC is very common and accessible, other options exist. For example, Microsoft offers the Remote Desktop Protocol (RDP) for sharing the desktop with a remote host. RDP is included by default on Windows 2003 and XP systems, and is available from Microsoft for other Windows versions (http://msdn.microsoft.com/library/en-us/termserv/termserv/remote_desktop_protocol.asp). On the Linux and Unix side, tools such as rdesktop (part of the default Ubuntu desktop) allow access to the shared Windows desktop from non-Windows systems. To use this program, you just need to provide the name of the windows server—for example:

```
rdesktop winserver
```

Other RDP client packages for Ubuntu include gnome-rdp and tsclient. For the KDE desktop, there is also krdc.

Although using a native Microsoft protocol is useful for accessing a Windows desktop, there are two significant limitations. First, the RDP server (shared desktop) is not available for all versions of Windows; second, only Windows can be a server. Currently, you cannot use any of these Ubuntu RDP tools to share your Ubuntu desktop with a Windows system.

Using the VNC Viewer

The VNC client for Ubuntu is provided by the xvncviewer package and is installed as part of the Ubuntu desktop. To use it, run: vncviewer. This pops up a small window that asks for the server's name.

Tip

I usually add the VNC viewer as a launcher on the top panel. This way, you can click on an icon and immediately get prompted for the server's name. If you include the server's name on the command-line, then vncviewer will immediately connect to the server.

VNC servers can be configured to require password. If one is needed, you will be prompted to enter it. Then the viewer's window will appear, showing you the shared desktop (see Figure 6-6). While your mouse is over the viewer, your cursor will become a small square. If the server allows you to interact (and not just "view only"), then the server's cursor will follow you. Every keystroke and every mouse click will be transmitted from your system to the server.

Even more importantly, the clipboard buffers on the server and client are linked. This enables you to copy and paste text between applications on the client and everything on the server.

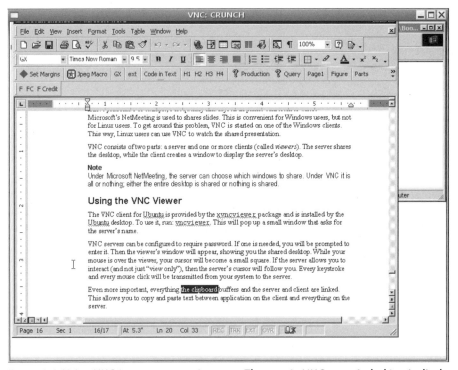

FIGURE 6-6: Using VNC to access a remote server. The remote VNC server's desktop is displayed within the VNC window.

Note If the server's desktop resolution is larger than the client's window, then the viewer's window will have scrollbars. This can be inconvenient. Also, if the server's color palette differs from the client's, then colors may look wrong.

Sharing Your Desktop

For an Ubuntu VNC server, there are two options. First, you can share your own desktop. In this setup, every client sees everything you have. Although this is usually not a problem, it can sometimes hinder your own productivity. For example, you can't search the web or check e-mail in privacy if everyone can see your desktop. The second option is to share a virtual desktop, where clients only see what you want them to see.

Sharing Your Complete Desktop

To share your complete desktop, you will need to install the server, x11vnc.

```
sudo apt-get install x11vnc
```

To start the server, simply run x11vnc. The basic server uses no passwords, allows one client to fully interact with the server, and exits when the client disconnects. There are many other options for x11vnc. Table 6-1 shows some of the more useful ones. These options can be combined. I usually use something like x11vnc -forever -passwd SeCrEt.

Table 6-1   Command-line options for x11vnc

Option	Example	Purpose
passwd	x11vnc -passwd SeCrEt	Assign a password to the server. It's not very secure, but it does keep the riff-raff out.
viewonly	x11vnc -viewonly	All clients can watch but cannot interact. This is useful for presentations.
forever	x11vnc -forever	The server continues running after the last client disconnects. The default setting is -once.
clip	x11vnc -clip 600x400+25+0	Restrict the desktop region. In this case, it is 600x400 pixels offset vertically 25 pixels— this is a region just below the top panel. Only items within this region are shared.

Sharing Independent Desktops

Although sharing your full desktop is useful, sometimes it is better to have a clean slate for sharing. X-Windows supports virtual desktops. These are desktops that exist in memory and do not conflict with your real desktop. The `tightvncserver` package provides a virtual desktop for sharing over VNC.

1. Install the Tight VNC server.

```
sudo apt-get install tightvncserver
```

2. Start the server. Be sure to specify the screen resolution (e.g., 800x600), color depth (e.g. 8, 16, or 32 bit), and the display number. Your normal desktop runs on display ":0", so you will need to choose an alternative display.

```
vncserver -geometry 800x600 -depth 16 :9
```

Tip   Although you can specify a desktop space that is larger than your real desktop and uses a higher resolution, don't. In most cases, it is more convenient to choose a geometry that is smaller than your desktop and has the same color depth (or less) to avoid scrollbars and ugly colors.

3. When you first start `vncserver`, it will ask you for a password. Clients will need to provide this when connecting to the server. If you restart the server, you won't need to specify the password. If you want to change the password later, use `vncpasswd`.

4. Use `xvncviewer` to connect to the server. For the server's name, include the display. For example, if the server's hostname is `vserver` then type in `vserver:9`.

The virtual desktop starts up in the background. To stop it from running, use the `-kill` option. For example, `vncserver -kill :9`.

The basic virtual desktop has a very simple configuration: it has one terminal window open. There are no menus, no icons, and no background beyond the default X11 "gray". The desktop is defined in the `$HOME/.vnc/xstartup` script. You can change this in order to give it a real desktop. For example, Listing 6-3 shows my `xstartup`. It has options for many different desktops, but currently starts up *my* Gnome desktop without showing any of the actual applications I have open (see Figure 6-7).

Listing 6-3: Sample $HOME/.vnc/xstartup with Different Desktops

```
#!/bin/sh

####################################################
# Select your desktop (only uncomment one window manager)
####################################################

#########################################
### For *your* Gnome Desktop
gnome-session --sm-disable &

#########################################
### For KDE (after: sudo apt-get install kubuntu-desktop)
#startkde &
```

Listing 6-3 *Continued*

```
#########################################
### For Tab Window Manager (after: sudo apt-get install twm)
#twm &

#########################################
### For plain X-Windows with a terminal
#xrdb $HOME/.Xresources
#xsetroot -solid grey
#x-terminal-emulator -geometry 80x24+10+10 -ls -title "$VNCDESKTOP Desktop"
&
#x-window-manager &

###################################################
### Add your own applications here.
### Be sure to background them using "&"
```

 Tip When using Firefox on the VNC virtual desktop, you may see errors about Firefox already running or the profile being in use. Consider using `firefox --no-xshm` or an alternate profile to overcome this problem. See Chapter 5 for tuning Firefox.

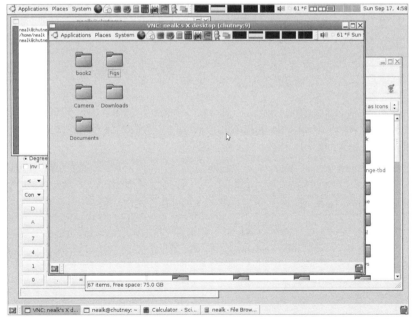

FIGURE 6-7: Tight VNC server running the Gnome desktop. The real Gnome desktop has applications running that do not appear in the VNC server.

Securing VNC Connections

The VNC password provides a basic level of security, but should not be trusted for safety over the Internet. Instead, you can tunnel VNC over an SSH connection. By default, the VNC server uses port 5900/tcp. Each VNC display increments this value. For example, if you are using Tight VNC and specify display :9, then the port is 5909/tcp. Then, using SSH port forwarding, you can tunnel the VNC port. For example, to tunnel the local VNC port to the server's VNC server running on :9, use:

1. On the remote server, start the Tight VNC server on display :9. For example:

```
vncserver :9
```

2. On your local system, use SSH to connect to the server and forward the local port 5900/tcp to the server's port 5909/tcp.

```
ssh -L5900:localhost:5909 server
```

3. In a different window on your local system, start the VNC client with:

```
xvncviewer localhost
```

This command tells the viewer to connect to the VNC server located on localhost:5900. However, 5900/tcp is actually tunneled through the SSH connection to the remote server. The connection is tunneled to the server's port 5909/tcp where the VNC server is running.

By tunneling VNC over SSH, you prevent attackers from seeing your desktop and, more importantly, you do not need to have the VNC server and its weak password system accessible to the world.

Seeing a Speed Difference

VNC transmits a lot of graphics and can be a bandwidth hog. If a dozen clients connect to a single server, then network traffic leaving the server can become a bottleneck and result in really slow updates for everyone.

If you need to have lots of viewers, consider farming out the load. The main server should only share the desktop with a few clients (for example, one server shares to four clients). Each of the clients also runs a server and shares with more clients. You can continue spreading the network load among computers until everyone has access. It only takes three levels of this "one server to four clients" for over 200 people to see the same thing. Although the people at the end of this chain may need to wait a second before seeing updates, this is much faster than having 200 clients access the same VNC server.

Tunneling VNC over SSH is not always fast. For better speed performance, enable compression (`-C`) and change the encryption selection to use the Blowfish algorithm: `ssh -C -c blowfish -L5900:localhost:5909` *server*.

Running Software in Emulators

Although nearly compatible software helps collaborators bridge a communication gap, nothing beats running the exact same application. For example, if you need to edit Word documents, then nothing does a better job than Microsoft Word. In the days of old, this true compatibility was accomplished with dual-boot systems. A single computer would have multiple operating systems installed and the user would reboot the computer into whatever operating system they needed. Although Ubuntu does support dual-boot environments (see Chapter 1), this is not as effective as being able to run applications from multiple operating systems at the same time. Today, people either run two separate computers with different operating systems and network connectivity (hardware is cheap), or they use hardware emulators.

A hardware emulator is an application that pretends to be an entire computer. Emulators replicate a computer in a virtual machine (VM): CPU, memory, devices (for example, hard drives), and even BIOS. A perfect emulator can run any operating system, and the operating system should not be able to tell that it is running in an emulator. For example, operating systems like Ubuntu and Windows expect standardized hardware. If the emulator mirrors the hardware, then either operating system will run without a problem. Most OSs do not need to know that the hardware is emulated.

There are many reasons to run an emulator, such as playing with hostile viruses, opening suspicious e-mails, or installing software without screwing up your main system. A true emulator is a perfect sandbox, where software can run without hurting the host operating system. But one of the main reasons to use an emulator is compatibility. Not all software can be used natively under Ubuntu, but an emulator running under Ubuntu can be installed with a non-Ubuntu operating system and used to run native applications. For example, if I really need to use Microsoft NetMeeting, then I can start a VM running Windows and use NetMeeting from within the emulation.

Choosing an Emulator

Emulators have three main components. The *host* operating system is where the emulator is running and the *guest* operating system runs in the emulator. For example, an Ubuntu host can run Windows 2000 as a guest within an emulator. The final component is a virtual hard drive. This is usually a file on the host system. I frequently install a guest operating system to a virtual hard drive (file), configure it just the way I like it, and make a backup of the file. Later, after playing with software in the guest system, I can copy back the image in order to reset the system. This is faster and cleaner than trying to remove undesirable software or perform a restore from a backup system.

If you want to see if a patch will make your system unstable, first install it in a VM. I have a VM installed with the same software as some of my critical computers. Before patching the real thing, I make sure the VM works after being patched.

There are three main emulators for Ubuntu: Qemu, VMware, and Xen. Although each provides solid emulation, they are all different. Table 6-2 shows some of the differences. All three emulators offer the same basic features. They all support multiple drives, offer solid i386 emulation, and support network access. The main differences come from licensing, architecture support, and speed. Qemu is the slowest of the emulators, but offers the widest hardware support. Xen 3.0 is arguably the fastest, but only supports Linux or BSD systems. VMware offers a commercial quality, fast emulation, and refined interface, but is proprietary and limited to Linux and Windows host systems.

There are two types of virtual machine: emulators and virtualizers. An emulator uses software to represent a computer system. A true emulator, such as Qemu and VMware, provide virtual hardware, BIOS, and even multiple CPUs. The benefit is that any operating system that is supported on the real hardware will work within an emulator. For example, if the emulator acts as an SMP Pentium Pro PC with 512 MB RAM, then it will support Windows, Linux, BSD, OS/2, E/OS, and any other PC operating system.

The biggest limitations with emulators are system resources and speed. If you configure an emulator to have 512 MB RAM but you actually have 128 MB RAM, then you can expect to spend time swapping RAM to disk. As speed goes, emulators interpret running opcodes. This means, the guest operating system runs slower than if it was on a dedicated computer. The speed can be less than 25 percent of the actual operating system's clock speed. For example, a 2.8 GHz host system may have a guest that appears to run at 300 MHz. Systems can run even slower if they are performing hardware-intensive commands. For example, when installing any guest operating system, the detection of attached peripherals may take a very long time. To overcome some of the speed limitations, kernel modules are available for boosting performance. These modules allow the emulator to directly link some functions into the host operating system. Drive, memory, and video access can all be performed faster with a kernel module. In the best cases, a kernel module can give you a nearly 1-to-1 performance ratio.

In contrast to emulators, *virtualizers* do not emulate hardware. Instead, they manage the existing host hardware and allow different guest systems to share the same resources. Xen is an example of a virtualizer. Xen allows multiple guest operating systems to run independently on the same hardware. Although Xen won't allow you to run different applications for collaboration, it can assist in dividing workloads, testing networked applications, and even benchmarking software. Xen is often used for security. Each independent operating system performs a specific task. If one Xen VM is compromised, it will not impact other VMs.

Table 6-2 Comparison of Hardware Emulators

Feature	Qemu 0.8.1	VMware 1.0.2	Xen 3.0.2
Licensing	GPL	Commercial	GPL
Open Source	Yes	No	Yes

Table 6-2   Continued

Feature	Qemu 0.8.1	VMware 1.0.2	Xen 3.0.2
VM Type	Emulator	Emulator	Virtualizer
Host Architectures	i386, PowerPC, Sparc; Linux, BSD, Windows, Solaris, MacOS X; portable to other host systems	i386; Linux and Windows	i386; Linux and BSD[4]
Guest Platforms	i386, PowerPC[1], ARM, MIPS, Sparc, and more	i386	i386[5]
Kernel Boost Module	Yes[2]	Yes	Yes
Ubuntu Support	Universe repository[3]	Generic Linux binary	Download source or Debian binary
Installation and Removal	`apt-get` for install and remove	Install script; manual removal	Manual install and removal

[1] Qemu 0.8.1 only supports Linux as a guest OS on a PowerPC.

[2] Qemu 0.8.1 includes a kernel boot module, but it does not work consistently under Ubuntu.

[3] The Ubuntu universe repository may not have the latest version of Qemu available.

[4] Xen 2.0 supported FreeBSD, but Xen 3.0 broke that support. Check with the Xen homepage for updates on BSD support.

[5] Xen virtualizes hardware, so it can only run multiple instances of the host's hardware.

Understanding Virtual Disks

In general, there are a few types of virtual drives you can use with emulators. The first is a disk image of an actual hard drive. After installing the guest OS, this image will contain a partition table, boot loader, and the guest OS—similar to the block device /dev/hda. This is the most flexible option. Unfortunately, this option is not always desirable since you cannot easily copy files off of the disk image. (Linux does not allow you to mount a file containing a partition table.)

The second option is a plain disk partition. This is a file (or device) missing the partition table and boot loader—similar to the block devices /dev/hda1 and /dev/hda2, which are partitions under /dev/hda. This option allows you to mount the file as a loop-back device. If you want to share files between the guest and host OSs, you can mount the partition image. For example, if the partition-file is called disk.img, then you can use:

```
sudo mkdir /mnt/img   # make sure the mount point exists
sudo mount -o loop disk.img /mnt/img  # mount the disk
```

By mounting the partition, you can copy any files you need to and from the VM.

A third option is to use an existing directory. The directory is used by the VM and treated as a disk partition. While not supported by all emulators, this does make it easier to copy files between the host and guest systems.

Differences Between VNC and VM

All of these emulators have the ability to grab the mouse. This means that the mouse's input is completely used by the VM. This is different from VNC, where the remote mouse is separate from the local mouse, and moving the mouse outside the window allows you to leave the remote window. To release the mouse from the emulator, press Control and Alt at the same time.

Note For Qemu, only the Ctrl+Alt keys on the left side of the keyboard release the mouse. The ones on the right are sent to the guest operating system. With VMware, any combination of Ctrl and Alt keys will release the mouse.

The other big difference concerns the clipboard. Under VNC, you can cut and paste between the remote (guest) and local (host) operating systems. Qemu 0.8.1 does not support this feature—the host and guest do not share a clipboard. Xen 3.0 and VMware do offer shared clipboards if the guest OS kernel is modified.

Emulating with VNC

The coolest feature provided by all three emulators is the ability to use VNC *as the display*. Normally when a VM is started, a window appears that acts as the display for the operating system. Qemu, VMware, and Xen allow you to specify a VNC display instead of a normal window. For example, under Qemu you would use `qemu -vnc 2` to start the display on the VNC server `localhost:2`. Now, if you want to collaborate, you can use any application on any supported guest operating system—you are not limited to sharing your Ubuntu desktop.

Using Qemu (Open Source)

The Q-Emulator (Qemu; `http://fabrice.bellard.free.fr/qemu/`) is the most flexible emulator option. Qemu supports a wide variety of host and guest architectures. Generally, if a pre-built Qemu binary is unavailable, you can download the source code and compile it. For Ubuntu, you can install Qemu from the universe repository; Qemu is the only emulator that offers Dapper-specific binaries.

```
sudo apt-get install qemu
```

You may want to compile Qemu from scratch since the Ubuntu package does not always contain the most recent code release.

Note You will need to have a developer's environment installed. See Chapter 4 for Programming with C.

1. Download the latest source code from `http://fabrice.bellard.free.fr/qemu/`.

2. Follow the installation instructions. They should be as simple as:

   ■ Extract the source code and `cd` into the source code directory.

   ■ Configure the build files with `./configure`.

- Compile Qemu using `make clean ; make`.
- Install it using `sudo make install`.

3. You will need to do one manual configuration step to specify the keyboard mapping for the Qemu VNC server:

```
sudo ln -s /usr/share/rdesktop/keymaps /usr/local/share/qemu/keymaps
```

Installing a Qemu VM

To get started using Qemu, you first need a virtual disk. There are a bunch of options for doing this:

- **Use** `qemu-img`—The program `qemu-img` creates a blank file that will act as a disk image. To create a two-gigabyte file called disk.img, use:

```
qemu-img create disk.img 2G
```

- **Create a blank disk**—You can use `dd` to create a blank disk. For example, `dd if=/dev/zero of=big1 bs=512 count=4194304`. This will do the same thing as using `qemu-img` (but not as fast).

- **Copy a working drive**—Use `dd` to make a copy of a working hard drive. This is much faster than installing a guest OS within the VM. If the disk is located at `/dev/hdb`, then you can copy it to `disk.img` using:

```
dd if=/dev/hdb of=disk.img
```

- **Use a real hard drive**—If the disk is installed as `/dev/hdb`, then you will just need read/write access to `/dev/hdb`.

Warning   Do not use the same boot device as your host system! If your host OS is using `/dev/had`, do not tell the VM to use `/dev/hda`. The drive may become corrupted if two operating systems use it at the same time.

If you have configured a blank disk, then you will need to install an operating system on it. This is usually done using a CD-ROM drive or ISO image. For example, if you downloaded the Ubuntu server ISO, then you can burn it to a CD-ROM or install directly from the ISO:

```
qemu -hda disk.img -cdrom /dev/cdrom -boot d
qemu -hda disk.img -cdrom ubuntu-6.06-server-i386.iso -boot d
```

Both of these commands will start the Qemu i386 VM and begin installing Dapper Drake. The main options for Qemu specify the images for hard drives (`-hda` and `-hdb` for the primary and secondary IDE drives), CD-ROM (`-cdrom`), and floppy drives (`-fda` and `-fdb`). By default, Qemu boots from the first hard drive (`-boot c`). If you want, you can specify booting from the floppy (`-boot a`) or CD-ROM (`-boot d`). There are other options for supporting USB devices, network cards, and video.

Tip   Qemu 0.8.1 does not support emulating DVD drives. If you need to access a DVD image, mount it to your local file system (for example, `sudo mount /dev/dvd /mnt/dvd`) and access it as a directory by using `qemu -hdb fat:/mnt/dvd`.

Installing Ubuntu under Qemu can take a very long time. Although a real Ubuntu installation may complete in under a half-hour, a Qemu-based installation may take two hours or longer. You can usually speed up VMs by increasing the amount of emulated RAM. Qemu defaults to 128 MB for each VM. With this default setting, I do not recommend booting off the Ubuntu desktop Live CD-ROM—you may grow old and die before the desktop loads (in can take over four hours). If you increase the VM's RAM to 256 MB (-m 256), then it should come up fully in a few minutes.

Running a Qemu VM

Although installations usually take a long time, installed operating systems are fast enough for real-time use. After you have installed the operating system, you can boot off the image drive using:

```
qemu -hda disk.img
```

The only limits to the number of operating systems you can run simultaneously are the speed of the host system and the amount of shared memory. Although you can increase the shared memory size (see Chapter 7), you cannot increase your computer's speed. On a dual 2.8 GHz computer with 1 GB RAM, I would not recommend running more than two graphical operating systems (or four text systems) at one time. Since the boot sequence for most guest systems consumes the most resources, I would also recommend booting them one at a time. After booting, it is very easy to run two emulators at once. Figure 6-8 shows two Qemu sessions running. One VM is running E/OS (a BeOS clone) with a VNC display. The other is running Windows 98 with the Firefox web browser. The host operating system is Ubuntu's Dapper Drake.

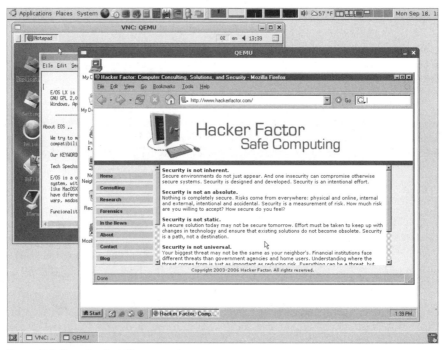

FIGURE 6-8: Running two Qemu sessions

Creating Partitions

Although having a disk partition for a file is great for loop-back mounts, Qemu and VMware cannot use a disk image as a drive unless it has a partition table. The challenge becomes: How do you create a partition table when all you have is a partition? The answer involves the dd and fdisk commands.

Let's assume you have a disk partition in a file (for example, part.img created from /dev/hda1) and you want to turn it into a disk image for Qemu (disk.img). First, you need to allocate space for the partition table. The partition table consumes the first 63 sectors of the drive. Using dd, you can replace your partition file (part.img) with a disk image (disk.img):

```
dd if=part.img of=disk.img bs=512 seek=63
```

Your disk file (disk.img) is 32,256 bytes larger than the partition image and has space for a partition table.

The next step is more complicated. Disks have sectors, heads, and cylinders. While old drives had a direct correlation between heads and physical read-write heads, newer drives simply use it as a numerical offset. Groups of sectors are grouped into cylinders. There are a maximum sizes are 63 sectors per cylinder, 255 heads, and 16,383 cylinders. For disks larger than 125 Gigs, sector sizes greater than 512 bytes are used.

Take a look at the size of your disk.img file and compute the number of cylinders. For example, let's say the size of disk.img is 1,073,774,080 bytes (a 1 GB partition plus partition table). Qemu prefers 16 heads and 63 sectors: 1,073,774,080 bytes ÷ (512 bytes per sector · 63 sectors · 16 heads) = 2080.5704 cylinders. Since you cannot have a fractional cylinder, round up to 2081. Now you can use fdisk to create the partition table:

```
fdisk -C 2081 -H 16 -S 63 disk.img
```

Tip   The fdisk command works on both block devices and files. You don't need to be root to modify a file, but fdisk will still try to synchronize disks. If you see errors about ioctl(), don't worry—only root has permission to call it and your changes are still saved.

Create one partition that spans the entire disk, from cylinder 1 to 2081. The final partition table should look like:

```
   Device Boot        Start        End       Blocks    Id  System
disk.img1                  1       2081     1048823+   83  Linux
```

Note   Based on the type of partition, you may need to change the system identifier in the partition table. If you plan to boot from this drive, you will also need to make the partition "active".

Your saved disk image is now usable as a disk by Qemu. Even though it may not be bootable (since there is no boot manager for Linux), you can boot from a live CD-ROM and setup a boot manager.

Using VMware (Commercial)

VMware is a commercial emulator. Although it has a more professional feel than Qemu and offers more configuration options, installing VMware is not as painless as Qemu.

Note Before you begin, check your system requirements. VMware only runs under Ubuntu on an i386. If you are using an IA64 or PowerPC system, then you cannot use VMware.

1. Go to www.vmware.com. VMware offers three different types of emulators. The VMware Player is free, but cannot be used to create a new image. In contrast, the VMware server and workstation are not free, but can create new images and make it easy to configure emulated hardware. Download the type of VMware system you plan to use. Be sure to download the Linux TAR image.

Tip If you plan to install the VMware server, get your serial number code *first*! While you can re-run the installer, the server will not run until you enter your serial number. The VMware workstation offers a short trial period, but then must be registered to use.

2. Extract the TAR file. For example, if you downloaded VMware-server-1.0.1-29996.tar.gz, then you would extract the contents—this creates a directory called vmware-server-distrib. Similarly, the VMware-player will create a directory called vmware-player-distrib.

   ```
   tar -xvf VMware-server-1.0.1-29996.tar.gz
   ```

3. For the VMware kernel module, you will need to install the headers for your kernel.

   ```
   sudo apt-get install linux-headers-`uname -r`
   ```

4. Now you can install VMware. Go into the VMware directory and run the install script.

   ```
   cd vmware-server-distrib  # or vmware-player-distrib
   sudo ./vmware-install.pl
   ```

   The install script will ask you a bunch of questions. Unless you have special needs, the default values should work fine.

Warning Unlike Qemu's apt-get package, VMware does not have an uninstall option. Once you install it, it is installed. And VMware scatters files all over the system.

Unlike Qemu, VMware provides lots of options for networking virtual machines. You can easily create a virtual subnet with lots of virtual machines. This is really useful for testing network software.

Creating a VMware Disk

If you purchased the VMware server or workstation, then you already have the ability to create a VM. But if you are cheap, then you installed the VMware player. The player can only run existing images, it cannot create new images. Fortunately, *you* can still create a boot image for use with the VMware player; the secret is to use Qemu. In this example, we'll install Dapper onto a 2 GB drive.

1. Install Qemu. (You will need `qemu-img`.)

2. You will need to create a VMware disk image (VMDK). You can do this with `qemu-img`.

   ```
   qemu-img create -f vmdk disk.vmdk 2G
   ```

3. Every VMware disk image also includes a configuration file. Listing 6-4 shows the configuration for booting off the Ubuntu server ISO. (Configurable portions appear in bold.) Call this file **disk.vmx**. If you plan to customize this example, then be sure to change the disk names.

Listing 6-4: Sample VMX Configuration File: disk.vmx

```
#!/usr/local/bin/vmware
config.version = "8"
virtualHW.version = "3"
memsize = "128"
nvram = "ubuntu.nvram"
ide0:0.present = "TRUE"
ide0:0.fileName = "disk.vmdk"
ide0:0.redo = ""
ide1:0.present = "TRUE"
ide1:0.fileName = "ubuntu-6.06-server-i386.iso"
ide1:0.deviceType = "cdrom-image"
ide1:0.autodetect = "TRUE"
floppy0.fileName = "/dev/fd0"
scsi0:0.redo = ""
usb.present = "TRUE"
sound.present = "TRUE"
sound.virtualDev = "es1371"
displayName = "Ubuntu"
guestOS = "other24xlinux"
uuid.location = "56 4d ad 0d c5 c8 b9 88-d2 f8 c0 01 12 5e 26 c4"
uuid.bios = "56 4d f3 a5 03 8c cb b9-ed bb 8f 10 a3 de b0 10"
ethernet0.addressType = "generated"
ethernet0.present = "TRUE"
ethernet0.connectionType = "nat"
ethernet0.generatedAddress = "00:0c:29:de:b0:10"
ethernet0.generatedAddressOffset = "0"
checkpoint.vmState = ""
tools.remindInstall = "TRUE"
```

4. Run the program `vmplayer`. This will ask you to select an image.

5. Select your `disk.vmx` file. Don't worry if some configuration items are not correct; `vmplayer` will correct them for you.

VMware is noticeably faster than Qemu, but installing Ubuntu still takes a very long time. After installing the operating system, you can boot the system off the virtual hard drive.

Note This hack enables you to test VMware, but is not intended for long-term use. For full support, consider purchasing the VMware server or workstation.

Converting Partitions

VMware and Qemu use different disk image formats. Qemu supports a variety of formats, but is usually used with either a copy-on-write disk (cow or qcow) or a raw disk image. In contrast, VMware uses the vmdk format that includes metadata along with the disk. Fortunately, you can easily convert between formats using `qemu-img`. To convert a raw Qemu image (for example, `disk.img`) to VMware disk (`disk.vmdk`), use:

```
qemu-img convert disk.img -O vmdk disk.vmdk
```

Similarly, you can convert a VMware disk to a Qemu disk using:

```
qemu-img convert -f vmdk disk.vmdk disk.img
```

Using this approach, you can use any Qemu disk under VMware and vice versa. Even though VMplayer cannot be used to create a virtual disk, Qemu can! And the Qemu disk can be quickly converted for use with VMware.

Using Xen (Open Source)

Xen is an operating system virtualizer designed for speed. This application replaces the host operating systems. At the time of this writing, Xen was not available from the Ubuntu repositories and only supported Linux and BSD guest operating systems.

Warning Installing Xen requires you to change your kernel and boot loader (Grub) configuration. If you screw up the installation then you can really hose your system. If you are not comfortable with a lot of manual configuration and troubleshooting, then don't try Xen. You might want to wait until the project matures a little more and you can use `apt-get` to install it.

Note Before you begin, check your system requirements. Xen only supports i386 and IA64, architectures with optional SMP support. If you are using a PowerPC system, then you cannot use Xen.

While there are many different ways to install Xen, I believe that the instructions at `www.howtoforge.com/xen_3.0_ubuntu_dapper_drake` are very helpful and detailed.

You will also receive instructions when you download the Xen source code—follow those instructions closely.

1. Install necessary packages. Xen uses these for installation and when it runs.

   ```
   sudo apt-get install python-twisted bridge-utils debootstrap
   ```

2. Edit /etc/mkinitramfs/modules and increase the number of loop-back devices.

   ```
   sudo bash -c 'echo "loop max_loop=64" >> /etc/mkinitramfs/modules'
   ```

3. Download Xen from www.xensource.com/xen/downloads/. You should download the pre-build installations (listed as *tarballs*). To download the code, you may need to provide an e-mail address where you will receive download installation instructions. Wait for the e-mail and follow the instructions. Be sure to check the prerequisites and follow the post-install steps! This should allow you to install Xen.

Tip

When downloading Xen, look for the open source downloads, not the commercial software.

Note

Why are the instructions not in this book? Xen is undergoing a lot of development and the installation instructions frequently change. It is likely that any instructions listed here would become outdated quickly. The best instructions are found in the README file for the Xen installer.

After you install Xen and reboot your system to use the Xen kernel, you can use the xm command to create a new VM, launch a VM, and remove a running VM.

Wine or Vinegar?

When people talk about emulators, the topic almost always turns to Wine. (Wine is a recursive acronym: Wine Is Not an Emulator.) Wine was created before most hardware emulators. It provides converted Windows libraries, enabling Windows applications to run under Linux. This is different than an emulator: emulators provide an entire system, while Wine provides support for Windows applications under Linux. Wine's support is very good for most Windows programs. In fact, it is so complete that it even permitted some Windows viruses to spread! (In http://os.newsforge.com/print.pl?sid=05/01/25/1430222, Matt Moen reported that Klez, Sobig, and a few other viruses worked under Wine.)

Continued

Wine or Vinegar? *Continued*

While many applications can be used with Wine (for example, Microsoft PowerPoint and Word), other applications are hit-and-miss. Even newer versions of supported programs do not always work because of changes in the Microsoft libraries. Wine is also a mostly unsupported application—it had no updates between August 2005 and August 2006. Even though it was created in 1993, it is still listed as beta code 13 years later.

Although Wine was an acceptable solution a few years ago, true emulators and virtualizers such as Qemu, VMware, and Xen provide better compatibility.

Sharing Files with Emulators

Regardless of your choice of emulator, you will need some way to exchange files between the guest and host systems. There are a variety of choices—you should choose the one(s) that best fit your needs.

- **FTP**—You can run an FTP server on the host OS and use the guest to connect and transfer files. This can also be done using Secure Shell's `scp` command. This option is almost universally supported by all guest operating systems.

- **NFS**—The host OS can export a partition to the guest OS. This works well if the guest is running a version of Linux or Unix.

- **SAMBA**—For a Windows guest OS, you can export a partition from the host OS using SAMBA.

- **Port forwarding**—Qemu and VMware allow you to forward ports between the host and guest operating systems. For example, the Qemu parameter `-redir tcp:10022:22` will redirect port `10022/tcp` on the host to the SSH server (`22/tcp`) on the guest. Port forwarding allows the host to communicate with the guest OS using whatever server is you require.

 Note All of these options require network access. Although network access is supported by each of these hardware emulators, you may want to disable the emulator's network access if you are evaluating viruses, performing disk forensics, or installing questionable software. If the network is disabled then there is no easy way to get data off of the virtual system.

Other Collaboration Tools

There are other collaboration tools beyond office applications, shared desktops, and virtual machines. Most common file formats, like PDF and PostScript have plenty of support under Ubuntu. Tools like xpdf, Ghostscript, and Ghostview can show you the contents of these common file types. With regards to networking, there are plenty of peer-to-peer applications. Packages like amule and peercast are available from the Ubuntu repositories.

Developers also have options for collaboration. The Concurrent Versioning System (cvs) and SubVersion (svn) file management systems are readily available and not too difficult to configure. Both svn and cvs support sharing source code across the network and are secure enough to use over the Internet (especially when they are tunneled over SSH).

Summary

Ubuntu offers plenty of options for collaboration. The available tools enable you to work with other people, regardless of operating system configuration. If you can't find a compatible tool, you can access a remote system where the tool is supported or run a virtual machine where the needed application runs natively.

Improving Performance

part

in this part

Chapter 7
Tuning Processes

Chapter 8
Multitasking Applications

Chapter 9
Getting Graphical with
Video Bling

Tuning Processes

T he default Ubuntu Dapper Drake installation includes some basic processes that check devices, tune the operating system, and perform housekeeping. Some of these processes are always running, while others start up periodically. Occasionally you might see your hard drive start up or grind away for a few minutes—what's going on? On mission critical servers, serious gaming boxes, and other real-time systems, unexpected processes can cause huge problems; administrators should know exactly what is running and when. The last thing a time-sensitive application needs is for a resource-intensive maintenance system to start at an unexpected time and cause the system to slow down.

In order to fine-tune your system, you will need to know what is currently running, which resources are available, and when processes start up. From there, you can tweak configurations: disable undesirable processes, enable necessary housekeeping, and adjust your kernel to better handle your needs.

Learning the Lingo

Everything that runs on the system is a *process*. Processes are programs that perform tasks. The tasks may range from system maintenance to configuring plug-and-play devices and anything else the user needs. *System processes* manage keep the operating system running, whereas *user processes* handle user needs.

Many processes provide *services* for other processes. For example, a web server is a service for handling HTTP network requests. The web server may use one or more processes to perform its task. Some services are critical to the system's operation. For example, if the system must support graphics but the X-Windows service is unavailable, then a critical service is missing.

Although most system processes are services, most user processes are *applications*. Applications consist of one or more processes for supporting user needs. For example, the Firefox web browser is an application that helps the user browse the web. In general, services start and end based on system needs, while applications start and end based on user needs.

None of these definitions—programs, processes, applications, and services—are very distinct. For example, the Gnome desktop consists of programs and processes that provide services to other programs and supports user needs. GDE can be called a set of programs, processes, applications, or services without any conflict.

in this chapter

☑ **Learning the Lingo**

☑ **Viewing running processes**

☑ **Identifying resources**

☑ **Finding process startups**

☑ **Tuning kernel parameters**

☑ **Speeding up boot time**

Time to Change

Different versions of Ubuntu (and Linux) use different startup scripts and run different support processes. Knowing how one version of Linux works does not mean that you know how all versions work. For example, one of my computers has a clock that loses a few minutes after every reboot. (It's an old computer.) When I installed Ubuntu Dapper Drake (6.06), I noticed that the time was correct after a reboot. I started to look around to find out how it did that and which timeserver it was using. The first thing I noticed was that there was no script in `/etc/init.d/` for setting the time. Eventually I tracked down the network startup scripts and found that the `ntpdate` script was moved from `/etc/init.d/` (in previous Ubuntu releases) to `/etc/network/if-up.d/`. This script allowed me to find the network time protocol (NTP) configuration file (`/etc/default/ntpdate`).

A similar problem came up when I started running Ubuntu Hoary Hedgehog (5.04). Periodically the hard drives would grind when I was not doing anything. At other times it happened when I was running processes that were impacted by disk I/O—when the drives began to grind, the critical process would detect a processing problem. I quickly narrowed the disk grinding to `updatedb`—a caching program that works with `slocate` for quickly finding files. What I could not find was how this program was being started. Eventually I discovered that `updatedb` was started by `anacron`, an automated scheduler.

While it is important to know what is running, it is even more important to know how to track down running processes and tune them to your needs.

When I talk about processes, I refer to anything that generates a running process identifier (see the next section for Viewing Running Processes). Programs are the executable files on the system that generate one or more processes. Users directly use applications, while the operating system uses services.

Viewing Running Processes

The only things that consume systems resources are running processes. If your computer seems to be running slower than normal, then it is probably due to some process that is either misbehaving or consuming more resources than you have available.

There are a couple of easy ways to find out what is running. From the command line, you can use ps and top to show applications, dependencies, and resources. For example, ps -ef shows every (-e) running process in a full (-f) detailed list (see Listing 7-1). The columns show the user who runs the process (UID), the process ID (PID), the parent process ID (PPID) who spawned this process, as well as when the process was started, how long it has been running, and of course, the process itself.

Listing 7-1: Sample Listing of Running Processes from ps -ef

```
UID         PID  PPID C STIME TTY        TIME CMD
root          1     0 0 Sep28 ?      00:00:01 init [2]
root          2     1 0 Sep28 ?      00:00:00 [migration/0]
root          3     1 0 Sep28 ?      00:00:00 [ksoftirqd/0]
root          4     1 0 Sep28 ?      00:00:00 [watchdog/0]
root       2406     1 0 Sep28 ?      00:00:00 [kjournald]
root       2652     1 0 Sep28 ?      00:00:00 /sbin/udevd --daemon
root       3532     1 0 Sep28 ?      00:00:00 [shpchpd_event]
root       4219     1 0 Sep28 ?      00:00:00 [kjournald]
daemon     4370     1 0 Sep28 ?      00:00:00 /sbin/portmap
root       4686     1 0 Sep28 ?      00:00:00 /usr/sbin/acpid -c /etc/acpi/eve
nts -s /var/run/acpid.socket
root       4857     1 0 Sep28 ?      00:00:00 /bin/dd bs 1 if /proc/kmsg of /v
ar/run/klogd/kmsg
klog       4859     1 0 Sep28 ?      00:00:00 /sbin/klogd -P /var/run/klogd/km  .
sg
root       5174     1 0 Sep28 ?      00:00:00 /usr/sbin/gdm
hplip      5213     1 0 Sep28 ?      00:00:00 /usr/sbin/hpiod
hplip      5217     1 0 Sep28 ?      00:00:00 python /usr/sbin/hpssd
nobody     5303     1 0 Sep28 ?      00:00:00 /usr/sbin/danted -D
nobody     5304  5303 0 Sep28 ?      00:00:00 /usr/sbin/danted -D
nobody     5306  5303 0 Sep28 ?      00:00:00 /usr/sbin/danted -D
nobody     5308  5303 0 Sep28 ?      00:00:00 /usr/sbin/danted -D
```

All in the Family

There are two main branches of Unix: BSD and System V. BSD is the older branch, and provides a standard that is used by operating systems such as FreeBSD, OpenBSD, SunOS, and Mac OS X. The BSD standard defines process management, device driver naming conventions, and system directory layouts. The younger branch, System V (pronounced "System Five"), includes operating systems like HP-UX, AIX, Solaris, and IRIX. System V follows the POSIX standards and differs slightly from the BSD family. For example, BSD places all device drivers in /dev—this directory may contain hundreds of devices. POSIX defines subdirectories in /dev, so all disks will be in /dev/disk (or /dev/dsk, /dev/rdsk, and so on) and all network drivers are in /dev/net. This makes /dev a cleaner directory.

Continued

All in the Family *Continued*

These differences also show up in the `ps` command. Typing `ps -ef` on System V generates similar output to `ps -aux` on BSD.

Not every operating system is strictly in the BSD or System V camp. Linux, for example, supports both BSD and POSIX. Under Linux, hard drives are usually listed in `/dev/` (for example, `/dev/hda` and `/dev/hdb`) and in `/dev/disk/`. There are a few places where the standards conflict (for example, what goes in specific directories); in these cases, the Linux selection seems almost arbitrary. For example, the `/sbin` directory under BSD contains system binaries. Under POSIX, they contain statically linked executables. Under Linux, they contain both.

The Linux `ps` command actually supports two different output formats: BSD and POSIX. Options that begin with a dash (for example, `-e`, `-f`, or combined as `-ef`) follow the POSIX standard. Without the dash (for example, `ps aux`) ps acts like BSD.

The `top` command shows all running processes and can order them by memory or CPU resource usage. Unlike `ps`, which provides a single snapshot of the currently running applications, `top` refreshes every few seconds to show you what is actively running. Processes that are spawned but not active will appear further down the `top` listing. You can interact with `top` in order to change the refresh rate (type **s** and then enter the refresh rate in seconds) or ordering (use < and > to select the order-by column). You can also press h to see a full list of the supported commands.

The graphical System Monitor (System ⇨ Administration ⇨ System Monitor) also enables you to see the list of running processes (see Figure 7-1).

Killing Processes

Under Linux, there are a maximum of 65,536 different PIDs—you cannot have more than 65,536 processes running at once. Under Ubuntu, the default maximum is 32,768 PIDs. (See "Tuning Kernel Parameters" later in this chapter; this parameter's name is `kernel.pid_max`.) Any new process is assigned the next available PID. As a result, it is possible to have a new process start with a lower PID than some older process. You can use the PID to kill processes using the `kill` command. For example to kill PID 123 use `kill 123`. The `kill` command can also be used to suspend processes (`kill -STOP 123`) and continue paused processes (`kill -CONT 123`). However, some processes do not die immediately.

Note Technically, PIDs are *handles* to processes and not actual processes. A multi-threaded process may have one handle for all threads, or one handle per thread. It all depends on how the process creates the threads.

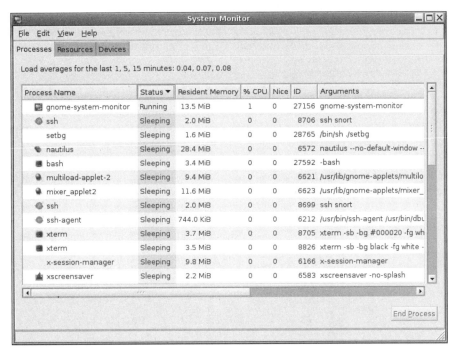

FIGURE 7-1: The System Monitor showing processes

Every process is assigned a dynamic PID, but there are two exceptions: kernel and `init`. The kernel uses PID 0 and is not listed by `ps`, `top`, or the System Monitor. You cannot kill the kernel (with the `kill` command). The `init` process (briefly discussed in Chapter 1) is the master parent process. Every process needs a running parent (PPID) to receive return codes and status from children. If a process' parent dies, then `init` becomes the parent.

Warning   While you can kill `init` (`sudo kill -9 1`), you don't want to do this! Killing `init` will eventually crash the system since `init` is used to clean up dead processes.

Killing a process kills it *once*; the kill signal does nothing to prevent the process from being started up again. In addition, there are some processes that cannot be killed.

- **Zombies**—When a process dies, it returns an error code to its parent (PPID). A dead PID whose return code has not yet been received by its parent becomes a zombie. Zombies take up no CPU, but do take up a PID. For programmers, calling the `wait()` function retrieves return codes and kills zombies. In contrast, sending a kill signal to a zombie does nothing since the process is already dead.

- **I/O Bound**—A process that is blocked on a kernel driver call may not process the kill signal until the kernel call returns. This is usually seen with network file system calls (NFS) when the network is down or on disk I/O when the drive is bad. For example, if you are using an NFS mounted directory and run `ls`, the command may hang if the network mount is bad. Sending a kill signal to the `ls` process will not immediately kill it. I've also experienced these hangs when using `dd` to copy a disk that was in the middle of a head-crash.

- **Interception**—Some kill signals can be intercepted by applications. For example, programs can intercept the default signal (`kill`, `kill -15`, or `kill -TERM`). This is usually done so the program can clean up before exiting. Unfortunately, some programs don't die immediately. Other kill signals, such as `kill -KILL` or `kill -9`, cannot be intercepted.

Tip

If you really want to kill a process, first use `kill PID` (e.g., `kill 1234`). This sends a TERM signal and allows well-behaved processes to clean up resources. If that does not get the result you want, try `kill -1 PID`. This sends a hang-up signal, telling the process that the terminal died. This signal is usually only intercepted by well-behaved processes; other processes just die. If that does not kill it, then using `kill -9 PID`. This is a true kill signal and cannot be intercepted by the process. (`Kill -9` always reminds me of Yosemite Sam shouting, "When I say whoa, I mean WHOA!")

Signals: Night of the Living Dead

Each signal is associated with a long name, short name, and number. The most common signals are:

- SIGHUP, HUP, 1—This is a hang-up signal that is sent to processes when the terminal dies.

- SIGINT, INT, 2—This is an interrupt signal. It is sent when the user presses Ctrl+C.

- SIGKILL, KILL, 9—The true kill signal. This cannot be intercepted and causes immediate death.

- SIGTERM, TERM, 15—This is a request to terminate signal and is the default signal sent by the `kill` command. Unlike KILL, TERM can be intercepted by the application.

- SIGSTOP, STOP, 19—This signal stops the process but does not terminate it. This is sent when you press Ctrl+Z to halt the current process.

- SIGCONT, CONT, 18—This resumes a process that is suspended by SIGSTOP. For a paused process at the command line (Ctrl+Z), typing `fg` will continue the process in the foreground and `bg` will continue the process in the background.

- SIGCHLD, CHLD, 17—Programmers who write spawning applications use this signal. CHLD is sent to the parent whenever any child dies.

Signals: Night of the Living Dead *Continued*

The full list of signals is in the man page for `signal` (`man 7 signal`). Any of these representations can be used by the `kill` command. Typing `kill -9 1234` is the same as `kill -KILL 1234` and `kill -SIGKILL 1234`.

Signals are flags; they are not queued up. If you send a dozen TERM signals to a process before the process can handle them, then the process will only receive one TERM signal. Similarly, if a program spawns six children and all die at once, then the parent may only receive one CHLD signal. If the parent fails to check for other dead children, then the remaining children could become zombies.

Killing All Processes

Every developer I know has, at one time or another, created a spawning nightmare. Sometimes killing a process only makes another process spawn. Since spawning happens faster than a user can run `ps` and `kill`, you won't be able to kill all of the processes. Fortunately, there are a couple of options.

- **Kill by name**—If all the processes have the same name, you can kill them all at once using `killall`. For example, if my process is called `mustdie`, then I can use `killall -9 mustdie` to end all running instances of it.

- **Kill all user processes**—There is a special `kill` command that will end all processes that you have permission to kill: `kill -9 -1`. As a user, this kills all of your processes, including your graphical display and terminals. But it will definitely kill any spawning loops you may have running.

Note Technically, the process ID -1 is a special case for the `kill` command. This means kill everything except the `kill` command (don't kill yourself) and `init` (don't kill the default parent).

Warning Never use `kill -9 -1` as root! This will kill every process—including shells and necessary system applications. This will crash your system before you can take you finger off the Enter key. If you need to kill all processes as root, use the power button or use the `reboot` or `shutdown` commands—don't use `kill -9 -1`.

- **Stop processes**—Infinite spawning loops usually happen because one process detects the death of another process. Instead of killing the processes, use the stop signal: `kill -STOP PID` or `killall -STOP Name`. This will prevent further spawning and enable you to kill all the sleeping processes without them re-spawning.

Identifying Resources

Your system has a lot of different resources that can be used by processes. These resources include CPU processing time, disk space, disk I/O, RAM, graphic memory, and network traffic. Fortunately, there are ways to measure each of these resources.

What's Up, /proc?

Linux provides a virtual file system that is mounted in the /proc directory. This directory lists system resources and running processes. For example:

```
$ ls -F /proc
1/      3910/   4133/   4351/   bus/          iomem       partitions
1642/   3930/   4135/   4352/   cmdline       ioports     pmu/
1645/   3945/   4137/   4363/   cpuinfo       irq/        scsi/
1650/   3951/   4167/   4364/   crypto        kallsyms    self@
1736/   3993/   4220/   4382/   devices       kcore       slabinfo
1946/   4/      4224/   5/      device-tree/  key-users   stat
2/      4009/   4237/   54/     diskstats     kmsg        swaps
20/     4027/   4250/   55/     dma           loadavg     sys/
3/      4057/   4270/   56/     driver/       locks       sysrq-trigger
3310/   4072/   4286/   57/     execdomains   mdstat      sysvipc/
3333/   4073/   4299/   6/      fb            meminfo     tty/
3335/   4081/   4347/   651/    filesystems   misc        uptime
3356/   4091/   4348/   apm     fs/           modules     version
3402/   4092/   4349/   asound/ ide/          mounts@     vmstat
3904/   4127/   4350/   buddyinfo interrupts   net/        zoneinfo
```

The numbered directories match every running process. In each directory, you will find the actual running command-line and running environment. Device drivers and the kernel use non-numeric directories. These show system resources. For example, /proc/iomem shows the hardware I/O map and /proc/cpuinfo provides information about the system CPUs.

Although /proc is useful for debugging, applications should be careful when depending on it. In particular, everything is dynamic: process directories may appear and vanish quickly and some resources constantly change.

Measuring CPU

The CPU load can be measured in a couple of ways. The uptime command provides a simple summary. It lists three values: load averages for 1 minute, 5 minutes, and 15 minutes. The load is a measurement of queue time. If you have one CPU and the load is less than 1.0, then you are not consuming all of the CPU resources. A load of 2.0 means all resources are being consumed and you need twice as many CPUs to reduce any wait-time. If you have two CPUs, then a load of 1.0 indicates that both processors are operating at maximum capacity. Although a load of 1.0 won't seem sluggish, a load of 5.0 can be noticeably detectable because commands may need to wait a few seconds few moments before being processed.

While uptime provides a basic metric, top gives finer details. While running top, you can press 1 to see the load per CPU at the top of the screen and you can see which processes are consuming the most CPU resources. The command ps aux also shows CPU resources per process.

Measuring Disk Space

The commands df and du are used to identify disk space. The disk-free command (df, also sometimes called *disk-full* or *disk-file system*) lists every mounted partition and the amount of disk usage. The default output shows the information in blocks. You can also see the output in a human-readable form (-h) and see the sizes in kilobytes or megabytes: df -h. The df command also allows you to specify a file or directory name. In this case, it will show the disk usage for the partition containing the file (or directory). For example to see how much space if in the current directory, use:

```
$ df .    # default output
Filesystem          1K-blocks      Used Available Use% Mounted on
/dev/hda1           154585604  72737288  73995748  50% /
$ df -h .  # human readable form
Filesystem           Size  Used Avail Use% Mounted on
/dev/hda1            148G   70G   71G  50% /
```

You can also use the System Monitor (System ⇨ Administration ⇨ System Monitor) to graphically show the df results (see Figure 7-2).

The disk-usage (du) command shows disk usage by directory. When used by itself, it will display the disk space in your current directory and every subdirectory. If you specify a directory, then it starts there instead. To see the biggest directories, you can use a command like du | sort -rn | head. This will sort all directories by size and display the top 10 biggest directories. Finally, you can use the -s parameter to stop du from listing the sizes from every subdirectory. When I am looking for disk hogs in my directory, I usually use du -s * | sort -rn | head. This lists the directories in size order. I can then enter the biggest directory and repeat the command until I find the largest files.

Tip The du command looks at every file in every subdirectory. If you have thousands of files, then this could take a while. When looking for large directories, consider the ones that take the longest to process. If every directory takes a second to display and one directory takes a minute, then you can press Ctrl+C because you probably found the biggest directory.

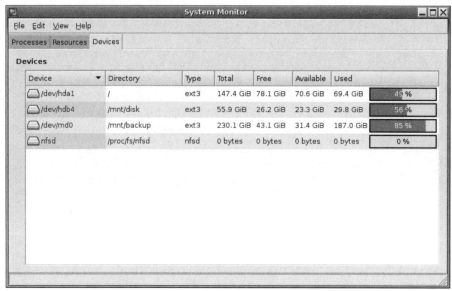

FIGURE 7-2: System Monitor showing available disk space

Measuring Disk I/O

All processes that access a disk do so over the same I/O channel. If the channel becomes clogged with traffic, then the entire system may slow down. It is very easy for a low-CPU application to consume most of the disk I/O. While the system load will remain low, the computer will appear sluggish.

If the system seems to be running slowly, you can use `iostat` (`sudo apt-get install sysstat`) to check the performance (see Listing 7-2). Besides showing the system load, the I/O metrics from each device are displayed. I usually use `iostat` with the `watch` command in order to identify devices that seem overly active.

```
watch --interval 0.5 iostat
```

Listing 7-2: Installing and Using iostat

```
$ sudo apt-get install sysstat   # install iostat
$ iostat
Linux 2.6.15-26-686 (chutney)    09/30/2006

avg-cpu:   %user   %nice %system %iowait   %steal   %idle
            0.22    0.00    0.13    0.10     0.00   99.55

Device:            tps   Blk_read/s   Blk_wrtn/s   Blk_read   Blk_wrtn
```

Listing 7-2 *Continued*				
hda	1.98	19.46	23.12	2805161	3332264
hdb	0.18	1.39	0.46	200903	66000
sda	0.01	0.06	0.01	8612	1536
sdb	0.01	0.07	0.01	9518	1536
md0	0.01	0.11	0.01	15450	1392

After finding which device is active, you can identify where the device is mounted using the mount command:

```
$ mount
/dev/hda1 on / type ext3 (rw,errors=remount-ro)
proc on /proc type proc (rw)
/sys on /sys type sysfs (rw)
varrun on /var/run type tmpfs (rw)
varlock on /var/lock type tmpfs (rw)
udev on /dev type tmpfs (rw)
devpts on /dev/pts type devpts (rw,gid=5,mode=620)
devshm on /dev/shm type tmpfs (rw)
```

Now that you know which device is active and where it is used, you can use lsof to identify which processes are using the device. For example, if device hda is the most active and it is mounted on /, then you can use lsof / to list every process accessing the directory. If a raw device is being used, then you can specify all devices with lsof /dev or a single device (for example, hda) using lsof /dev/hda.

Note Unfortunately, there is no top-like command for disk I/O. You can narrow down the list of suspected applications using lsof, but you cannot identify which application is consuming most of the disk resources.

Measuring Memory Usage

RAM is a limited resource on the system. If your applications allocate all available RAM, then the kernel will begin swapping memory to disk. Although swap space can allow you to run massively large applications, swap is also very slow compared to just using RAM. There are a couple of ways to view swap usage. The command swapon -s will list the available swap space and show the usage. There is usually a little swap space used, but if it is very full then you either need to allocate more swap space, install more RAM, or find out what is consuming the available RAM. The System Monitor (System ⇨ Administration ⇨ System Monitor) enables you to graphically view the available memory usage and swap space and identify if it is actively being used (see Figure 7-3).

To identify which applications are consuming memory, use the top or ps aux commands. Both of these commands show memory allocation per process. In addition, the pmap command can show you memory allocations for specific process IDs.

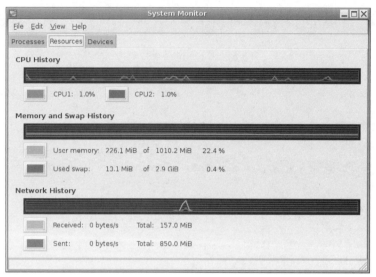

FIGURE 7-3: The System Monitor displaying CPU, memory, swap, and network usage

Measuring Video Memory

The amount of memory on your video card will directly impact your display. If you have an old video card with 256 KB of RAM, then the best you can hope for is 800x600 with 16 colors. Most high-end video cards today have upwards of 128 MB of RAM, allowing monster resolutions like 1280x1024 with 32 million colors. More memory also eases animation for games and desktops. While one set of video memory holds the main picture, other memory sections can act as layers for animated elements.

There is no simple way to determine video memory. If you have a PCI memory card, then the command `lspci -v` will show you all PCI cards (including your video card) and all memory associated with the card. For example:

```
$ lspci -v | more
0000:01:00.0 VGA compatible controller: nVidia Corporation NV18 [GeForce4 MX 400
0 AGP 8x] (rev c1) (prog-if 00 [VGA])
        Subsystem: Jaton Corp: Unknown device 0000
        Flags: bus master, 66MHz, medium devsel, latency 248, IRQ 177
        Memory at fa000000 (32-bit, non-prefetchable) [size=16M]
        Memory at f0000000 (32-bit, prefetchable) [size=128M]
        Expansion ROM at fbee0000 [disabled] [size=128K]
        Capabilities: <available only to root>
```

This listing shows an NVIDIA NV18 video card with 128 MB of video RAM.

Tip

On large supercomputers, `lspci` not only shows what is attached but also where. For example, if you have eight network cards then it can identify which slot each card is in. This is extremely useful for diagnostics in a mission-critical environment with fail-over hardware support. One example is to use (`lspci -t ; lspci -v`) | `less` to show the bus tree and each item's details.

Measuring Network Throughput

Just as disk I/O can create a performance bottleneck, so can network I/O. While some applications poll the network for data and increase CPU load when the network is slow, most applications just wait until the network is available and do not impact the CPU's load.

If the computer seems sluggish when accessing the network, then you can check the network performance using netstat -i inet:

```
$ netstat -i inet
Kernel Interface table
Iface  MTU Met   RX-OK RX-ERR RX-DRP RX-OVR   TX-OK TX-ERR TX-DRP TX-OVR Flg
eth0   1500 0   338386      0      0      0  737350      0      0      0 BMRU
lo    16436 0     786      0      0      0     786      0      0      0 LRU
vmnet  1500 0       0      0      0      0     465      0      0      0 BMRU
vmnet  1500 0       0      0      0      0     465      0      0      0 BMRU
```

This shows the amount of traffic on each network interface as well as any network errors, dropped packets, and overruns. This also shows the name of the network interface (for example, eth0). When checking network usage, I usually use netstat with the watch command so I can see network usage over time:

```
watch --interval 0.5 netstat -i inet
```

Tip The netstat -i inet command shows the number of packets from every interface. You can also use ifconfig (for example, ifconfig eth0) to see more detail; ifconfig shows the number of packets and number of bytes from a particular network interface.

The netstat -t and netstat -u commands allow you to see which network connections are active. The -t option shows TCP traffic, and -u shows UDP traffic. There are many other options including --protocol=ip to show all IP (IPv4) connections, and IPv6 connections are listed with --protocol=ip6.

To identify which processes are using the network, you can use lsof. The -i4 parameter shows which processes have IPv4 connections, -i6 displays IPv6, -i tcp lists TCP, and -i udp displays applications with open UDP sockets:

```
$ lsof -i4 -n # show network processes and give IP addresses as numbers
COMMAND  PID  USER   FD   TYPE DEVICE SIZE NODE NAME
ssh     8699 mark    3u   IPv4 120398      TCP 10.3.1.5:41525->10.3.1.3:ssh
(ESTABLISHED)
ssh     8706 mark    3u   IPv4 120576      TCP 10.3.1.5:41526->10.3.7.245:ssh
(ESTABLISHED)
```

Finding Process Startups

While the `ps` command can list what is running now, and other tools show what resources are being used, there is no good tool for telling how something started in the first place. Although `ps` can identify the PPID, in many cases the PPID is 1—indicating `init` owns it. Instead, there are plenty of places where a process can be started, including boot scripts, device configuration scripts, network changes, logins, application initialization scripts, and scheduled tasks.

Inspecting Boot Scripts

The directory `/etc/init.d/` contains scripts for starting and stopping system services (these are detailed in Chapter 3). These scripts are activated by links in the different `rc` directories (`/etc/rc0.d`, `/etc/rc1.d`, and so on). As `init` enters each run level, the appropriate S links are executed. For example, at run level 1, all S links in `/etc/rc1.d/` are started. This includes `S20single` for single-user mode configuration. When the system changes levels, all K (for kill) scripts are executed before changing run levels. To find the current run level, you can either use `who -r` or the `runlevel` command.

Note   The `runlevel` command displays the previous and current run levels. Usually the previous one is not defined (since you probably booted into the current level) and is displayed as an N (for not defined).

```
$ who -r
         run-level 2   2006-09-28 20:32                        last=S
$ runlevel
N 2
```

During boot, all output from the init scripts is sent to `/var/log/messages`. You can use this log file to identify which processes were executed.

Note   Under Dapper Drake and earlier Ubuntu versions, `init` is the top-most process and is critical for managing running processes. New to Edgy Eft, the System V `init` is being replaced with Upstart—an event driven process manager.

Inspecting Device Startups

Dynamic device configuration is managed by udev (see Chapter 3). The udev process watches and manages plug-and-play devices. Based on the configuration in `/etc/udev/rules.d/`, different applications may be launched.

Inspecting Network Services

New network interfaces are managed by a couple of different systems. First, udev identifies the network interface (`/etc/udev/rules.d/25-iftab.rules`). This rule runs the interface table helper (`iftab_helper`) command. The helper consults the file `/etc/iftab` in order to identify the proper device handle. After the interface is identified, it can be brought up or down. There are four directories of scripts for managing network interfaces:

- `/etc/network/if-pre-up.d/`—This contains steps that must be completed before (pre) the interface is brought up. For example, the scripts may need to load wireless drivers.

- `/etc/network/if-up.d/`—These scripts are used after bringing up the configured network interface. For example, this is where the system clock is set—every time any network is brought up, the computer's clock is set.

- `/etc/network/if-down.d/`—These scripts are used to remove any running configuration. For example, if you have the Postfix mail server running, then there is a script that tells Postfix to reload its configuration when an interface is taken down.

- `/etc/network/if-post-down.d/`—This directory contains any cleanup stages that are needed after (post) the interface is taken down. For example, unnecessary wireless drivers can be unloaded.

Tip The `/etc/network/` scripts are used when an interface is brought up and down. The `/etc/init.d/networking` script is used to actually bring up and down the interfaces. Interfaces are configured based on the `/etc/network/interfaces` file, described in Chapter 11.

Although `/etc/network/` is used only when interfaces are brought up or down, other programs like `xinetd` can run applications based on network connections. If you installed `xinetd` (`sudo apt-get install xinetd`), the configuration file `/etc/xinetd.conf` and the `/etc/xinetd.d/` directory contain the list of executables that can be started by `xinetd`.

Inspecting Shell Startup Scripts

Each time you log in, log out, or create a new shell, configuration scripts are executed. Each of these scripts run processes. Since `bash` is the default shell under Ubuntu, you are likely to use the configuration scripts in Table 7-1.

Table 7-1   Shell Startup Scripts

Initialization Script	Purpose
`/etc/profile`	Used by every login shell, system-wide.
`$HOME/.bash_profile`	Used on a per-user basis. Each user can have a personalized login script.
`/etc/bash.bashrc`	Every interactive shell runs this system-wide configuration script.
`$HOME/.bashrc`	Every interactive shell runs this user-specific configuration script.

Continued

Table 7-1 *Continued*

Initialization Script	Purpose
/etc/bash.logout	If you create it, this system-wide script is executed every time a user logs out.
$HOME/.bash_logout	User-specific script that is used during logout.

All of these scripts are divided into two situations: login/logout and interactive shells. Whenever you log into your Ubuntu system, the login and interactive shell scripts are executed. When you open a terminal window, only the interactive scripts are used.

Tip The default user-specific shell scripts are stored in /etc/skel/. Use ls -la /etc/skel/ to list all of the default files. Changing these defaults will give all new user accounts the modified configuration files, but you will still need to modify existing user accounts. For system-wide changes, modify /etc/profile and /etc/bash.bashrc instead.

Inspecting Desktop Scripts

Beyond user-level shell scripts, the graphical desktop can also run scripts. First, X-Windows runs. This starts up applications by running the script /etc/X11/xinit/xinitrc, /etc/X11/Xsession, and /etc/X11/xinit/xserverrc. Each of these scripts set environment variables and can run applications. There are also startup scripts in /etc/X11/Xsession.d/ that are started after a user logs in, and individual users can have a $HOME/.xsession script for running applications at startup.

After X-Windows, the desktop starts. Under Ubuntu, this is Gnome. Gnome runs lots of applications that, in turn, can run many more applications. The main places to look for automatically running Gnome processes are in the /etc/X11/gdm/ directory, in the file $HOME/.gnomerc, and under System ⇨ Preferences ⇨ Sessions. The /etc/X11/gdm directory contains system-wide startup scripts. The $HOME/.gnomerc script enables you to configure your own startup applications, and the graphical session configuration tool (see Figure 7-4) enables you to easily customize non-standard startups.

FIGURE 7-4: The Gnome graphical session manager showing the list of startup applications

All of these startup options can become very confusing. For example, if you want to automatically start Firefox on login, then you can add it to `/etc/X11/Xsession`, `/etc/X11/gdm/Xsession`, `/etc/X11/gdm/PostSession/Default`, `/etc/X11/Xsession.d/99start_firefox`, `$HOME/.xsession`, `$HOME/.gnomerc`, or use the graphical Gnome Session editor to add a startup applications. The main question to ask is, "who will want this?"

- **Everyone running X-Windows?**—Use `/etc/X11/Xsession` or place the startup script under `/etc/X11/Xsession.d/`.

- **Just you running X-Windows?**—Use `$HOME/.xsession`.

- **Everyone running Gnome?**—Use `/etc/X11/gdm/PostSession/Default`. This will work for Gnome users, but not KDE or other desktops. KDE, XDM, and other desktops have their own configuration directories and files.

- **Just you running Gnome?**—Use `$HOME/.gnomerc` or the graphical session editor.

Note These are not all of the possible startup hooks. There are plenty of places where code can be told to start running. If you are trying to find where an application starts, look here first or use `ps` and start tracking down parent processes. Most graphical processes use configuration files and any of those files could potentially run applications.

Inspecting Gnome Applications

Just as `udev` watches for plug-and-play devices, so does Gnome. The Gnome desktop can identify some devices and automatically run applications. The default settings are found under System ➪ Preferences ➪ Removable Drives and Media. The tabs show you the items you can change:

- **Storage**—When a CD-ROM is inserted, the default action is to either browse the disk or start the CD-ROM burner (see Figure 7-5). I usually disable the option Burn a CD or DVD when a blank disc is inserted. This does not disable your ability to right-click on an ISO image and select the burn option—it only stops the default CD-Writer application from starting. This tab also covers other types of removable media, including USB thumb drives.

- **Multimedia**—When you first insert an audio CD or a DVD, the default media player starts up. From the Multimedia tab (see Figure 7-6), you can change the default applications or disable the automatic startup. If you disable it, you can still run the multimedia players from the Applications ➪ Sound & Video menu.

- **Cameras**—When a camera is connected, the default action is to import pictures (see Figure 7-7). On my main workstation, I usually disable this option—if I want to import pictures, then I will do it myself. This is because I usually want to download a single, specific picture, and not all of them. In contrast, my laptop is configured to automatically import pictures since I am probably traveling and want to quickly transfer pictures before taking more photos.

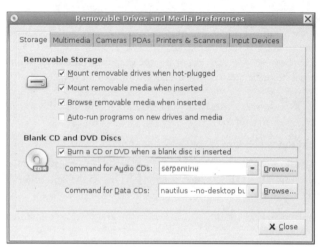

FIGURE 7-5: The Removable Drives and Media preferences, showing drive handlers

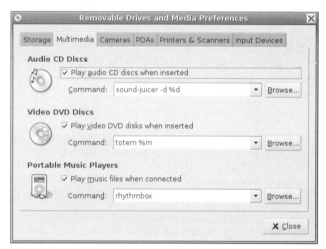

FIGURE 7-6: The Removable Drives and Media preferences, showing the default audio and video applications

- **PDAs**—If you have a PDA such as a Palm or PocketPC, then you can automatically connect and synchronize with these devices.

- **Printers & Scanners**—If you have a USB scanner or printer, then it may not always be connected. Normally, no programs (beyond udev) run when a printer is attached, but you could enable the default setting and add the printer to the printing system. For scanners, xsane automatically runs. You can change the default action that occurs when these devices are attached (see Figure 7-8).

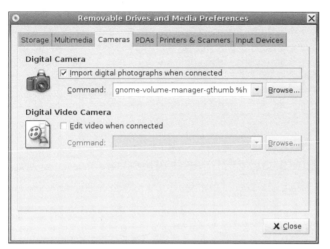

FIGURE 7-7: The Removable Drives and Media preferences, showing the default camera settings

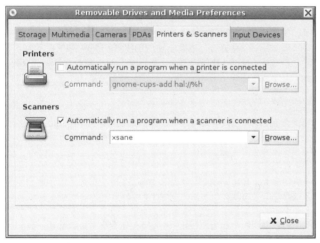

FIGURE 7-8: The Removable Drives and Media preferences, showing the default actions for printers and scanners

- **Input Devices**—This is an interesting tab because it really does not do anything. In theory, you can connect a USB mouse, keyboard, or tablet and have an application run. In practice, the X-Windows server normally uses these devices. If they are not configured and connected before the X-server starts, then they will not be recognized as pointer devices (see Chapter 3 for configuring pointer devices). However, if you have a special application that can handle the device, then you can use these settings to run the application.

Although other spawning subsystems, such as udev and /etc/init.d/, are configurable and extendable, Gnome is fairly inflexible. You can only configure auto-run settings for items listed in this applet. If you have a new plug-and-play device that is not listed (for example, a GPS system) then you cannot make Gnome spawn an application. Instead, you will need to configure udev run the application.

Tip

Configuring udev to run programs is covered in Chapter 3. See the section on Associating Applications with USB.

Inspecting Schedulers: at, cron, and anacron

Programs that should run periodically are usually placed in a scheduler. The three common schedulers are at, cron, and anacron.

Scheduling with at

The at command specifies that an application should run at a specific time. This is used for run-once commands. For example, to start xclock in 15 minutes, you could use:

```
echo "DISPLAY=:0 xclock" | at now + 15 minutes
```

The at command takes one or more command-line statements as input. The time format can either be in an HH:MM with am or pm (for example, 3:45 pm or 3:45 PM), a date format (for example, 03/15/07), or as an offset (for example, noon + 3 hours or 8am + 6 days). Scheduled at jobs are stored in the /var/spool/cron/atjobs/ directory. You can query them using atq and remove jobs using atrm. After the process runs, any text output is e-mailed back to the user.

Scheduling with cron

While at is used for one-time applications, cron is used for repeated tasks. Each user has a crontab entry where processes can be scheduled. For example, mine has this entry:

```
3,18,33,48 * * * * fetchmail -U -n --invisible > /dev/null 2>&1
```

Each cron entry has six elements per line. The first five specify when to run, and the last element is a single command line to actually execute. The time fields are:

- **Minute**—The minute to run. This can be a single value (0-59) or a comma-separated list of times (for example, 3,18 means run at 3 and 18 minutes after the hour). A star can also be used to mean *every minute*.

- **Hour**—The hour to run. This can be a single value (0-23), a range (for example, 9-17 means hourly from 9 am to 5 pm), a comma-separated list, or a division indicating how often. For example, 9-17 means hourly from 9 am to 5 pm, but 9-17/3 means every 3 hours between 9 am and 5 pm (9 am, 12 pm, and 3 pm). A star can be used to mean *every hour*, and when combined with a divisor, "*/4 means every four hours.

- **Day**—Day of the month to run. As with the other fields, this can be a single value (1-31), a range, or a list and can use a divisor. A star means *every day*.

- **Month**—Month of the year to run. This can be a single value (1-12), a range, or a list and can use a divisor. A star means *every month*.

- **Day of week**—You can specify which weekday to run on. The days are numbers: 0-6 for Sunday through Saturday (7 can also mean Sunday). Again, this can be a value, list, or range and may include a divisor.

Usually the date specification is simple. For example, `0 12 * * 0` means to run every Sunday at noon. But it can be very complex: `*/3 */3 */3 */3 */3` says to run every three minutes, every third hour of every third day in every third month, but only when it corresponds with every third day of the week.

Tip

Try to space cron jobs so they do not all run at once. Although I could use `*/15` to run `fetchmail` four times per hour, I use the list `3,18,33,48` instead. This prevents lots of applications from all trying to start on the hour.

To schedule a `cron` task, use `crontab -e`. This edits your `crontab` file (found in `/var/spool/cron/crontabs/`). You can also use `crontab -1` to list your crontab entries. A `#` at the beginning on a crontab line is a comment. I usually put the following comment at the start of my file just so I can remember what the time fields mean:

```
# mm ss DD MM WW command
```

As with `at`, every text output from the cronjob is e-mailed back to the user. If you don't want to receive e-mail, then add `> /dev/null 2>&1` to the end of the command. This directs all output to `/dev/null`.

Scheduling with anacron

While `cron` runs tasks repeatedly, it makes no distinction as to the system state. The `anacron` service is similar to `cron`, but allows tasks to be run based on a relative period rather than an absolute date. For example, the default `anacron` installation runs `updatedb` (to update online man-page indexes) daily, starting at five minutes after the computer first boots up.

The configuration schedule for `anacron` is found in the `/etc/anacrontab` file. The default scripts are in `/etc/cron.d/`, `/etc/cron.daily/`, `/etc/cron.weekly/`, and `/etc/cron.monthly/`.

If you run a mission-critical system, or a computer with limited resources, then you should seriously consider looking at these configuration settings and tuning them to your needs. For example, if it is a deployed server, then you probably do not need `updatedb` running daily. In fact, you could disable `anacron` completely and move any required functionality into root's crontab (`sudo crontab -e`). This way, tasks such as log file rotation will happen on a predictable schedule.

Tuning Kernel Parameters

Many of the tunable performance items can be configured directly by the kernel. The command `sysctl` is used to view current kernel settings and adjust them. For example, to display all available parameters (in a sorted list), use:

```
sudo sysctl -a | sort | more
```

Note There are a few tunable parameters that can only be accessed by root. Without `sudo`, you can still view most of the kernel parameters.

Each of the kernel parameters are in a *field = value* format. For example, the parameter `kernel.threads-max = 16379` sets the maximum number of concurrent processes to 16,379. This is smaller than the maximum number of unique PIDs (65,536). Lowering the number of PIDs can improve performance on systems with slow CPUs or little RAM since it reduces the number of simultaneous tasks. On high-performance computers with dual processors, this value can be large. As an example, my 350 MHz iMac is set to 2,048, my dual-processor 200 MHz PC is set to 1024, and my 2.8 GHz dual processor PC is set to 16,379.

Tip The kernel configures the default number of threads based on the available resources. Installing the same Ubuntu version on different hardware may set a different value. If you need an identical system (for testing, critical deployment, or sensitive compatibility), be sure to explicitly set this value.

There are two ways to adjust the kernel parameters. First, you can do it on the command line. For example, `sudo sysctl -w kernel.threads-max=16000`. This change takes effect immediately but is not permanent; if you reboot, this change will be lost. The other way to make a kernel change is to add the parameter to the `/etc/sysctl.conf` file. Adding the line `kernel.threads-max=16000` will make the change take effect on the next reboot. Usually when tuning, you first use `sysctl -w`. If you like the change, then you can add it to `/etc/sysctl.conf`. Using `sysctl -w` first allows you to test modifications. In the event that everything breaks, you can always reboot to recover before committing the changes to `/etc/sysctl.conf`.

Computing Swap

The biggest improvement you can make to any computer runnning Ubuntu is to add RAM. In general, the speed impact from adding RAM is bigger than the impact from a faster processor. For example, increasing the RAM from 128 MB to 256 MB can turn the installation from a day job to an hour. Increasing to 1 GB of RAM shrinks the installation to minutes.

There is an old rule-of-thumb about the amount of swap space. The conventional wisdom says that you should have twice as much swap as RAM. A computer with 256 MB of RAM should start with 512 MB of swap. Although this is a good idea for memory limited systems, it isn't practical for high-end home user systems. If you have 1 GB of RAM, then you probably will never need swap space—and you are very unlikely to need 2 GB of swap unless you are planning on doing video editing or audio composition.

There is a limit to the amount of usable RAM. A 32-bit PC architecture like the Intel Pentium i686 family can only access 4 GB of RAM. This is a hardware limitation. Assuming you can insert 16 GB of RAM into the computer, only the first 4 GB will be addressable. The second limitation comes from the Linux 2.6 kernel used by Ubuntu's Dapper Drake (as well as other Linux variants). The kernel can only access 1 GB of RAM. Any remaining RAM is unused. For this reason, it is currently not worth investing in more than 1 GB of RAM. Also, since the total virtual memory (RAM + swap) is limited to 4 GB, you should not need to allocate more than 3 GB of swap on a 1 GB RAM system.

Note If you compile the kernel from scratch, there is a HIGHMEM flag that can be set to access up to 4 GB of RAM on a 32-bit architecture. Unfortunately, there is a reported performance hit since most hardware drivers cannot access the high memory. If you set this flag, then do not bother with any swap space—the total amount of memory (RAM + swap) cannot be larger than 4 GB.

Modifying Shared Memory

Some sections of virtual memory can be earmarked for use by multiple applications. Shared memory allows different programs to communicate quickly and share large volumes of information. Applications such as X-Windows, the Gnome Desktop, Nautilus, X-session manager, Gnome Panel, Trashcan applet, and Firefox all use shared memory. If programs cannot allocate or access the shared memory that they need, then programs will fail to start.

The inter-process communication status command, `ipcs`, displays the current shared memory allocations as well as the PIDs that created and last accessed the memory (see Listing 7-3).

Tip There are many other flags for `ipcs`. For example, `ipcs -m -t` shows the last time the shared memory was accessed, and `ipcs -m -c` shows access permissions. In addition, `ipcs` can show semaphore and message queue allocations.

Listing 7-3: Viewing Shared Memory Allocation

```
$ ipcs -m
------ Shared Memory Segments --------
key        shmid      owner      perms      bytes      nattch     status
0x00000000 327680     nealk      600        393216     2          dest
0x00000000 360449     nealk      600        393216     2          dest
0x00000000 196610     nealk      600        393216     2          dest
0x00000000 229379     nealk      600        393216     2          dest
0x00000000 262148     nealk      600        393216     2          dest

$ ipcs -m -p
------ Shared Memory Creator/Last-op --------
shmid      owner      cpid       lpid
327680     nealk      7267       7307
360449     nealk      7267       3930
196610     nealk      7182       7288
229379     nealk      7265       3930
```

Continued

Listing 7-3 Continued

```
262148    nealk    7284    3930
393221    nealk    7314    3930
425990    nealk    7280    3930
458759    nealk    7332    3930

$ ps -ef | grep -e 3930 -e 7280  # what processes are PID 3930 and 7280?
root     3930  3910  0 09:24 tty7    00:00:02 /usr/bin/X :0 -br -
audit 0 -auth /var/lib/gdm/:0.Xauth -nolisten tcp vt7
nealk    7280    1  0 15:22 ?       00:00:01 update-notifier
```

Programs can allocate shared memory in two different ways: temporary and permanent. A temporary allocation means the memory remains shared until all applications release the memory handle. When no applications remain attached (the ipcs nattch field), the memory is freed. In contrast, permanent allocations can remain even when no programs are currently using it. This allows programs to save state in a shared communication buffer.

Sometimes shared memory becomes abandoned. To forcefully free abandoned memory, use ipcrm. You will need to specify the shared memory ID found from using ipcs (the shmid column).

More often than not, you will be more concerned with allocating more shared memory rather than freeing abandoned segments. For example, databases and high-performance web servers work better when there is more shared memory available. The sysctl command shows the current shared memory allocations:

```
$ sysctl kernel | grep shm
kernel.shmmni = 4096
kernel.shmall = 2097152
kernel.shmmax = 33554432
```

In this example, there is a total of 33,554,432 bytes (32 MB) of shared memory available. A single application can allocate up to 2 MB (2,097,152 bytes), and the minimal allocation unit is 4096 bytes. These sizes are plenty for most day-to-day usage, but if you plan to run a database such as Oracle, MySQL, or PostgreSQL, then you will almost certainly need to increase these values.

Changing Per User Settings

Beyond the kernel settings are parameters for configuring users. The ulimit command is built into the bash shell and provides limits for specific application. Running ulimit -a shows the current settings:

```
$ ulimit -a
core file size          (blocks, -c) 0
data seg size           (kbytes, -d) unlimited
max nice                       (-e) 20
```

```
file size               (blocks, -f) unlimited
pending signals               (-i) unlimited
max locked memory       (kbytes, -l) unlimited
max memory size         (kbytes, -m) unlimited
open files                    (-n) 1024
pipe size            (512 bytes, -p) 8
POSIX message queues     (bytes, -q) unlimited
max rt priority               (-r) unlimited
stack size              (kbytes, -s) 8192
cpu time               (seconds, -t) unlimited
max user processes            (-u) unlimited
virtual memory          (kbytes, -v) unlimited
file locks                    (-x) unlimited
```

These setting show, for example, that a single user-shell can have a maximum of 1,024 open files and core dumps are disabled (size 0). Developers will probably want to enable core dumps, with ulimit -c 100 (for 100 blocks). If you want to increase the number of open files to 2,048, use ulimit -n 2048.

The user cannot change some limits. For example, if you want to increase the number of open files to 2,048 then you would use ulimit -n 2048, except only root can increase this value. In contrast, the user can always lower the value.

Note Some values have an upper limit defined by the kernel. For example, although root can increase the number of open file handles, this cannot be increased beyond the value set by the kernel parameter fs.file-max (sysctl fs.file-max).

On a multi-user system, the administrator may want to limit the number of processes any single user can have running. This can be done by adding a ulimit statement to the /etc/bash.bashrc script:

```
# Only change the maximum number of processes for users, not root.
if [ `/usr/bin/id -u` -ne 0 ] ; then
  ulimit -u 2048 2>/dev/null # ignore errors if user set it lower
else
  ulimit -u unlimited # root can run anything
fi
```

Speeding Up Boot Time

The default init scripts found in /etc/init.d/ and the /etc/rc*.d/ directories are good for most systems, but they may not be needed on your specific system. If you do not need a service then you can disable it. This can reduce the boot time for your system. In some cases, it can also speed up the overall running speed by freeing resources. Use sysv-rc-conf (sudo apt-get install sysv-rc-conf) to change the enable/disable settings. Some of the services to consider disabling include:

- anacron—As mentioned earlier, this subsystem periodically runs processes. You may want to disable it and move any critical services to cron.

- `atd` and `cron`—By default, there are not `at` or `cron` jobs scheduled. If you do not need these services, then they can be disabled. Personally, I would always leave them enabled since they take relatively few resources.

- `apmd`—This service handles power management and is intended for older systems that do not support the ACPI interface. It only monitors the battery. If you have a newer laptop (or are not using a laptop), then you probably do not need this service enabled.

- `acpid`—The `acpid` service monitors battery levels and special laptop buttons such as screen brightness, volume control, and wireless on/off. Although intended for laptops, it can also support some desktop computers that use special keys on the keyboard (for example, a www button to start the browser). If you are not using a laptop and do not have special buttons on your keyboard, then you probably do not need this service.

- `bluez-utiles`—This provides support for BlueTooth devices. If you don't have any, then this can be disabled.

- `dns-clean`, `ppp`, and `pppd-dns`—These services are used for dynamic, dial-up connections. If you do not use dialup, then these can be disabled.

- `hdparm`—This system is used to tune disk drive performance. It is not essential and, unless configured, does not do anything. The configuration file is `/etc/hdparm.conf` and it is not enabled by default.

- `hplip`—This provides Linux support for the HP Linux Image and Printing system. If you do not need it, then it can be disabled. Without this, you can still print using the `lpr` and CUPS systems.

- `mdadm`, `mdadm-raid`, and `lvm`—These provide file system support for RAID (`mdadm` and `mdadm-raid`) and Logical Volume groups (`lvm`). If you do not use either, then these can be disabled.

- `nfs-common`, `nfs-kernel-server`, and `portmap`—These are used by NFS—they are only present if you installed NFS support. If you do not need NFS all the time, then you can disable these and only start the services when you need them:

```
sudo /etc/init.d/portmap start
sudo /etc/init.d/nfs-common start
sudo /etc/init.d/nfs-kernel-server start
```

- `pcmcia` and `pcmciautils`—These provide support for PCMCIA devices on laptops. If you do not have any PCMCIA slots on your computer, then you do not need these services.

- `powernowd` and `powernowd.early`—These services are used to control variable-speed CPUs. Newer computers and laptops should have these enabled, but older systems (for example, my dual-processor 200 MHz PC) do not need it.

- `readahead` and `readahead-desktop`—These services are used to preload libraries so some applications will initially start faster. In a tradeoff for speed, these services slow down the initial boot time of the system and consume virtual memory with preloaded libraries. If you have limited RAM, then you should consider disabling these services.

- rsync—This is a replacement for the remote copy (rcp) command. Few people need this—it is used to synchronize files between computers.

- vbesave—This services monitors the Video BIOS real-time configuration. This is an ACPI function and is usually used on laptops when switching between the laptop display and an external display. If your computer does not support APCI or does not switch between displays, then you do not need this service.

Tip There is a System ⇨ Admin ⇨ Services applet for enabling and disabling some services. However, this applet only knows of a few services; it does not list every available service. The sysv-rc-conf command recognizes far more services and offers more management options.

The sysv-rc-conf command shows most of the system services. However, it does not show all of them. If the service's name ends with .sh, contains .dpkg-, or is named rc or rcS, then it is treated as a non-modifiable system service. To change these services, you will need to manually modify the /etc/init.d/ and /etc/rc*.d/ directory contents.

Leave It On!

Although there are many services that you probably do not need, there are a few that are essential. You should not turn off these essential services unless you really know what you are doing:

- dbus—Provides messaging services.

- gdm—This is the Gnome Desktop. Only disable this if you do not want a graphical desktop.

- klogd—This is the kernel log daemon. Removing it disables system logging.

- makedev and udev—These create all device nodes.

- module-init-tools—Loads kernel modules specified in /etc/modules.

- networking and loopback—These start and stop the network. Disabling removes the network configuration at boot.

- procps.sh—Any kernel tuning parameters added to /etc/sysctl.conf are processed by this service.

- urandom—This seeds the real random number generator that is used by most cryptographic system. You should leave it enabled.

As a rule of thumb, if you do not know what it is, then leave it on. Also, if the service only runs in single-user mode (rcS) that it is usually smart to not change it. Single user mode is where you should go when everything fails in order to repair the system.

Summary

Ubuntu is designed for the average computer user. As a result, there are some running processes that may not be needed and some resources that are not used optimally. Using a variety of commands, you can see what is running, what resources are available, and what resources are being used. The system can be tuned by adjusting kernel parameters, shell parameters, and settings for specific applications.

Multitasking Applications

☑ Switching
   applications

☑ Tweaking the
   workplace switcher

☑ Customizing
   application
   windows

☑ Buffering buffers

☑ Automating tasks

☑ Tracking projects

T wenty years ago, computers did one thing at a time. You either used a
word processor *or* used a spreadsheet *or* printed a document—but not
all at once. Today, people rarely use computers for just one thing. While
using a spreadsheet, you may be modifying a document in a word processor,
watching the stock market, reading news, and checking the weather—all at
the same time! In my experience, the only times a computer does one dedicated task today is when (a) it is an embedded system, (b) it is devoted to a
game that consumes all resources, (c) it is solving some computationally
complex formula (for example, cracking passwords, modeling, or data min-
ing) and needs all of the system's computing power, or (d) it's a *really* old
computer.

Multitasking does not just mean running two programs at once. The defini-
tion encompasses your ability to switch between programs, communicate
between applications, and find running programs. In the corporate world, it
also means accountability: you need to be able to say how much time was
spent on each project. Fortunately, Ubuntu has many options for addressing
these needs.

Switching Applications

Starting up an application on the Ubuntu desktop can be as easy as clicking
an icon or choosing from a menu. However, after you have a few dozen programs running, it can be a challenge to find the right program again.
Without a good application management scheme, I frequently find myself
clicking through windows before finding the right one. The worst is when I
select text from one application, and cannot find the right window to paste
into; and after finding the right destination, discovering that I had lost the
selection buffer. After a couple of times, this becomes frustrating.

Fortunately, Ubuntu has many options for finding the right application.
These include the Window List, Window Selector, and keyboard for
switching between applications.

Using the Window List and Window Selector

The two most common window management tools are the Window List and the Window Selector (see Figure 8-1). By default, the Window List appears in the display's bottom panel. It opens a new button every time you start a new application window. To switch between applications, simply click on the button. You can also right-click a button in the Window List to see a menu for maximizing, minimizing, moving, or closing the window.

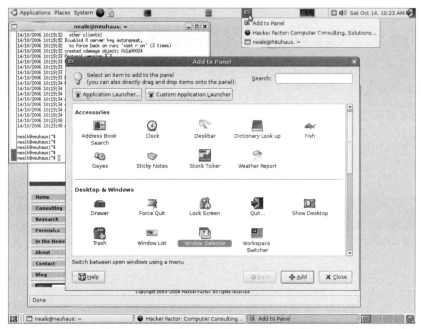

FIGURE 8-1: The Window List is visible on the bottom panel. The Window Selector has been added to the top panel and is open, showing three processes.

The Window Selector provides a drop-down menu of all windows on the desktop. To set up the Window Selector, you will need to add it to the panel.

1. On an empty space on the top (or bottom) panel, right-click to bring up the panel menu.

2. Select Add to Panel... from the menu. This will bring up the Add to Panel applet.

3. The default applets are divided into sections. In the second section, titled Desktop and Windows, is the Window Selector applet. Select this applet and drag it to the top panel. Releasing the mouse button will place the applet on the panel.

Note Earlier versions of Ubuntu installed the Window Selector in the top right corner of the panel. If you upgraded from Hoary or Breezy to Dapper, then you probably have the Window Selector already on the top panel. However, if you did a clean install of Dapper, then you will need to add it to the top panel.

Although the Window Selector and Window List show the same information, I find that they have different use models. The Window List is very useful if you have fewer than eight open windows. However, if you have more open windows, then the text in the buttons becomes truncated down to almost nothing and the buttons become indistinct. When I have many open windows, I rely on the Window Selector to help me locate the windows I need.

Using Alt+Tab

Another method to switch between applications uses Alt+Tab. When you press the Alt and Tab keys at the same time, a small window manager appears in the middle of the screen (see Figure 8-2). This window manager shows the icons for each open window. As long as you hold down the Alt key, this window manager will remain up. By holding down the Alt key and repeatedly pressing Tab, you can select different windows. Releasing the Alt key selects the window.

Tip   Each selected window shows the window title in the window manager and highlights the window on the screen using a black rectangle. If the window is partially covered, then you can see where it will appear.

The icons in this window manager are ordered from left to right by usage; the left-most icon represents the window that was just used. If you switch between two windows, then the two icons on the left will represent them. An infrequently used window will be shuffled to the right. Pressing Alt+Tab moves the selector from left to right; pressing Alt+Shift+Tab moves the selector from right to left.

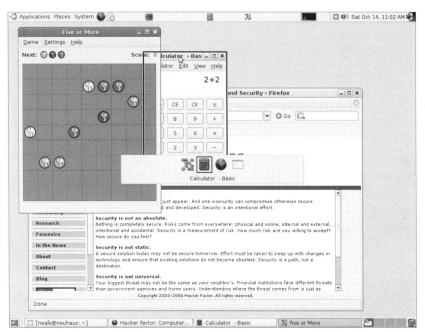

Figure 8-2: The Alt+Tab window manager. The calculator is selected but partially covered by another application.

Using Ctrl+Alt+Tab

Although Alt+Tab allows you to quickly switch between applications, it does not allow you to select different panels. Pressing Ctrl+Alt+Tab brings up a window manager that is similar to Alt+Tab, but it lists the different panels and the desktop rather than individual applications (see Figure 8-3).

Tip   Using Ctrl+Alt+Tab can be very handy if your mouse ever stops working (or was not working when the computer started up). Using the keyboard, you can select the top panel and logout or shutdown. You can also open a terminal window for fixing the problem.

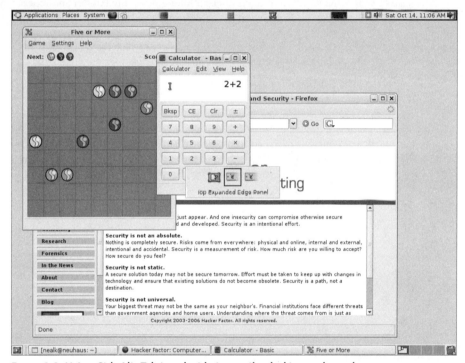

FIGURE 8-3: Using Ctrl+Alt+Tab to select between the desktop and panels

Switching Between Firefox Tabs

Some applications also enable you to have multiple windows within the application and then switch between the windows. Firefox, for example, can open web pages in different windows or in different tabs within one browser. If you use multiple windows, then Alt+Tab can be used to switch between them. However, if you use tabs within one Firefox window, then you need some other way to switch between web pages. Pressing Ctrl+Tab in Firefox allows you to select the next tabbed web page. Similarly, Ctrl+Shift-Tab allows you to select the previous tabbed web page.

The tab management in Firefox (Ctrl+Tab and Ctrl+Shift-Tab) has two big differences from the desktop's Alt+Tab and Ctrl+Alt+Tab. First, Firefox does not display a dialog in the middle of the screen. Instead, watch the Firefox tabs to see which one is highlighted. Second, the tabs are ordered from left to right, not based on last usage. If you want to change the order of the tabs, grab a Firefox tab by right-clicking it and drag it left or right to reposition it.

Tweaking the Workplace Switcher

It does not take long before you have a desktop with dozens of open windows. When this happens, no amount of Alt+Tab combinations will help you become organized. Fortunately, there is the Workplace Switcher. This applet gives you multiple desktops—you can put all work windows on one workplace, games on another, short projects on a third, and so on. By default, the Workplace Switcher is placed in the right corner of the bottom panel—I usually move mine to the top right so the Window List has more room. If you don't have the Workplace Switcher, you can add it by opening the Add to Panel... menu and dragging the applet to your panel.

Switching Workspaces with Ctrl+Alt+Arrows

The Workplace Switcher gives you a tiny view of each desktop (see Figure 8-4). Although you cannot see icons or window titles, you can see the general layout—there are gray boxes that represent each window on each desktop. To switch between desktops, you can either click on the Workspace Switcher or use the Ctrl+Alt+Arrow keys. For example, Ctrl+Alt+LeftArrow switches the workspace to the left; Ctrl+Alt+RightArrow moves to the workspace on the right.

Tip If you open the Workspace Switcher's Preferences, then you can add more desktops and change their layout. The default uses four desktops arranged in one row. If you add more rows, then you can use Ctrl+Alt+UpArrow and Ctrl+Alt+DownArrow to navigate between them.

FIGURE 8-4: The Workspace Switcher, showing four distinct desktops

Managing Workspaces

By default, there are four workspaces available. You can add additional workspaces by right-clicking the Workspace Switching and selecting Preferences (see Figure 8-5). From here, you can name workspaces, adjust the layout, or add more workspaces (you can also remove workspaces, but who would want to do that?). For example, I usually name my middle workspace *Games*—I can always go to this workspace when the boss is not around. (And if he suddenly shows up, I can use Ctrl+Alt+LeftArrow to quickly hide my games and show real work-in-progress.)

Windows do not need to stay in one workspace. Your active window appears highlighted in the Workspace Switcher. You can drag an application's window onto any other desktop in the Workspace Switcher. I usually do this when one window becomes cluttered, or when popup windows come from a different application. For example, when the Evolution mailer pops up a To Do list alert, I'll drop it in the appropriate window. (There is no reason to have "Write Status Report" appear in the middle of my Games workspace.)

Some application windows are small and may be hard to grab in the Workspace Switcher. Another way to move windows is to click on the top right corner of any window. This will open a menu that displays options such as Move to Workspace Right and Move to Another Workspace ⇨ Workspace 1. You can also pull up this menu by right-clicking any of the buttons in the Workspace List.

Finally, some application windows may be very important. These are ones that you will want to appear on every workspace, and not just one workspace. In the window's top-left corner menu is an option titled, Always on Visible Workspace. If you select this, then the window will be visible regardless of the selected workspace. I find this option to be very handy for important online conversations (for example, IRC and Jabber), and when using xawtv (watching TV while working—see Chapter 3). This way, I won't miss any communications when I switch workspaces. Without this option, something may happen in a window and I won't notice it until I switch back to that workspace.

FIGURE 8-5: The Workspace Switcher
preferences window

Customizing Application Windows

When graphical applications start up, the X-Windows system sets elements such as the placement and dimensions (geometry), whether the window is visible or hidden, maximized or minimized, and always on top or bottom. Usually the application defaults are fine, but sometimes they need to be tweaked. For example, xawtv (discussed in Chapter 3) always seems to get buried under other windows—that makes it hard to watch *Myth Busters*. If I want it to always start on top, I either need to press t (an interactive command to the program) to tell xawtv to always be on top, create an X-resource file to specify properties, or use a program like Devil's Pie (see the section on this tool) to automatically set the graphical properties.

Creating X-resources

Many X-Windows applications support a set of externally configurable parameters. These resources enable you to customize everything from a program's startup position to its size, fonts, and colors. The type of resource depends on the type of executable. There are Gnome Toolkit (Gtk) resources, used by most applications that start with a g like gedit and gnobots2. There is the Qt library, used by many KDE applications, and there is the X Toolkit (Xt), which is used by most applications that start with an x (for example, xedit, xman, and xterm).

Most Gtk and KDE applications get their resource configurations from application-specific configuration files. For example, gedit uses $HOME/.gnome2/gedit-2, $HOME/.gnome2/gedit-metadata.xml, and $HOME/.gnome2/accels/gedit. Unfortunately, the location, name, format, and contents of these configuration files are application specific (if they exist at all).

In contrast to Gtk and Qt, most Xt applications follow a standard configuration format: application*resource: value. For example, xterm*scrollBar: true sets the scrollBar resource for the xterm application to true (the default is false). This way, all new xterm windows will start with a scrollbar. To create a set of Xt X-resources:

1. Identify the application name. If you run the program from the command line, then this is the program's name. If you click an icon or menu item to run the program, then xprop to identify the name of the program. The xprop program will turn your cursor into a crosshair. By clicking the window, you will see the running application's name in the WM_CLASS string.

   ```
   xprop | grep WM_CLASS
   ```

Tip   There may be multiple class strings for an application. Some are specific, while others are general. Any will work as a resource name. However, if you choose a specific string, then keep in mind that the resource must match the specific string. This can be very useful if you want one set of properties for Xterm"and another for xterm (remote via TELNET).

2. Identify the name of the resource. Unfortunately, there are few standards here. Sometimes you can find the resource names and properties in the man pages for your particular application, but not always. For example, man xterm and man xman lists lots of X-resources, while man xeyes provides no information. The few almost-universal resources include:

   ▪ geometry—Specifies the dimension and location for an application. For example, 80x42+150+180 creates a window that is 80x42, located at the screen coordinates 150x180.

Note The dimensions are application specific. 80x42 for `xterm` means 80 columns wide and 42 characters tall, while 80x42 for `xeyes` specifies 80 pixels wide and 42 pixels tall.

- `font`—Specifies the font name to use. This can be a short name, such as `serif` or a long name that describes the exact font, such as `-*-serif-medium-r-normal -iso9241-*-*-75-75-p-*-iso8859-1` for a regular serif font at 75 dpi. You can use the program `xfontsel` to browse the available fonts and determine the exact font name.

- `background`—Specifies the background color. This can be a standard color name (for example, yellow or black) or a set of three hex values representing the red, green, and blue components (for example, `#ff0010` for red with a little bit of blue).

- `foreground`—Specifies the foreground color.

3. Add your resource to the X-resource file. By default, the resource file is `$HOME/ .Xdefaults` (create it if it does not exist). For example, my `$HOME/.Xdefaults` specifies the dimensions of the default `xterm` window and turns on the scrollbars:

```
xterm*VT100*geometry: 80x42+150+180
! this line is a comment (! denotes a comment)
!xterm*scrollBar: false
*scrollBar: true
```

4. Load the resource file. The command `xrdb` is used to load the X-resources. There are many options for this, but I usually use: `xrdb -merge $HOME/.Xdefaults`. This says that all values should be lexically sorted and then loaded into memory. Existing values are replaced and new values are added. Alternately, you can use `xrdb $HOME/.Xdefaults`, which will load the file in order (unsorted) and replace existing values.

Tip Under other window managers, changes to .Xdefaults are loaded automatically. Under Gnome, you will need to explicitly run `xrdb`. To automatically load your defaults, add `xrdb -merge $HOME/.Xdefaults` to your `$HOME/.profile` script. This way, it will run every time you log in.

While individual users can have a `$HOME/.Xdefaults` file for personalizing applications, there are also system-wide configurations. The directory `/etc/X11/app-defaults/` contains a file for every application and the default X-resource values. Changing these defaults will impact the entire system. Also, you don't need to use `xrdb` for the system-wide defaults— changes take affect immediately because applications know to look here for default configuration information.

Using Devil's Pie

Some applications don't use X-resources, and configuring other applications can be inconvenient. An alternative configuration method is to use a tool called Devil's Pie (`sudo apt-get install devilspie`). This program watches for new X-Windows applications and configures them as they appear. Unlike the Xt X-resources, Devil's Pie works with all X-Windows applications (Xt, Gtk, and Qt).

Devil's Pie uses a configuration file that describes what to look for and how to modify the X-resources.

1. Make a $HOME/.devilspie/ directory. Any file in this directory will become a resource for Devil's Pie.

2. Create a resource file. For example, I have a file called $HOME/.devilspie/games.ds that opens all games on workspace #4:

```
(begin
(if (is (application_name) "gnobots2") (begin (set_workspace 4)) )
(if (is (application_name) "iagno") (begin (set_workspace 4)) )
(if (is (application_name) "same-gnome") (begin (set_workspace 4)) )
)
```

Similarly, I have an xawtv.ds configuration file that says:

```
(if (is (application_name) "xawtv") (above) )
```

3. Run devilspie. As long as it is running, it will monitor new windows and adjust their X-resources as needed.

Tip   If you like Devil's Pie, consider adding it to your startup: System ➪ Preferences ➪ Sessions ➪ Startup Programs. Alternately, you can use devilspie & to run this command in the background.

Each clause in the configuration file contains a condition (is, contains, or matches), item to match against (window_name, window_role, window_class, or application_name), and one or more actions. Table 8-1 lists the set of available actions and associated values (if any).

Table 8-1   List of common actions for Devil's Pie

Action	Value	Example	Purpose
geometry	widthxheight+xpos+ypos	geometry 80x42+100+20	Start the application with the specified dimensions
fullscreen	n/a	fullscreen	Make full-screen
focus	n/a	focus	Give the application focus
center	n/a	center	Center the application on the desktop
maximize	n/a	maximize	Maximize the window
minimize	n/a	minimize	Start the window minimized

Continued

Table 8-1   *Continued*

Action	Value	Example	Purpose
above	n/a	above	The window should always be on top of other windows
below	n/a	below	The window should always be below other windows
set_workspace	workspace number	set_workspace 4	Place the window on a specific workspace

Devil's Pie can match an X-Windows application based on the window's name, role, or class. To identify these values, use:

```
xprop | grep -E "^(WM_NAME)|(WM_WINDOW_ROLE)|(WM_CLASS)"
```

This will list any or all of the available values for any given window. Using Devil's Pie, you can automatically make windows appear in the right place on the right workspace and with the right settings. You can even handle dynamic popup windows like those created by Firefox, Gaim, and Evolution. For example, to have Gaim's chat window start maximized in a different workspace, you can use:

```
(if
  (and
    (contains (application_name) "gaim")
    (contains (window_role) "conversation")
  )
  (begin (set_workspace 3) (maximize))
)
```

Buffering Buffers

I don't think there is anybody who uses a graphical interface without periodically cutting and pasting information between windows. Under some operating systems (for example, Microsoft Windows), there is only one commonly used clipboard. This clipboard can be used to share information between applications. Under Ubuntu, X-Windows and the Gnome Desktop provide *two* clipboards for common use. The first is the selection clipboard. Whenever you highlight any text, it gets placed in this buffer. Using the middle mouse button, you can paste the contents.

The second clipboard (called the *primary clipboard*) is used when you use Ctrl+C to copy, Ctrl+X to cut, and Ctrl+V to paste. Word processors (for example, OpenOffice) and graphic editors (for example, Gimp) usually use this buffer. Also, some text applications, like gnome-terminal, change cut-and-paste to use Shift+Ctrl instead of Ctrl (for example, Shift+Ctrl+C to copy).

Note X-Windows actually provides a couple of different clipboard buffers. *Clipboard* is used for selection, *primary* is used by Ctrl+C and Ctrl+V, and *secondary* is usually unused.

I usually come across two problems with the default clipboards. First, the selection clipboard loses information too quickly. Simply clicking in a window to bring it forward could accidentally select a space or other character, wiping out the current selection. Although you could click the title bar to bring the window forward and prevent clipboard changes, other windows usually cover my title bars. Second, when doing a lot of development or editing, I sometimes need more than just two clipboards. I usually end up pasting text into a temporary file and then grabbing the temporary data when I need it.

Fortunately, there is a better way to manage clipboards. The program `xclip` (`sudo apt-get install xclip`) enables you to manipulate the clipboard contents. You can dump the clipboard contents to a file or load a file into the clipboard. Using `xclip`, you can easily give yourself one or more additional clipboards. You can even save clipboard contents between system reboots! Think of it like a calculator with a memory button—do you want one storage area, or many? Do you want to lose the memory when the calculator shuts off, or retain the memory?

The basic `xclip` usage specifies whether you want to write out (`-o`) or read in (`-i`) clipboard data, and which clipboard (p for primary, s for secondary, and c for the selection clipboard). For example:

- To store the primary clipboard to a file, use:

  ```
  xclip -o -selection p > buff
  ```

- To load a file into the secondary clipboard, use:

  ```
  xclip -i -selection s < buff
  ```

- To copy the selection clipboard into the primary clipboard, use:

  ```
  xclip -o -selection c | xclip -i -selection p
  ```

These commands can be mapped to keys. For example, Listing 8-1 creates three additional clipboards. Ctrl+F1 copies the primary clipboard into the first storage area, Ctrl+F2 uses the second storage area, and Ctrl+F3 creates the third storage area. To recall these buffers, use Ctrl+Shift+F1, Ctrl+Shift+F2, or Ctrl+Shift+F3. Using this hack, you can copy text into the primary clipboard (Ctrl+C) and then move it into the second storage area (Ctrl+F2). Later, you can recall this buffer using Ctrl+Shift-F2 and paste it using Ctrl+V.

Tip This hack also enables you to inspect and easily replace the contents of the clipboard. The storage buffers from the hack (see Listing 8-1) are in `$HOME/.xclip/`. You can view, edit, or replace the contents and then use the Ctrl+Shift keys (for example, Ctrl+Shift+F1) to load them into the clipboard buffer.

A similar hack can be used to exchange the contents of the selection and primary buffers (Listing 8-1, mapped to Ctrl+F4). This way, if you press Ctrl+C to copy a buffer and then use Ctrl+F4 to swap clipboards, allowing the middle mouse button to paste the contents rather than using Ctrl+V.

Tip

Swapping the clipboards may sound overly complicated or unnecessary, but some applications use specific clipboards. For example, `xterm` only uses the primary buffer. Anything copied into the clipboard buffer (e.g., using Ctrl+C in a word processor) cannot be pasted into an `xterm` window. Using Ctrl+F4, you can now paste the content.

Listing 8-1: Using xclip to Create Three Additional Clipboards

```
mkdir ~/.xclip  # create space for the clipboard buffers

# Map commands to actions
## Map the save commands
gconftool-2 -t str --set /apps/metacity/keybinding_commands/command_1 \
  'bash -c "xclip -o -selection p > ~/.xclip/clip.1"'
gconftool-2 -t str --set /apps/metacity/keybinding_commands/command_2 \
  'bash -c "xclip -o -selection p > ~/.xclip/clip.2"'
gconftool-2 -t str --set /apps/metacity/keybinding_commands/command_3 \
  'bash -c "xclip -o -selection p > ~/.xclip/clip.3"'
## Map the recall commands
gconftool-2 -t str --set /apps/metacity/keybinding_commands/command_4 \
  'bash -c "xclip -i -selection p < ~/.xclip/clip.1"'
gconftool-2 -t str --set /apps/metacity/keybinding_commands/command_5 \
  'bash -c "xclip -i -selection p < ~/.xclip/clip.2"'
gconftool-2 -t str --set /apps/metacity/keybinding_commands/command_6 \
  'bash -c "xclip -i -selection p < ~/.xclip/clip.3"'

# Map keys to commands
gconftool-2 -t str --set /apps/metacity/global_keybindings/run_command_1 \
  '<Control>F1'
gconftool-2 -t str --set /apps/metacity/global_keybindings/run_command_2 \
  '<Control>F2'
gconftool-2 -t str --set /apps/metacity/global_keybindings/run_command_3 \
  '<Control>F3'
gconftool-2 -t str --set /apps/metacity/global_keybindings/run_command_4 \
  '<Control><Shift>F1'
gconftool-2 -t str --set /apps/metacity/global_keybindings/run_command_5 \
  '<Control><Shift>F2'
gconftool-2 -t str --set /apps/metacity/global_keybindings/run_command_6 \
  '<Control><Shift>F3'

# Make Control-F4 swap the primary and selection clipboards
# Do this by using the secondary clipboard as a temporary buffer
```

Listing 8-1 *Continued*

```
gconftool-2 -t str --set /apps/metacity/keybinding_commands/command_10 \
   'bash -c "xclip -o -selection p | xclip -i -selection s ;
            xclip -o -selection c | xclip -i -selection p ;
            xclip -o -selection s | xclip -i -selection c"'
gconftool-2 -t str --set /apps/metacity/global_keybindings/run_command_10 \
   '<Control>F4'
```

Automating Tasks

There are some tasks that we end up doing over and over by hand. For example, I frequently convert DOC and PDF files to text. Rather than opening a command prompt and running `pdftotext` or `antiword` every time I need to convert a file, I created an automated conversion directory.

The `dnotify` program watches a specified directory for any change. A change may be a file creation, update, renaming, deletion, permission modification, or all of the above. When a change happens, `dnotify` can run a script. I have a script that converts DOC and PDF files to text, and the directory being monitored is on my desktop. Using `dnotify`, I can convert files by simply dropping them into a directory on my desktop.

1. Install `dnotify` as well as any conversion tools you need. In this example, `pdftotext` and `antiword` will perform text conversions.

Tip

For graphic conversion, consider installing the `netpbm` package. This provides programs such as `giftopnm`, `jpegtopnm`, `pnmtopng`, `pnmtogif`, and `pnmtojpeg`.

```
sudo apt-get install dnotify
sudo apt-get install xpdf-utils  # provides pdftotext
sudo apt-get install antiword
```

2. Create a small script to convert all files in a directory. Listing 8-2 shows my `convert2text` script. This script takes a directory name on the command-line and scans the directory for all DOC and PDF files. Any file not already available as text is converted.

Listing 8-2: Simple convert2text Script to Convert Files to Text

```
#!/bin/sh
# Be sure to make this executable: chmod a+x convert2text
# Be sure to place it in your $PATH (e.g., sudo cp convert2text /usr/local/bin/)
if [ "$1" = "" ] ; then
  echo "Usage: $0 directory"
  exit
fi

# Get list of files in the directory
find "$1" -type f |
while read Name ; do
  # Based on the file name, perform the conversion
  case "$Name" in
    (*.pdf) # convert pdf to text
      NameTxt="${Name%.pdf}.txt"
      if [ ! -f "${NameTxt}" ] ; then pdftotext "${Name}" "${NameTxt}"; fi
      ;;

    (*.doc) # convert doc to text
      NameTxt="${Name%.doc}.txt"
      if [ ! -f "${NameTxt}" ] ; then antiword "${Name}" > "${NameTxt}"; fi
      ;;
  esac
done
```

3. Create a directory to monitor.

```
mkdir $HOME/Desktop/convert2text
```

4. Run the dnotify program. Specify the convert2text script and the directory to monitor. In this case, the action to watch for is file creation (-C). The dnotify program changes the '{}' string to the directory name.

```
dnotify -C $HOME/Desktop/convert2text -e convert2text '{}'
```

Now, dragging or pasting any PDF or DOC file into this folder will create a text file. The text file will have the same name as the original document, but will end with the .txt extension. For example, ch08.doc will generate ch08.txt. If you are using the command line then you can copy (cp) or move (mv) files into $HOME/Desktop/convert2text/ for automatic conversion. Figure 8-6 shows a sample conversion directory.

Tip If you are like me and frequently use the convert2text directory, then you can add the dnotify command to your Gnome startup (System ⇨ Preferences ⇨ Sessions ⇨ Startup Programs). This way, the automatic conversion will be enabled immediately after you login. Also, you can use the -b option to run it in the background: dnotify -b -C $HOME/Desktop/convert2text -e convert2text '{}'.

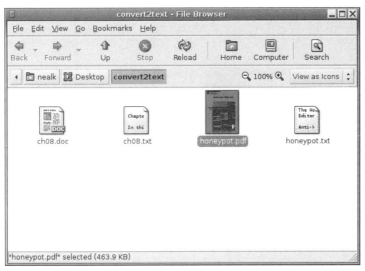

FIGURE 8-6: Automatic file conversion using dnotify and the convert2text directory

Tracking Projects

Many corporate and government environments require employees to keep track of their time. For example, when consulting, I track my time in 15-minute intervals. I once had a job where the employer required accountability down to every 6-minute interval. With today's operating systems, multitasking becomes a blessing and a problem. The good news is that you can do many things at once. The bad news is: tracking billable time on projects can get very confusing when you're multitasking (and double-billing clients is a definite no-no). If the accounting people require you to track your work, then Ubuntu is definitely what you want.

Tracking Time on Projects

There are a variety of packages that enable you to track your time on projects. Some examples include `gnotime`, `gtimer`, `gtimelog`, `wmwork`, and `worklog`. Each of these packages allows you to create a project, start and stop a work-time clock, and easily switch between projects. They also allow you set the accumulation interval (from one minute to hourly) and display total time spent summaries.

My personal preference is the Gnotime Time Tracker (`sudo apt-get install gnotime`). After installing it, you can run the Gnotime Time Tracker from Applications ⇨ Office ⇨ GnoTime Tracking Tool. Besides being able to add projects and diary entries, it allows you to specify billable rates on a per-project basis. You can also mark projects with a priority and urgency. Figure 8-7 shows the main window for `gnotime`. Simply double-click any task to start the clock. Diary entries can be added to help track what work was being done.

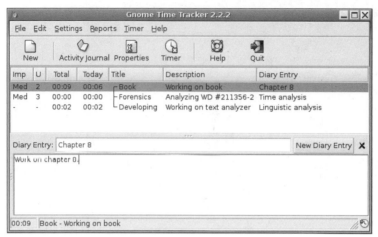

FIGURE 8-7: The Gnotime Time Tracker

Gnotime can generate a variety of reports including a journal of time spent (see Figure 8-8) and a billing list (see Figure 8-9). Each report includes clickable items with menus so you can add more diaries, annotations, adjust times, change rates, and so on. Reports can be saved as HTML or exported to a web server, FTP site, or e-mailed.

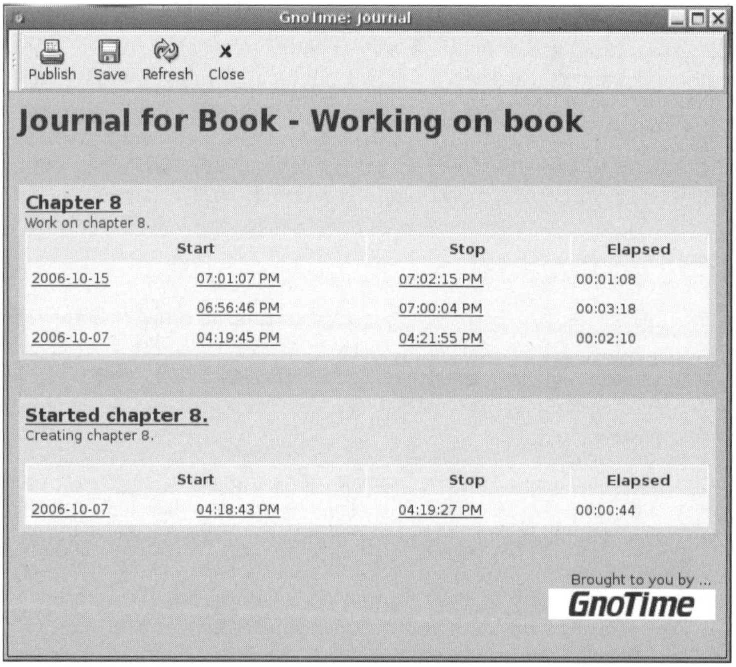

FIGURE 8-8: The work journal

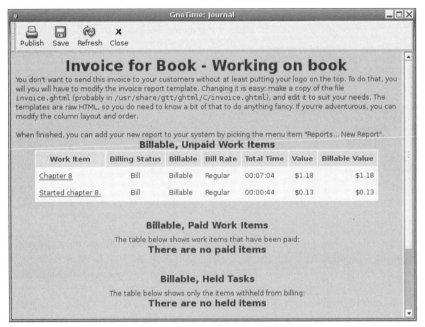

FIGURE 8-9: Invoice report showing billable hours. (Wow! $1.18 in just 7 minutes!)

Gnotime isn't perfect. It cannot merge times from multiple people or export to a spreadsheet. However, it is more than enough for tracking the work from a single individual. For group tracking, consider a collaborative project tracking system such as gforge.

Tracking CPU Usage

In some cases, projects need to be tracked by the resources they consume. The two most common billable resources are CPU time and disk space. Unfortunately, there are no nice GUI applications for tracking a project's CPU consumption. Instead, this is done using the time command. This keeps track of the real elapsed time, time spent in user-space, and system time (time spent in the kernel). For example, time bash monitors the command bash (a shell) and every process created by bash. When the shell finally exists, a run-time summary is displayed:

```
$ time bash
# run some commands
$ exit
real    1m12.428s
user    0m0.292s
sys     0m0.588s
```

The example summary shows that the shell was running for a little more than a minute, but most of the time was spent idling—0.588 seconds were spent in the kernel and 0.292 seconds were spent in user-space. If you need to know how long a process was running, preface the command with time. When the process exists, you will know how much time was spent.

The `time` command has trouble monitoring spawned processes. If the program being timed kicks off a CPU intensive process, then `time` will only see the total duration, not the kernel or user-space times. Also, if a process is separated from its parent (for example, scheduled to run using `at`) then `time` will not measure the spawned application.

Tracking Disk Usage and Quotas

Disk space is much easier to compute. The `df` command (discussed in Chapter 7) shows you the current disk usage, but this is usually inadequate for billing. Another way to track disk usage is to install the `quota` package. Enabling quotas is not the easiest system, but the command line tools allow you to specify how much disk space a user can have on a specific file system.

When using `df` to determine disk space, be aware that this is only a snapshot. There may have been a time between snapshots when the disk space exceeded the current allotment.

Although quotas may seem unnecessary for the average home user, they can be very useful for project tracking. Quotas enable you to track disk use, bill by the megabyte, and identify when a project dramatically increases in size. Quotas can also stop runaway processes from filling your hard drive. For example, the default installation for Ubuntu places all files in one partition. If you are running a mail server then you might want to enable quotas for the e-mail system. This prevents a massive e-mail (or flood of small e-mails) from filling your disk.

Understanding Your Limits

Under Ubuntu, the quota system enables you to specify limits for files, links, and disk space per user. There are soft limits and hard limits, and an allotted grace period. These limits can be set for users or groups. This way, a group can share files within a given quota.

- **Hard limits**—A hard limit specifies the maximum allocation for a user or group. For example, if you are allotted 10,000 files, then you cannot create any new files if you are over your quota. The only way to get under your quota is to either delete files, or have the administrator increase your limit.

- **Soft limits**—Soft limits are used to provide a warning to users. If they go over their soft limit quota, then the grace time kicks in. The grace time says how long they have to remove files and get under their quota. If the grace time is set to seven days, then users have seven days to get under their quota. After the grace period, the soft limit is treated as a hard limit and the user is blocked from creating or updating new files. Soft limits are really useful since sometimes you might go a little over your quota for a short duration.

- **Disk limits**—Soft and hard limits can be set based on disk space. For example, a user may be allocated a 100 MB soft limit at 110 MB hard limit. Small systems may have limits set in the megabyte range, while large systems may use gigabyte quotas.

- **File limits**. This limit allows you to specify how many files a user (or group) can have. Files are anything that consumes an inode—this includes real files, device files, and links to other files. Small systems, such as local e-mail servers, may be limited to a few hundred or a few thousand files. In contrast, large file repositories may be allowed hundreds of thousands of files, or have no limit at all.

Note The file system uses *inodes* to store meta-data information about files. This includes the actual file name (since it is not found inside the file contents), permissions, timestamps, and directory information.

Enabling Quotas

1. Install the quota package.

```
sudo apt-get install quota
```

2. Quotas are set on a per-file-system basis. Edit /etc/fstab and add the mount options usrquota and grpquota to your file system. In my case, I have added user quotas to my Ubuntu file system (/dev/hda1), and both user and group quota to second hard drive (/dev/hdb4). My /etc/fstab file looks like:

```
# /etc/fstab: static file system information.
# device  mount        fs      options                     dump   pass
proc      /proc        proc    defaults                      0      0
/dev/hda1 /      ext3  defaults,errors=remount-o,usrquota 0      1
/dev/hda5 none         swap    sw                            0      0
/dev/hdc  /media/cdrom0 udf,iso9660 user,noauto              0      0
/dev/hdb4 /mnt/disk    ext3    defaults,usrquota,grpquota    0      0
```

Tip Don't enable quotas on read-only devices such as CD-ROM drives. Since a user has no way to add or remove files, quota information provides no value. Similarly, removable devices such as floppy disks and USB thumb drivers usually should not have quotas enabled.

3. Since the partitions are already mounted, you will need to remount each of the quota-enabled file systems in order to load the new mount flags. Since the changes are in /etc/fstab, you won't need to do this after a reboot. Since I added quotas to / and /mnt/disk, I can remount using:

```
$ sudo mount -o remount /
$ sudo mount -o remount /mnt/disk
$ mount | grep quota  # check results
/dev/hda1 on / type ext3 (rw,errors=remount-ro,usrquota)
/dev/hdb4 on /mnt/disk type ext3 (rw,usrquota,grpquota)
```

4. Before quotas can be enabled, you need to check for existing problems (even through there shouldn't be any problems). This is done using the quotacheck command. The parameters -augmv means all file systems, all user and group quotas, and don't remount the partitions. For large disks, this check might take a few minutes. If you don't have user quotas, then you do not need -u, and -g is only used when group quotas are enabled. Specifying the -g without the grpquota mount option will generate a warning, but won't cause problems.

```
$ sudo quotacheck -augmv
quotacheck: Scanning /dev/hdb4 [/mnt/disk] quotacheck: Cannot stat old
user quota file: No such file or directory
```

```
quotacheck: Cannot stat old group quota file: No such file or directory
quotacheck: Cannot stat old user quota file: No such file or directory
quotacheck: Cannot stat old group quota file: No such file or directory
done
quotacheck: Checked 10254 directories and 228748 files
quotacheck: Old file not found.
quotacheck: Old file not found.
```

The first time you run `quotacheck -augmv`, you will see a bunch of warnings about files not existing. This is because the system has not been checked before. After it is checked, the quota version 2 files `/mnt/disk/aquota.user` and `/mnt/disk/aquota.group` (or `quota.user` and `quota.group` if you are using the older quota version 1 system) will be created and these errors should not appear again.

Note Even if you are not enabling both user and group quotas on a file system, you should create both files. Otherwise some quota commands may generate warnings.

5. Now quotas can be turned on.

```
sudo quotaon -augv
```

Tip Running `sudo /etc/init.d/quota start` will perform the quota check (Step 4) and turn on quotas (step #5).

Editing Quotas

After quotas are enabled you can edit them using `edquota`. Using `edquota -u`, you can edit the quota for any particular user. Similarly, `edquota -g` edits group quotas.

```
sudo edquota -u bill
sudo edquota -g users
```

The `edquota` command opens an editor that allows you to specify the soft and hard limits for disk space (blocks) and files (inodes). Each partition where quotas are enabled is listed. The current values are also displayed. For example, my quota settings look like:

Filesystem	blocks	soft	hard	inodes	soft	hard
/dev/hda1	68866148	0	0	247947	0	0
/dev/hdb4	31153944	0	0	238603	0	0

This says that I am currently using about 65 GB on /dev/hda1, and using 247,947 inodes. On /dev/hdb4 I am using about 30 GB and 238,603 inodes. This also says that I have no quota limits. Changing and saving the soft and hard values will immediately enable quotas. If I am over quota, then the soft and hard limits are immediately enforced.

The grace times default to seven days, but can be edited using `sudo edquota -t`. This brings up an editor that displays the current settings per device and allows you to change the values.

```
Grace period before enforcing soft limits for users:
Time units may be: days, hours, minutes, or seconds
   Filesystem            Block grace period      Inode grace period
   /dev/hda1                   7days                   7days
   /dev/hdb4                   7days                   7days
```

Tip Don't worry about maintaining the correct column spacing when editing with `edquota`. The system only checks the number of columns separated by spaces, not the actual number of spaces. Saving changes and then running `edquota` again will reformat the columns.

Reporting Quotas

After enabling quotas, you can generate periodic reports using the `repquota` command. These can either be in the raw system format or in a human-readable form (`-s`).

```
$ sudo repquota -a
*** Report for user quotas on device /dev/hda1
Block grace time: 7days; Inode grace time: 7days
                        Block limits                 File limits
User            used    soft    hard   grace    used  soft  hard  grace
----------------------------------------------------------------------
root       -- 3953944      0       0          189921     0     0
nealk      -- 68866148     0       0          247947     0     0
postfix    --       56     0       0              41     0     0
test       --       28     0       0               8     0     0

*** Report for user quotas on device /dev/hdb4
Block grace time: 7days; Inode grace time: 7days
                        Block limits                 File limits
User            used    soft    hard   grace    used  soft  hard  grace
----------------------------------------------------------------------
root       --   36628      0       0             192     0     0
nealk      -- 31153944 41153944 51153944      238603 59153944 61153944
postfix    --        4     0       0               1     0     0
test       --    32472     0       0             207     0     0

$ sudo repquota -as
*** Report for user quotas on device /dev/hda1
Block grace time: 7days; Inode grace time: 7days
                        Block limits                 File limits
User            used    soft    hard   grace    used  soft  hard  grace
----------------------------------------------------------------------
```

```
root      --    3862M      0        0              190k     0      0
nealk     --   67253M      0        0              248k     0      0
postfix   --      56       0        0               41      0      0
test      --      28       0        0                8      0      0
```

```
*** Report for user quotas on device /dev/hdb4
Block grace time: 7days; Inode grace time: 7days
                      Block limits                 File limits
User          used    soft    hard   grace    used   soft   hard   grace
--------------------------------------------------------------------------
root      --   36628      0      0             192      0      0
nealk     --   30424M  40190M  49956M         239k  59154k 61154k
postfix   --      4       0      0               1      0      0
test      --   32472      0      0             207      0      0
```

You can also generate quota e-mails using `warnquota`. By default, e-mails are sent to each user when they are over quota, and root also receives a copy of each e-mail. You can change the e-mail sender's information by editing `/etc/warnquota.conf`.

When I need to track projects by disk space, I usually create a user account just for the project and enable a cron job to generate a nightly (or hourly) report for the project's user (`sudo repquota -a | grep` *projectusername*).

Summary

Ubuntu provides many different options for managing concurrent applications. Whether your needs are for task switching, window management, or project tracking, there are plenty of options available. Using simple scripts, you can enhance clipboard usage and create directories that automate tasks. And best of all, you can literally budget your time.

Getting Graphical with Video Bling

W hen you install the Ubuntu desktop, the video display becomes the single most important system. If the mouse doesn't work, you can use the keyboard. If the keyboard does not work, then you can remotely login. However, if the display does not work, then you cannot see what you are doing and are completely out of luck.

Some Linux versions install very basic VGA or SVGA graphics support. It is up to the user to upgrade the driver to something other than the default low resolution (for example, 800 × 600 with 256 colors).

Ubuntu takes the next step. During the installation of the graphical desktop, it tries to detect your video card. In most cases, you will end up with at least 1024 × 768 and 24-bit color (16 million colors). Although this is good for getting started, it might not be the best you can do.

Note If you start off with 800 × 600 and 256 colors, then you probably have an unsupported video card. Video cards have really come down in price—you can get a decent one that can do 1024 × 768 (or higher resolution!) with true color for under $30. See `https://wiki.ubuntu.com/HardwareSupport` for a list of supported video cards.

With graphics come customizable elements such as screen savers and animated background. I've seen some people spend hours selecting and tuning screen savers. Other customizations that are becoming really common are dual-monitors and cross-desktop systems. With Ubuntu (and a little tweaking) you can enable two monitors on the same computer, or use a second computer as a second monitor.

Tuning Graphics

During the installation, Ubuntu detects the graphics card and installs a usable driver. The detection is done using the `ddcprobe` and `xresprobe` commands. For example, to list all of the resolution information about my video card and monitor, I can use:

```
$ sudo ddcprobe -?
vbe: VESA 3.0 detected.
oem: NVIDIA
vendor: NVIDIA Corporation
product: NV18 Board - p160nz Chip Rev A4
memory: 131072kb
mode: 640x400x256
mode: 640x480x256
mode: 800x600x16
mode: 800x600x256
mode: 1024x768x16
...
$ sudo xresprobe any
id: L1780U
res: 1280x1024 1024x768 800x600 720x400 640x480
freq: 30-83 56-75
disptype: crt
```

Note For `xresprobe`, you may also need to specify the type of driver. For example, `sudo xresprobe ati` works for the ATI driver. Other drivers include `vesa`, `nvidia`, `nv`, and `i810`.

These commands identify the video card and monitor. During the desktop install, they are used to identify the maximum resolution and to configure the `/etc/X11/xorg.conf` file.

Unfortunately, `ddcprobe` does not always know about your monitor, especially if you are using old equipment. If your graphics card supports 1280 × 1024 but your monitor supports only 1024 × 768, then you won't be able to see the display at 1280 × 1024. Unless you have a really old CRT monitor, your display probably supports 1024 × 768. Thus, this is usually the default resolution. To change the default resolution, use the System ⇨ Preferences ⇨ Screen Resolution applet (see Figure 9-1). From here, you can select the desired resolution and refresh rate. You can also choose to set new resolution for your login account or make it a system-wide change.

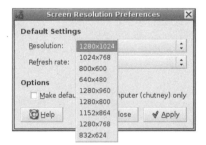

FIGURE 9-1: The Screen Resolution applet

Changing Screen Resolution (xrandr)

The System ➪ Preferences ➪ Screen Resolution applet does not list all of your available screen resolutions and settings. The full list of supported screen resolutions can be found with the X-Windows rotate and reflection command: xrandr. For example, to list the screen resolutions supported by the video driver, you would use:

```
$ xrandr -q
 SZ:      Pixels             Physical          Refresh
*0    1280 x 1024    ( 342mm x 271mm )   *75   60
 1    1024 x 768     ( 342mm x 271mm )    75   70   60
 2     800 x 600     ( 342mm x 271mm )    75   72   60   56
 3     640 x 480     ( 342mm x 271mm )    75   73   60
 4    1280 x 960     ( 342mm x 271mm )    60
 5    1280 x 800     ( 342mm x 271mm )    60
 6    1152 x 864     ( 342mm x 271mm )    75
 7    1280 x 768     ( 342mm x 271mm )    60
 8     832 x 624     ( 342mm x 271mm )    75
 9     640 x 512     ( 342mm x 271mm )    75   60
 10    720 x 450     ( 342mm x 271mm )    60
 11    640 x 400     ( 342mm x 271mm )    60
 12    576 x 432     ( 342mm x 271mm )    75
 13    640 x 384     ( 342mm x 271mm )    60
 14    512 x 384     ( 342mm x 271mm )    75   70   60
 15    416 x 312     ( 342mm x 271mm )    75
 16    400 x 300     ( 342mm x 271mm )    75   72   60   56
 17    320 x 240     ( 342mm x 271mm )    75   73   60
```

In this example, my video driver supports 18 different screen resolutions, and up to 4 different refresh rates. These resolutions are not necessarily the same as the ones listed in /etc/X11/xorg.conf (for X-Windows), and may not be supported by your monitor.

Warning

Your video card, video driver, and monitor many not all support the same resolutions. The xrandr command shows your video driver resolutions and allows you to set a screen resolution that is *not* supported by your montior. This could damage your monitor and video card!

You can use xrandr to change resolutions by specifying one of the listed sizes. Using the example, you can set the screen to 1024 × 768 with any of these commands:

```
xrandr -s 1                # screen size 1 is 1024x768
xrandr -s 1024x768         # specify by dimensions
xrandr -s 1024x768 -r 70   # for 70 Hz (default listed is 75 Hz)
xrandr -s 1 -r 70          # screen size 1 at 70 Hz
```

Note

If you specify an invalid screen resolution or refresh rate, then xrandr will fail with a cryptic error message. However, it won't make any screen changes.

Thinking Safety

When the Screen Resolution applet makes changes, it gives you 20 seconds to undo the change. This way, if the resolution is not supported and the display becomes dark or unreadable, then you just need to wait 20 seconds for it to switch back. Unfortunately, with xrandr, you do not have that luxury. The xrandr command will change the resolution immediately and it assumes you know what you are doing.

If you want to test a screen change with xrandr, use a small script (see Listing 9-1) to save the current resolution, change the screen, and then change back. If you like the resolution, you can press Ctrl+C to kill the script, or run xrandr without the test script to set the resolution.

Listing 9-1: Script to Test a Screen Resolution

```
#!/bin/sh
# Temporarily change resolutions (great for testing)
# Example usage: ./testres -s 1   (to set to xrandr screen setting #1)

# Save current resolution
Resolution=`xrandr -q | grep '*' |  awk -F'*' '{print $2}' | \
         awk '{print $2 $3 $4}'`
Rate=`xrandr -q | grep '*' |  awk -F'*' '{print $3}' | awk '{print $1}'`
echo "Old: Resolution: $Resolution  Refresh rate: $Rate Hz"

# Set the resolution using the command-line options.
xrandr $*
echo "New: `xrandr -q | grep '*'`"

# Wait 20 seconds, then change back
sleep 20
xrandr -s $Resolution -r $Rate
echo "Switching back"
echo "Current: `xrandr -q | grep '*'`"
```

Flipping Cool!

Some video drivers support flipping the screen. If your video driver supports this, then you can use xrandr -x to flip the screen horizontally, making a mirror reflection. The xrandr -y command flips the screen vertically, and xrandr -x -y flips both. Similarly, the -o option can change the orientation from normal (-o normal) to rotated 90 degrees (-o right), 180 degrees (-o inverted), and 270 degrees (-o left).

However, not every video driver supports flipping and rotation. If your driver does not support these commands, then xrandr will give you a cryptic error message such as:

```
X Error of failed request:  BadMatch (invalid parameter attributes)
  Major opcode of failed request:  155 (RANDR)
  Minor opcode of failed request:  2 (RRSetScreenConfig)
  Serial number of failed request:  12
  Current serial number in output stream:  12
```

Practical Uses for xrandr

By now you're probably thinking, "xrandr is cool, but it has no long-term practical use." Most people set the display and that's it. However, sometimes there is a need to switch between display resolutions. For example, web designers may want to quickly switch screen resolutions to see what their web pages look like with different settings. This is important since not everyone uses 1280 × 1024. On the laptop that I use for presentations, I use xrandr to quickly change the display to something that will work with the overhead projector; I've seen too many conferences where people spend more time fighting with the projector rather than actually presenting. And for this book, I used a quick script (see Listing 9-2) to change the screen resolution, set the background, colors, etc. to match the publisher's guidelines for screen shots. This script ensures that every screen shot is taken the same way.

Listing 9-2: The setbg Script for Taking *Hacking Ubuntu* Screen Shots

```
#!/bin/sh
# Set background to white for a screenshot, then put it back.
# Publisher requirements:
#   - White background (so hide my background)
#   - 1024x768 (so lower the resolution from my normal 1280x1024)
# Wait for a key press, then put it all back.

# Save current settings (background colors, settings, and image)
RES=`gconftool-2 --get /desktop/gnome/screen/default/0/resolution`
BG1=`gconftool-2 --get /desktop/gnome/background/primary_color`
BG2=`gconftool-2 --get /desktop/gnome/background/secondary_color`
BG=`gconftool-2 --get /desktop/gnome/background/draw_background`
BGI=`gconftool-2 --get /desktop/gnome/background/picture_filename`

# Set change
xrandr -s 1024x768
gconftool-2 -t str --set /desktop/gnome/screen/default/0/resolution "1024x768"
gconftool-2 -t str --set /desktop/gnome/background/primary_color "#ffffff"
gconftool-2 -t str --set /desktop/gnome/background/secondary_color "#ffffff"
gconftool-2 -t boolean --set /desktop/gnome/background/draw_background "False"
gconftool-2 -t str --set /desktop/gnome/background/picture_filename ""

# Wait
echo "Use Control-Alt-D to hide all windows (and later restore)"
read

# Put it back
xrandr -s 0  # this is my default resolution
gconftool-2 -t str --set /desktop/gnome/screen/default/0/resolution "$RES"
```

Continued

Listing 9-2 *Continued*

```
gconftool-2 -t str --set /desktop/gnome/background/primary_color "$BG1"
gconftool-2 -t str --set /desktop/gnome/background/secondary_color "$BG2"
gconftool-2 -t boolean --set /desktop/gnome/background/draw_background "$BG"
gconftool-2 -t str --set /desktop/gnome/background/picture_filename "$BGI"
```

Changing Video Drivers

X-Windows supports dozens of graphics cards. For a quick list, use `apt-cache search video driver`. Most of these video drivers are installed on the system during the default Ubuntu installation and are found in `/usr/lib/xorg/modules/drivers/`. The enabled graphic card is listed in the `/etc/X11/xorg.conf` file, under the "Device" section. For example:

```
Section "Device"
        Identifier      "ATI Technologies, Inc. Rage 128 RL/VR AGP"
        Driver          "ati"
        Option          "UseFBDev"               "true"
EndSection
```

This specifies the use of the `ati` driver found in `/usr/lib/xorg/modules/drivers/ati_drv.so`. If you want to change the driver, then you will need to change the `xorg.conf` configuration and restart the X-server.

Tip You can restart the X-server by either rebooting or pressing Ctrl+Alt+Backspace. Since this will kill all your X-Window applications, you should logout before restarting the server.

Warning If you install the wrong video driver, then X-Windows will fail to start. Be sure to make a backup of the `xorg.conf` file before making modifications. This way, if X-Windows breaks, then you will have a working configuration that you can put back.

Enabling OpenGL

The Open Graphics Library (OpenGL) provides a set of extensions for accelerated 2D and 3D rendering. Without this extension, some graphics must be explicitly drawn by each application, leading to slower graphic rendering.

Some video card drivers support OpenGL without any additional steps. For example, if you have an Intel, SiS, or Matrox video card, then OpenGL may already be supported and enabled. However, if you have an NVIDIA or ATI video card, then you will need to change drivers and install the accelerated graphics extensions.

To tell if you need to enable OpenGL, use the `glxinfo` command:

```
$ glxinfo | grep "direct rendering"
direct rendering: No
```

If it says yes, then OpenGL is already enabled. However, if it says no, then either OpenGL is not supported, or you need to enable it.

1. To enable OpenGL, make sure your video card is either NVIDIA or ATI. Use the `lspci` command to list your video cards. If the result does not say "nVidia" or "ATI" (in lowercase, uppercase, or mixed case), then you do not need these steps.

```
$ lspci | grep -i -e Display -e VGA  # on an iMac
0000:00:10.0 Display controller: ATI Technologies Inc Rage 128 RL/VR
AGP
$ lspci | grep -i -e Display -e VGA  # on a PC
0000:01:00.0 VGA compatible controller: nVidia Corporation NV18
[GeForce4 MX 4000 AGP 8x] (rev c1)
```

Not every ATI and NVIDIA card is supported. Make sure the model listed by the `lspci` command matches a supported card:

- ATI must be a 9*xxx* series, 9500 series (or higher), or have TV-out support. Your monitor must also support at least 60 Hz.

- NVIDIA supports GeForce, nForce and Quadro models with AGP, TV-out, and flat panel displays.

- NVIDIA supports older TNT, TNT2, and GeForce models with legacy drivers.

Note   The two example `lspci` commands show an ATI Rage 128 video card in an iMac system that is not supported, and a NVIDIA GeForce4 MX 4000 card in a PC system with AGP that is supported.

2. Back up your `xorg.conf` file. If anything does not work, you'll need this backup copy to return to a working display.

```
sudo cp /etc/X11/xorg.conf /etc/X11/xorg.conf.bak
```

3. Regardless of your video card, you will need to install the restricted drivers for your kernel (if they are not already installed).

```
sudo apt-get install linux-restricted-modules-`uname -r`
```

At this point, you must perform some card-specific configurations.

If you have an ATI video card...

1. Install the ATI drivers:

```
sudo apt-get install xorg-driver-fglrx fglrx-control
```

2. Run these commands to configure your `xorg.conf` file:

```
sudo aticonfig --initial
sudo aticonfig --overlay-type=Xv
```

3. Reconfigure the X-server:

```
sudo dpkg-reconfigure xserver-xorg
```

This auto-detects your video card. Be sure to select fglrx and not ATI. For the remaining prompts (and there are a lot of prompts), you can just press enter and select the default values. (Since you're already running the X-server, the default values work.)

4. Check your `/etc/X11/xorg.conf` settings and make sure the driver in the "Device" section says: `Driver "fglrx"`.

5. Restart your X-server. You can do this by rebooting or by logging out and then pressing Ctrl+Alt+Backspace.

If all goes well, then your display will start. Otherwise, you should be stuck at a text prompt— skip to the "Debugging X-Windows" section for resolving the problem.

If you have an NVIDIA card...

1. Install the NVIDIA drivers for the current or legacy card. *Do not install both.* (Actually, `apt-get` will not allow you to install both.)

```
sudo apt-get install nvidia-glx nvidia-kernel-common
```

If you have a legacy card, use:

```
sudo apt-get install nvidia-glx-legacy nvidia-kernel-common
```

2. If you previously made changes to your `xorg.conf` file, then make sure it is archived:

```
md5sum /etc/X11/xorg.conf | sudo tee /var/lib/x11/xorg.conf
```

Note While archiving `xorg.conf` is always a good thing, the NVIDIA configuration script will not continue if it is not archived.

3. Configure the driver:

```
sudo nvidia-glx-config enable
```

4. Edit `xorg.conf` and check the "Device" section. The driver should be `nvidia` and not `nv`. If it says nv, then change it to `nvidia`.

5. When you are editing `xorg.conf`, add the following line to the "Device" section to disable the NVIDIA splash screen (and speed up the boot time):

```
Option "NoLogo" "true"
```

The full Device section should look something similar to this example (although your video card model and BusID may be different):

```
Section "Device"
    Identifier   "NVIDIA Corporation NV18 [GeForce4 MX 4000 AGP 8x]"
    Driver       "nvidia"
    BusID        "PCI:1:0:0"
    Option       "NoLogo"        "true"
EndSection
```

6. Restart your X-server. You can do this by rebooting or by logging out and then pressing Ctrl+Alt+Backspace.

If all goes well, then your display will start. Otherwise, you should be stuck at a text prompt—skip to the next section, "Debugging X-Windows", for resolving the problem.

Debugging X-Windows

When X-Windows fails, it either drops you at a text prompt, or leaves the screen blank. In the worst case, you will need to reboot the computer in order to get to a text login prompt. The X-Windows system logs everything—including cryptic error messages—in `/var/log/Xorg.0.log`. Check the log for a place to start debugging. Fortunately, problems usually fall into one of four categories:

1. Human error. Make sure you didn't type something wrong. The `xorg.conf` file is not very forgiving of typographical errors.

2. Your card is not supported.

3. You installed multiple, conflicting drivers.

4. Your card was not recognized properly.

The first problem can be resolved by checking everything that you entered into the `xorg.conf` file. The other items are a little more complicated and are covered in the next subsections.

Putting Things Back

If your card is not supported or your changes were not correct, then put back your `xorg.conf` file. You should be able to run `startx` from the command line. This will start the graphics system and let you know if you put it back correctly.

Tip

Hopefully you made a backup of `/etc/X11/xorg.conf`. If you didn't, then all is not lost. Some drivers make backups automatically when they install. Look in the `/etc/X11/` directory for files like `xorg.conf~` and `xorg.conf.backup`. These are probably functional configuration files. In the worst case, you can run `sudo dpkg-reconfigure xserver-xorg` to generate a new configuration file.

Although `startx` is good for running the server and debugging the `xorg.conf` file, it runs the server from your text login. This means that logging out or shutting down from the graphical desktop will return you to your text command prompt; it will not actually log you out or reboot the system. To get the automatic login working, use:

```
sudo /etc/init.d/gdm restart
```

Debugging the Wrong Driver

Usually people will blindly install one driver and, if it does not work, then try the other. (Ok, I admit that I've done that.) If you're going to do this, be sure to remove the unused driver first; otherwise, neither driver will work.

- To remove the ATI drivers, use:

  ```
  sudo apt-get remove xorg-driver-fglrx fglrx-control
  ```

- To unconfigure the NVIDIA drivers, use:

  ```
  sudo /usr/bin/nvidia-installer --uninstall
  sudo apt-get remove nvidia-glx         # for current cards
  sudo apt-get remove nvidia-glx-legacy # for legacy cards
  ```

- To copy back your `xorg.conf` file, use:

  ```
  sudo cp /etc/X11/xorg.conf.bak /etc/X11/xorg.conf
  ```

- Restart your X-Windows system by either rebooting or logging out and pressing Ctrl+Alt+Backspace.

Forcing Drivers to Install

For ATI, some cards are claimed to be unsupported even through they will work. For example, the Radeon Mobility 9600 (found in laptops) is reported as unsupported by the ATI drivers. You can change the PCI ID and try to fake the driver into thinking the card is supported. For example, the Radeon Mobility 9600 uses PCI ID 4e53 (found using the `lspci -n` command). You can add a line to the `xorg.conf` "Device" section to specify a supported ID (for example, 4e50—the Radeon 9600 M10—is supported and seems to be compatible with the 4e53). For example:

```
Section "Device"
  Identifier "ATI"
  Driver     "fglrx"
  ChipID     0x4e50
  ...
EndSection
```

The full list of PCI IDs is found in /usr/share/misc/pci.ids. Vendors usually follow a consistent ID convention, so the 4e50, 4e51, 4e52, and 4e53 are all ATI Radeon cards. If one does not work, try another. However, forcing an ATI ID onto a non-ATI card (for example, Cirrus GD 5440) has virtually no chance of working.

Adjusting with xvidtune

Many newer computers come with flat LCD displays. This means the picture is usually centered. (And if it isn't, then there should be an auto or manual adjustment setting.) However, CRT monitors are not always centered. The desktop may appear slightly cut off at the top, bottom, left, or right. (In the case of some monitors, the desktop may be cut off by more than a little.) The xvidtune program allows you to adjust the screen width, height, and position by tuning the horizontal and vertical scan frequencies.

The xvidtune program does not actually perform the system changes (although it does allow you to test the settings). Instead, it generates code that can be inserted into /etc/X11/xorg.conf for adjusting the monitor automatically.

1. Open a terminal and run the xvidtune program. This will display a warning about possible damage to your monitor (see Figure 9-2). Take this warning seriously, then smile, and click OK.

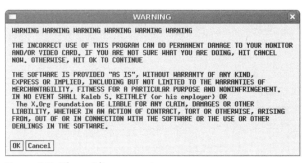

FIGURE 9-2: The xvidtune warning screen

Note   You will need to run xvidtune from a terminal window (for example, Applications ⇨ Accessories ⇨ Terminal). This is because the final output from xvidtune will be printed in the terminal window.

2. The xvidtune menu may not be pretty, but it is functional (see Figure 9-3). At the top of the window are the actual horizontal and vertical scan synchronization values used to denote the start of an analog video scan. I usually ignore these. The more important items are the buttons. These enable you to adjust the screen.

   The xvidtune adjustment options are:

   ◦ **Left, Right, Up, Down**—These shift the screen's position.

   ◦ **Wider, Narrower, Shorter, Taller**—These options adjust the screen's width and height.

   ◦ **Test**—This temporarily applies the changes to the screen so you can see what it looks like.

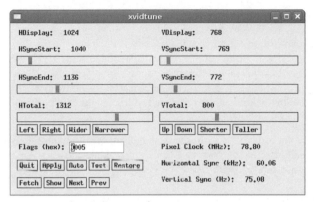

FIGURE 9-3: The xvidtune configuration settings

- **Auto**—Rather than making adjustments and clicking Test, you can click Auto to automatically apply the changes as you make them. These changes are not permanent, but they allow you to see what they will look like.

- **Restore**—If you think you really screwed up, you can click this button to return to the current settings.

- **Show**—This displays the current settings in the text console where you started running xvidtune.

- **Quit**—This exits the program. You can also type **q** to quit.

3. Make your adjustments. Use Test or Auto to view your changes.

Tip   On some monitors, clicking Left or Right may really swing the display over to the side. Before making adjustments, move the xvidtune window into the middle of the screen. This way, it will not accidentally go out of view.

4. After finding a good adjustment setting, click Show. The terminal window should display a line with your settings. It should look similar to:

```
"1024x768"  78.80    1024 1040 1136 1304   768 769 772 796 +hsync +vsync
```

This line lists the resolution (in quotes) and the scan settings.

5. Edit /etc/X11/xorg.conf and scroll down to the Monitor section. Add a ModeLine option that includes the output from xvidtune. For example, mine (including a very long line that wraps on the screen) looks like:

```
Section "Monitor"
        Identifier      "iMac"
        Option          "DPMS"
        HorizSync       60-60
```

```
        VertRefresh      75-117
        ModeLine         "1024x768"      78.80   1024 1040 1136 1308
768  769  772  796 +hsync +vsync
EndSection
```

6. Save your changes, log out, and restart the X-server using Ctrl+Alt+Backspace.

Tip

If you use multiple screen resolutions, then run `xvidtune` *after* changing each resolution. You can have multiple ModeLine entries in the `xorg.conf` file—as long as they all have different resolutions. Don't change screen resolutions while running `xvidtune` since it will not detect changes.

Improving Performance

When you have a slow display, everything else can seem to be slow. Much of this may be because the display is consuming CPU and memory resources. Fortunately, there are a few things you can do to improve the display's performance.

- **Install the accelerated drivers**—The NVIDIA and ATI accelerated 3D drivers (mentioned in the Enabling OpenGL section) significantly improve performance. If you have the option to install either of these, then do it!

- **Disable the Nautilus background**—Nautilus is used to place icons on the background (see Chapter 2). If this is disabled, then memory and CPU resources are freed up. Otherwise, Nautilus may need to redraw the background every time something on the screen changes. To disable it, use:

```
gconftool-2 --type bool \
   --set /apps/nautilus/preferences/show_desktop FALSE
```

- **Disable Gnome background images**—Drawing a background takes time and memory. If you don't need a background image, then turn it off. This can either be done by the background applet (System ➪ Preferences ➪ Desktop Background, select No Wallpaper) or with `gconftool-2`.

```
gconftool-2 --type string \
   --set /desktop/gnome/background/picture_options none
```

- **Disable thumbnails**—Nautilus can generate thumbnail icons and preview audio. If Nautilus opens a directory with lots of images in it, the overhead from creating thumbnails can be very noticeable (especially on slow systems). To disable previews, use:

```
gconftool-2 --type string \
   --set /apps/nautilus/preferences/show_image_thumbnails never
```

Tip

If you want some thumbnail icons, use `local_only` instead of `never`. This gives you icons in local folders, but disables it for networked file systems. This way, you don't need to wait for the network to transfer all of the images—an action required for making thumbnail images.

■ **Disable icons in menus**—By default, every menu items includes an icon. While these icons are cached, they can take time to load (especially on a slow system). You can disable the icons using:

```
gconftool-2 --type bool \
  --set /desktop/gnome/interface/menus_have_icons FALSE
```

Accessibility

Not everyone optimizes the display for cool graphics and speed. People with sight disabilities can optimize the display for their own needs. By default, Ubuntu includes many themes for addressing accessibility. For example, under System ➪ Preferences ➪ Theme, you can select High Contrast Large Print, Low Contrast Large Print, Large Print, Low Contrast, and so on. Even without my glasses, I can read the screen using the High Contrast Large Print theme without being inches from the monitor.

For people who have little or no sight, the default Ubuntu installation supports Braille displays. This is done using `brltty`. The `brltty` driver supports many different Braille displays and input devices. You can start it by opening a terminal window and running `sudo brltty`.

After you connect your Braille terminal, you can use Orca to map specific events, such as window actions, to the Braille terminal.

1. Install Orca using `sudo apt-get install gnome-orca`.

2. Configure it in a terminal by running orca-setup. It will ask you questions such as:

   ```
   Use key echo?  Enter y or n:
   ```

   Orca supports some text-to-speech systems. If you have more than one speech server installed, it will ask you to select one of them.

3. After it is configured, Orca will finish tuning Gnome and create a `$HOME/.orca` directory. You will need to log out and log back in for the changes to take affect.

4. (Optional) You may also want to change the default init level in `/etc/inittab` from run-level 2 to run level 3.

   ```
   id:3:initdefault:
   ```

   Run level 3 is intended for accessibility needs and automatically starts the Braille display. See Chapter 3 for modifying init scripts and the run level.

Switching Screensavers

Under Dapper Drake, the default screen saver is `gnome-screensaver`. (Prior to Dapper, Ubunty Hoary and Breezy used `xscreensaver`.) Although `gnome-screensaver` does the basic job of preventing the screen from being burned in, it has some serious limitations. For example, it is missing many of the configuration options found in `xscreensaver`, and more importantly: it sometimes kicks in while applications are running full-screen. When I first upgraded to Dapper, I started playing my favorite game: `bzflag`. This is a full screen networked tank game. Ten minutes into the game, the screen would fade to black! At first I thought it was the game, then I realized that it was the screen saver. The game was intercepting all keyboard and mouse inputs. As a result, the screen saver thought the computer was inactive.

While I could have chosen to write a script around the game to temporarily disable the screen saver, I opted for a better solution: replace `gnome-screensaver` with `xscreensaver`. This gave me all the missing functionality, as well as a screen saver that was game-aware. This change requires a couple of steps:

1. Install `xscreensaver`.

   ```
   sudo apt-get install xscreensaver
   ```

2. Disable the Gnome screensaver.

   ```
   gconftool-2 --type boolean \
      -s /apps/gnome_settings_daemon/screensaver/start_screensaver false
   ```

 Warning Do not try to uninstall `gnome-screensaver` since there are dependencies that will remove the entire desktop!

3. Stop the running `gnome-screensaver`.

   ```
   sudo killall gnome-screensaver
   ```

4. Configure `xscreensaver` to start when you log in. Go to System ➪ Preferences ➪ Sessions ➪ Startup Programs. Click Add and enter:

   ```
   xscreensaver -no-splash
   ```

   Then click Close. This makes the new screen saver start when you login.

5. Change the menu preferences so that they use `xscreensaver`:

   - Right-click the System menu and select Edit Menus. This brings up the Menu Editor applet.

   - In the Menu Editor, scroll to the bottom of the left window and click Preferences.

   - In the right window, scroll down and right-click Screensaver (see Figure 9-4). Select Properties from the item menu.

- Change the command from `gnome-screensaver` to `xscreensaver-demo`. (see Figure 9-5).
- Close all of the Menu Editor windows.

FIGURE 9-4: The Menu Editor properties for the Screensaver item

FIGURE 9-5: The properties for the Screensaver menu item

6. As root, edit the file `/usr/share/applications/gnome-screensaver-prefer-ences.desktop`. Near the bottom you will see the line, `Exec=gnome-screensaver-preferences`. Change this line to `Exec=xscreensaver-demo`. Also, comment out (or delete) the following lines:

```
X-GNOME-Bugzilla-Bugzilla=GNOME
X-GNOME-Bugzilla-Product=gnome-screensaver
X-GNOME-Bugzilla-Component=general
X-Ubuntu-Gettext-Domain=gnome-screensaver
```

Warning If you use `sudo apt-get upgrade` (or Synaptic's automatic upgrade) and refresh the screen saver package, then you may need to do this change again.

7. Open the screen saver preferences (System ➪ Preferences ➪ Screensaver) and deselect all of the grayed out screensaver options. If you do not disable them, then the default random screensaver may try to run missing screensavers, resulting in errors.

Note If you open the preferences before starting the screen saver (per these instructions), then you will receive a pop-up saying that the XScreenSaver daemon is not running. Click OK to launch it now. If the daemon is already running, then you won't see this pop-up message.

8. Select your desired screen saver, adjust the properties as you see fit, and close the window.

Now, `xscreensaver` is your default screen saver and will start from boot.

I have only found one limitation from installing `xscreensaver`: it does not work from the System ➪ Quit... menu. This menu normally brings up a window with options including Log Out, Restart, and Shutdown. The Lock Screen option breaks when you install `xscreensaver`. To get around this limitation, I installed an applet on the top panel that runs the command: `xscreensaver-command -lock`. (When you install `xscreensaver`, it even gives you an icon that looks like a monitor with a flame coming out of it.) In order to quickly lock the screen, I can click the `xscreensaver` icon on my top panel. Although this does not fix the Lock Screen option in the Quit... window, I find it is more convenient to click-and-lock rather than drill down menus in order to lock the screen.

Adding New Screensavers

The default Ubuntu installation includes some screensavers that are not installed under `xscreensaver`. For example, Lattice (my favorite GL screensaver) is not installed by default. To install Lattice, you'll need an OpenGL video driver (see the section on "Enabling OpenGL"). However, non-GL screensavers can also be added with the following steps:

1. As root, edit `/etc/X11/app-defaults/XScreenSaver`. This file lists all the screensavers that `xscreensaver` knows about.

2. Search for `fliptext`—this is another screensaver that *does* exist. You'll use it as a template.

3. Duplicate the line and change `fliptext` to `lattice`. Keep the `GL:` since Lattice is a GL screensaver.

```
GL:                    fliptext -root                    \n\
GL:                    lattice -root                     \n\
```

4. Search further down for `fliptext` (there will be a second line). Duplicate this line and change `fliptext` and `FlipText` to `lattice` and `Lattice`.

```
*hacks.fliptext.name:      FlipText
*hacks.lattice.name:       Lattice
```

5. Save your changes.

When you are all done, log out and restart the desktop using Ctrl+Alt+Backspace. When the graphics comes back up, it will be using your new screen saver and Lattice will be installed. You can select this screen saver using System ➪ Preferences ➪ Screensaver. If you followed the previous section on installing `xscreensaver` then this will run `xscreensaver-demo` and allow you to select Lattice—the interlocking rings.

Animating the Desktop Background

The default Ubuntu desktop can either be a solid color or a static image. With a few simple scripts, you can change the background image or color (see Chapter 2), but this isn't real animation. The secret to really animating the desktop is to run an X-Windows application that draws the background. Here's an example where the background is drawn by a screen saver.

1. You'll need to tell Nautilus to not draw the desktop. This means that you will lose all your desktop icons, but who needs icons when you can animate the desktop!

```
gconftool-2 -t bool /apps/nautilus/preferences/show_desktop -s false
```

2. Start the X-application that will draw the background. In this case, I'll use the Lattice screen saver, tell it to draw the full background (`-root` window), render rings that look like circuits (as apposed to doughnuts, brass, etc.) and consume fewer CPU cycles (`-n` and `nice`). The other options specify the rendering rate (20 frames per second), motion speed (`-e 1`), field of view (`-o 30`), and a background fog (`-f`). All of these options are detailed in the man page for `lattice`.

```
nice /usr/lib/xscreensaver/lattice -root --circuits \
    -n -s -e 1 -f -o 30 -x 20
```

This creates an animated background with moving rings (see Figure 9-6).

Note Lattice is a GL screen saver. If your video driver does not have GL support, Lattice will not work. In addition, if your OpenGL video driver does not have direct rendering enabled, then Lattice will consume all of your CPU resources, making the system sluggish. You can always choose a different screen saver that is better supported by your display.

Any application that can render to the root window can be used as a background image. However, there are a few caveats:

- **Applications do not store the images behind them**—As a result, a background that does not redraw the screen (for example, `/usr/lib/xscreensaver/sonar -root`) can have large gaps when a window is moved or closed. The best backgrounds render the entire screen at least 5 times per second—20 times per second is better.

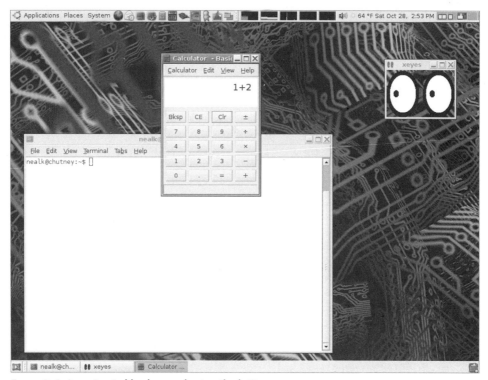

FIGURE 9-6: An animated background using the lattice screen saver

- **Some background applications consume lots of resources**—For example, running `/usr/lib/xscreensaver/colorfire --root` can noticeably slow down your system. Good backgrounds consume few resources, and many screen savers have options to lower their resource consumption.

- **As funny as it may sound, moving backgrounds can give some people a sense of motion sickness**—Although `sonar` probably won't cause a problem, the constant motion from `lattice` can be both fun and not so fun. Consider testing the background before you make it permanent.

Disabling Animated Backgrounds

If you decided to turn off the animated background, you'll need to follow a few steps:

1. Kill the background animation. For example, if you are running `lattice` then use `killall lattice`. This will stop the background from being drawn. However, it won't put back your default background and moving windows will start erasing parts of the background.

2. Tell Nautilus that it is OK to draw the background.

```
gconftool-2 -t bool /apps/nautilus/preferences/show_desktop -s true
```

3. Even though Nautilus now has permission to draw the background, you still need to force it to redraw the background once. You can do this by logging out and logging back in, or running: `nautilus -q ; nautilus`. This will quit Nautilus and—if it does not automatically restart—start it.

Configuring Dual Monitors

The graphical display has a limited amount of screen real estate. As more windows are opened, space on the desktop becomes an issue. Using the Workplace Switcher (see Chapter 8) is a good start, but eventually you will find yourself rapidly switching back and forth between desktops as you try to use two applications at once. For serious power users, one monitor is usually not enough. Ubuntu offers a couple of different options for adding multiple monitors:

- **Two headed systems**—One computer can have multiple graphics cards. This is an ideal solution for people with extra hardware. Alternately, some graphics cards are capable of driving more than one monitor.

- **Networked desktops**—Two different computers combine to form one virtual desktop. This is a great option when you have spare computers lying around.

- **Shared desktops**—There is no reason why all of the desktops need to run the same operating system. This is a must-have for anyone with a need to use Windows, Mac OS X, and Linux at the same time.

Using Two Heads

If your computer has multiple video ports, then you can frequently use them to drive two different monitors. Although most workstation computers don't have multiple video cards installed, you can always plug in an extra one. However, many laptops include two video sources: one for the LCD display and one for an external monitor. In some cases, these video ports can be configured to work together, forming one large display, while other laptops must display the same thing on both ports.

 Note The computer display is commonly called a *head*. A computer with two displays is a *dual-headed* system. Many servers are *headless*, since they have no display attached.

There are two ways to have a dual-headed system. The first is to combine monitors using TwinView. However, TwinView is strictly limited to nVidia video cards. The more universal option is Xinerama.

Using Two Heads with TwinView

If you have an NVIDIA graphics card *and* it supports two monitors, then you can use TwinView to combine both monitors into one desktop. TwinView is an NVIDIA-specific graphics extension for managing multiple monitors.

1. Create a backup of your working `xorg.conf` file.

```
sudo cp /etc/X11/xorg.conf /etc/X11/xorg.conf.orig
```

2. Tell X-Windows about the second monitor. In the file `/etc/X11/xorg.conf` is a section titled "Device". This contains the video card attributes. Add in TwinView options for the second monitor. For example:

```
Section "Device"
        Identifier   "NVIDIA Corporation NV18 [GeForce4 MX 4000 AGP 8x]"
        Driver       "nvidia"
        BusID        "PCI:1:0:0"
        Option       "TwinView"
        Option       "MetaModes"   "1280x1024,1280x1024; 1024x768,1024x768"
        Option       "TwinViewOrientation"    "RightOf"
        Option       "ConnectedMonitor"        "CRT,CRT"
        Option       "SecondMonitorHorizSync"          "UseEdidFreqs"
        Option       "SecondMonitorVertRefresh"        "UseEdidFreqs"
#       Option       "SecondMonitorHorizSync"          "24-80"
#       Option       "SecondMonitorVertRefresh"        "50-75"
EndSection
```

These options include pairs of video resolutions (one for each monitor), the location of the second monitor (right of the first), and the monitor scan rates (either using defaults or specifying range).

3. Save your new `xorg.conf` file and restart the X-server. Log out and use Ctrl+Alt+ Backspace to restart the server. If it does not come up, then refer to the section "Debugging X-Windows" earlier in this chapter. (If it does come up, then you're done and you should have two working displays.)

Using Two Heads with Xinerama

If your system has two different video ports, then you can use Xinerama to link them into one virtual display. Before you can use two monitors, you will need to make sure the computer actually has two video devices. Use the `lspci` command to list all display devices:

```
lspci -X | grep -i -e VGA -e DISPLAY
```

If only one display controller is listed, then you won't be able to use this option. However, if you see multiple video cards, then you can configure your X-server to use both cards. This requires editing the `/etc/X11/xorg.conf` file.

1. Create a backup of your working `xorg.conf` file.

```
sudo cp /etc/X11/xorg.conf /etc/X11/xorg.conf.orig
```

2. Tell X-Windows about the second monitor. In the file /etc/X11/xorg.conf is a section titled "Monitor". This contains a unique identifier and monitor attributes. Create a second one for your second monitor. For example:

```
Section "Monitor"
        # Default monitor
        Identifier      "LCD"
        Option          "DPMS"
EndSection

Section "Monitor"
        # Second monitor that I added
        Identifier      "CRT"
        Option          "DPMS"
        HorizSync       31.5 - 57.0
        VertRefresh     50-100
        # You may want to add ModeLine items later
EndSection
```

3. Each monitor in the xorg.conf file may display different desktop screens. You need to tell X-Windows about the second screen. In the file /etc/X11/xorg.conf is a section titled "Screen". This contains a unique identifier and information about the graphics modes. Create a second screen section with a different identifier for the second monitor. For example:

```
Section "Screen"
  # Define the first screen
  Identifier    "Default Screen"
  Device        "NVIDIA Corporation NV18 [GeForce4 MX 4000 AGP 8x]"
  Monitor "LCD"
  DefaultDepth  24
  BusID         "PCI:1:0:0" # optional for distinguishing cards
  SubSection "Display"
    Depth       24
    Modes       "1024x768"
  EndSubSection
EndSection

Section "Screen"
  # Define the second screen
  Identifier    "Second Screen"
  Device "ATI Technologies, Inc. M9+ 5C63 [Radeon Mobility 9000 (AGP)]"
  Monitor       "CRT"
  DefaultDepth  24
  SubSection "Display"
    Depth       24
    Modes       "1280x1024"
  EndSubSection
EndSection
```

Note Be sure the labels in your `Screen` section's "Monitor" lines match the unique identifiers from the Monitor sections. The `Device` name and option `BusID` value should match the results from the `lspci -X` command.

Tip Use the `BusID` option when you have two of the same type of video card in one computer. This distinguishes one card from the other.

4. In the `/etc/X11/xorg.conf` file is a section titled "ServerLayout". This is where you will specify the geometry of the desktop. Using the screen identifiers, you need to specify the X-display number (for example, 0 for DISPLAY=:0, 1 for DISPLAY=:1, and so on) and their relationship in forming the desktop: Above, Below, LeftOf, or RightOf. For example, if my CRT monitor is located to the right of the LCD monitor, then I can use:

```
Section "ServerLayout"
        Identifier "Default Layout"
        Screen 0 "Default Screen"
        Screen 1 "Second Screen" RightOf "Default Screen"
        InputDevice "Generic Keyboard"
        InputDevice "Configured Mouse"
        InputDevice "stylus" "SendCoreEvents"
        InputDevice "cursor" "SendCoreEvents"
        InputDevice "eraser" "SendCoreEvents"
        InputDevice "Synaptics Touchpad"
EndSection
```

5. (Optional) If you want to have the displays linked as one desktop, rather than being treated as individual displays, then you will need to add a Xinerama option. This can be done by creating a section titled "ServerFlags" and setting the `Xinerama` option to true.

```
Section "ServerFlags"
        Option "Xinerama" "true"
EndSection
```

Alternately, you can add the `Option` line to the "ServerLayout" section.

6. If you have everything in place, then you should be able to save your new `xorg.conf` file and restart the X-server. Logout and use Ctrl+Alt+Backspace to restart the server. If it does not come up, then you'll need to go to the section in this chapter titled "Debugging X-Windows." (If it does come up, then you're done and you should have two working displays.)

Xinerama

The big trick to making a multi-display desktop is the Xinerama extensions to X-Windows. This library is installed by default and allows you to chain multiple X-Windows displays into one large, virtual desktop. Without the flag, multiple displays can be used, but they do not appear as one coherent desktop.

How can you tell if you need the flag?

- If you cannot drag a window across the desktop, from one monitor to the other, then you need the Xinerama flag.

- If your graphical desktop (Gnome or KDE) replicates the background image and panels in every window, then you need the Xinerama flag. Without the flag, each display is treated independently. With the flag, they are linked into one large desktop. However, as one large desktop all panels will only appear in the first display. This allows the secondary displays to be used for presentation projectors and not be cluttered with panels and widgets.

Using Two Computers and One Desktop

If you have a high-end computer or two high-end video cards in one system, then connecting two monitors to one computer is definitely the way to go. However, there are some situations where it is more desirable to use a second computer to run the second display. For example:

- You do not have a second video card to put into your system. In my case, I have no spare video cards available, but I have plenty of spare computers that have video cards built into their motherboards.

- Your computer does not have available expansion slots for a second video card. Some low-end PCs are not expandable. Many times, motherboards have only one high-bandwidth slot for a high-end video card. You may have extra expansion slots, but may be unable to use them for graphics.

- Your second monitor is built into a stand-alone computer (for example, My grape iMac has a monitor built into the computer housing.)

Whatever your situation might be, you can extend your virtual display such that it spreads across computers. All you need are two or more networked computers running X-Windows.

Tip   Ideally you'll want the network to be fast. In some corporate environments, physically adjacent computers may actually be on different subnets. Since transmitting video consumes bandwidth, consider investing in a cheap router and putting all of the display computers on the same subnet. Latency across a slow network can be very noticeable.

1. Your virtual display will have one primary display (for the mouse and keyboard) and one or more secondary displays that will provide the desktop. Install the Distributed Multihead X Project server (Xdmx) on the primary computer. This will be used to bridge different X-Windows systems.

```
sudo apt-get install xdmx
```

2. Each of the machines that will be part of the virtual desktop will need to allow remote access to their X-Windows system. The problem is, the default Ubuntu installation disables all remote access. Thus, you will need to enable it. How you enable it depends on your desktop.

   - For Ubuntu's default window manager, Gnome, you must edit `/etc/gdm/gdm.conf`. Change `DisallowTCP=true` to `DisallowTCP=false`.

   - For the Kubuntu KDE window manager, you must edit `/etc/kde3/kdb/kdbrc` and change `ServerArgsLocal=-nolisten tcp` to `ServerArgsLocal=` (no parameters).

   - For other window managers, such as TWM, you will need to edit `/etc/X11/xinit/xserverrc` and change `exec /usr/bin/X11/X -dpi 100 -nolisten tcp` to `exec /usr/bin/X11/X -dpi 100`.

   After making this change, you will need to restart the X-server. Pressing Ctrl+Alt+Backspace won't cut it (that only re-reads configuration files). Instead, you will need to either reboot the system or restart the display. For example, to restart Gnome you can use:

   - Stop Gnome using: `sudo /etc/init.d/gdm stop`.

   - At the text screen, press Alt+F2 to get to a text login screen.

   - Log in.

   - At the command-line prompt, run: `sudo /etc/init.d/gdm start`.

3. Use `xhost +hostname` to enable remote access for the display server. For example, if my primary server is named `alpha`, then I would use `xhost +alpha`. You can also specify an IP address such as `xhost +10.1.2.15`.

4. On the primary display server, enable local access.

```
xhost +local:
```

5. Now you can use Xdmx to link all of the displays together. For example, if my secondary display is on the computer named `bravo`, then on the primary system I would run:

```
Xdmx :1 -display :0 -display bravo:0
```

This assigns the virtual desktop as display `:1`. The virtual desktop spans `:0` on the primary system (the normal display) and `bravo:0` is located to the right. If I had a third system (for example, `charlie`), then I could use:

```
Xdmx :1 -display :0 -display bravo:0 -display charlie:0
```

Xdmx takes a variety of different options. For example, the primary display does not need to be on the left. However, if it is not on the left, then you will need to specify which display will provide the keyboard and mouse input.

```
Xdmx :1 -input :0 -display bravo:0 -display :0 -display charlie:0
```

Other useful options include:

- +xinerama—If you need to enable to Xinerama flag, then use Xdmx +xinerama.

- -ignorebadfontpaths—It's not uncommon to have default font paths in the X configuration when they don't actually exist. This flag tells Xdmx to ignore bad font paths.

- -configfile and -config—The virtual display does not need to be horizontal. You can also specify vertical alignment. The -configfile option identifies the configuration file, while the -config option allows you to choose which virtual display layout you would like. Listing 9-3 shows an example configuration file with different layouts.

Listing 9-3: A Sample Xdmx Configuration File (xdmx.conf)

```
# A basic horizontal (left to right) alignment. Use -config 12r
virtual 12r
  {
  display :0 @0x0;          # the top corner will be at 0x0
  display bravo:0 @1024x0;  # place it 1024 pixels to the right
  }

# A vertical alignment using a 1x2 grid. Use -config virtual_stack
virtual vertical_stack { wall 1x2 bravo:0 :0; }

# A huge 3x3 display. Use -config grid3x3.
virtual grid3x3
  {
  wall 3x3
  bravo:0 charlie:0 delta:0
  echo:0   :0        foxtrot:0
  golf:0  hotel:0   india:0;
  }

# Specify two displays with absolute position 200x200
# This will overlay the displays (good for projection systems)
virtual overlay { display alpha:0 @200x200; display :0 @0x0; }
```

The Xdmx command creates the X-Windows desktop, but does not start any window managers. This means that every display will have the plain X-Windows gray color. For a more usable desktop, you will need to start a window manager. Listing 9-4 is an example startup script that runs Xdmx and starts the Gnome window manager. You can extend this script to start specific applications like a terminal or graphical monitor.

Tip   To quickly shut down Xdmx, press Ctrl+Alt+Q. This will kill the Xdmx system and immediately close all windows.

Listing 9-4: Sample Startup Script for Xdmx with a Window Manager

```
#!/bin/sh
# Give permission to open an X application.
xhost +local:
unset XAUTHORITY

# Save the displays
export REALDISPLAY=$DISPLAY
export NEWDISPLAY=:1

# Start Xdmx (use -configfile or -display to specify the virtual
display)
Xdmx $NEWDISPLAY +xinerama -ignorebadfontpaths \
  -input $REALDISPLAY -configfile xdmx.conf -config l2r &
export DISPLAY=$NEWDISPLAY
sleep 2  # give it time to come up

# Select your window manager
# Gnome should not have a SESSION_MANAGER variable set.
unset SESSION_MANAGER
gnome-session --sm-disabled &
#startkde & # run KDE as the window manager
#twm &      # run TWM as the window manager
#xterm &    # run a plain terminal
```

Tip

If you always want to run the virtual display, then you can add the startup script to your $HOME/.xinitrc. This way, it will always start up after you log in to a graphical desktop.

The Xdmx command has two significant limitations. First, if the network goes down or one of the virtual desktop computers crashes, then the program will abruptly exit. If you lose one of the desktops, then you will lose all of them. Second, creating a virtual desktop between two very different hardware platforms (for example, PC and Mac) can result in screwed up colors—even if all of the platforms are running Ubuntu with true 24-bit color. For best results, stick with the same hardware platforms.

Using Two Computers with Different Desktops

In the corporate world, few Linux users work strictly with other Linux users. Usually you need to interact with a wide variety of Windows, Linux, and Unix users (and the rare OS/2 fanatic). I know plenty of people who run two computers, one Linux and one Windows, for full compatibility. The problem is, they spend a lot of time either transferring files or using shared hard drives. Taking output from a Linux program and pasting it into a Microsoft Outlook e-mail is definitely a multi-step solution. While Part II of this book (and Chapter 6 in particular) covered many of the ways to share information between different operating systems, there is another option.

Using a tool called Synergy, you can connect the desktops from completely different operating systems. Although you cannot drag applications off desktops, you can use one mouse and keyboard to navigate the linked desktops. And most importantly: you can share the clipboard. This way, you can copy text from a Linux application and paste it into a Windows program without a dozen steps.

Installing and configuring Synergy is much simpler than using Xdmx.

1. Install Synergy on each of the virtual desktop systems. Under Ubuntu, this is simply `sudo apt-get install synergy`. For other operating systems, you will need to visit `http://synergy2.sourceforge.net/`. They have precompiled binaries available for Windows (from Windows 95 to Windows XP and Windows ME), Linux, and Mac OS X. If you need other platforms, then you can download and compile the source code.

2. Synergy uses a central server as the primary system, and one or more clients for the shared desktops. The server is the system that has the mouse and keyboard, and this system uses a configuration file to manage the screen relationships. Unlike Xdmx, Synergy can handle non-rectangular relationships and loops where, for example, moving off the far left takes you to the far right.

   ▪ For an Ubuntu Synergy server (and Mac OS X server), the configuration file is a text file that contains hostnames and relationships. My configuration file (Listing 9-5) has three hosts: a Windows client named `willy`, a Mac OS X named `matt`, and an Ubuntu system named `udo`. The computers are arranged with the Windows box (`willy`) sitting above the Ubuntu system (`udo`), and the Mac (`matt`) is to the right of the Ubuntu system.

   ▪ For Windows systems, the Synergy server uses an application for specifying systems and relational positions (see Figure 9-7).

   Regardless of the server's platform, the configuration has three main components. First, all of the possible clients are listed. Second, the links between the displays are defined. Finally, any special options can be listed. The links form the most complicated part; they define what happens when the mouse goes off the edge of a screen. You can specify left, right, above, and below relationships. Only defined relationships exist——nothing is assumed.

Tip   Synergy links do not have to be symmetrical. For example, my system named `matt` may be located to the right of `udo`, but `udo` may not be left of `matt`. You can also create loops. For example, moving right from `udo` goes to `matt`, and continuing to the right can cycle back to `udo`.

Warning   Be sure to define both directions of a link. If I only define `matt` as being right of `udo` without specifying the return link (for example, `udo` is left of `matt`) then I will not be able to move the cursor back.

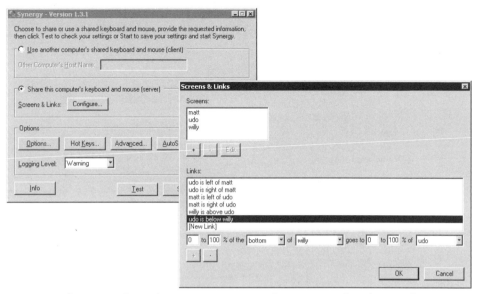

FIGURE 9-7: The Microsoft Windows Synergy server configuration window showing the same relationships as Listing 9-5

Listing 9-5: A Sample Synergy Configuration File (synergy.conf) with Three Systems

```
# The layout:
#     willy           -- is above udo
#       udo    matt   -- matt is right of udo

section: screens
  # List every known client by name, and any special mappings
  udo:
  matt:
    meta = super  # this is a Mac and uses the command/super key
  willy:
end

section: links
  # Define every link relationship.
  # It does not need to by symmetrical!
  udo:
    right = matt
    left = matt # make a horizontal loop
    up = willy
  matt:
```

Continued

Listing 9-5 *Continued*

```
    left = udo
    right = udo # make a horizontal loop
  willy:
    down = udo
end

section: options
  # Make all screensavers turn on at the same time
  screenSaverSync = true
end
```

---

3. Check your client configuration. Synergy supports pretty much any Windows, Mac OS X, Linux, and Unix system. For X-Windows systems, be sure to have the XTEST extension enabled. You can check this with `xdpyinfo | grep XTEST`. This should display the word XTEST. For Windows and Mac systems, no special configurations are needed.

4. Start the client. Each client requires two elements. First, it needs to know the host name of the server. Second, it needs a unique name that is listed in the server's configuration (in the `screens` section). By default, the name is the client's host name. However, you can specify an alternate client name.

   - Under Linux, Unix, and Mac OS X, the client is `synergyc`. The server's name is specified on the command line. You can also include an optional name for the client. Following the example above, I used this command to connect my Mac (`matt`) to my Ubuntu server (`udo`).

     ```
     synergyc --name matt udo
     ```

   - Under Windows, use the Synergy client to specify the server's name and optional client's name (see Figure 9-8).

5. Start the server. On Ubuntu, Mac OS X, and other Unix and Linux systems, the command is `synergys`. You specify the configuration file using:

   ```
   synergys --config synergy.conf
   ```

   On Windows systems, open the Synergy application, select Share this computer's keyboard and mouse (server) and click Start.

Tip

By default, `syngergys` and `synergyc` detach from the console and run in the background. To prevent the process from becoming a daemon, use `-f`. For example, `synergys -f --config synergy.conf`.

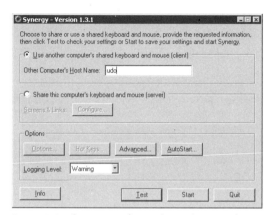

FIGURE 9-8: The Microsoft Windows client configuration for Synergy

Although the server and clients all need to be started, the order does not really matter. Clients regularly poll the server until a connection is achieved. As each system connects, the rules for the links are applied. Following the example, the cursor will be unable to move off the right side of udo until matt connects. When matt connects, the movement to the right will follow the established link.

Note Under Synergy, systems are either clients or a server. You do not need to run a server on the client.

When all of the clients connect to the server, you can start sharing desktops. Moving the mouse between windows allows you to set the focus for the keyboard. And most importantly: if you copy text from any desktop then you can paste it into application on any other desktop.

Tip With Xdmx, if any system disconnects for any reason, the entire Xdmx session aborts. In contrast, Synergy allows all clients to connect and disconnect without notice. If you have systems that crash or reboot often, Synergy is definitely a good productivity solution since you can continue working while one part of the desktop is down.

Dual heads, Xdmx, and Synergy are not independent solutions. You can actually run two displays on one computer (a dual head solution) *and* use Xdmx to link it to more displays *and* use Synergy to link in desktops from other operating systems. The only limitation to your virtual desktop size becomes your physical desktop. Just how many monitors can your desk hold?

Tip Consider installing a Synergy client in a virtual machine, such as Qemu (see Chapter 6). This enables you to cut and paste between the virtual computer and the real desktop. In many cases, this is much more convenient than transferring data across a network or through a shared partition.

Summary

Although the basic Ubuntu desktop is good for beginners, its flexibility enables you to change it from good for most things to excellent for your specific requirements. Whether you simply want a different screen resolution, display adjustment, or something more complicated, there are hacks for customizing the system to fit your needs. Using these tweaks, you can enable cool screen savers, animated backgrounds, and even massively large desktops that span multiple screens and operating systems.

Securing Your System

in this part

Chapter 10
Locking Down Ubuntu

Chapter 11
Advanced Networking

Chapter 12
Enabling Services

Locking Down Ubuntu

in this chapter

☑ Understanding Ubuntu security defaults

☑ Hacking with sudo

☑ Using Gnu Privacy Guard (GPG)

☑ Encrypting file systems

☑ Managing logs and caches

From a fresh install, Ubuntu Dapper Drake starts as a very secure operating system. Without applying any security patches, it poses few risks from external and remote attackers. However, maintaining security after the installation is *your* responsibility. There are a couple of tricks you can do to keep your files and data secure. These include using Sudo for root privileges, GPG to encode messages, enabling encrypted files systems, and even log file and cache management. Ubuntu is usually safe enough from the start, but with a few hacks, it can be made much safer.

Outside of the security field, many people view encryption and cache removal as a sign of guilt. The basic feeling is usually, "why are you covering your tracks if you have nothing to hide?" Just because you are encrypting data and cleaning temporary files does not mean you are doing anything illegal. Consider it like closing curtains on your bedroom window—it means you want privacy, not that you're doing anything wrong. Privacy is also preventative. If your laptop gets stolen, do you want the thief to see all your bank account information in your web cache? How about the source code from some big project you're working on? The same goes for your computer(s) at home. Thieves are just as likely to steal your desktop workstation, as they are your TV and stereo.

Locking down your system limits the amount of damage a bad guy can cause. Furthermore, many of these preventative steps require no additional work beyond installation and initial configuration.

Understanding Ubuntu Security Defaults

Ubuntu installs using a basic security model that consists of no network accessible services, and no root logins. These basic principles ensure that a clean install cannot lead to a remotely compromised host. If you need a network service, then you will need to explicitly install it (see Chapter 12). Even after installing the network services, it usually takes a couple of steps to fully enable it.

There are a few basic steps to maintaining a secure Ubuntu system:

- **Don't use root**—The default Ubuntu installation does not assign a root password and you cannot log in as root. Instead, the default user account can use Sudo (see the next section) to run commands as root. Additional user accounts cannot even run Sudo unless they are given explicit permission. Restricting root access limits your ability to accidentally (or intentionally) screw up the entire operating system.

- **Limit network services**—Only enable services that you need. If you don't need a mail server, then don't install one. If you do not host web pages, then don't install a web server. Attackers can only exploit network services that are running on your system.

- **Use trusted software sources**—Chapter 4 describes how to modify /etc/apt/sources.list in order to change the supported repository list. The default repositories come from a trusted location: the four official Ubuntu repositories. However, there are literally hundreds of unofficial repositories. Installing software from an unknown and untrusted repository could result in the installation of hostile software. Don't change the default repository settings or install software from untrusted providers unless you know what you are doing. Remember: just because *they* say it is safe does not mean it really is safe.

- **Limit scripts**—web browsers, chat room software, and other programs can transfer potentially hostile software from the network, download files, and run programs. If you don't need this functionality, then disable it. For example, if you don't need Java or JavaScript in your web browser, then disable it (see Chapter 5).

- **Use strong passwords**—If you are the only person with physical access to your computer and you do not allow remote network access, then you can probably get away with having *abcd* or your pet's name as your password. (One of my home computers is usually logged in and the screen saver does not demand a password—this is as effective as having no password.) However, if you are in a corporate environment with many users, or enable remote access, or are at home with young kids (or cats) who like to press the delete button, then consider a strong password. Remote access and physical access attacks can use brute force approaches that include:

  - **Dictionary words**—If your password is found in a dictionary (English, French, Chinese, and so on) then it can be easily guessed.

  - **Words with numbers**—Simple word-number combinations, like *apple12* or *288cereal* can be easily guessed. The same goes for punctuation (*hello!* and *?what?*).

  - **Keyboard patterns**—Sequences like *asdfghjk* (adjacent keys on the keyboard) are very easy to guess.

  - **Common data**—License plates, dates (birthday, anniversary, and so on), kids names, and other types of public information are very easy to guess.

- Programs like John the Ripper (sudo apt-get install john) are designed to crack passwords through dictionary attacks and common password patterns like the ones listed above. In my experience, John can crack about 20 percent of user-chosen passwords in the first few minutes, and up to 80 percent in a few hours. The best passwords will not be based on dictionary words or simple patterns, and will be memorable. Good passwords should make sense to only you and not anyone else.

Tip

If you are an administrator with lots of users on your system, consider using John the Ripper to look for weak passwords. It is much safer if you find the weak ones and ask the users to proactively change their passwords than wait for a hostile user to find them and exploit the accounts.

- **Don't compromise your security**. Telling people "I have a really cool password—it's my student ID number from high school and nobody will guess that!" is a huge hint to an attacker. Don't hint at your password, don't e-mail it, and don't tell it to anyone in public. If you think that somebody might have a clue about your password, then change it immediately. Remember: the only person inconvenienced by a password change will be you. Beyond passwords, don't give accounts with Sudo access to anyone, don't install software from strangers, and don't run with scissors. Your security is as strong as its weakest link, and that is often the user.

Warning

Don't use your Ubuntu system's password anywhere else. Many people use the same password for their Yahoo!, Gmail, and eBay accounts as well as other online services. If you use your password everywhere, then one compromised site will compromise all of your accounts. Most people underestimate the blackhat hacker's ability to find your other accounts. I'm a good guy (whitehat) and I spend a lot of time tracking people online—believe me, finding your other accounts is easy.

Secure by Default

The default Ubuntu server and desktop installations do not include any remote network services. This way, a clean install can be patched and prepared without the risk of an external attacker compromising the system. You can place a clean install of Dapper Drake on the Internet without a firewall and not risk any remote compromises. (You cannot compromise a network service when no network services exist.)

After the installation, you can update the system (`sudo apt-get update ; sudo apt-get upgrade`) and begin adding in services and user accounts. This minimizes the risk from remote exploitation.

The basic idea of "no default network services" is a concept that could benefit other operating systems. For example, Microsoft Windows, HP-UX, and RedHat Fedora Linux all enable some basic network services during the installation. This can lead to big problems. For example, if you work for a large company that has a few infected Windows systems, then installing a new Windows system on the network could face a problem: the new system may be infected over the open network services before the first security patch is applied.

Hacking with Sudo

Throughout this book we have used the sudo command for running commands as root. Sudo allows you to run a command with root privileges. The default installation of Ubuntu includes the Sudo command (sudo) and gives the default user account access to this command. If you need something to run as root, you can use sudo. A related command, sudoedit, allows you to edit a file as root. For example, to edit the root-only file /var/spool/anacron/cron.daily, you can use wither of the following commands:

```
sudo vi /var/spool/anacron/cron.daily
sudoedit /var/spool/anacron/cron.daily
```

Tip   The sudoedit command uses the editor defined in the $EDITOR environment variable. If this editor is not defined, the nano editor is used. See "Tuning the Shell" in Chapter 2 for setting the $EDITOR variable.

Sudo Coup

When Unix was young (circa 1970), administrators needed a way to change between user access privileges. This was accomplished with the su command. Although originally designed to **s**witch **u**ser access, it was mainly used to change privileges from a regular user to root. (The su command is sometimes called the **s**uper-**u**ser command for this reason.)

There are a couple of huge risks with using su to run commands as root. Most notably, all commands are executed with root privileges. Many times, only one command within a long list of commands really needs root access. Also, when a terminal is logged in as root, users may forget which user they are running as. Accidentally deleting files from a directory as root can be much more devastating than doing so as a regular user.

Sudo was created to limit the commands that can run as root. Rather than changing all privileges, only the privileges for a specific command are changed. Furthermore, Sudo can even limit which commands can be run as root. When the command completes, you are back to your regular user access. This way, only the required steps run as root, and you won't accidentally leave a terminal logged in a root.

Although very old Unix systems still rely on su to change access levels, it is being forcefully replaced by sudo. Furthermore, in most BSD and Linux distributions (including Ubuntu), Sudo has become standard for using root privileges. Although the su command is included with the Ubuntu installation, you cannot use it to run commands as root unless you first set a root password using sudo passwd root.

Adding Users to Sudo

The configuration file for `sudo` is `/etc/suders`. This lists who can run commands as root, which commands they can run, and any configuration preferences. Listing 10-1 shows the default `/etc/sudoers` file. Although this file can be edited using `sudo vi /etc/sudoers` or `sudoedit /etc/sudoers`, this is not recommended. Instead, the command `sudo visudo` (short for `vi sudo`) is the preferred approach. The `visudo` command ensures that only one person edits the file at a time. It also checks for syntax errors before installing the new file. (The last thing you need is to corrupt `/etc/sudoers` and lose the ability to run `sudo` for fixing the problem.)

The default `/etc/sudoers` file gives access to everyone who is part of the `admin` group. Non-`admin` users are blocked from running commands as root. If you want to add someone to the `admin` group, use:

1. Use the `vigr` command to edit the `/etc/groups` file.

```
sudo vigr
```

2. The `/etc/groups` file lists each group name, group ID number, and a comma-separated list of users. Search for the line that begins with admin. It should list one account name (your default Ubuntu account). For example, my default account name is *neal* and the line says:

```
admin:x:112:neal
```

3. Add the new user name to this line. Use a comma to separate usernames. For example, if I want to add the user *marc* to this line, I would have:

```
admin:x:112:neal,marc
```

4. Save your changes and quit the editor.

Note Changes to `/etc/groups` do not propagate to running applications. If the user is currently logged in, he or she will need to log out before noticing the group changes.

If you want to give a user Sudo access without adding them to a group, then you can add them as a privileged user.

1. Edit the `/etc/suderers` file using `sudo visudo`.

2. Look for the line that says `root     ALL=(ALL)  ALL`.

3. Create a similar line with the user's account name. For example, if I want to give the account "marc" access, I will use:

```
root    ALL=(ALL) ALL
marc    ALL=(ALL) ALL
```

This addition says that the users "root" and "marc" can use `sudo` and can run any command with root privileges.

4. Save your changes and exit the `visudo` command.

Listing 10-1: The Default /etc/sudoers File

```
# /etc/sudoers
#
# This file MUST be edited with the 'visudo' command as root.
#
# See the man page for details on how to write a sudoers file.
# Host alias specification

# User alias specification

# Cmnd alias specification

# Defaults

Defaults            !lecture,tty_tickets,!fqdn

# User privilege specification
root    ALL=(ALL) ALL

# Members of the admin group may gain root privileges
%admin ALL=(ALL) ALL
```

Tweaking other Sudo Options

The default sudo command has three options enabled: !lecture, tty_tickets, and !fqdn. These options are flags—the ! in front of any flag disables the option. Other options can be added that include values. All the options belong on the Defaults line in the /etc/suders file (use sudo visudo to edit this file). Some command options that you might want to tweak include:

- lecture—When this flag is enabled, the sudo command will display a warning about running commands as root. This can be useful if there are lots of administrators on a system. However, people usually ignore the warning. The default installation disables the lecture message: !lecture.

- timestamp_timeout—This option lists the number of minutes before sudo requires you to re-enter your password. If you are running many sudo commands in a row, then it can become very inconvenient to re-enter your password after every command. The default configuration is 15 minutes (timestamp_timeout=15)—if your last sudo command was executed more than 15 minutes ago, then you will need to re-enter your password to run sudo. Setting the value to zero will always prompt for a password; setting the value to a negative number disables the timeout. If you are in a very sensitive environment, then you may want to lower this value (or set it to zero).

- tty_tickets—If you have lots of windows open, then you will notice that you need to enter your password the first time you run sudo in any window. This is due to the tty_tickets flag—every terminal (tty) has its own sudo environment. If you disable this flag (!tty_tickets), then entering your password for sudo in one window will stop the sudo password prompts in all other windows.

- fqdn—When host names are used in the sudoers file, this flag specifies the use of fully qualified domain names (fqdns).

- passwd_tries—This sets how many password attempts the user gets before sudo fails. The default is passwd_tries=3.

- insults—This is a fun flag. If the user enters in a bad password, then sudo will generate a random message. (The default is !insults.) For example:

```
$ sudo id
Password: [wrong]
Just what do you think you're doing Dave?
Password: [wrong]
It can only be attributed to human error.
Password: [wrong]
My pet ferret can type better than you!
sudo: 3 incorrect password attempts
```

Tip

There are many other advanced configuration options including logging and user-based restrictions. If you have specific needs, look at the manual for sudoers (man sudoers).

Becoming Root

Although the Ubuntu security model has all administrative commands issued through sudo, there are some times when you really would be better off with a command prompt as root. Fortunately, there are many ways to accomplish this with sudo. A few examples:

```
sudo -s            # run a shell as root
sudo bash -o vi    # run a specific shell as root
sudo -i            # set root's initial login environment
sudo su - root     # become root and run root's login environment
```

In the first two cases, the shell runs as root, but environment variables (for example, $HOME) are inherited. In the other two cases, the environment is replaced with root's real environment settings.

If you *really* need to be able to login as root, then you can use sudo passwd root to give the root account a password. As soon as you set the password, the root account can log in. You can always undo this change with sudo passwd -l root to lock the account.

Warning

Enabling root logins is usually a bad idea. Logins give a trail of accountability. If someone logs in without a personalized account, then there is no way to identify the person who really logged in. sudo gives an audit trail in /var/log/auth.log (even though users with sudo access have the ability to blow away the logs).

Using Gnu Privacy Guard (GPG)

Security and encryption are frequently used in the same sentence. If you want to keep something private, use cryptography. In 1991, Phil Zimmerman made public a cryptographic system called *Pretty Good Privacy* (PGP). This became the basis of his company, PGP, Inc. The PGP system was rewritten and licensed under the Gnu Public License (GPL). This new system, the Gnu Privacy Guard (GnuPG or GPG), has become a de facto standard for file and e-mail encryption among Linux and Unix systems. As such, it is included during the default Ubuntu installation.

Tip Many people use the names GPG and PGP interchangeably. Both systems use the same encryption method and the tools have similar use models. A file encrypted with PGP can be decrypted with GPG. The most significant differences are licensing and availability; GPG is open source, GPL, and more widely used.

GPG is included with every Ubuntu installation, even a minimal install. GPG enables you to create public and private keys, securely exchange keys, and encrypt and decrypt messages. Many e-mail programs either natively integrate with PGP (and GPG) or have plug-ins available. For example, Dapper Evolution mailer natively supports GPG. The `mutt` text-based mailer also supports PGP, and even Microsoft Outlook users can get a plug-in for PGP encryption.

There are many parts to using GPG:

- Key generation
- Searching keys
- Exchanging keys
- Defining trust for keys
- File encryption and decryption
- Cryptographic signatures
- E-mail integration

Creating Keys

GPG uses asymmetrical key cryptography. This means that one key is used to encrypt the data, and a different key is required to decrypt the data. The two keys are called *private* and *public*. Basically, the private key is never passed out (it is kept private), while anyone and his dog can have a copy of the public key. Messages that are encrypted with the private key can only be decrypted with the public key.

Creating keys under GPG is pretty painless: `gpg --gen-key`. This provides a series of text prompts for creating a private-public key pair (see Listing 10-2). All users have their own set of keys (called a *key ring*) that are stored in `$HOME/.gnupg/`. The main key rings are `$HOME/.gnupg/pubring.gpg` and `secring.gpg`. The former stores public keys, whereas the latter stores private keys.

Although giving out your public keys is expected, your private keys should be kept as secret as possible. During the generation of your key pair, GPG prompts you for a password. Although this password is not used during the cryptography (only the keys are used for that), it *is* used to encrypt your private keys while they are on the hard drive. This deters some other user on the system from stealing your private keys and using them to access your encoded data (or impersonating you—see the section on Signing Data).

Tip Passwords are not required. Many automated tools use GPG, so it can be very desirable to not use a password at all. If you leave the password blank (just hit enter when generating the key), then you will never be prompted for a password.

Listing 10-2: Generating GPG Public and Private Keys

```
$ gpg --gen-key
gpg (GnuPG) 1.4.2.2; Copyright (C) 2005 Free Software Foundation, Inc.
This program comes with ABSOLUTELY NO WARRANTY.
This is free software, and you are welcome to redistribute it
under certain conditions. See the file COPYING for details.

Please select what kind of key you want:
   (1) DSA and Elgamal (default)
   (2) DSA (sign only)
   (5) RSA (sign only)
Your selection? 1
DSA keypair will have 1024 bits.
ELG-E keys may be between 1024 and 4096 bits long.
What keysize do you want? (2048) 2048
Requested keysize is 2048 bits
Please specify how long the key should be valid.
        0 = key does not expire
      <n>  = key expires in n days
      <n>w = key expires in n weeks
      <n>m = key expires in n months
      <n>y = key expires in n years
Key is valid for? (0) 2y
Key expires at Mon 10 Nov 2008 10:56:00 AM MST
Is this correct? (y/N) y

You need a user ID to identify your key; the software constructs the user ID
from the Real Name, Comment and Email Address in this form:
    "Heinrich Heine (Der Dichter) <heinrichh@duesseldorf.de>"

Real name: John Travolta
Email address: travolta@discomania.tv
Comment:
You selected this USER-ID:
    "John Travolta <travolta@discomania.tv>"
```

Continued

Listing 10-2 *Continued*

```
Change (N)ame, (C)omment, (E)mail or (O)kay/(Q)uit? O
You need a Passphrase to protect your secret key.
Enter passphrase: *******
Repeat passphrase: *******

We need to generate a lot of random bytes. It is a good idea to perform
some other action (type on the keyboard, move the mouse, utilize the
disks) during the prime generation; this gives the random number
generator a better chance to gain enough entropy.
.+++++++++..+++++++++..+++++.++++++++++++++++++++++++++++++||||||||++++++.+++++++
+++.+++++++++++++++++++++++++++++++++++++++++++.++++++++++.++++++++++..>
+++++..................................+++++
public and secret key created and signed.

gpg: checking the trustdb
gpg: 3 marginal(s) needed, 1 complete(s) needed, PGP trust model
gpg: depth: 0  valid:   1  signed:   0  trust: 0-, 0q, 0n, 0m, 0f, 1u
gpg: next trustdb check due at 2008-11-10
pub   1024D/EB66D0E2 2006-11-11 [expires: 2008-11-10]
      Key fingerprint = 6D01 42F6 C58E CC52 6B32  CEC7 475E 92D3 EB66 D0E2
uid                   John Travolta <travolta@discomania.tv>
sub   2048g/50AFB0BA 2006-11-11 [expires: 2008-11-10]
```

Can You Repeat That?

Private keys are supposed to be unique, and GPG uses some of the strongest cryptographic algorithms available. If you lose your password, delete your private key, or corrupt your key ring without a backup available, then you are screwed. You will not be able to recover the data.

Similarly, don't delete private keys unless you are positive that you will never need them ever again. Since they are unique, there is no going back after you make this decision. My key ring contains many old and expired keys because they are needed to decode some old messages and verify signatures.

When sending GPG-encoded e-mails, be sure to send a copy to yourself. Otherwise, you won't be able to decode your sent mail. Simply saving a copy of the sent message is not enough since your key is not added to the encryption. I occasionally receive e-mails where the sender asks me to send them back the e-mail so they can have a copy of their own text.

Searching Keys

After you create the keys, you can view them using the `--list-keys` option. The `gpg --list-keys` command will list every public key in your key ring. You can also specify filter words for searching the key ring. For example, `gpg --list-keys EB66D0E2` returns the key matching this unique identifier. You can also specify words, like `gpg --list-keys disco` to list every key where the string *disco* appears in the person's name or e-mail address.

Tip Since keys contain e-mail addresses, I use `gpg --list-keys` as a cheap Rolodex. For example, if I need to remember Marc See's e-mail address, then I use `gpg --list-keys marc` and his entry (Marcus T. See <msee@test.lan>) comes right up.

Other search options include `gpg --list-secret-keys` and `gpg --fingerprint`. The former lists all of your private keys and the latter shows key-unique hashes that can be used to validate keys. Since anyone can create any key with anyone's name and e-mail address, the unique fingerprint allows you to make sure the key is from the right person (see Transferring Keys).

Note You can delete keys using `--delete-key` and `--delete-secret-key`. However, you probably will never need to delete keys, and deleting a secret key is irreversible unless you have a backup.

Search for keys based on name, e-mail address, or unique ID is used by most of the GPG operations. For example, when encrypting a message you will be asked to provide a list of keys for encrypting the message. These can be found by searching names, e-mail addresses, or IDs.

Tip You can specify multiple search terms on the `gpg` command line. These terms form a logical OR—any key that matches any of the terms will be displayed.

Transferring Keys

After you create your keys, you will need to pass around your public key. Only people with your public key can encrypt messages to you. To do this, you will need to export the public key from your key ring. The command `gpg --export -a` will export *all* of your private keys. You can use the search strings to narrow down the keys being exported. For example, `gpg --export -a travolta` will export my public key for John Travolta. The result from this command is an ASCII-encoded text block that can be e-mailed or passed to other people. The block should look similar to this one:

```
-----BEGIN PGP PUBLIC KEY BLOCK-----
Version: GnuPG v1.4.2.2 (GNU/Linux)

mQGiBEVWXVkRBAC3TPV0zQC85SlEXJtcMiphzUzbqG76fRhAAYwcL5NfnoObKRD7
```

```
uEJMb4mphXSz5zMTBxKehPiLTGUm9CDjKyVCGkAahOGAXeGdrcYyL17As8ZZNc7f
64ehXB+VSVQiRTkAdqVMje/qqT8x7vyCkfAoNZxs4zOPF0xt434AD/2rOwCgtcrp
ryIimx0b/a2QPHjGhxJ0AY0D/2MlwvQUakMOZJNRyqkhTN0FHx1toLaNI/I8l+v4
E4FTPpyf343n1anAyf44iMzU2/k4ErDMaBuSgWfiDsxFvDuMVS+tN0S86iYLswGX
DVKxhMWJ7HRBSiHJhEpdvUlnYM4wxdAoORL6p1tpHRMod6MakHInxYmJelH55bxo
G/1rA/4+n3rmnnf0wC4O0LHT9uIsLyRMVDGVFfeSKy3YNOn28KV42ZUFXQguytAZ
31yo+kyYvrjqfjBskGrIg5aEUJqwJjrXirjtHf6K6l0W3LgxllwFmAxSOLEfMEvR
T+wbpCmvf+QUvRITNPLxTZH1Z2UNjIZHZjDvHm1ZH94xqViTZrQmSm9obiBUcmF2
b2x0YSA8dHJhdm9sdGFAZGlzY29tYW5pYS50dj6IZgQTEQIAJgUCRVZdWQIbAwUJ
A8JnAAYLCQgHAwIEFQIIAwQWAgMBAh4BAheAAAoJEEdektPrZtDiRFsAnj+hHR7z
BwNqiDN1/nwbNLtotrU6AJ9lRv2/i5ExejDDNEcDe+YH7FjHvbkCDQRFVl1fEAgA
pOel0yQROIyA7Bceky8ZVacEbozbcuHWT/hicNvh8LXtTdBrWXLvTeWZVSvzgACs
Kei5yppb7St0i0W/PtkjnfrbBxIMZZG4LeuavAB6eAYqPi+lr1TYnGFbD4wOtrxu
0Q1nrm4O3xAYmAYwzf+87TsONFyh3OSA9x6ZDT73l1rE5J6HawtBzNZ9bbAJj6Tf9
Y6Yduyi2k/n9VmG5RRHbyn268+tsFs+U2wo/5U8WzJ0X5K/7JleAdyC/1SLDRJfZ
zxa0njgg7ccrnNSntPZxu7BCdTmSSd+mVEbtZqtqdU7+5A2kY1edj5PXR6kU9mnd
e4uBeWTvtnCHE9/LNI1CnwADBwf8CWucwS3EMxh5BAoBcDvsn6D1PZv4AJ4nhsxQ
1s5G23eEDuIGcP0yODz8PI2ETnU6bopJGS8ryLLG7y+rnLamRMxYqx61+j5q5cCE
HxutP5ZnqmZeTbb7hE4/RSctmLUgoRDwEHjWfRnkhqMfQYW1tY1KltFI2pg08sA7
i38ggrREQ+oQScJaibvNUNC3NlfZHhhulyl648zW3KMTPIrNkHYqkIX35GCI5iT3
pIZYA7L1tw6jN1F2aG6Zbt/wWL/D9+0Q7F/zRLnbZ5sG08quJ7AUB005Gjs5MunT
YpaW4bSGJeKE+F7NB1gM9OHFpaJNF8an+S3qqu8K60cejfiziohPBBgRAgAPBQJF
Vl1fAhsMBQkDwmcAAAoJEEdektPrZtDiNecAnAu1qZeNexAZCPb3C37pRSRyZb/C
AJ4lM3ZXyeabTebxnl/ebpM/IoJiZQ==
=SQwU
-----END PGP PUBLIC KEY BLOCK-----
```

When you receive a message like this, you can import it using `gpg --import`. For example:

```
gpg --export -a travolta > travolta.pub  # export public key
gpg --import travolta.pub                 # import public key
gpg --import < travolta.pub               # inline import public key
```

The `import` command looks for the BEGIN and END markers, so you don't even need to separate it from the rest of the file before doing the import. For example, if you have a bunch of keys in an e-mail file (for example, `e-mail.mbox`), then you can import all of them using:

```
gpg --import e-mail.mbox
```

Defining Trust

GPG has a well-defined notion of trust. Although a new key that you import can be used to decode a message, you shouldn't communicate with keys you do not trust. Using the `gpg` command, you can set an explicit trust level for a key. The basic levels are:

- **Undefined**—You can use the key to decode messages, but probably shouldn't use it for encryption.

- **Do not trust**—This key is a known forgery or is otherwise evil.

- **Marginal trust**—The key is probably authentic.

- **Fully trust**—You know the key is valid. Most likely, you were given a hash fingerprint and have compared it using `gpg --fingerprint` and you know it is correct.

- **Ultimately trust**—This usually means it is your own key.

Listing 10-3 shows an example for setting the trust level on the example Travolta key.

> **Note** Few programs that use GPG actually use the trust level. The main one that I have found is Evolution. If a public key is not explicitly trusted, then you cannot send an encrypted e-mail to that user.

Listing 10-3: Setting the Trust Level

```
$ gpg --edit-key travolta trust
gpg (GnuPG) 1.4.2.2; Copyright (C) 2005 Free Software Foundation, Inc.
This program comes with ABSOLUTELY NO WARRANTY.
This is free software, and you are welcome to redistribute it
under certain conditions. See the file COPYING for details.

Secret key is available.

gpg: checking the trustdb
gpg: 3 marginal(s) needed, 1 complete(s) needed, PGP trust model
gpg: depth: 0  valid:   1  signed:   0  trust: 0-, 0q, 0n, 0m, 0f, 1u
gpg: next trustdb check due at 2008-11-10
pub  1024D/EB66D0E2  created: 2006-11-11  expires: 2008-11-10  usage: CS
                     trust: undefined      validity: unknown
sub  2048g/50AFB0BA  created: 2006-11-11  expires: 2008-11-10  usage: E
[ unknown] (1). John Travolta <travolta@discomania.tv>

pub  1024D/EB66D0E2  created: 2006-11-11  expires: 2008-11-10  usage: CS
                     trust: undefined      validity: unknown
sub  2048g/50AFB0BA  created: 2006-11-11  expires: 2008-11-10  usage: E
[ unknown] (1). John Travolta <travolta@discomania.tv>

Please decide how far you trust this user to correctly verify other users' keys
(by looking at passports, checking fingerprints from different sources, etc.)

  1 = I don't know or won't say
  2 = I do NOT trust
  3 = I trust marginally
  4 = I trust fully
  5 = I trust ultimately
  m = back to the main menu
```

Continued

Listing 10-3 *Continued*

```
Your decision? 4

pub  1024D/EB66D0E2  created: 2006-11-11  expires: 2008-11-10  usage: CS
                     trust: full          validity: unknown
sub  2048g/50AFB0BA  created: 2006-11-11  expires: 2008-11-10  usage: E
[ unknown] (1). John Travolta <travolta@discomania.tv>
Please note that the shown key validity is not necessarily correct
unless you restart the program.

Command> q
```

Encrypting Files

GPG has two ways to encrypt files. The first way, `gpg -e file`, will prompt you to select all of the public keys that should be use to encrypt the data. If you select three public keys, then any of those three people (with the private keys) can decrypt the data. The output from this command is a binary file with the `.gpg` extension. If you use `file`, then the output becomes `file.gpg`, and if you use cow.txt, then the output is `cow.txt.gpg`. Because this is a binary file, the contents will look like random gibberish. When you transfer the file, be sure to use a system that can transfer binary files—pasting `file.gpg` into an e-mail will likely corrupt the data.

Warning

If you have a file encrypted with GPG and you lose the keys, then the file will be unreadable.

A second encryption method uses ASCII armoring. In this approach, the binary data is encoded into text characters. The content is wrapped with BEGIN and END labels and is ready for e-mailing. Using `gpg -e -a file` or `gpg -e --armor file` will create `file.asc`, containing the ASCII armored encrypted message. An armored message should look like a random jumble of characters within the BEGIN and END labels:

```
-----BEGIN PGP MESSAGE-----
Version: GnuPG v1.4.2.2 (GNU/Linux)

hQIOA3OCbECpKQX7EAf/b0G1/zBQjyWPPywwZmqFEiZdnTH9r+6Q1hAhMfIvh22S
b21nyAQReRFE05NUdAIj3eE4nYOpILIXqvun3HfRph9dNpAvRTWrUHeJYoJCfhau
Ut/JFo6JexikBr2pT1zOXAyrCdohxAKAG1TW+r1p2o/2MFykPJeScD02cXR4UggK
NLQQwV5zKkHUJ9ZgJSirCNveU5zWtE/PUWRLStZNcpmEuVdhrZfmDv5781u63BvW
A5IAjF971QphbKMYLVg0qsIV8FJwiztxkNo4Env2bZ9A0No8DvlPTzLedJBINHvq
Znfk0rxeBN+8PRpwJA3qu3K7OYUq4IDCghaAAl0+egf/Tp1vUJPfk8iXDpnFoLyc
```

```
RIF1cytqa5hk41sh2mt9Fbby11FLAg0NLfoxnnyEKpb5qzx//9RwBl4KzP9aD411
ekQfkoKldau8+pc/PCM2cj0KNhG7I28wQkcPZQ7kkrX5f6S4QnnnMjKmyn3qUzQ7
9m8mFZXR9I/T7cG0SFiQg7CbzWdcZc8WLmUAwOcakouV16jdFkxx8WxvlyqsNWNa
TK/jw0Y7jlrvvX60rL9I5xwPYXjhuYDEYMrahRsYFMzSxlXWsxP5GZfw/RXvFRzp
GTc/pbYDh0AyfP81tbagRt/fyOwISrlXvs3VnNIIrS6ZyH9p01/7SQ+VnuPyd6cc
0tJQAae9GyP09mF3SfWQL6sCiy0wclEaxPBZ9FxnauCjvgF94w3xJ+1uiiOPk+eS
Xup6VZoDIcC0TqKJExTbmDg1gHAKVbBEWf+4YPLxyjosw6E=
=qzqu
-----END PGP MESSAGE-----
```

Warning

Don't modify anything between the BEGIN and END markers or you will corrupt the data.

Decoding a GPG message is a snap. The -d parameter means *decode* and the command line specifies the file to decrypt. The decoded contents are sent to standard-out.

```
gpg -d file.gpg > file  # decoding a binary GPG file
gpg -d file.asc > file  # decoding an ASCII armored GPG file
```

During the decryption, you will be asked to provide your private key's password.

Signing Data

Usually public keys are used to encrypt data, so only the private key can decrypt the file. This way, anyone can encrypt a message and only you can decrypt it. However, GPG does allow you to reverse the process. GPG can be used to sign messages using the private key—anyone with the public key can validate the cryptographic signature. This allows recipients to know that the data has not been tampered and that it is authentic. To sign a file, use:

```
gpg -s file        # creates a signed binary file.gpg
gpg -a -s file     # creates a signed ASCII armored file.asc
gpg -e -a -s file  # creates a signed and encrypted ASCII armored file.asc
```

When signing a file, you will be asked to provide your private key's password. During the decoding process (gpg -d), the signature will be tested and validated.

Tip

Even if you don't have a copy of the public key, you can still view the signed contents using gpg -d. However, you will not be able to authenticate the signature without the public key, and if the file is encrypted then you will not even be able to view the contents.

Although signing data may sound like a neat idea, it serves a critical purpose. In some jurisdictions, a digital signature is legal and binding. If you are sending contracts or making business agreements, consider using GPG to digitally sign a document. Doing this will prevent forgeries and is much more secure than faxing your signature on a piece of paper. (Be sure to first check with your legal council to make sure a digital signature is binding.)

Integrating with e-mail

PGP and GPG are most commonly used for encrypted e-mail. The Ubuntu mail program, Evolution, natively supports GPG (although it calls it PGP). When composing an e-mail, select the PGP options from the Security menu (see Figure 10-1).

FIGURE 10-1: Enabling PGP encryption and digital signatures

Evolution has one big limitation when using PGP: you will only be able to send encrypted e-mail when the trust level is defined on the public key. If the trust for a key is not defined, or a public key is unavailable for the recipient, then you will be unable to send an encrypted e-mail. (See the section on "Defining Trust" earlier in this chapter.) This can become a big problem if the key is associated with one e-mail address, but the user has a couple of different e-mail addresses.

Evolution is not the only e-mail program that supports PGP. I frequently use mutt (see Figure 10-2). This is a text-only mail program (sudo apt-get install mutt). This program enables me to easily send my public key to other people (by pressing Esc, then k) and I can enable encryption or signing by pressing p. Unlike Evolution, if mutt cannot find the appropriate keys, then it allows me to search for alternate keys. However, mutt is not a graphical application—HTML contents and images cannot be viewed using this tool.

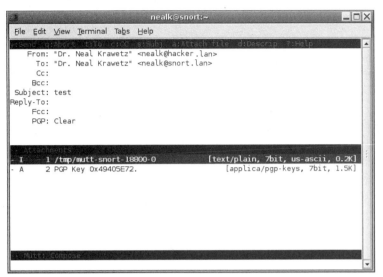

Figure 10-2: Sending an e-mail with using mutt. In this example, a public key is being forwarded as an attachment

PGP does have one large limitation when used with e-mail: different e-mail programs may be incompatibility. A PGP e-mail sent with Microsoft Outlook may not be immediately readable with `mutt` or Evolution. This is because different mailers use different mail headers to identify an encrypted message. With `mutt`, you can usually resolve incompatible formats by pressing Ctrl+E and changing the `Content-Type` to `application/pgp`. In contrast, with Evolution you will need to save the e-mail to a file and decrypt it by hand.

Encrypting File Systems

Why encrypt individual files, when you can encrypt entire file systems? Although Ubuntu does not provide any built-in cryptographic systems for this, you can install EncFS, the Encrypted File System. Using EncFS, you can encrypt directories and files. The decrypted file systems only exist as long as the encrypted system is mounted.

Installing and Configuring EncFS

EncFS is not an independent file system. Instead, it is a file system plug-in that encrypts and decrypts files on the fly. It uses the existing file system for storing data, but all data is encrypted on a file-by-file basis. File names are also cloaked to ensure that the encrypted directory has limited usefulness to someone without the password.

1. Install EncFS. This will also install the FUSE (Filesystem in Userspace) utilities.

```
sudo apt-get install encfs
```

2. Make sure the command `fusermount` can run as root.

```
sudo chmod u+s /usr/bin/fusermount
```

3. Each user who will need to use EncFS must be added to the fuse group. Use `sudo vigr` to add users to this group. Find the line that starts with `fuse` and add user names to the end of the line.

4. Changes to `/etc/groups` do not impact current logins. Make sure the user is in the group fuse by running the command `groups`. If the group fuse is not listed, then the user must log out and log back in for the change to take effect.

5. Make sure the FUSE kernel module is loaded. You may also want to add fuse to `/etc/modules` so it is always loaded after a reboot.

```
sudo modprobe fuse
```

6. Using the `encfs` command, create the encryption and decryption directories. For example, I use `encrypt/` and `decrypt/`. If the directories do not exist, then you will be prompted to create them. You will also be prompted for a password.

Note   The `encfs` command tries to run in the background. To do this, you must use absolute paths. If you specify a relative path, then you will need to use the `-f` option and it will not run in the background.

```
$ encfs `pwd`/encrypt `pwd`/decrypt
The directory "/.../encrypt/" does not exist. Should it be created? (y,n) y
The directory "/.../decrypt" does not exist. Should it be created? (y,n) y
Creating new encrypted volume.
Please choose from one of the following options:
 enter "x" for expert configuration mode,
 enter "p" for pre-configured paranoia mode,
 anything else, or an empty line will select standard mode.
?> [enter]

Standard configuration selected.

Configuration finished.  The filesystem to be created has
the following properties:
Filesystem cipher: "ssl/blowfish", version 2:1:1
Filename encoding: "nameio/block", version 3:0:1
Key Size: 160 bits
Block Size: 512 bytes
Each file contains 8 byte header with unique IV data.
Filenames encoded using IV chaining mode.

Now you will need to enter a password for your filesystem.
You will need to remember this password, as there is absolutely
no recovery mechanism.  However, the password can be changed
```

```
later using encfsctl.

New Encfs Password: [password]
Verify Encfs Password: [password]
```

Warning Do not forget your password! There is no way to recover a lost password.

Now you have two directories: `decrypt/` contains the decoded file system, and `encrypt/` contains the real encrypted files. If you copy files into the `decrypt/` directory, then you will see encrypted counterparts in the `encrypt/` directory.

Note An attacker who views the `encrypt/` directory can see the number of files, owner's name, permissions, and timestamps. He can also see the approximate file sizes. However, he cannot see the actual file names or file contents.

Maintaining EncFS

When you are all done with the decrypted directory, you un-mount it using `fusermount -u decrypt`. Although the encrypted files still exist in the `encrypt/` directory, the `decrypt/` directory will appear empty (because it is not mounted). Later, when you need to access the encrypted files, you can use: `encfs` `pwd`/encrypt `pwd`/decrypt. This will only ask you for your password. The files will only appear in the decrypted/ directory if you enter the correct password.

If you ever need to change the password, you can use the `encfsctl passwd encrypt/` command. This will prompt you for your old and new passwords.

Note You do not need to un-mount the directory in order to change the password. The password is only used during the initial file mounting. However, if you change the password, then you will need the new password in order to re-mount the encrypted files.

Using EncFS

EncFS is great for storing files if you are worried about someone stealing the media or accessing the stored data. Here are some sample situations where you might want to use EncFS:

- **Encrypt an entire directory**—If you have a directory that you don't want people to access, then you can encrypt it. For example, I have a source code repository containing sensitive information. The actual files are stored using EncFS. If you are worried about your web cache, consider encrypting `$HOME/.mozilla/`.

- **Encrypt your home directory for more privacy**—Using EncFS, you can encrypt your entire home directory. This can become a little complicated since you cannot mount and un-mount without logging in multiple times. However, this is an option. The secret is to mount the encrypted file system over your existing file system.

  1. You will need a directory outside of your home directory for storing the encrypted files. If my home directory is /home/neal then I can use /home/neal2. For example:
  ```
  sudo mkdir ${HOME}2
  sudo chown `id -un`:`id -gn` ${HOME}2
  mkdir ${HOME}2/encrypt
  ```

  2. Create a temporary encrypted directory and copy your home directory into it.
  ```
  encfs ${HOME}2/encrypt $HOME/tmp
  [Answer the prompts and give it a password]
  mv $HOME/* $HOME/tmp  # ignore error about copying same directory
  ```

  3. Un-mount $HOME/tmp
  ```
  fusermount -u $HOME/tmp
  ```
  At this point, you have all of your file encrypted at ${HOME}2/encrypt, and no files in your home directory.

  4. After you log in, mount your directory using:
  ```
  encfs ${HOME}2/encrypt $HOME -- -o nonempty,use_ino,allow_root
  ```
  The options tell EncFS to place the decrypted home directory over the regular home directory.

  5. Now log out and log back in. The decrypted home directory will be visible.

  6. To un-mount, you will need to log out, log in as a different user, and use Sudo to un-mount the directory.

- **Encrypt a CD-ROM**—Rather than burning a regular directory to a CD-ROM, you can burn an encrypted directory. The CD-ROM will appear to have garbage file names and random data in each file. However, you can then use `encfs` to mount it and access the decrypted data. If you are worried about someone stealing a CD-ROM that contains sensitive information, then this is an excellent solution. The CD-ROM is as secure as your password.

- **Encrypt a USB drive**—You can specify a USB thumb drive for storing the encrypted files. This is similar to the CD-ROM solution, except you can read and write to the drive.

- **Encrypt a networked file system**—NFS does not offer encryption, and SMB provides few security options. Rather than exporting unprotected files, you can export the encrypted file system. Network clients can mount the NFS (or SMB) partition containing the encrypted files, and then use `encfs` to access the decrypted files. This way, the file system's data is encrypted as it is passed along the network. (See Chapter 6 for configuring NFS and Samba.)

Knowing EncFS Limitations

EncFS is very flexible and is supported by a variety of file systems. You can download EncFS for Windows and other versions of Linux—see http://arg0.net/encfs/ for details. However, there are some limitations with this type of encrypted file system.

- **Supported platforms**—EncFS is not supported on every operating system. BSD and Mac OS X are just two examples. If you need EncFS on these platforms, consider running a supported platform using a virtual machine like Qemu (see Chapter 6) and exporting the decrypted directory to the host operating system.

- **EncFS does not un-mount when you log out**—Unmounting needs to be a conscious effort. Consider placing `fusermount -u -z decoded/` in your `$HOME/.bash_logout` script. This will un-mount the directory after all processes end.

- **EncFS does not protect the decrypted directory**—If you successfully run `encfs` and can access the decrypted files, then anyone on the system can access the decrypted files.

- **EncFS is not for automated systems**—Some people have tried to configure EncFS to mount automatically, when the system boots (or when a user logs in). Doing this defeats the security. For example, if the encrypted file system is mounted when the system powers up, then a thief who steals the system only needs to power up the computer in order to access the sensitive files.

Managing Logs and Caches

Backups are essential for security, but not everything needs to be backed up. For example, cache files and really old logs probably do not need to be archived. Some files, like logs, also need to be maintained. Without the occasional pruning, logs may expand to fill all available disk space.

Besides consuming unnecessary disk space and slowing down backup systems, temporary files and cache files can pose a security risk. Cache files allow someone to look at a history of your activities and possibly recover sensitive information. While deleted files may be recoverable with forensic tools, this is usually more effort than a simple attacker can manage. Deleting an unnecessary cache file is better than leaving it around.

Clearing Temporary Files

Many applications need to use temporary files for storage. Although some programs write to the current directory, others write to `/tmp` or `/var/tmp`. Without periodic maintenance, these directories can become cluttered. In addition, because `/tmp` is usually part of the `/` partition, temporary files can consume all available space on the root partition.

By default, Ubuntu flushes most files from `/tmp` during boot. This happens during the initial file mounting: init calls `/etc/rcS.d/S35mountall.sh`, which calls `/etc/init.d/boot-clean.sh`, which deletes files from `/tmp`. However, nothing cleans files from `/var/tmp`. Also, the `bootclean.sh` script only runs during boot up, not during shutdown. To clean both temporary directories during shutdown and boot up, I use my own init script called `cleantmp` (see Listing 10-4). This script deletes all temporary files except root-owned system files.

Listing 10-4: /etc/init.d/cleantmp for Cleaning Temporary Directories

```
#!/bin/sh

PATH=/bin:/usr/bin:/sbin:/usr/sbin
. /lib/lsb/init-functions

cleantmp()
{
  # EXCEPT list for system files
  for i in /tmp /var/tmp ; do
  EXCEPT="! ( -path $i )
           ! ( -path $i/lost+found -uid 0 )
           ! ( -path $i/quota.user -uid 0 )
           ! ( -path $i/aquota.user -uid 0 )
           ! ( -path $i/quota.group -uid 0 )
           ! ( -path $i/aquota.group -uid 0 )
           ! ( -path $i/.journal -uid 0 )
           ! ( -path $i/.clean -uid 0 )
           ! ( -path '$i/...security*' -uid 0 )"
    # Find everything in the directory (except the exceptions)
    find $i -maxdepth 1 $EXCEPT -exec rm -rf "{}" \;
  done
}

case "$1" in
  start|stop|restart|reload)
    log_begin_msg "Cleaning tmp directories..."
    cleantmp
    ;;
  *)
    log_success_msg "Usage: /etc/init.d/cleantmp" \
      "{start|stop|restart|reload}"
    exit 1
esac

exit 0
```

To make the cleantmp script run during boot and shutdown, I added it to /etc/rcS.d/and /etc/rc0.d/.

```
sudo chmod a+rx /etc/init.d/cleantmp
cd /etc/rcS.d
sudo ln -s ../init.d/cleantmp S36cleantmp  # for startup
cd /etc/rc0.d
sudo ln -s ../init.d/cleantmp K78cleantmp  # for shutdown
```

Erasing Web Caches

Web browsers store lots of cache files. The default setting for Firefox is 50 MB per profile per user! (See Chapter 5 for managing profiles and configuring browsers.) Most of the time, these cache files do not need to be kept by backup systems. For a list of the Firefox cache files, use:

```
sudo ls -d /home/*/.mozilla/firefox/*/Cache
```

Most of the time, you can safely blow away (or not back up) these files. However, you should leave the empty cache directory so that Mozilla won't need to re-create it next time you start the browser.

 Note   If you installed Konquerer (part of the Kubuntu desktop), then look for user-owned cache files in `/var/tmp/kdecache*/`.

Firefox stores a history of every URL accessed. This can also become a very big file and is usually not critical to system operation. All history files can be found using:

```
sudo ls -d /home/*/.mozilla/firefox/*/history.dat
```

If you want to remove the cache files during boot, you can add them to find command in the `/etc/init.d/cleantmp` script (see Listing 10-4) by changing the `for`-loop to:

```
for i in /tmp /var/tmp /home/*/.mozilla/firefox/*/Cache ; do
```

You may also want to add a line to zero-out history files. For example:

```
for i in /home/*/.mozilla/firefox/*/history.dat ; do cat /dev/zero > $i ; done
```

Cleaning APT Cache

The APT command can be another source of large, unnecessary files. For example, if you install some software and then remove it, the installation files may still be on the system. By default, APT does not automatically remove these files. However, the command `sudo apt-get autoclean` will remove these residues.

You can also configure APT to periodically remove old files by editing: `/etc/apt/apt.conf.d/10periodic`. For example, you can tell APT to periodically remove old files by adding different command directives:

- Set the auto-clean interval to once a week (the interval is specified in days).

  ```
  APT::Periodic::AutocleanInterval "7";
  ```

- Tell APT to remove cache packages older than seven days.

  ```
  APT::Periodic::MaxAge "7";
  ```

- If you disabled the periodic Synaptic update check (or installed the minimal Ubuntu server and don't have Synaptic installed), then you can enable a weekly (seven days) check for new packages:

  ```
  APT::Periodic::Update-Package-Lists "7";
  ```

These changes are processed by `anacron` in `/etc/cron.daily/apt`. (See Chapter 7 for configuring `anacron`.)

Rotating Logs

There are many different system log files. Some are rotated daily, others are rotated weekly, and some are never rotated. If you don't manage your log files, then they can grow indefinitely. And since most log files are stored in `/var/log`, filling the disk can lead to system failures.

The basic command for rotating a log file is `savelog`. This will rename the log file. So, `savelog test.log` will move `test.log` to `test.log.0` (or `test.log.0.gz` if it is big enough to compress), and any old `test.log.0` will become `test.log.1`, `test.log.1` becomes `test.log.2`, and so on. The default settings keep seven levels of backups (`test.log.0` to `test.log.7`). Anything older is deleted. You can change the number of rotated copies with the `-c` parameter. For example, `savelog -c 20 test.log` will keep 20 rotations.

If you want to create your own log file then you should add it to a rotation system. The main rotation system is `logrotate`, and is called by `anacron` (see `/etc/cron.daily/logrotate`). This command consults a directory of rotation command scripts: `/etc/logrotate.d/`. In this directory are a bunch of files that define log files and rotation schedules. For example, `/etc/logrotate.d/acpid` looks like:

```
/var/log/acpid {
    weekly
    rotate 4
    compress
    missingok
    postrotate
        /etc/init.d/acpid restart >/dev/null
    endscript
}
```

This specifies four log rotations of `/var/log/acpid` on a weekly basis. After rotating the log, the service `/etc/init.d/acpid` is restarted. Everything between the `postrotate` and `endscript` lines form a script that will be executed. For some processes, you may need to use `prerotate ... endscript` to stop a process before rotating the logs.

Some log files don't always need to be rotated. In the `logrotate` configuration file you can add a `size` parameter. For example, `size 10M` will only rotate the log if it is bigger than 10 MB. You can also use other sizes such as `50k` or `1G`. The single letters k, M, and G are recognized as kilobytes, megabytes, and gigabytes. If no size modifier is specified, bytes are assumed.

If you run a high-volume service, like a web server that gets millions of hits per day, then you will probably want to rotate logs more often than daily or weekly. I'd suggest putting the `logrotate` command in your `crontab` (see Chapter 7) so it runs more often. For example, to rotate logs hourly (at 1 minute after the hour):

```
1 * * * * logrotate /etc/logrotate.d/mylog
```

Alternately, you can use `savelog`:

```
1 * * * * savelog -c 48 /var/log/mylogfile  # save last 48 hours as 0..47
```

If you notice a log that is growing too large, or never being rotated, then look for a log configuration files in `/etc/logrotate.d/`. If it does not exist, consider adding it. If it does exist, then maybe it needs to be rotated more often.

Summary

The default Dapper Drake installation is a good start for a secure system. Although it does reduce risks from remote attackers, it is vulnerable to local data exposure. Restricting root access, encrypting files, and removing unnecessary files all provide additional security. Tools such as Sudo, GPG, and EncFS help protect files and access, while `savelog` and `logrotate` manage files that would otherwise grow without bounds.

Advanced Networking

Most of the time, people will install Ubuntu, configure the network during the installation, and not need to change it again. However, there are some situations where you will want to configure the network. This can happen if you have a laptop and frequently move between different networks, if you add in a second network card, or if you need more security than the default settings.

In many cases, changing the network configuration can be as simple as using a GUI. In other cases, you'll need to edit some configuration files in order to properly configure some adapters.

As mentioned in Chapter 10, the default Ubuntu installation is pretty secure because no network services are enabled. However, all your network traffic is probably still being sent unencrypted across the network. There are a couple of different ways you can enable encryption, authentication, and anonymity when accessing the network.

If you start turning on network services (see Chapter 12), you will need to make sure that your network is hardened. Tools like `iptables` can definitely help lock down a system.

Finally, when everything goes wrong, you will need to know how to debug the network. This is where tools like `tcpdump`, `snort`, and `ethereal` (a.k.a. Wireshark) come in handy.

in this chapter

☑ Configuring network devices

☑ Configuring wireless networks

☑ Securing the network

☑ Enabling proxies

☑ Debugging the network

Configuring Network Devices

The simplest way to configure the network is through a GUI. From the main menu, use System ➪ Administration ➪ Networking to bring up the network configuration menu (see Figure 11-1). This menu shows each of the available network adapters and enables you to configure them. You can enable or disable interfaces, and set addresses statically or through DHCP. For modems, you can enter the ISP's phone number, login credentials, and whether to reconnect after any disconnects.

If you are configuring the network without a GUI, you can still configure the network device. The command `ifconfig -a` lists all known network devices. The `lo` device is the local loop-back, `eth0` is usually the first wired Ethernet adapter, and `sit0` is used to bridge IPv4 and IPv6. Additional network devices may be enumerated, such as `eth1` and `eth2` for two additional Ethernet cards.

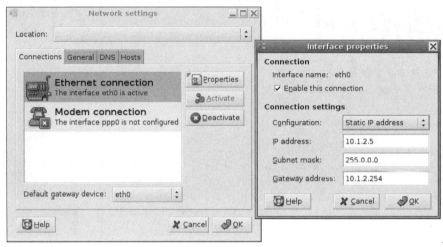

FIGURE 11-1: The Network Settings applet, showing the properties for eth0

The configuration for each device is stored in file /etc/network/interfaces. This is where you can define static or dynamic configurations, and whether they start up automatically or only as needed. For example, my computer has two Ethernet cards, but only the first one is automatically configured (see Listing 11-1).

Listing 11-1: Sample /etc/network/interfaces

```
# This file describes the network interfaces available on your system
# and how to activate them. For more information, see interfaces(5).

# The loopback network interface
auto lo
iface lo inet loopback

# The primary network interface
auto eth0
iface eth0 inet static
address 10.1.2.30
netmask 255.0.0.0
gateway 10.1.2.254

# The second network interface
auto eth1
iface eth1 inet dhcp
```

Table 11-1 shows some of the common fields for /etc/network/interfaces. For additional information, see the online manual (man 5 interfaces).

Table 11-1 Common Fields for /etc/network/interfaces

Field Name	Example	Purpose
iface	iface eth0 inet dhcp	Defines an interface. The parameters are the interface name (for example, eth0), protocol (inet for IPv4 or inet6 for IPv6), and whether the configuration is static, dhcp, ppp, or bootp.
address	address 10.1.2.5	Static IP or IPv6 address.
netmask	netmask 10.255.255.255	Static subnet mask.
gateway	gateway 10.1.2.254	Static default gateway.
hostname	hostname myhost.local.lan	When using DHCP, this is the host name to request.
auto	auto eth0 lo	Set one or more interfaces to automatically come up configured. If you want an interface to *not* come up automatically, then leave it off the auto field.
wireless-essid	wireless-essid home	For wireless networks, specifies the Service Set Identifier (SSID) to connect to (for example, "home").
wireless-key	wireless-key 0123456789abcdef0011223344	For wireless networks that use WEP for security, this string specifies the WEP key as 10 or 26 hex digits (for 64-bit or 104-bit encryption, respectively).
pre-up	pre-up /usr/local/bin/ myscript	Run this script before bringing up the network interface.
post-up	post-up /usr/local/bin/ myscript	Run this script after bringing up the network interface.
pre-down	pre-down /usr/local/bin/ myscript	Run this script before taking down the network interface.
post-down	post-down /usr/local/bin/ myscript	Run this script after taking down the network interface.

After configuring the `/etc/network/interfaces` file, you can load the settings using:

`sudo /etc/init.d/networking restart`

For interfaces that are not brought up automatically, you can use `ifconfig` to bring them up and down. For example, `sudo ifconfig eth1 up` and `sudo ifconfig eth1 down`. You can only use an interface when it is up.

Configuring Wireless Networks

Although wired network cards are pretty easy to configure, wireless cards usually pose some problems. For example, many wireless cards only include Windows drivers, not Linux. Without drivers, there is no way to use the hardware. Fortunately, `ndiswrapper` enables you to use some Windows drivers under Ubuntu!

Assuming you have a working wireless network card, configuring new wireless network configurations is not always automatic. Also, WEP, WAP, and other wireless security protocols can be hard to configure.

Looking for Drivers

Wireless network drivers can come from many different sources. Some network interface cards (NICs) are identified during the Ubuntu installation and immediately installed. These include the Intel ipw2100 and ipw2200, Cisco Aironet cards, and NICs based on the Prism chipsets (for example, Prism 2, 2.5, and 3). If you go to System ➪ Administration ➪ Networking and see your wireless card listed, then it is already supported and ready for configuration. You can just jump to the "Hacking with Wireless Tools" section.

While some manufacturers provide wireless network drivers for Ubuntu (for example, Intel), other drivers have been reverse-engineered. For example, the Broadcom drivers were built by people in the open source community and not by Broadcom.

If the wireless NIC is not supported by the base installation, consider using `apt-cache` to search for an appropriate Ubuntu driver. (See Chapter 4 for using `apt-cache`.) You may need to search based on the wireless card's chipset and not the NIC's model number or manufacturer. For example, the Madwifi driver in the linux-restricted-modules package (`apt-cache search linux-restricted-modules`) provides support for Atheros-based adapters. Atheros-based wireless adapters are found in many laptops as well as NICs by 3Com, D-Link, Netgear, and many other manufacturers.

Be sure to install the correct linux-restricted-modules package for your kernel. Use `sudo apt-get install linux-restricted-modules-`uname -r``. Since this comes from the restricted repository, the drivers are not necessarily free or open source.

If all else fails and you cannot find a native Linux driver for your wireless card (and purchasing a natively supported wireless NIC is not a viable option), then you can try using `ndiswrapper` to use the Microsoft Windows driver under Ubuntu.

Using ndiswrapper

Chapter 6 discusses some different emulators that work under Ubuntu. Using these emulators, you can install an entire operating system in a virtual environment. However, everything in the virtual environment stays in the virtual environment. In contrast, the Network Driver Interface Specification wrapper (`ndiswrapper`) program enables you to install some network drivers for Microsoft Windows in your actual Linux environment. The wrapper provides enough emulation to support Windows device drivers.

Warning Using `ndiswrapper` may hang your computer! Save all critical files and close all unnecessary processes before attempting to install any drivers using this tool.

Installing a Driver

Before installing a Windows driver under Linux, you need a few things.

- **Install** `ndiswrapper`—This can be installed using `sudo apt-get install ndiswrapper-utils`. This will give you the `ndiswrapper` program as well as a loadable kernel module.

- **Get the Windows driver**—The `ndiswrapper` tool works only with Microsoft Windows XP drivers. If you have drivers for Windows 95, 98, or ME (or some other version), then it won't work unless it also says that the driver will work with Windows XP. If you don't have the Windows XP driver, then you can stop here because it won't work.

- **Unpacked INF files**—Most Windows drivers come bundled in a self-extracting archive. You'll need to extract the files before you can use them. Try using `unzip` to expand a self-extracting zip file, `cabextract` for Windows Cabinet files, or `unshield` for unpacking Install Shield files. You can install these tools using:

```
sudo apt-get install unzip cabextract unshield
```

- You will know that you have extracted the right files if you see an INF file and some device drivers (likely SYS files). You can check for them using:

```
find . -type f -name '*.inf' -o -name '*.INF'
```

After you have gathered the necessary programs and files, you can install the drivers.

1. If the device is an external USB device, then disconnect it before installing the drivers. Some drivers may hang the operating system if the device is installed before the drivers.

2. Find the INF files needed to install the program. In my case, there are two files needed, although other network devices may only need one INF file.

```
$ find . -name '*.inf' -o -name '*.INF'
./athfmwdl.inf
./net5523.inf
```

3. Use `ndiswrapper` to install the files. For my USB network adapter, there were two drivers that needed to be installed, and they needed to be installed in a specific order (see "Debugging Driver Problems").

```
sudo ndiswrapper -i ./net5523.inf
sudo ndiswrapper -i ./athfmwdl.inf
```

4. Load the kernel module.

```
sudo modprobe ndiswrapper
```

5. If the device needs to be plugged in (for example, a USB network adaptor), then plug it in now.

 Warning If the system is going to lock up and hang, it will do it here. If it hangs, then go to the next section, "Debugging Driver Problems."

6. If you made it this far, then it didn't hang (that's great!). Use `ifconfig -a` to list all network devices. You should see a device called `wlan0`—this is the default name given to `ndiswrapper` devices. You can then configure it using System ➪ Administration ➪ Networking.

7. To automatically start `ndiswrapper` on boot, add the kernel module to `/etc/modules`.

```
sudo bash -c 'echo "ndiswrapper" >> /etc/modules'
```

A graphical alternative to using the command line `ndiswrapper` is `ndisgtk`.

```
sudo apt-get install ndisgtk
sudo ndisgtk
```

This tool offers a front end to `ndiswrapper` and makes it a little easier to install devices (see Figure 11-2). You can also click the Configure Network button to quickly open the Network Settings applet.

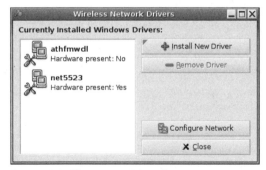

FIGURE 11-2: The `ndisgtk` interface

Debugging Driver Problems

Installing a driver with `ndiswrapper` is fairly straightforward, although there are a few places where things can go very bad. If the drivers are going to hang the computer, then it will likely happen when the kernel module is loaded or when the device is plugged in. However, drivers may also cause your system to hang when the devices are unloaded or detached, or when resuming after being suspended (like on a laptop).

If the drivers are not working for you, then you can try the following:

- **Unload the drivers**—If the drivers hang your system, then you should probably unload them.

    - Reboot the system (usually with the front panel's reset button since the computer probably hangs).

    - When Ubuntu begins to come up, press Alt+F1 so you can see all of the `init` steps as they happen.

    - When you see the text "Configuring network interfaces," press Ctrl+C. This will skip the network configuration. As long as the network does not configure, the NDIS drivers will not load and the system will not hang. If you don't stop it here, then the system will hang again.

    - Allow the rest of the initialization stages to come up.

    - Log into the system.

    - Use `ndiswrapper -l` to list each of the loaded drivers.

    - Use `ndiswrapper -e` to erase (remove) the offending driver. For example, you can use:

    ```
    $ ndiswrapper -l
    Installed ndis drivers:
    athfmwdl                    driver present
    net5523            driver present, hardware present
    $ sudo ndiswrapper -e net5523
    ```

    8. Reboot the system (`sudo reboot`) and allow it to come up completely.

Tip

For some USB network devices, simply unplugging the device and rebooting the system enables you to boot without hanging. In this case, you only need to remove the devices (`ndiswrapper -e`) and do not need to reboot the system a second time.

    - **Check the drivers**—In some cases, there may be newer or more stable Windows XP drivers available. Also, drivers from compatible network devices may work better than official ones from the manufacturer.

    - **Check official forums**—The `ndiswrapper` tool is very well supported and there are hundreds of network interfaces that are documented as being compatible, incompatible, or requiring additional steps. Visit `http://ndiswrapper`.

`sourceforge.net/mediawiki/` for tips and hints for specific cards. In many cases, this forum also provides links to the actual Windows drivers, ensuring that you are installing the right one.

- **Check for compatible devices**—Many manufacturers may use the same chipsets in different cards. Using `lsusb` or `lspci -n`, identify your four-byte unique identifier for your network adapter. It should look something like "0123:89ab" (although the exact hex numbers will be different). Check the official forums for the identifier and see if any other devices use the same drivers. For example, the EnGenius EUB-862 uses the same chipset as the Airlink101 (both use the USB identifier "0cf3:0001"). Although the Windows drivers that came with the EUB-862 consistently hung my system, the drivers for the Airlink101 worked well.

Hacking with Wireless Tools

Ubuntu includes many different tools for configuring the network. The most important ones are `iwconfig` and `iwlist`. Using these, you can configure and reconfigure most wireless options.

The `iwconfig` command is used to configure wireless devices. When used by itself, it lists every network device and, if it is a wireless device, the current configuration. For example:

```
$ iwconfig
lo        no wireless extensions.
eth0      no wireless extensions.
sit0      no wireless extensions.
wlan0     IEEE 802.11b  ESSID:"My SSID"
          Mode:Managed  Frequency:2.437 GHz  Access Point: Not-Associated
          Bit Rate:108 Mb/s
          Power Management min timeout:0us  mode:All packets received
          Link Quality:0  Signal level:0  Noise level:0
          Rx invalid nwid:0  Rx invalid crypt:0  Rx invalid frag:0
          Tx excessive retries:0  Invalid misc:0   Missed beacon:0
```

Using the `iwlist` command, you can scan for available access points (APs), as demonstrated in Listing 11-2.

Listing 11-2: Example iwlist Scan

```
$ sudo iwlist wlan0 scan
wlan0     Scan completed :
          Cell 01 - Address: 00:18:39:CC:F8:C7
                    ESSID:"logo1"
                    Protocol:IEEE 802.11g
                    Mode:Managed
                    Frequency:2.412 GHz (Channel 1)
```

Listing 11-2 *Continued*

```
                    Quality:0/100   Signal level:-87 dBm   Noise level:-256 dBm
                    Encryption key:on
                    Bit Rates:1 Mb/s; 2 Mb/s; 5.5 Mb/s; 11 Mb/s; 18 Mb/s
                              24 Mb/s; 36 Mb/s; 54 Mb/s; 6 Mb/s; 9 Mb/s
                              12 Mb/s; 48 Mb/s
                    Extra:bcn_int=100
                    Extra:atim=0
                    Extra:wpa_ie=3d180050f21101020050f21201002050f20211002050f20
          Cell 02 - Address: 00:14:BF:9B:CA:D3
                    ESSID:"My SSID"
                    Protocol:IEEE 802.11g
                    Mode:Managed
                    Frequency:2.437 GHz (Channel 6)
                    Quality:0/100   Signal level:-36 dBm   Noise level:-256 dBm
                    Encryption key:on
                    Bit Rates:1 Mb/s; 2 Mb/s; 5.5 Mb/s; 11 Mb/s; 18 Mb/s
                              24 Mb/s; 36 Mb/s; 54 Mb/s; 6 Mb/s; 9 Mb/s
                              12 Mb/s; 48 Mb/s
                    Extra:bcn_int=1000
                    Extra:atim=0
          Cell 03 - Address: 00:18:39:2C:2B:51
                    ESSID:"linksys"
                    Protocol:IEEE 802.11g
                    Mode:Managed
                    Frequency:2.437 GHz (Channel 6)
                    Quality:0/100   Signal level:-85 dBm   Noise level:-256 dBm
                    Encryption key:off
                    Bit Rates:1 Mb/s; 2 Mb/s; 5.5 Mb/s; 11 Mb/s; 18 Mb/s
                              24 Mb/s; 36 Mb/s; 54 Mb/s; 6 Mb/s; 9 Mb/s
                              12 Mb/s; 48 Mb/s
                    Extra:bcn_int=100
                    Extra:atim=0
```

Tip   When used as a regular user, `iwscan wlan0 scan` will only display previous results. These may expire after a few minutes. However, if you run the command as root, it will initiate a new scan.

The example in Listing 11-2 shows a scan from `iwlist`. In the example, there are three APs that are within range of the Ubuntu system. You can combine the results from `iwlist` with `iwconfig` and connect to a specific AP. For example:

```
sudo iwconfig essid "My SSID"           # connect to an AP using the SSID
sudo iwconfig essid "My SSID" channel 6 # connect to SSID on a specific channel
```

Enabling Wireless Security with WEP

The Wired Equivalent Privacy (WEP) protocol is a common method for encrypting wireless connections. The `iwconfig` program allows you to specify the physical connection. It also allows you to provide a WEP key for connecting to an AP. This can be specified on the command line as a series of hex digits or as a string. Table 11-2 shows some of the common key formats.

Note Although it has some security weaknesses, WEP is universally available and certainly better than using no security.

Table 11-2   Example `iwconfig` **Key Formats**

Example	Description
iwconfig wlan0 key 0123456789	Specify a 10-digit (hexadecimal) key for 64-bit WEP.
iwconfig wlan0 key 0123-4567-89ab-cdef-0123-4567-89	Specify a 26-digit (hexadecimal) key for 104-bit WEP. Hyphens are optional.
iwconfig wlan0 key 's:Secret Key'	An ASCII string can be used as the key if it is prefaced by an "s:". Be sure to quote the string if it has spaces.

The key value for `iwconfig` can also be placed in the `/etc/networking/interfaces` file. In addition, you can specify multiple keys—if one key does not work, then it will try the next one. Multiple keys can be really useful if your home and office use the same SSID but different keys. (Or if your office has meeting rooms, each with the same SSID but different keys.) For example, to specify three keys and set the default to be #2, you could have lines similar to these in your `/etc/networking/interfaces` file:

```
auto wlan0
iface wlan0 inet dhcp
wireless-essid My SSID
wireless-key1 0123456789abcdef0123456789
wireless-key2 abcdef0123
wireless-key3 s:Top Secret
wireless-defaultkey 2
```

Enabling Wireless Security with WPA

Although WEP is certainly better than no security, there are other ways to secure wireless networks. Wi-Fi Protected Access (WPA) is steadily growing in popularity and offers stronger options for privacy and authentication.

1. To configure WPA, you will need to generate a WPA configuration file. This is done using wpa_passphrase. You will need to provide your SSID and a passphrase, and it will generate a configuration file.

Tip

Specifying the passphrase on the command line (as done in this example) is usually not very secure—particularly if multiple people have access to the computer. If you don't specify the passphrase, you will be prompted for it. (Prompting is much better since the passphrase won't be stored in your shell's history.)

```
wpa_passphrase "My SSID" "Secret Password" > tempfile
sudo cp tempfile /etc/wpa_supplicant.conf
```

The contents of /etc/wpa_supplicant.conf lists your network's name and the associated WPA key. Although they should be autodetected, some drivers may need to you to add proto and key_mgmt fields. Listing 11-3 shows a sample /etc/wpa_supplicant.conf file (bold indicates optional fields).

Listing 11-3: Sample /etc/wpa_supplicant.conf File

```
network={
        ssid="My SSID"
        #psk="Secret Password"
        psk=aa380927bc23c6a736a69fa2b395b442bade145973b3a39c25cee0c9d55b0711
        proto=WPA
        key_mgmt=WPA-PSK
}
```

Tip

For security on multi-user systems, you should consider removing the #psk line that contains the decoded key and changing the file permissions so it is only accessible by root: sudo chmod 600 /etc/wpa_supplicant.conf ; sudo chown root:root /etc/wpa_supplicant.conf.

2. After creating the /etc/wpa_supplicant.conf file, you should test it to make sure it works. In this example, the wireless interface is wlan0 and it uses the generic wireless LAN extensions (-D wext). Other possible control extensions are listed in man wpa_supplicant and include ndiswrapper, ndis, madwifi (for Atheros adapters), and wired for wired Ethernet cards with WPA support.

```
sudo wpa_supplicant -D wext -i wlan0 -c/etc/wpa_supplicant.conf
```

3. To make the changes take effect every time the network interface is used, pre-up and post-down scripts can be added to /etc/networking/interfaces. These scripts will start and stop WPA support. For example:

```
auto wlan0
iface wlan0 inet dhcp
pre-up wpa_supplicant -B -w -D wext -i wlan0 -c/etc/wpa_supplicant.conf
post-down killall -q wpa_supplicant
```

Note The -B option to wpa_supplicant means to run the command in the background. The "-w" option means to wait for the interface to be added in case the wlan0 interface is not immediately available (or created) when the script starts.

Securing the Network

When you enable a network interface, you create a bi-directional path. Just as you can go out over the network, there is a path for attackers to come into your system. Firewall software, such as Tcpwrappers and IP Tables, enable you to restrict, modify, and manage network packet handling.

Using the network usually has one other limitation: there is no security. Although a user may connect remotely using SSH or some other secure protocol, the ability to connect in the first place can lead to security risks in highly sensitive environments. Fortunately, Dapper includes IPsec and IPv6. These network layer protocols can authenticate, validate, and encrypt network traffic. It's one thing to require a user-login using SSH; it's another thing to block SSH connections in the first place if they are not authenticated.

Configuring Firewalls with Tcpwrappers

The basic Ubuntu installation includes two types of firewalls: Tcpwrappers and IP Tables. Tcpwrappers is usually used with automated services such as inetd and xinetd. This system consults two files (/etc/hosts.allow and /etc/hosts.deny) and grants access based on these settings. Both files are in the same format: *daemon* : *clients*. For example, to restrict access for incoming FTP requests to only machines in the mydomain.lan domain, you can use:

```
in.ftpd : .mydomain.lan
```

Note There are many different FTP servers available. In this example, the server's executable is called in.ftpd. For the full list, use apt-cache search ftpd. You will need a server that supports libwrap or starts from inetd. See the section "Enabling Tcpwrappers" later in this chapter.

When a new network request for the daemon is received, Tcpwrappers first checks /etc/ hosts.allow and then /etc/hosts.deny. If the restriction is found in /etc/hosts.allow, then the connection is permitted to contact the daemon. The /etc/hosts.deny restriction blocks the request from ever reaching the daemon. And if there is no restriction, then the connection is permitted.

If you don't want to list specific daemons and hosts, then you can use the keyword ALL. Very secure systems usually have an /etc/hosts.deny that says:

ALL: ALL

This creates a default-deny configuration and blocks access to every service from every client except when they are explicitly permitted by /etc/hosts.allow.

Warning If you set /etc/hosts.deny to ALL: ALL and forget to grant access in /etc/hosts.allow, then new remote access connections will fail! You may not notice this immediately if you are already remotely connected; Tcpwrappers impacts only new connections, not established ones.

Testing the Tcpwrappers Configuration

You can check your Tcpwrappers configuration using the tcpdmatch command. For example, to check if the host myhost.mydomain.lan can access the service in.ftpd, you can use:

tcpdmatch in.ftpd myhost.mydomain.lan

This displays any host name warnings, service issues, and whether access is granted or denied. In addition, if any rule is matched then it will tell you which file (/etc/hosts.allow or /etc/hosts.deny) and which line.

Enabling Tcpwrappers

The active program for running Tcpwrappers is called tcpd (/usr/sbin/tcpd). This is usually found in /etc/inetd.conf for starting services. For example:

netbios-ssn   stream tcp   nowait root   /usr/sbin/tcpd /usr/sbin/smbd

This line says to run the SMB daemon when there is a connection on port 139/tcp (the netbios-ssn TCP port). Before running the smbd daemon, Tcpwrappers is used to check if the connection is permitted.

Not every program that uses Tcpwrappers runs the tcpd program; Tcpwrappers is commonly compiled into some network daemons. For example, the SSH daemon (sudo apt-get install openssh-server) has Tcpwrappers built-in. You can check for this by using the ldd command to list all linked libraries and search the libwrap shared library.

```
$ ldd /usr/sbin/sshd | grep libwrap
        libwrap.so.0 => /lib/libwrap.so.0 (0xb7eee000)
```

This means that the SSH server will consult `/etc/hosts.allow` and `/etc/hosts.deny` before allowing connections. You can generate a list of `libwrap`-enabled applications using a small script:

```
# find all executables and test for libwrap
find /bin /usr/bin /sbin /usr/sbin -type f -perm -1 | \
while read filename ; do
  haslib=`ldd "$filename" | grep libwrap.so`;
  if [ "$haslib" != "" ] ; then echo "$filename" ; fi ;
done
```

Configuring Firewalls with IP Tables

Tcpwrappers operates on the network's transport layer. It can filter TCP or UDP ports, but can not filter network layer (IP, IPv6, and so on) traffic. For this type of filtering, you can use IP Tables. Unlike Tcpwrappers, which runs as an application, IP Tables are provided as a kernel module. As a result, IP Tables impact all applications, not just those designed or configured to use it.

By default, IP Tables stores three types of filters:

- INPUT—This table identifies what type of incoming packets to accept. For example, to block SSH packets that use TCP on port 22 from the subnet 172.16.23.0/24, then you can use:

  ```
  sudo iptables -A INPUT -p tcp --dport 22 \
      --source 172.16.23.0/24 -j REJECT
  ```

- OUTPUT—This table is used to filter outbound network traffic (from your system to a remote system). For example, to block all connections to Microsoft, you can use:

  ```
  sudo iptables -A OUTPUT --destination 207.46.0.0/16 -j REJECT
  ```

- FORWARD—This table is used to forward traffic, in case you want to use your Ubuntu system as a network firewall. For example, to allow all traffic from my local LAN (10.0.0.0/8) to relay through my Ubuntu system, I can use:

  ```
  sudo iptables --table nat -A POSTROUTING \
      --out-interface eth0 -j MASQUERADE
  sudo iptables -A FORWARD --in-interface eth0 \
      --source 10.0.0.0/8 -j ACCEPT
  ```

  However, if I only want to forward web traffic, then I can specify a destination port:

  ```
  sudo iptables -A FORWARD --in-interface eth0 \
      --source 10.0.0.0/8 -p tcp --dport 80 -j ACCEPT
  ```

  After configuring your system to forward traffic, you can use it as the network gateway for other systems on your network.

The `iptables` command manages a set of tables and rules, called *chains*. A single table may have many different chains. The default table is called `filter` and has the INPUT, OUTPUT, and FORWARD chains. Other tables include `nat` (for network address translations), `mangle` (for packet modification), and `raw` for low-level packet management.

The `iptables` command takes a variety of options. Table 11-3 lists some of the more common parameters. The full list can be found in the man page for `iptables`.

Table 11-3   Common Parameters for `iptables`

Parameter	Example	Purpose
`-t, --table`	`-t nat`	Specify the table to act on, such as `filter`, `nat`, `mangle`, or `raw`. The default table is `filter`.
`-A, --append`	`-A INPUT`	Append rules to a particular chain, such as INPUT, FORWARD, or OUTPUT.
`-s, --source; -d, --destination`	`-s 10.0.0.0/8`	Specify the source (`-s` or `--source`) and destination (`-d` or `--destination`) network address. You may include an optional subnet mask.
`-p, --proto`	`-p tcp`	Specify the transport layer protocol, such as tcp, udp, icmp, or all. Without this option, all protocols match the rule.
`--sport, --dport, --port`	`--port 22`	If you specify a protocol with `-p`, then you can also specify the port number. This can be a source port (`--sport`), destination port (`--dport`), or either (`--port`).
`--in-interface and --out-interface`	`--in-interface eth0`	Specify the port used for receiving (`in`) or sending (`out`) packets.
`-j, --jump`	`-j ACCEPT`	Identify how to handle the rule. Common rules usually use ACCEPT, REJECT, or DROP. There are a variety of other rules including ones for rewriting packets, triggering logs, or generating specific packet responses.

When you are finished, you can view your tables using `sudo iptables -L`. For example:

```
$ sudo iptables -L
Chain INPUT (policy ACCEPT)
target     prot opt source              destination
REJECT     tcp  --  172.16.23.0/24      anywhere            tcp dpt:ssh
reject-with icmp-port-unreachable
REJECT     tcp  --  172.16.23.0/24      anywhere            tcp dpt:ssh
reject-with icmp-port-unreachable

Chain FORWARD (policy ACCEPT)
target     prot opt source              destination
ACCEPT     tcp  --  10.0.0.0/8          anywhere            tcp dpt:www

Chain OUTPUT (policy ACCEPT)
target     prot opt source              destination
REJECT     all  --  anywhere            207.46.0.0/16       reject-with
icmp-port-unreachable
```

Saving IP Tables Settings

Changes made using IP Tables are not permanent. To make them happen every time you reboot, you will need to save the settings and re-load them during boot.

1. Configure IP Tables and test them to make sure they do what you want.

Custom Filtering

Usually when administrators configure IP Tables, it is done to block external attack paths or enable routing through an existing computer. However, there is another use.

Many different types of viruses, spyware, and worms call out to remote control systems. Using the OUTPUT chain from the `filter` table, you can block known communication protocols. For example, if nobody without your network should be accessing IRC servers, then you can block TCP ports 6666 and 6667 since these are commonly used for IRC:

```
sudo iptables -A OUTPUT -p tcp --dport 6666 -j REJECT
sudo iptables -A OUTPUT -p tcp --dport 6667 -j REJECT
```

On mail servers, you can use this to block access from known spam subnets, and on proxy servers you can block access to sites that are infected with malware.

Personally, I have a different use. I perform computer network audits and some systems may be off limits or outside the scope of the audit. To prevent accidental access, I block outbound traffic to the restricted hosts. In some cases, hosts may only be accessed during certain hours (to prevent interference with regular customers). In this case, I use a cron job to add and remove access as needed. (See Chapter 7 for scheduling tasks with cron.)

2. Save your changes to a configuration file.

```
sudo iptables-save > iptables.conf
sudo mv iptables.conf /etc/iptables.conf
```

3. Make an init script for IP Tables. I created /etc/init.d/iptables and the contents are in Listing 11-4. Be sure to make the script executable: chmod 755 /etc/init.d/iptables.

Listing 11-4: The /etc/init.d/iptables Startup Script

```
#! /bin/sh
PATH=/usr/local/sbin:/usr/local/bin:/sbin:/bin:/usr/sbin:/usr/bin
NAME=iptables
DESC="IP Tables"

[ -f /etc/iptables.conf ] || exit 1

case "$1" in
  start)
        echo "Starting $DESC: $NAME"
        /sbin/iptables --flush -t filter
        /sbin/iptables --flush -t nat
        /sbin/iptables-restore /etc/iptables.conf
        ;;
  stop)
        /sbin/iptables --flush -t filter
        /sbin/iptables --flush -t nat
        ;;
  restart|reload|force-reload)
        echo "Restarting $DESC: $NAME"
        /sbin/iptables --flush -t filter
        /sbin/iptables --flush -t nat
        /sbin/iptables-restore /etc/iptables.conf
        ;;
  *)
        echo "Usage: $0 {start|stop|restart|force-reload}" >&2
        exit 1
        ;;
esac
exit 0
```

4. Add the script to the startup configuration. It is configured to be one of the first scripts to run.

```
cd /etc/rcS.d
sudo ln -s ../init.d/iptables S37iptables
```

Now, any configuration saved in `/etc/iptables.conf` will be included during startup. If you make new changes using `iptables`, you can save them using `sudo iptables-save`.

Enabling IPsec

Although firewalls prevent some connections, they do nothing to actually authenticate the connection and offer no privacy options. If you really need to make sure the connection is permitted and don't want someone to see what you are doing, then consider using IPsec, the security extension to IP. IPsec offers digital signatures for authentication and encryption for privacy.

Note There are two common versions of the Internet Protocol: the older IP (also called IPv4) and the newer IPv6. IPv6 uses the same security options found in IPsec. The only difference: the availability of these security functions is optional for IPv4, but mandatory for IPv6. However, *available* is not the same an *enabled*. The security in IPv6 is normally turned off unless you explicitly enable it. Turning on the security for IPv6 is exactly the same as configuring the security for IPsec.

IPsec provides point-to-point security that can be used as a secure path or as a virtual private network (VPN). The configuration happens in two stages. First you define the keys to use, and then you define the security policies.

The main program for configuring IPsec is called `setkey` and it comes from the `ipsec-tools` package.

```
sudo apt-get install ipsec-tools
```

Unmasking Racoon

There is an alternate package to `ipsec-tools` called `racoon`. (Yes, it is spelled with one c, not like the animal with the same name.) Although `racoon` is popular with some Linux and BSD distributions, `ipsec-tools` was the first one included in the main repository for older versions of Ubuntu. This historical precedence gives it slightly more popularity with Ubuntu users. Both packages include the `setkey` program and both have nearly identical usage. Ironically, the man page for `setkey` from the `ipsec-tools` package explicitly references `racoon`, even if you don't install `racoon`.

So, what is the difference between `racoon` and `ipsec-tools`? Not much from my viewpoint. `ipsec-tools` accepts configuration commands from a file or stdin, while `racoon` also supports configurations on the command-line. The `racoon` package also uses a different configuration file location: `/etc/racoon/racoon-tool.conf` instead of `/etc/ipsec-tools.conf`.

Creating IPsec Keys

Warning I strongly recommend against *remotely* using `setkey` to configure IPsec. As soon as you run the command, it becomes implemented. If you configure a rule to require a key, then your network connection may be immediately terminated. Unless you have an alternate route onto the system, you can easily become locked out.

To create a key, you need to know the IP addresses for the source and destination hosts, the algorithm, and the key. For example, to define a key for 3DES encryption using cipher block chaining (CBC), I can use:

```
echo 'add 10.1.1.5 10.1.2.10 esp 0x201 -m tunnel
  -E 3des-cbc "Twenty-four characters!!"
  -A hmac-md5 0xdeadbeefcafe1234deadbeefcafe1234 ;' |
  sudo setkey -c
```

In this case, the 3DES key for encryption is the string `Twenty-four characters!!`, and the secret password used for authenticating the packet is the hexadecimal value `0xdeadbeef-cafe1234deadbeefcafe1234`.

The `setkey` program either reads in commands from a file or from stdin. If you just want to run one setting, then place the command in an `echo` statement and pipe the data into `setkey` `-c`. The `-c` option to `setkey` says to read from stdin, whereas `-f` says to read from a file. The lines that it reads are commands such as `add` or `delete` and include configuration options. Each command needs to end with a semicolon.

The `add` option within the `setkey` command is used to specify a Security Association Database (SAD) entry. These are basically combinations of encryption, authentication, and compression definitions along with network addresses.

- **Addresses**—The first two options to the `add` command are the source and destination IP addresses. These can be IP or IPv6 address (although they must both be IP or both be IPv6).

- **Protocol**—The next parameter specifies the type of protocol. The available values are usually either `esp` for encapsulating security payload or `ah` for authenticated header. The former defines a protected payload, while the latter is only used for authenticating the sender. Other protocols include `esp-old` and `ah-old` (from obsolete standards), `ipcomp`, and `tcp` for using TCP with MD5 for validation.

- **SPI**—The protocol is followed by a Security Parameter Index used to identify the SAD entry.

- **Mode**—The `-m` option identifies the type of protocol. It can be `tunnel`, `transport`, or `any`. A `tunnel` is used for a VPN, while `transport` is only used for protecting the transport layer (TCP or UDP traffic). Other protocols, such as ICMP, will not pass through the secure connection when using `transport`. Specifying `-m any` allows the SAD to be used for either `tunnel` or `transport` security.

■ **Encryption**—The -E option specifies an encryption algorithm and a secret key used for the encryption. The length of the key depends on the selected encryption algorithm. For example, -E 3des-cbc requires a 24-byte key. Table 11-4 lists the available encryption algorithms and the required key lengths. Keys can be provided as hexadecimal values (beginning with 0x) or as quoted strings. If you do not specify an encryption algorithm, then the entire packet will be sent unencrypted—the same as using the null cipher with no key.

Warning

The setkey program will not load the command if the key length is wrong. It will only say that the key length is wrong; it won't tell you what the key length should be. Also, the man page for setkey only gives you the key length in bits, not bytes or characters.

Table 11-4   Available Encryption Algorithms and Required Key Sizes for setkey

Algorithm	Key size in bits	Key size in bytes
des-cbc	64	8
3des-cbc	192	24
Null	0–2048	0–256
blowfish-cbc	40–448	5–56
cast128-cbc	40–128	5–16
des-deriv	64	8
3des-deriv	192	24
rijndael-cbc	128, 192, or 256	16, 24, or 32
twofish-cbc	0–256	0–32
aes-ctr	160, 224, or 288	20, 28, or 36

■ **Authentication**—The -A option specifies the algorithm for digitally signing the packet. This authentication header allows the recipient to know that the packet is actually from the sender. As with encryption, the key can either be a hexadecimal value (beginning with 0x) or a quoted string, and the key size depends on the algorithm (see Table 11-5). If this option is not specified, then the header is not authenticated.

■ **Compression**—The -C option can be used to specify packet compression. The only available algorithm is deflate, based on the same algorithm used to compress gzip files (see RFC2394). However, unlike gzip, you cannot specify the compression level. Although compression is useful in some situations, such as transmitting large text files, it isn't ideal for all situations. For example, most encryption algorithms generate random looking data that may not compress well. Also if the data being transmitted is already compressed, then it won't compress any further. Trying to compress data again may only consume more CPU resources. If you're transmitting small packets or not using encryption, then it might be worthwhile to enable compression since the TCP header (a significant transmission overhead) will be compressed. However, for large blocks of streaming data through an encrypted tunnel, you might see better performance without using encryption. This is because the TCP header no longer accounts for a significant amount of data, and encrypted data does not compress well. For these reasons, this option is usually not enabled.

Table 11-5   Available Authentication Algorithms and Required Key Sizes for Setkey

Algorithm	Key size in bits	Key size in bytes
hmac-md5	128	16
hmac-sha1	160	20
keyed-md5	128	16
keyed-sha1	160	20
Null	0–2048	0–256
hmac-sha256	256	32
hmac-sha384	384	48
hmac-sha512	512	64
hmac-ripemd160	160	20
aes-xcbc-mac	128	16
tcp-md5	8–640	1–80

Both ends of an encrypted tunnel need to have the same configuration. Otherwise, they will be unable to communicate. However, both directions of an encrypted tunnel do not need to use the same configuration. For example, transmitting IPsec packets may use an authenticated header with one key, and responses may use authentication and encryption with different keys.

Configuring the Security Policy Database

While the Security Association Database (SAD) is used to match algorithms to a particular configuration, the Security Policy Database (SPD) says when to use the SAD entries. The setkey option spdadd defines the requirements. For example:

```
spdadd 10.1.2.10 10.1.1.5 any -P in
  ipsec esp/tunnel/10.1.2.10-10.1.1.5/require;
```

As with the add command, spdadd takes a series of parameters.

- **Addresses**—The first two parameters specify the source and destination addresses. These can be provided as IP or IPv6. They can also contain an optional subnet mask and port number. For example, 10.1.2.10 is the same as 10.1.2.10/32 and 10.1.2.10/32[any]. If you want to allow an entire subnet, then you can use something like 10.1.2.0/24. You can specify port (for example, port 80) as 10.1.2.10[80] or 10.1.2.0/24[80]. Specific ports are very useful if you are configuring a static VPN.

- **Policy**—The -P option specifies policy requirements. This starts with the direction of packet traversal; -P in, -P out, or -P any. While both sides of an IPsec connection need to have the same SAD values, the -P option in the SDP need to be reversed. If one system says -P in then the other needs to say -P out. The policy also defines what should happen. The options are ipsec for enabling IPsec, discard to deny access, or none to allow unsecured connections.

- **IPsec**—If the policy specifies using ipsec, then you also need to specify which SAD to associate with the SPD and when to associate it. The specification has four parameters, separated by slashes.

  - *Protocol*—This can be either esp or ah.

  - *Mode*—This can be either tunnel or transport.

  - *Addresses*—This is only required for tunnels; it lists the source and destination addresses with optional ports. For transport mode, this field can be blank (denoted by //).

  - *Level*—This says when to enable IPsec. The value must be either default, use, or require. The default setting will consult the esp_trans_deflev kernel variable (see Chapter 7 for sysctl). If you have not changed anything, then this means no IPsec. The use value will try to use IPsec, but fall back to regular IP if a connection cannot be established. Finally, the require value demands IPsec and will not establish a connection without it—this is the most secure option.

Configuring IPsec

There is a startup script called /etc/init.d/setkey that configures IPsec at boot. It does this by consulting the configuration file /etc/ipsec-tools.conf. If you want to configure IPsec, place your settings in this file. Listing 11-5 shows a sample configuration file that uses encryption and authenticated headers between two hosts.

Listing 11-5: Sample /etc/ipsec-tools.conf

```
#!/usr/sbin/setkey -f
# Flush the SAD and SPD
flush;
spdflush;

#########
# My host is 10.1.1.5
# The remote host is 10.1.2.10
```

Listing 11-5 *Continued*

```
#########
# Set a tunnel between 10.1.1.5 and 10.1.2.10
add 10.1.1.5 10.1.2.10 esp 0x201 -m tunnel
  -E 3des-cbc "Twenty-four characters!!"
  -A hmac-md5 "0123456789abcdef" ;

add 10.1.2.10 10.1.1.5 esp 0x301 -m tunnel
  -E 3des-cbc "Twenty-two plus two more"
  -A hmac-md5 0xdeadbeefcafe1234deadbeefcafe1234;

########
# Security policies
# NOTE: If this file is placed on the remote host, then
# swap the "-P out" and "-P in" values.
# All outbound traffic must go through the tunnel
spdadd 10.1.1.5 10.1.2.10 any -P out
  ipsec esp/tunnel/10.1.1.5-10.1.2.10/require;

# All inbound traffic must come from the tunnel
spdadd 10.1.2.10 10.1.1.5 any -P in
  ipsec esp/tunnel/10.1.2.10-10.1.1.5/require;
```

After creating the configuration file, you can test it using:

```
sudo setkey -f /etc/ipsec-tools.conf
```

If there are any errors when it loads, they will be cryptic but at least you will know that there is a problem. Errors are likely due to typographical mistakes or oversights. After it loads, you can use setkey -D and setkey -DP to view the current settings.

```
$ sudo setkey -D
10.1.1.5 10.1.2.10
        esp mode=tunnel spi=513(0x00000201) reqid=0(0x00000000)
        E: 3des-cbc  5477656e 74792d66 6f757220 63686172 61637465 72732121
        A: hmac-md5  30313233 34353637 38396162 63646566
        seq=0x00000000 replay=0 flags=0x00000000 state=mature
        created: Nov 25 16:53:50 2006    current: Nov 25 16:53:55 2006
        diff: 5(s)       hard: 0(s)       soft: 0(s)
        last:                     hard: 0(s)       soft: 0(s)
        current: 0(bytes)         hard: 0(bytes)  soft: 0(bytes)
        allocated: 0     hard: 0 soft: 0
        sadb_seq=1 pid=9861 refcnt=0
10.1.2.10 10.1.1.5
        esp mode=tunnel spi=769(0x00000301) reqid=0(0x00000000)
        E: 3des-cbc  5477656e 74792d74 776f2070 6c757320 74776f20 6d6f7265
        A: hmac-md5  deadbeef cafe1234 deadbeef cafe1234
        seq=0x00000000 replay=0 flags=0x00000000 state=mature
        created: Nov 25 16:53:50 2006    current: Nov 25 16:53:55 2006
```

```
        diff: 5(s)      hard: 0(s)      soft: 0(s)
        last:                   hard: 0(s)      soft: 0(s)
        current: 0(bytes)       hard: 0(bytes)  soft: 0(bytes)
        allocated: 0    hard: 0 soft: 0
        sadb_seq=0 pid=9861 refcnt=0
$ sudo setkey -DP
10.1.2.10[any] 10.1.1.5[any] any
        in prio def ipsec
        esp/tunnel/10.1.2.10-10.1.1.5/require
        created: Nov 25 16:53:50 2006  lastused:
        lifetime: 0(s) validtime: 0(s)
        spid=32 seq=2 pid=9864
        refcnt=1
10.1.1.5[any] 10.1.2.10[any] any
        out prio def ipsec
        esp/tunnel/10.1.1.5-10.1.2.10/require
        created: Nov 25 16:53:50 2006  lastused:
        lifetime: 0(s) validtime: 0(s)
        spid=25 seq=1 pid=9864
        refcnt=1
10.1.2.10[any] 10.1.1.5[any] any
        fwd prio def ipsec
        esp/tunnel/10.1.2.10-10.1.1.5/require
        created: Nov 25 16:53:50 2006  lastused:
        lifetime: 0(s) validtime: 0(s)
        spid=42 seq=0 pid=9864
        refcnt=1
```

Finally, you can test the connection. If you can ping the host or connect using a known service such as SSH or HTTP, then you know it is working.

Enabling Proxies

Another way to add security to the network is to relay through a proxy. Chapter 5 covers how to install a SOCKS server for assisting privacy. The example relays web traffic through a SSH tunnel. However, this example works because the web browser was configured to use a proxy. Under Dapper, there are many different ways to configure proxies. For example, there is a general system proxy setting that few applications use. There are also some generic proxy settings that are supported by a variety of applications.

Proxies can add more than a level of indirection. Some proxy systems, like Tor, can provide network anonymity.

Using the General System Proxy

Individual applications can be independently configured to each use a proxy, In contrast, Ubuntu's Gnome desktop supports a global proxy configuration. The theory is that all applications will immediately use the proxy rather than directly access the Internet. In reality, only specific applications use these settings and you may need to log out and log back in for all applications to use the configuration. General system proxy configurations are commonly required for corporate networks that have specific outbound relays for accessing the Internet.

To set the general proxy, use System ⇨ Preferences ⇨ Network Proxy. This opens the Network Proxy Preferences applet (see Figure 11-3). In this applet, you can declare your SOCKS, HTTP, HTTPS, and FTP proxy servers. You will need to know the host names (or network address) as well as the proxy port number. Under the Advanced Configuration tab, you can specify local hosts and networks that do not require proxy access.

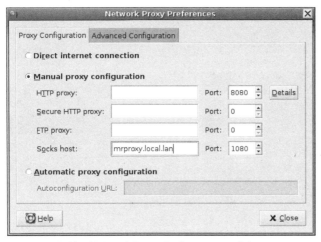

FIGURE **11-3: The Network Proxy Preferences applet.**

Enabling Application-Specific Proxy Configurations

Although the global proxy settings are a nice idea, they are currently not supported by many applications. For example, the settings may be ignored by `firefox`, `ssh`, `wget`, and `apt-get`. If you want more general proxy support, you can use environment variables. Many applications look for HTTP, HTTPS, and FTP proxy definitions in variable names that have become de facto standards. Table 11-6 lists the more common definitions. In general, if the variable is in all capitals, only the server name and port number are specified. Lowercase variables need entire URLs.

Warning

Setting the general system proxy defines many of these variables for new shells and applications. However, they are only set for Gnome applications. For example, if you start the Gnome Terminal, they will be set; however, if you start an `xterm`, they will not be set. They will also not necessarily be available if you remotely log in and you may also need to log out and log back in for the changes to take affect. If you need these proxy settings, you should probably define them manually.

Table 11-6   Common Proxy Environment Variables

Variable	Example	Purpose
HTTP_PROXY	export HTTP_PROXY=10.1.2.45:8080	Define an HTTP proxy.
FTP_PROXY	export FTP_PROXY=10.1.2.45:8081	Define an FTP proxy.
ftp_proxy	export ftp_proxy= "http://10.1.2.45:8081/"	Specify a proxy for relaying FTP traffic.
http_proxy	export http_proxy= "http://10.1.2.45:8080/"	Specify an HTTP proxy.
https_proxy	export https_proxy= "http://10.1.2.45:8082/"	Specify an HTTPS proxy.
gopher_proxy	export gopher_proxy= "http://10.1.2.45:8083/"	Although few networks still support the GOPHER protocol, you can specify a proxy if you need it.
wais_proxy	export wais_proxy= "http://10.1.2.45:8084/"	As with GOPHER, you can specify a WAIS proxy if you need it.

Tip   In many corporate environments, the same server and port are used for all proxy services. They do not need to all be different.

These proxy definitions can be added to your $HOME/.profile (or $HOME/.bashrc) for individual user declarations. For system-wide support, they should be added to /etc/bash.bashrc or /etc/profile.

Note   Setting proxy variables does not impact running applications. You will need to log out and log back in to set the variables for all of your running processes.

Defining these proxy variables will give you proxy support for some applications, but other applications need their own configurations. For example:

- **Firefox**—Proxy settings for the web browser must be specified through the Firefox preferences. If you have multiple profiles, then you will need to set the preferences in each one of them.

- **APT**—The `apt-get` command looks for proxies in `/etc/apt/apt.conf`. The default install says:

```
Acquire::http::Proxy "false";
```

This setting disables all proxies. If you need to use a proxy, then you can change the line to something like:

```
Acquire::http::Proxy "http://proxyserver:port/";
```

This tells `apt-get` to use this specific proxy for HTTP access. If you have multiple proxies available, then you can specify multiple proxy definitions.

Enabling SOCKS Clients

While HTTP and FTP proxies forward specific protocols, SOCKS servers can forward almost any protocol. This can be specified using the SOCKS_SERVER environment variable. For example:

```
export SOCKS_SERVER=10.1.2.251:1080
```

Unfortunately, most applications do not support SOCKS, even if the environment variable is defined. For SOCKS support, you will need to socksify applications.

1. If you have not already installed it, then install the dante-client package. This will give you a SOCKS client.

```
sudo apt-get install dante-client
```

2. Edit the `/etc/dante.conf` configuration and declare your SOCKS server. You will need to know the server's network address, port, and version (either SOCKSv4 or SOCKSv5). My configuration specifies a SOCKS server at 10.1.2.251 and uses the standard port 1080. The configuration looks like this:

```
route {
      from: 0.0.0.0/0 to: 0.0.0.0/0 via: 10.1.2.251 port = 1080
      protocol: tcp udp                # server supports tcp and udp
      proxyprotocol: socks_v4 socks_v5 # server supports both versions.
      method: none #username           # no authentication needed
}
```

3. To enable SOCKS support for non-SOCKS applications, run the application through the `socksify` wrapper. For example to use `ssh` to connect to the host `outside.local.lan` via the SOCKS server, I can use:

```
socksify ssh outside.local.lan
```

Similarly, I can force Firefox to use the SOCKS server without changing the Firefox proxy settings:

```
socksify firefox
```

Socksifying Firefox will only work if there are no other open Firefox windows. This is because Firefox uses inter-process communications when there are multiple instances running, and will use the existing instance instead of creating a new one. You can overcome this limitation by using `socksify firefox --no-xshm`.

Anonymizing with Tor

A simple proxy is good for relaying traffic, but a group of proxies can provide network anonymity. A system called The Onion Router (Tor) uses groups of linked proxies to relay traffic. The connection between each proxy is encrypted, so anyone observing the network traffic will be unable to see what is going on. From the client's end, Tor looks like just another SOCKS proxy server (although it may have significantly higher network delays).

Installing Tor is relatively easy:

```
sudo apt-get install tor
```

The installation packages include startup scripts for `/etc/init.d/` and intelligent default configurations.

To run an application over the Tor network, either set the proxy to be `localhost:9050`, or use the program `torify` the same way you would use `socksify`. For example, to run Firefox through the Tor network, you can use: `torify firefox --no-xshm`. When Firefox runs using Tor, your external IP address may be anywhere in the world. Connecting to sites like Google (`www.google.com`) may display text in English, German, Italian, or some other language depending on where Google thinks you are coming from.

Understanding Tor's Limitations

Although Tor does make all of the SOCKS connections effectively anonymous, there are still some ways to breach the anonymity.

The most significant leak is due to UDP traffic. Tor only proxies TCP. However, host name lookups use UDP. If you connect to a site by specifying the host name, then the host name lookup may be traceable back to your system. To overcome this limitation, install the `privoxy` package.

```
sudo apt-get install privoxy
```

The `privoxy` system provides an HTTP proxy interface to Tor. Since HTTP proxies do not need the client to perform host name lookups, UDP traffic is never generated by the client. You can then use the HTTP_PROXY and `http_proxy` environment variables (or the Firefox HTTP proxy connection preference) to specify using the `privoxy` server on `local-host:8118`.

While `privoxy` provides anonymity for web requests, it offers no security for other protocols. For example, SSH through a Tor connection will generate a host name lookup that is traceable.

Another limitation to Tor comes from unproxied requests. For example, if your web browser spawns a RealPlayer or Totem player for streaming video, then these players may not use the proxy server.

Debugging the Network

In my own experience, configuring networks to use proxies or encryption doesn't always work right the first time. Between typographical errors and missed steps, it might take a few tries to get it right. You are probably going to need a network sniffer to diagnose bad connections and make sure the good connections are working right. (There's no point in setting up an IPsec tunnel only to discover later that all traffic is transmitted in plain text, or to configure a proxy and find that your critical applications are not using it.)

You can use a couple of different tools to diagnose network issues. They range in complexity from "pretty pictures" to hard-core packet analysis. The main tools that I use are EtherApe, Snort, and Ethereal.

Packet sniffers are only as good as the network that they are connected to. If your network adaptor is located on an isolated network (or behind a network switch), then you are not going to see many packets. In contrast, if you are connected to a busy network then you will see lots of packets.

Note Sniffers can only capture packets that reach the network adaptor. The range is limited by physical connectivity. There is no way for a remote packet sniffer to capture packets on your local network.

Using EtherApe

EtherApe is a simple packet sniffer that graphically displays all network connections. This is a great tool if you just want to know where the connections are going, without the details found in every packet.

To use EtherApe, you just need to install it and run it.

```
sudo apt-get install etherape
sudo etherape
```

The graphical display shows a large black field with every node heard on the network represented by dots (see Figure 11-4). Lines between nodes show connections, and line thickness represents the amount of traffic. Lines are color-coded based on protocols and listed in the protocol key on the left side. You can also hover your mouse over any of the lines and see the protocol's name at the bottom of the window.

EtherApe can be a quick way to identify that a proxy or secure tunnel is being used. For example, if all of your network connections should pass through a proxy or VPN, then the only connections should go to one host. Similarly, ports map to protocols. If connections are supposed to use a specific port, then you can make sure that the specific port is being used. Also, if you are using IPsec and the packet should be encrypted, then you should see an unknown protocol being displayed.

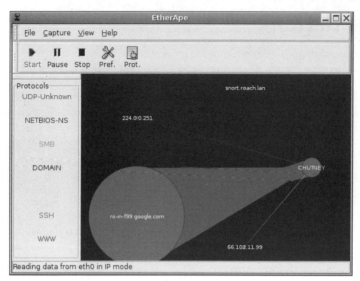

FIGURE 11-4: EtherApe capturing packets

Using Ethereal

Although EtherApe can give you a very quick view of what is happening, it does not allow you to tell what traffic is being transmitted. For example, if everything should use a proxy and EtherApe shows some traffic outside of the proxy's connection, then you need some way to debug it. Ethereal (also known as Wireshark) is absolutely the most powerful packet analyzer I've ever come across. Not only can it collect and display packets, but it can also disassemble the packet fields and decode most protocols. If something should be encrypted, then you can confirm that the packet contents are encrypted. If some packets are unexpected, then you can capture the packets and analyze them and investigate what is really going on.

Running Ethereal is almost as easy as running EtherApe:

1. Install the Ethereal package.

```
sudo apt-get install ethereal
```

2. Run Ethereal.

```
sudo ethereal
```

The Ethereal user interface allows you to capture packets or analyze packets, but capturing and analyzing are usually done in two separate steps.

3. Capture some packets by selecting Capture ⇨ Interfaces from the menu. This will display a list of available interfaces. From this popup window, you can click the Capture button for the appropriate interface.

4. As packets are being captured, a capture status window is available. It shows the number of each packet type collected. When you are done capturing packets, you can click Stop. This moves you from the collection phase to the analysis phase.

5. The analysis window is divided into three segments (see Figure 11-5). The top shows each packet that was collected in the order that it was collected. You can click any packet to reveal the contents in the lower two window sections. The middle section shows the decoded components and the lower section shows the raw packet. You can click any part of the decoded section and the raw bytes in the lower section will be highlighted. Similarly, you can click any of the raw bytes to see what the decoded bytes mean.

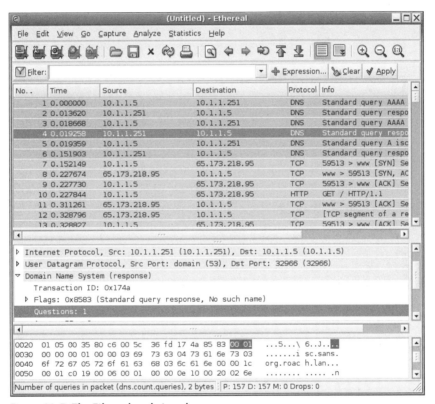

FIGURE 11-5: The Ethereal packet analyzer

Although Ethereal is relatively easy to use, it has some very complex packet filtering options. Some functions have a very steep learning curve. If you have a need to use Ethereal for anything other than basic capture-and-analysis, then you probably should get a book dedicated to Ethereal; there are plenty of available resources. Another source for more information is the Ethereal web site www.wireshark.org.

Sharks and Lawyers

If you start digging into resources dedicated to Ethereal, then it won't take long until you see a product named *Wireshark*. Wireshark *is* Ethereal. Due to some legal wrangling, the creators of Ethereal are no longer permitted to use that name. Although the new name is Wireshark, you will still see the program called Ethereal; Ubuntu still delivers the `ethereal` package. In the future, the package may be renamed as well as the executable, but for now, *Wireshark* stands for *Ethereal*.

Using Snort and Tcpdump

Ethereal and EtherApe are very useful if you have a graphical workstation. However, if you are using a command-line terminal, remote login, or the Ubuntu Server installation, then you really need a command-line tool. The two most common are Tcpdump and Snort.

Tcpdump comes standard on Ubuntu systems. It allows you to capture packets and apply simple packet filters. For example, to capture all UDP packets, you can use: `sudo tcpdump udp`. If you want to capture all packets, use `sudo tcpdump`.

Each packet that is captured displays a line on the console. For example:

```
14:32:28.958743 IP ubuntu.roach.lan.32966 > dns.roach.lan.domain:  31917+
A? cow.rats. (26)
14:32:28.959476 IP ubuntu.roach.lan.32967 > dns.roach.lan.domain:  35645+
PTR? 251.1.1.10.in-addr.arpa. (41)
14:32:28.960760 IP dns.roach.lan.domain > ubuntu.roach.lan.32967:  35645*
1/1/0 PTR[|domain]
14:32:28.960929 IP ubuntu.roach.lan.32967 > dns.roach.lan.domain:  33818+
PTR? 5.1.1.10.in-addr.arpa. (39)
14:32:28.961467 IP dns.roach.lan.domain > ubuntu.roach.lan.32967:  33818*
1/1/0 PTR[|domain]
14:32:28.997905 IP dns.roach.lan.domain > ubuntu.roach.lan.32966:  31917
NXDomain 0/1/0 (101)
```

Each line includes a timestamp, the protocol, source and destination addresses with ports, and some of the decoded packet flags. Tcpdump can be configured to write packets to a file and the file can be later used by Ethereal for analysis.

Snort (`sudo apt-get install snort`) is an alternative to Tcpdump. Just as Ethereal is more complex than EtherApe, Snort is more complex than Tcpdump. Using Snort, you can capture packets, display contents, trigger rules and alerts, and even create your own plug-in filters. As with Ethereal, if you need to use Snort for anything more complicated that displaying packets with basic filters (for example, `sudo snort -v udp`), then I strongly recommend the Snort homepage (`www.snort.org`) as a resource. There are also plenty of books on basic and advanced Snort configurations.

Tip When Snort is installed, it enables the Snort Intrusion Detection System (IDS). This IDS (covered in Chapter 12) generates one e-mail per day, summarizing the possible network attacks that were detected. If you want to disable the IDS, you can remove the S20snort and K20snort initialization scripts from the /etc/rc*.d/ directories.

Summary

Networking with Ubuntu does not need to be static. At any time you can enable new network adaptors and reconfigure existing ones. Network connections may be direct, routed through proxies, or protected through encrypted network connections. With tools like ndiswrapper, you are not limited to hardware with Linux drivers, and IPsec and Tor add security to your connections.

Configuring new network routes is not always simple. Ubuntu offers a variety of powerful packet analysis tools that you can use to diagnose network problems.

Enabling Services

I find it somewhat ironic that the final chapter in this book covers turning on essential network servers such as FTP, e-mail, and the web. Part I of this book covers installation and system tweaking, mainly focusing on the local system, not network services. Part II discusses collaboration systems, where your Ubuntu system primarily operates as a client and details some services such as SMB, SSH, SOCKS, and LPD. Part III aims at improving performance, but not network services. That leaves Part IV. In Chapters 10 and 11, I show you how to lock down your system and network. In this chapter, I show you how to open it up.

Any time you make a network service externally accessible, you open yourself up to a possible network attack. For this reason, it is very important to know exactly what services you are offering and to limit access to only the services you explicitly want to offer. You will also want to monitor your system for possible threats. Basic network services, like web and e-mail systems, should expect to receive literally hundreds of probes and attack attempts per day. As luck usually has it, the day you stop monitoring for these events will be the day one of them becomes successful in compromising your system.

Finally, when you understand the risks and how to handle them, you should feel confident enough to open a network service to other people, including everyone on the Internet. Common services that you will probably want to run include SSH, FTP, e-mail, and web servers.

 Warning While booting from a USB drive is arguably the most difficult hack in this book (see Chapter 1), opening a network service (especially to the Internet) is the most dangerous. The question is not "will you be attacked?"—you will. You will probably be probed and attacked within a few hours, and the attempts will *never* end. Eventually some attack method may succeed. The only real question is, "when will you notice?"

in this chapter

☑ Understanding the Ubuntu default services

☑ Recognizing network threats

☑ Mitigating risks before going public

☑ Monitoring attacks

☑ Running services

Understanding the Ubuntu Default Services

Ubuntu has a simple default setting: no default network services. Although software firewalls are not configured (see Chapter 11), they are also not needed until you begin turning on services.

Although externally accessible services are disabled, some programs do use network connections to communicate between processes on the same system. For example, X-Windows uses some local network connections to communicate between applications. There are two common ways to identify what services are running: `netstat` and `nmap`.

Using netstat

As mentioned in Chapter 7, the `netstat` command provides useful statistics about the network interfaces on your system. Besides summarizing traffic flows, `netstat` can also show established network connections and open network services. Running the command all by itself generates a long list of current TCP, UDP (datagram), and Unix sockets.

Tip   The `netstat` command usually generates a large amount of data. You should pipe the output into a pager such as `more` or `less`. (The `less` command is similar to `more`, but enables you to scroll backwards.)

```
$ netstat | more
Active Internet connections (w/o servers)
Proto Recv-Q Send-Q Local Address            Foreign Address        State
tcp        0      0 marvin.local.lan:55419   bugs.local.lan:ssh     ESTABLISHED
tcp        0      0 localhost:44235          localhost:46274        ESTABLISHED
tcp        0      0 marvin.local.lan:38446   foghorn.local.lan:ssh  ESTABLISHED
tcp        0      0 localhost:46274          localhost:44235        ESTABLISHED
tcp6       0      0 chutney.local.lan:ssh    foghorn.local.lan:1074 ESTABLISHED
Active UNIX domain sockets (w/o servers)
Proto RefCnt Flags       Type       State         I-Node Path
unix  4      [ ]         DGRAM                     13124361 /dev/log
unix  2      [ ]         DGRAM                     5610     @/org/kernel/udev/udevd
unix  2      [ ]         DGRAM                     12548    @/org/freedesktop/hal/u
dev_event
unix  2      [ ]         DGRAM                     13232791
unix  2      [ ]         DGRAM                     13198909
unix  2      [ ]         DGRAM                     13124142
unix  3      [ ]         STREAM     CONNECTED      13123939 /var/run/cups/cups.sock
unix  3      [ ]         STREAM     CONNECTED      13123938
unix  2      [ ]         DGRAM                     13123531
—More—
```

The first part of the `netstat` output shows TCP connections. This can also be shown using `netstat -t`. Connections show the local address (in this case, my localhost is named *marvin*), the connected remote systems (bugs and foghorn), and the connection state. The states represent the TCP connection's status. There are two states that you will often see:

- **ESTABLISHED**—A network connection exists between the two systems.

- **TIME_WAIT**—A connection has terminated and the system is just waiting for any final packets before tearing down the connection.

Along with these common states, there are many other states that exist for very short durations. For example, SYN_SENT and SYN_RECV indicate that a connection is starting. These will quickly switch over to the ESTABLISHED state. There are also plenty of states that indicate a connection is closing. For example, FIN_WAIT1, FIN_WAIT2, CLOSE, and CLOSE_WAIT. These states rarely exist for more than the blink of an eye before switching over to the TIME_WAIT state.

The second part of the `netstat` output shows Unix services. These include connectionless UDP packets (DGRAM) and connection-oriented sockets (STREAM). You can limit the display to just these packets by using `netstat -x`.

Identifying Servers with netstat

Besides showing established connections, `netstat` can display waiting network services. The command `netstat -l` shows all the listening servers.

```
$ netstat -l | more
Active Internet connections (only servers)
Proto Recv-Q Send-Q Local Address           Foreign Address         State
tcp        0      0 *:nfs                   *:*                     LISTEN
tcp        0      0 *:printer               *:*                     LISTEN
tcp        0      0 *:40867                 *:*                     LISTEN
tcp        0      0 localhost:42309         *:*                     LISTEN
tcp        0      0 *:935                   *:*                     LISTEN
tcp        0      0 *:netbios-ssn           *:*                     LISTEN
tcp        0      0 localhost:44235         *:*                     LISTEN
tcp        0      0 *:sunrpc                *:*                     LISTEN
tcp        0      0 localhost:8118          *:*                     LISTEN
tcp        0      0 localhost:socks         *:*                     LISTEN
tcp        0      0 *:smtp                  *:*                     LISTEN
tcp        0      0 localhost:9050          *:*                     LISTEN
tcp        0      0 localhost:6010          *:*                     LISTEN
tcp        0      0 *:668                   *:*                     LISTEN
tcp        0      0 *:microsoft-ds          *:*                     LISTEN
tcp6       0      0 *:ssh                   *:*                     LISTEN
tcp6       0      0 ip6-localhost:6010      *:*                     LISTEN
udp        0      0 *:32768                 *:*
udp        0      0 *:nfs                   *:*
udp        0      0 *:netbios-ns            *:*
—More—
```

This example shows a large number of available network services including Tor (port 9050), NFS and LPD (printer), and even Samba (netbios). If you only want to list TCP or UDP services, you can use `netstat -lt` or `netstat -lu`, respectively. `netstat -lx` shows the local Unix services and sockets.

Running nmap

Although `netstat` usually shows many services, not all are accessible from across the network. For example, the Unix services are usually restricted to the local system and are not externally accessible. In addition, many TCP and UDP services may be bound to the loopback interface rather than the external network interface. These are denoted by the *localhost* interface name.

A better way to identify running services is with the `nmap` command (`sudo apt-get install nmap`). This network-mapping tool can identify every network-accessible service on a host and can even scan an entire subnet in minutes.

Warning In some sensitive network environments, `nmap` will trigger intrusion detection systems. Before you scan a host cross a network, make sure you won't get in trouble with your local network administrators.

Table 12-1 lists some of the common command line parameters that I use with `nmap`. Other parameters are described in the man page for `nmap`.

Table 12-1 Common nmap Command-line Parameters

Parameter	Purpose
`-p portlist`	By default, `nmap` only scans a set of well-known and common ports. This option can be used to specify one or more ports (for example, `-p 80` or `-p 80,443`) or a range of ports (for example, `-p 0-65535` or `-p 1-1023`).
`-P0`	Normally `nmap` pings the host before scanning it. However, if you enabled `iptables` or a firewall to drop ICMP packets, then the host cannot be pinged. This option disables pinging hosts before scanning them.
`-sS`	This performs a SYN-scan. Rather that performing a full TCP connection, only the initial connection is performed. This type of scan is not detected by some logging systems. I use it because it is faster than performing a full TCP scan.
`-sU`	Rather than scanning for TCP services, this will scan for UDP services.
`-sV`	When a network service is identified, only the port number is known. This option tells `nmap` to profile what is running on the port. In many cases, it will identify the name and version of the server.
`-O`	While `-sV` profiles individual services, `-O` profiles the actual operating system. Using the option, `nmap` can try to determine the running operating system and version.

The results from an nmap scan show all of the accessible network services. For example:

```
$ sudo nmap -sS -sV -p 0-65535 -O 127.0.0.1
Starting Nmap 4.10 ( http://www.insecure.org/nmap/ ) at 2006-12-02 10:56 MST
Interesting ports on localhost (127.0.0.1):
Not shown: 65518 closed ports
PORT       STATE SERVICE     VERSION
21/tcp     open  ftp         vsftpd 2.0.4
22/tcp     open  ssh         OpenSSH 4.2p1 Debian-7ubuntu3 (protocol 2.0)
25/tcp     open  smtp        Postfix smtpd
111/tcp    open  rpcbind      2 (rpc #100000)
139/tcp    open  netbios-ssn Samba smbd 3.X (workgroup: WORKGROUP)
445/tcp    open  netbios-ssn Samba smbd 3.X (workgroup: WORKGROUP)
515/tcp    open  printer
668/tcp    open  mountd      1-3 (rpc #100005)
935/tcp    open  status      1 (rpc #100024)
1080/tcp   open  socks?
2049/tcp   open  nfs         2-4 (rpc #100003)
6010/tcp   open  unknown
8080/tcp   open  http-proxy  Microsoft ISA Server http proxy
8118/tcp   open  http-proxy  Junkbuster/Privoxy webproxy
9050/tcp   open  tor-socks   Tor SOCKS Proxy
40867/tcp open  nlockmgr    1-4 (rpc #100021)
42309/tcp open  hpssd       HP Services and Status Daemon
44235/tcp open  hpiod       HP Linux Imaging and Printing System
Device type: general purpose
Running: Linux 2.4.X|2.5.X|2.6.X
OS details: Linux 2.4.0 - 2.5.20, Linux 2.4.18 - 2.4.20, Linux 2.5.25 - 2.6.8
or Gentoo 1.2 Linux 2.4.19 rc1-rc7, Linux 2.6.0 (x86), Linux 2.6.3 - 2.6.10
Service Info: Host:  localhost; OSs: Unix, Linux, Windows
Nmap finished: 1 IP address (1 host up) scanned in 36.204 seconds
```

Using nmap to scan your local system won't generate the same results as scanning from a remote host. This is because some network services are restricted to the local host. Also, some network services do their own filtering (for example, Tcpwrappers from Chapter 11) and only permit local connections. Ideally, you will want to scan your system from a different host on the same local network. Scanning my host from a remote system shows:

```
$ sudo nmap -sS -sV -O -p 0-65535 marvin
Starting Nmap 4.10 ( http://www.insecure.org/nmap/ ) at 2006-12-02 11:00 MST
Interesting ports on marvin (10.1.3.5):
Not shown: 65525 closed ports
PORT       STATE SERVICE     VERSION
21/tcp     open  ftp         vsftpd 2.0.4
22/tcp     open  ssh         OpenSSH 4.2p1 Debian-7ubuntu3 (protocol 2.0)
25/tcp     open  smtp        Postfix smtpd
111/tcp    open  rpcbind      2 (rpc #100000)
```

```
139/tcp    open   netbios-ssn Samba smbd 3.X (workgroup: WORKGROUP)
445/tcp    open   netbios-ssn Samba smbd 3.X (workgroup: WORKGROUP)
515/tcp    open   printer
668/tcp    open   mountd       1-3 (rpc #100005)
935/tcp    open   status       1 (rpc #100024)
2049/tcp   open   nfs          2-4 (rpc #100003)
40867/tcp  open   nlockmgr     1-4 (rpc #100021)
MAC Address: 00:11:D8:AB:39:2C (Asustek Computer)
Device type: general purpose|broadband router
Running: Linux 2.4.X|2.5.X|2.6.X, D-Link embedded
OS details: Linux 2.4.0 - 2.5.20, Linux 2.4.18 - 2.4.20, Linux 2.4.26,
Linux 2.4.27 or D-Link DSL-500T (running linux 2.4), Linux 2.4.7 - 2.6.11,
Linux 2.6.0 - 2.6.11
Service Info: Host:  localhost; OSs: Unix, Linux
Nmap finished: 1 IP address (1 host up) scanned in 25.491 seconds
```

Note that the remote scan shows fewer ports and a slightly different operating system profile. (In this case, it discovered my D-Link router as well as my Linux system.)

Tip   Some of the `nmap` options require root privileges. These include `-O` and `-sS`. If you are the only user on your system and you plan to use `nmap` often, consider making it run with root permissions: `sudo chmod u+s /usr/bin/nmap`. This way, you don't need to use `sudo` to do scans.

Recognizing Network Threats

Every network service that is remotely accessible offers a path onto your system. If there is an exploit (available today *or* some time in the future), then you will have a risk that needs to be addressed. In addition, many network services run with root privileges; an exploit can potentially access your entire file system as root. Even if the exploit only gives user-level access, there are plenty of options for escalating privileges from a "regular" local user to root.

Tip   As far as bug discovery goes, local exploits are much more common than remote exploits. However, if you periodically update your system with `apt-get update` and `apt-get upgrade`, then you should have most of the local exploits under control. Periodically updating your system will also take care of any known remote exploits.

Having open ports accessible within your home or office network is usually not as serious as having ports accessible to anyone on the Internet. For example, I'm not too worried about my RedHat system having access to my Ubuntu box. On the other hand, I certainly don't want everyone in the world to access my Ubuntu NFS service.

What's My Motivation?

Security is a measurement of risk. A good system is "secure enough" for your needs. With security comes tradeoffs for performance, accessibility, and functionality. In order to understand your risks, you need to understand your potential attacker. For example, in your home environment, your main risks are probably restricted to physical access from kids, cats, and the occasional guest (anyone who might download a virus or accidentally delete something critical). However, other risks may include burglary, disk crashes, and viruses that you accidentally download.

Threats at home are different than threats at work. In your office are dozens or hundreds of people with network access, including a few disgruntled employees, and sensitive or company confidential information. However, local access is still limited to people who are usually trusted. This is different from Internet-accessible services, where anyone in the world has access and you *know* that you cannot trust everyone.

The big question becomes: who is your likely attacker, and what does the attacker probably want? In directed attacks, someone wants something on your system—files, passwords, credit cards, secret files, or anything else of value. However, more common are broadcast attacks, where the attacker wants *a* computer and not specifically *your* computer. Even if you have a slow CPU and very little disk space, the fact that you have Internet access means that you can relay spam, act as a proxy for anonymous attacks, or become part of a botnet. If you happen to have a fast computer or a few gigabytes of disk space, then that's just icing on the cake for the attacker. They can use your computer to store porn or warez (stolen software), crack passwords, host chat rooms for other undesirable associates, or worse. That one network service that you temporarily opened to the Internet could be the reason you are at the epicenter of a massive network attack and child pornography ring.

Attackers are constantly scanning the Internet for computers with vulnerable network services. If you open up a web, FTP, or e-mail server, then potential attackers will probably discover it within a few hours. If you open some other service, then it might take longer to be discovered, but eventually someone will find it.

Mitigating Risks Before Going Public

There are a couple of things you can do to mitigate risks before opening a network service to the Internet.

- **Remove defaults**—Any sample scripts and default documentation should be removed. In many cases, sample code can be used to exploit a system, and documentation usually tells an attacker what they are up against. If there is a default login or account name, then change it.

- **Limit service access**—Restrict Internet access to only the necessary services. For example, if you only want to give access to your SSH server, then you don't need to offer your HTTP server to the world. You can restrict access with Tcpwrappers or IP Tables (see Chapter 11). Some services can be bound to the loopback interface rather than the network card. A better alternative to local access restrictions is to use a stand-alone firewall. This way, hostile network traffic never reaches your computer in the first place.

- **Limit services per system**—Ideally, each open network service should be on a different computer system. This way, an attacker who compromises your web server won't also have access to your e-mail, SSH, and other services. In reality, you may not have many computers sitting around, acting as dedicated service providers. Maintenance may also be a hassle. However, if you have a particularly critical service, definitely consider placing it on a standalone system.

- **Limit host access**—If only a few hosts will be accessing the service, consider restricting connections to just those hosts. The restrictions may be based on IP addresses (if they are static), or on VPN technology such as IPsec (see Chapter 11) or SSH (see Chapter 5).

- **Use a firewall**—Anyone using a computer connected to the Internet (or an ISP) without a firewall is just asking for trouble. A simple NAT-based home firewall usually costs under $50 and is well worth the investment.

- **Use a DMZ**—A DMZ (de-militarized zone) is a network buffer region that is surrounded by firewalls. The concept is pretty simple: all inbound traffic must stop at the computer in the DMZ before continuing into the internal network. The DMZ provides a choke point for monitoring suspicious network traffic and authenticating desirable traffic. Configuring a DMZ requires two firewalls and one computer (the computer can even be that old 75 MHz Pentium that you have collecting dust in your closet).

- **Configure an IDS**—An IDS (Intrusion Detection System) watches network traffic for potential threats and alerts you when something questionable is identified.

- **Monitor logs**—Local network services usually generate log files. So do firewalls and IDSs. If you don't periodically look at the logs, then you will never see attacks when they happen.

- **Keep backups**—Being able to recover from a compromise is just as important as knowing how and when the compromise happens. Chapter 3 offers a very simple backup system, but your backups should really match your needs.

- **Patch! Patch! Patch!**—While a home computer with no services may only need to be updated monthly, systems with Internet-accessible services should be patched much more often. Attackers won't wait for you to catch up with the latest exploit.

Monitoring Attacks

Regardless of the type of network service you want to enable, you should have lots of log files that identify what happened and when. You're going to need a way to sort through all the noise and clutter for those few items that might indicate a possible attack—or a successful attack.

What Should You Look For?

There are a couple of different types of attacks, each of which should show up in various log files.

- **Brute force**—Brute force attacks are usually tried against login systems. You should see logs that have a high number of failed connection attempts.

- **Reconnaissance scans**—Before attacking a target, many systems initially perform some type of reconnaissance. This should appear in the logs as a scan. Scans usually look like a bunch of connections or simple queries. There may be one per host, or a suite of connections per host. If the scan finds anything useful, then the attack will come later.

- **One-time tries**—Many automated attack systems blindly try exploits. If the attack works, then you are compromised. If it fails, then you're safe. These should appear in log files as one-time oddities. Or in the case of a massive worm, lots of the same oddity as each infected system tries to spread.

A quick hack for analyzing log files simply looks at file size. If you rotate logs hourly or daily, then look for a sharp increase in log size—this will indicate some new worm or network scan. As far as one-time attacks go, look over some logs to get an idea of "normal" and then look for things that stand out as odd.

Periodic scans of your own systems with tools like nmap should be used to look for new, unexpected services. If there is a new, unexpected service running on your system, then take the time to find out why. If there are lots of new ports, then it is a good sign that the system is compromised. Similarly, look for unexpected network traffic. If you never use IRC and start seeing IRC traffic, then find out where it is coming from!

What Now? After a Compromise...

Ok, so you started a new network service, you put it on the Internet, and you've been compromised. Do you know what you will do? Turning off the system is a good start, but how and when will you turn it back on? Do you reset or restore the system? This could simply reintroduce the same environment that led to the initial compromise!

Regardless what you plan to do, have a plan in place *before* making a service public. For example, what will you do if you are on vacation and you suddenly hear that your hobby FTP server is sending millions of spam e-mail messages? It is better if you take care of it than having your ISP disconnect you.

I have a very simple plan: there is always someone available to pull out the power cord if a system is acting fishy. Later, I can remove the hard drive and mount it under a different Linux system and see what went wrong and recover log files. Later, I can restore from a backup and apply the most recent patches as needed.

Logging Logins

Many types of services provide login access. Failed logins should be placed in log files. Under the default Ubuntu installation, successful logins are stored in `/var/log/wtmp`. This is a binary file that stores the login account name, date of access (login and logout), and if it is a remote connection, then the name of the remote host. You can access this log file with the `last` command.

```
$ last
nealk     pts/2      foghorn.local.lan   Sun Dec  3 10:36   still logged in
nealk     :0                             Sat Dec  2 15:31   still logged in
reboot    system boot 2.6.15-26-686      Sat Dec  2 15:30      (1+00:51)
wtmp begins Sat Dec  2 11:10:17 2006
```

Unfortunately, Ubuntu does not normally log failed login attempts. To log failed attempts, you will need to create a `/var/log/btmp` file. Simply creating this file enables logging and all new login failures will be recorded.

```
sudo touch /var/log/btmp
sudo chown root:utmp /var/log/btmp
sudo chmod 660 /var/log/btmp
```

Tip   The `/var/log/btmp` file is usually used by text-based login windows. The graphical login screen, such as Dapper's `gdm` version 2.14, does not record login failures to `btmp`. To test `btmp`, press Alt+F2 and try a few failed logins, then login and use `lastb` to see the results.

You can access the `btmp` logs using the `lastb` command:

```
$ sudo lastb
UNKNOWN                               Sun Nov 12 15:36 - 15:36  (00:00)
root                                  Sun Nov 12 15:36 - 15:36  (00:00)
root                                  Sun Nov 12 15:35 - 15:35  (00:00)
111                                   Sun Nov 12 12:05 - 12:05  (00:00)
ggg                                   Sun Nov 12 12:05 - 12:05  (00:00)
UNKNOWN                               Sun Nov 12 12:01 - 12:01  (00:00)
UNKNOWN                               Sun Nov 12 12:01 - 12:01  (00:00)
UNKNOWN                               Sun Nov 12 12:00 - 12:00  (00:00)
nealk                                 Sun Nov 12 11:58 - 11:58  (00:00)
nealk                                 Sun Nov 12 11:58 - 11:58  (00:00)
UNKNOWN                               Sun Nov 12 11:56 - 11:56  (00:00)
UNKNOWN                               Sun Nov 12 11:56 - 11:56  (00:00)
btmp begins Sun Nov 12 11:56:40 2006
```

Tip   The `wtmp` and `btmp` log files rotate. You may need to use `lastb -f` to specify a specific log file. For example, `sudo lastb -f /var/log/btmp.1`.

Normally `btmp` only logs valid user names and the time of the failed login attempts. Unknown user names are logged as UNKNOWN. You can change `btmp` to log all unknown usernames, enabling you to see what user names are used by a brute force attack:

1. As root, edit `/etc/login.defs`.

2. Change LOG_UNKFAIL_ENAB from `no` to `yes`. There is no need to restart the system—this change takes affect immediately.

Warning   Users sometimes accidentally enter their password instead of a user name. This means that their passwords will be logged to `/var/log/btmp`. If you accidentally enter your password at the login prompt of a multi-user system, then login and immediately change your password.

Tip   Make sure `btmp` is not world-readable (`sudo chmod o-r /var/log/wtmp`) to prevent other users from potentially seeing login-password mistakes.

Although `last` and `lastb` record login events, not every remote-access system uses them. For example, the SSH daemon logs to `/var/log/auth.log`. To see the list of failed logins, you will need to search the log files:

```
$ zgrep "Invalid user" /var/log/auth.log* | sed -e 's/^.*: //' | sort | uniq -c
      2 Invalid user bill from 127.0.0.1
      1 Invalid user cow from 10.1.3.251
      3 Invalid user dog from 127.0.0.1
```

This command searches all of the `auth.log` files for the lines containing `Invalid user`. It then displays each invalid user name, where the attempt came from, and how many times it was tried (sorted by user name).

Tip   The `zgrep` command searches regular logs and compressed (.gz) files.

Enabling Intrusion Detection Systems

Snort is a very powerful tool. As mentioned in Chapter 11, it can be used to sniff packets. However, Snort can do much more than just collect packets. The default installation (`sudo apt-get install snort`) enables an Intrusion Detection System (`/etc/init.d/snort`).

This constantly watches for suspicious traffic and generates an activity report. To generate a report, you can use the snort-stat command:

```
$ sudo id   # make sure the next sudo command does not prompt for a password
$ sudo cat /var/log/snort/alert | snort-stat -a | less
Events between  11 28 05:29:52  and  12 02 10:26:15
Total events: 1289
Signatures recorded: 21
Source IP recorded: 8
Destination IP recorded: 21


Events from same host to same destination using same method
========================================================================
 # of  from            to              method
========================================================================
 1088  10.1.3.10       10.255.255.255  NETBIOS name query overflow attempt UDP
   73  10.1.3.5        65.19.187.154   WEB-IIS %2E-asp access
   24  204.11.52.67    10.1.3.5        ATTACK-RESPONSES 403 Forbidden
   21  64.127.105.40   10.1.3.5        ICMP Destination Unreachable
Communication with Destination Host is Administratively Prohibited
    9  64.127.105.44   10.1.3.5        ICMP Destination Unreachable
Communication with Destination Host is Administratively Prohibited
    6  10.1.3.5        209.97.46.5     (http_inspect) DOUBLE DECODING ATTACK
    4  10.1.3.251      10.1.3.5        SNMP trap tcp
    4  10.1.3.251      10.1.3.5        SNMP AgentX/tcp request
    3  10.1.3.5        72.21.210.11    WEB-CGI redirect access
    3  10.1.3.251      10.1.3.5        (spp_rpc_decode) Multiple RPC Records
    3  10.1.3.5        203.0.178.91    WEB-CGI count.cgi access
    2  10.1.3.30       10.1.3.5        (portscan) TCP Portscan
    2  10.1.3.251      10.1.3.5        (portscan) TCP Portscan
    2  10.1.3.251      10.1.3.5        (portscan) TCP Portsweep
—More—
```

The log report shows the number of suspicious packets, as well as the type of attack. For example, there were a couple of port scans and port sweeps identified, as well as some suspicious web traffic, but the main concern is a NETBIOS name query overflow attempt. (In this case, it was due to a misconfigured OS/2 system running an old SMB configuration.) Although there are likely to be many false-positive findings, some items such as port scans and known attacks should be closely examined. All of the suspicious packets are saved in /var/log/snort/tcpdump.log.* files. These can be viewed using Ethereal (see Chapter 11).

The actual set of IDS rules used by Snort are found in /etc/snort/rules/. There are dozens of attack signatures that trigger alerts. If you have some known false-positives, you can remove the IDS rule by commenting out the rule in the /etc/snort/snort.conf configuration file. Similarly, if you learn of a new rule, then you can easily add it to the rules directory and tell snort.conf to include the new rule. After changing any of the rules, be sure to restart the IDS: sudo /etc/init.d/snort restart.

The Snort IDS configuration files (`/etc/snort/snort.conf` and `/etc/snort/snort.debian.conf`) have a large number of configuration items, and most have excellent default values. The main items you may want to change are your home network (the `HOME_NET` variable) and the interface. For example, one of my systems has two network adapters: `eth0` and `eth1`. One adapter (`eth0`) is used for regular network traffic, while the other (`eth1`) is connected to a hub in the DMZ and monitors suspicious traffic. To change Snort so that it watches only the second network card, I changed the interface name in `/etc/snort/snort.debian.conf` from `DEBIAN_SNORT_INTERFACE="eth0"` to `DEBIAN_SNORT_INTERFACE="eth1"`.

Running Services

There are literally hundreds of different types of servers that you can install and use. However, when it comes to services on the Internet, there are a couple of main ones that you will probably want to enable. These include SSH, FTP, e-mail, and web.

Hardening SSH

The Secure Shell server (`sshd`) provides encrypted and authenticated remote connectivity for logins, file transfers, and remote command execution. The basic SSH server installation (`sudo apt-get install openssh-server`, discussed in Chapter 5) is secure enough to immediately place on the Internet. However, there are some parameters in the `/etc/ssh/sshd_config` file that you might want to modify for added security (see Table 12-2).

Table 12-2   Commonly Modified SSH Server Parameters

Option	Default Value	Purpose
AllowUsers	AllowUsers *	Restricts login access to a list of user names (separated by white space). You can also specify *user@host* to restrict access to a specific user logging in from a specific host. If only some users should have remote access, then you can use this to explicitly block all other users.
AllowGroups	AllowGroups *	Similar to AllowUsers, you can specify group names found in `/etc/group`. Only users who are members of the specified groups are allowed to login. To find the groups you are in, use the `groups` command.

Continued

Table 12-2   *Continued*

Option	Default Value	Purpose
LoginGraceTime	LoginGraceTime 120	Specifies the number of seconds a user should sit at the password prompt before being disconnected. The sshd has a limit on the number of concurrent connections. If someone is trying to block your connection by tying up all available connections, then consider lowering this value from 120 seconds to 5. You may also want to lower this value if you have users who connect but take too long trying to remember their passwords.
MaxStartups	MaxStartups 10	Specifies how many concurrent login attempts are permitted (before successfully entering your password). The default is 10 concurrent, unauthenticated connections. You should consider changing this to 10:30:60. This specifies allowing 10 concurrent. If the 10 are connected, then drop them at a rate of 30/100—there is a 30-percent chance that some connection will be dropped before LoginGraceTime. This will continue until the maximum of 60 connections is reached; then all new connections are dropped.
Port	Port 22	For servers on the Internet, consider moving them to a port other than 22/tcp. Although this is technically "security by obscurity", it will deter most simple reconnaissance attacks from finding your server and attempting brute-force logins.

Tip   There are two parameters in /etc/ssh/sshd_config that are serious risks any to system on the Internet: PermitRootLogin and PermitEmptyPasswords. By default, users with empty passwords cannot log in. Although the default setting does permit root logins, Ubuntu does not give root a password. Still, setting either of these to yes is a serious risk for system on the Internet. You should consider changing both of them to no.

After you change anything in the /etc/ssh/sshd_config file, you will need to restart the server:

```
sudo /etc/init.d/ssh restart
```

Restarting the server will apply all the changes to new connections, but existing connections will be unaffected.

Using SSH Keys

SSH supports different types of authentication. Basic password authentication is the most common approach. However, password authentication isn't very good for automated tasks like cron jobs (see Chapter 7) that use SSH for network administration.

Another form of authentication uses keys. These can be used in place of passwords. The SSH keys are similar to PGP (see Chapter 10) in that they are asymmetrical; there is a public and a private key. Creating SSH keys requires generating keys on the client and transferring the public key to the server.

1. The ssh-keygen program is used to generate SSH keys on the client. You will need to specify the algorithm (DSA or RSA) and the bit size. For security, use a key size of at least 2048 bits.

```
% ssh-keygen -t dsa -b 2048
Generating public/private dsa key pair.
Enter file in which to save the key (/home/user/.ssh/id_dsa): [enter]
Enter passphrase (empty for no passphrase): [password][enter]
Enter same passphrase again: [password][enter]
Your identification has been saved in /home/user/.ssh/id_dsa.
Your public key has been saved in /home/user/.ssh/id_dsa.pub.
The key fingerprint is:
82:be:37:65:df:d9:f6:20:0a:fc:85:76:8a:c6:61:10 user@ubuntu
```

Generating keys longer than 2048 bits may take awhile. Be patient and it will eventually ask you where to save the keys.

Tip

The passphrase is used to protect the key from theft. If you are not worried about other users on the system stealing your SSH key file, then you can leave this blank. For automated system, you should probably leave it blank.

2. Generating keys creates two files. $HOME/.ssh/id_dsa (or id_rsa) holds the private key, whereas $HOME/.ssh/id_dsa.pub (or id_rsa.pub) is the public key. Transfer the public key from the client to the remote server.

```
scp $HOME/.ssh/id_dsa.pub remote:id_dsa.pub
```

This will use SSH to copy the public key from your local system to the server named *remote*. The file will be copied to $HOME/id_dsa.pub (not $HOME/.ssh/id_dsa.pub on the remote host).

3. You will need to tell the server which keys are permitted for logins. Copy the contents of id_dsa to $HOME/.ssh/authorized_keys. If the file exists, then you can just append to it.

```
mkdir $HOME/.ssh    # in case it does not exist
cat $HOME/id_dsa.pub >> $HOME/.ssh/authorized_keys
```

4. On some SSH servers, you may need to make sure the server accepts keys. Edit (or have the administrator edit) the /etc/ssh/sshd_config file and make sure RSAAuthentication and PubkeyAuthentication are both set to yes. (Under the default installation for Ubuntu, they are already set to yes.) If you made changes, then you will also need to restart the SSH server.

5. Test the connection. You should be able to use ssh and connect to the host using only your key. If you entered a passphrase for the key, then you will be prompted for it but it will not be transferred across the network. Without a passphrase, you should immediately get a command-line prompt.

Tip

If the server does not accept the key, then it will regress to using the user's login password. If you want to disable password-based logins, then set PasswordAuthentication to no in /etc/ssh/sshd_config.

Debugging SSH Connections

The most common problem with SSH is an unknown server key. During the server installation, a server key is generated. The OpenSSH client caches this key the first time you connect to the server, and then compares new keys during subsequent connections. There are only a few real reasons why the server key may not match. First and most common, the server was reinstalled for some reason and generated a new key, or was replaced by a different server with a different key. The alternative is that someone is trying to hijack your connection. Both will appear as a message that looks something like this:

```
@@@@@@@@@@@@@@@@@@@@@@@@@@@@@@@@@@@@@@@@@@@@@@@@@@@@@@@@@@@
@    WARNING: REMOTE HOST IDENTIFICATION HAS CHANGED!    @
@@@@@@@@@@@@@@@@@@@@@@@@@@@@@@@@@@@@@@@@@@@@@@@@@@@@@@@@@@@
IT IS POSSIBLE THAT SOMEONE IS DOING SOMETHING NASTY!
Someone could be eavesdropping on you right now (man-in-the-middle attack)!
It is also possible that the RSA host key has just been changed.
The fingerprint for the RSA key sent by the remote host is
7f:23:ac:9d:4f:6d:88:eb:db:61:85:af:8b:c6:f3:21.
Please contact your system administrator.
Add correct host key in /home/user/.ssh/known_hosts to get rid of this message.
Offending key in /home/user/.ssh/known_hosts:7
RSA host key for localhost has changed and you have requested strict checking.
Host key verification failed.
```

To resolve this problem, you'll need to remove the offending server's key from the SSH cache file: $HOME/.ssh/known_hosts. In this case, delete line 7 as specified in the warning: /home/user/.ssh/known_hosts:7.

Warning

Although hijacking is extremely rare, it is definitely possible! Do not just fix the cache file without making sure that it isn't a real attack. If you are at a coffeehouse (or hacker conference) and you own this server and nothing should have changed, then don't try to fix the connection to the server! If nothing should have changed then this probably *is* an attack and removing the cached entry can allow the attacker access to your system.

Enabling FTP

I use a variety of operating systems—some new and some very old. Using SSH to log in and transfer files between Unix and Linux systems is convenient. However, other operating systems may not be as convenient for using SSH. For example, in my opinion the best SSH clients for Windows are commercial and costly (although some free ones do exist). In some cases (for example, my OS/2 system) SSH is unavailable.

Since I need to transfer files between systems, I have found that FTP is ubiquitous, and usually a little faster than SSH even if it is not as secure. For a local network, FTP is a great file transfer option. For direct Internet access, FTP can be secure enough as long as you lock down the system and recognize that anyone may gain access to the server. Besides being universally available to all clients, FTP also overcomes one serious limitation found in SSH: SSH does not permit anonymous logins. With FTP, anyone can connect to a shared directory for collaboration.

Installing VSFTPD

Ubuntu offers a variety of FTP servers (`apt-cache search ftpd`). My personal preference is the Very Secure FTP Daemon (VSFTPD). I like all of the customizable features and the fact that it is secure enough to be given direct Internet access immediately after being installed. However, you'll probably want to customize the system since the basic installation gives no access.

Installing the server is straightforward:

```
sudo apt-get install vsftpd
```

The installation will start the server as a stand-alone process (not requiring `inetd`), configure the `/etc/init.d/vsftpd` startup script, and create the user *ftp* for anonymous access. The server immediately permits anonymous read-only access to the directory `/home/ftp`. You can log in using the user name *anonymous* or *ftp* with any password.

```
$ ftp localhost
Connected to localhost.
220 (vsFTPd 2.0.4)
Name (localhost:ubuntu): anonymous
331 Please specify the password.
Password: ********
230 Login successful.
Remote system type is UNIX.
Using binary mode to transfer files.
ftp> ls -la
200 PORT command successful. Consider using PASV.
150 Here comes the directory listing.
drwxr-xr-x    2 0         65534        4096 Dec 09 16:30 .
drwxr-xr-x    2 0         65534        4096 Dec 09 16:30 ..
226 Directory send OK.
```

Any files or directories placed in the /home/ftp/ directory will be accessible by the anonymous FTP user. However, regular users do not have access until you explicitly enable it (see the section "Adjusting Regular FTP Access" later in this chapter).

Adjusting Anonymous FTP Access

If you don't want anonymous FTP access, then you can disable it.

1. As root, edit /etc/vsftpd.conf.

2. Change the configuration value anonymous_enable=YES to anonymous_enable=NO.

3. Restart the FTP server:

```
sudo /etc/init.d/vsftpd restart
```

Tip

You will need to restart the server any time you make a change to /etc/vsftpd.conf.

However, if you want to enable FTP access, then there are many configuration options you might want to change. Table 12-3 shows some of the anonymous FTP configuration options. Other options can be found in the online manual (man vsftpd.conf).

Table 12-3   Anonymous FTP Options for /etc/vsftpd.conf

Option	Example	Purpose
anon_upload_enable	anon_upload_ enable=YES	Allow anonymous users to upload files to the /home/ftp/ directory.
anon_mkdir_write_enable	anon_mkdir_write_ enable=YES	Allow anonymous users to create directories under /home/ftp/ with the mkdir FTP command.
anon_other_write_enable	anon_other_write _enable=YES	Allow anonymous users to rename or delete files under /home/ftp/.
anon_max_rate	anon_max_rate=131072	Throttle file transfer rates for anonymous users. This specifies 131,072 bytes per second (or 1 megabit per second).

Table 12-3 *Continued*

Option	Example	Purpose
anon_world_readable_only	anon_world_readable_only=YES	Restrict anonymous users to downloading only files that are world-readable. This way, the user *ftp* may have private files that cannot be downloaded.
hide_ids	hide_ids=YES	Changes all user and group IDs so they look like ftp. By default, all IDs are shown by their numeric values.
secure_email_list_enable	secure_email_list_enable=YES	Force anonymous users to provide a valid password. You will need to create the file /etc/vsftpd.email_passwords and give it a list of passwords, one per line. Any of these passwords are acceptable for anonymous access.

Tip If you allow anonymous users to upload files, consider enabling disk quotas for user ftp (see Chapter 8). This way, anonymous FTP users won't consume all of your disk space.

Adjusting Regular FTP Access

By default, VSFTPD disables FTP access for regular users. To enabling FTP access for local (non-anonymous) users:

1. Edit /etc/vsftpd.conf.

2. Uncomment the local_enable=YES line.

3. Restart the server:

```
sudo /etc/init.d/vsftpd restart
```

After these changes, any user may FTP to his or her account by specifying a valid username and password. There are other local user options for /etc/vsftpd.conf that you may want to modify (see Table 12-4).

Table 12-4 Local User FTP Options for /etc/vsftpd.conf

Option	Example	Purpose
max_clients	max_clients=20	Limit the number of client connections. In this case, up to 20 clients can be connected at once. The default value is 0 meaning *no limit*.
max_per_ip	max_per_ip=2	Specify how many FTP connections may come from the same IP address. The default is 0 meaning *no limit*.
local_max_rate	local_max_rate=1048576	Specify the number of bytes per second for throttling FTP connections. This example sets a limit of one megabyte (eight megabit) per second. If you have an 8 Mbps connection, then consider setting the limit to 6 Mbps or less so the FTP server will not consume all available network bandwidth. The default value has no limit.
chroot_local_user	chroot_local_user=YES	Restrict local users to their home directories rather than letting them access anything on the system.
chroot_list_enable	chroot_list_enable=YES	Specify a list of users that should or should not be limited to their home directories. If chroot_local_user is NO, then this is a list of users who should be restricted. If chroot_local_user is YES, then this is a list of users who should not be restricted. The list of users (one user name per line) is stored in /etc/vsftpd.chroot_list (you'll need to create this file).

Tip   VSFTPD logs every connection, file transfer, and anonymous login password to the file `/var/log/vsftpd.log`. If your system is connected to the Internet, then you should monitor this log file for possible attacks or abuse. The log file is rotated weekly by the `logrotate` configuration file `/etc/logrotate.d/vsftpd` (see Chapter 10 for rotating log files).

Securing Internet FTP

FTP is not a secure protocol. Every user name and password is transmitted in plain text across the network. If your server is accessible from the Internet, then anyone capable of capturing your packets will see your valid user name and password. If you need to give users FTP access, consider creating a second account strictly for FTP access. By default, new accounts are given a unique group name. You can create an FTP-only account for each user, and assign the accounts to the user's group name. For example, user bill can be given the account bill-ftp in the group bill:

```
sudo useradd -m -g bill -c "FTP for Bill" bill-ftp
```

Be sure to give bill write-access to the `bill-ftp` directory:

```
sudo chmod -R g+w /home/bill-ftp
```

Then you can give this account a different password than Bill's regular account.

```
sudo passwd bill-ftp
```

Finally, you can block SSH and remote login access for any account containing `-ftp` in the account name.

1. Edit `/etc/ssh/sshd_config`.

2. Add the following option: `DenyUsers *-ftp`

3. Restart the SSH server: `sudo /etc/init.d/ssh restart`

This way, user bill can access the directory `bill-ftp`. But if his login credentials are ever compromised, then the attacker will be unable to access the account through SSH.

Enabling Postfix

E-mail is pretty much a mandatory network service. If you don't want to host your own e-mail, then you just need an e-mail client (see Chapter 5). However, if you plan to actually receive e-mail on your own system, then you will need an e-mail server. In addition, many applications generate status reports using e-mail. You will need a server if you want to send the e-mails directly to yourself.

Tip I have a home firewall that can e-mail its system logs. Rather than sending the logs out to my ISP, I have them sent directly to my own, internal mail server running on an Ubuntu system.

Ubuntu offers many different e-mail servers. However, Sendmail, Qmail, and Postfix are the most common under Linux. Of these servers, Sendmail is the oldest and most widely used, but it is also historically the most insecure. My personal preference is Postfix because of its security, speed, and reliability. Each of these mail servers support configurations that vary from plug-and-play simple to extremely complex. Unfortunately, none of these mail servers are trivial to configure. (Sendmail is one of the most complicated ones to configure—another reason that I like Postfix.)

To get started with your mail server, you will need to install the server package, configure it, and test it. If it tests well and seems to work, then you can be really daring and open it to the world.

1. Install the Postfix server. This will create the appropriate startup scripts, place default files, and start the server:

```
sudo apt-get install postfix
```

2. During the installation, you will be prompted for the type of installation. Your options are:

   ▪ **No configuration**—Install the server but leave it unconfigured. (Probably not what you want unless you are trying to repair a broken installation.)

   ▪ **Internet Site**—Assume the server will be directly connected to the Internet. Use this if you actually intend to send and receive e-mail directly. This is the default option but it is probably not what you want if you are installing on a home system, private network, or for a small business.

   ▪ **Internet with smarthost**—This configuration is useful for most home users who need to relay out-bound e-mail through an ISP's smart mail relay. This can be used to provide a mail server to a local never even if the host is not accessible from the Internet.

Note A *smarthost* is a mail relay that knows how to route e-mail across the Internet. Many ISPs provide a smarthost for sending e-mail. You'll need to ask your ISP if they have an SMTP server for outbound delivery.

   ▪ **Satellite system**—This option configures Postfix as a system for sending e-mail through a smart mail relay, but not for receiving. This is a great option if your actual e-mail is stored on some other server.

   ▪ **Local only**—Choose this configuration if you have no external systems that will be relaying e-mail through this host.

I usually choose the Internet Site or Internet with smarthost option for primary servers. However, for secondary servers and workstations, I use the Satellite system. Depending on the option you choose, you will be prompted to supply your own mailing domain, smarthost name, and other configuration values. Then the installation will complete and the server will start up.

Post-Installation Configuration

There are a couple of options in `/etc/postfix/main.cf` that you might want to modify or add after the installation.

- `relayhost`—This option is the IP address or host name of the smarthost. If it is blank, then no smarthost is used.

- `mydestination`—This is a comma-separated list of host names and domains that are used for local delivery. You probably should add your system's host name to this list. Also, if this server is expected to receive e-mail for multiple domains, then you'll want to add every domain here.

- `myhostname`—This option specifies you host's Internet host name that is revealed when sending e-mail. I usually make this my Internet domain name rather than my private LAN's domain since seeing e-mail from neuhaus.roach.lan won't make sense to anyone but me.

- `mydomain`—Similar to `myhostname`, this specifies your Internet domain name. If you have a vanity (personal) domain, you can put it here rather than using your ISP or any private domain name.

- `inet_interfaces`—You can specify one or more network interfaces for receiving e-mail. If your system has multiple network interfaces but only one that should receive e-mail, then you definitely need to modify this line. If you're just testing, you can always say `inet_interfaces = loopback-only` and only receive e-mail from yourself.

- `mynetworks`—If other systems will be relaying e-mail through your server, then you will need to specify the networks that can relay e-mail. For example, I use:

```
mysetworks = 127.0.0.0/8, 10.0.0.0/8
```

This setting enables me to send e-mail from localhost (the 127.0.0.1 subnet) and from my private, local network: 10.*x.x.x*. All other machines (not on these networks) that connect to my mail server can only deliver e-mail directly to this host; they cannot relay. This way, my host will not be used to relay spam to other networks.

- `smtpd_banner`—This is the welcome banner that is displayed any time a mail client connects to the mail server. For security, it should display as little information as possible about the system—don't display the server's version since that can be used by an attacker to gain knowledge about the server. The default setting does not give a version, but it does state Ubuntu (I recommend removing that). I usually make a simple banner:

```
smtpd_banner = Private System - All connections are logged.
```

There are many more configuration options. The file `/usr/share/postfix/main.cf.dist` is a template that describes every default option and configuration. Alternately, you can consult the man page: `man 5 postconf`. When you finish tweaking your configuration file, you need to tell Postfix to reload it:

```
sudo /etc/init.d/postfix reload
```

Testing Postfix

When you have it all configured, try sending an e-mail to yourself—both locally and to a remote system so that you can verify network access. Also, if any systems on your network will be relaying through your server, then try relaying e-mail. If there are any problems or errors, you should see them logged in `/var/log/mail.log`.

Opening Postifx

If you are going to be making your mail server publicly accessible from the Internet, then you will need to open port 25/tcp in your firewall. This traffic should go to your mail server. After opening the firewall, you can try e-mailing yourself from outside your network and see if you receive it.

Warning Opening your mail server to the Internet is not as easy as opening a port in a firewall. You're also going to need to configure your DNS entry for your domain so the server is listed as a mail exchanger (DNS MX record). How to do this depends on your domain registrar or DNS hosting provider. Contact them if you have questions.

Enabling Apache

Web servers play an important role on most networks. You can use them to create official web sites, or to test web pages before making them public. On internal networks, placing a file on a web site for download can be more convenient than using an FTP server. In addition, server-side scripts such as CGI scripts and PHP can create dynamic content. As a software developer, I frequently use HTML and CGI scripts to mock up graphic interfaces and user flows before devoting time to creating the final "real" interface.

The Ubuntu repositories contain a wide variety of web servers. For example, `thttpd` is a tiny server that is ideal for minimal-resource systems. Other server packages include `dhttpd`, `fnord`, and the Roxen Challenger server (`roxen4`). However, Apache is by and far the most common server. Although it isn't tiny, it is fast, stable, secure, and extremely flexible.

The basic Apache package installs the core web server: `sudo apt-get install apache`. This provides the server (`httpd`), startup script (`/etc/init.d/apache`), and log management file (`/etc/logrotate.d/apache`). You should be able to connect to it using `http://localhost/` and see a generic web page (see Figure 12-1).

Are You Being Served?

There are actually two different branches of Apache web servers: 1.x and 2.x. The Apache Software Foundation supports both versions. Basically, the 2.x branch is a complete rewrite and offers features such as IPv6 support and a new software API. However, unless you plan to create plug-ins for Apache (not CGI), you'll probably never notice a difference.

For Ubuntu, the `apache` package installs Apache 1.x, while `apache2` installs the 2.x version. My preference is usually for Apache 1.x since it seems a little faster to me. (Unless I'm developing plug-ins, in which case I like the 2.x API). However, if I'm just creating web pages and CGI scripts, or installing web applications like Wikis and blogs, then either version works well.

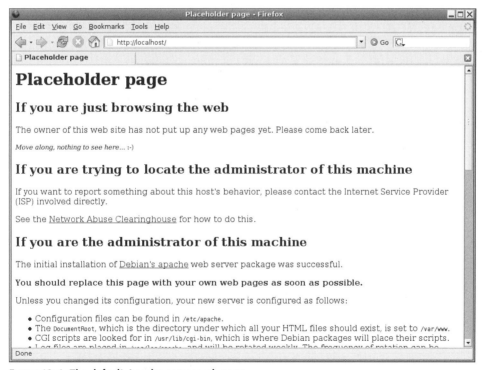

FIGURE 12-1: The default Apache server web page

Post-Installation Configuration

After installing Apache, there are a few configuration items that you will want to tweak. These are stored in the `/etc/apache/httpd.conf` file.

- `ServerName`—This configuration option specifies the host name to use during a redirection. It defaults to localhost—that's fine for testing but it really should be a network identifiable host name. Use either the machines public IP address or public domain name instead of localhost.

- `ServerAdmin`—This is the person to contact in case of a problem. It defaults to webmaster@localhost. I recommend creating a webmaster account for your domain and setting that as the contact. I try not to use specific users since people in companies have a tendency to move around—it's easier to change the mail alias than contact everyone who has the webmaster e-mail address.

- `DocumentRoot`—The default root is `/var/www/`. I usually change this to `/home/www-data/` (after creating a directory for the www-data user). I mainly do this because on my systems `/home/` usually has more disk space than `/var/` and if I'm enabling disk quotas, then `/home/` usually has quotas enabled.

Beyond the basic contact and host name configurations, I also modify some of the default directories and files listed in the `/etc/apache/httpd.conf` file. Most of this is done for additional security.

- **Remove unneeded aliases**—Anything that is not needed on the server can be used to profile and potentially attack the server. I usually remove the web server's `/doc/` entry, `/images/`, and `/perl/`. For example, `/doc/` is defined as:

```
<IfModule mod_alias.c>
 Alias /doc/ /usr/share/doc/
</IfModule>

<Location /doc>
  order deny,allow
  deny from all
  allow from 127.0.0.0/255.0.0.0
  Options Indexes FollowSymLinks MultiViews
</Location>
```

I remove all of this. Even though `/doc/` is only accessible from the local system, I have never needed to use any of these files from the web browsers. Providing these over the web could tell an attacker exactly what software (and vulnerabilities) are on my system.

- **Disable indexes**—Throughout the configuration file are Options lines that reference `Indexes`. For example:

```
<Directory /var/www/>
Options Indexes Includes FollowSymLinks MultiViews
  ...
```

Just remove the `Indexes` keyword. With this option, a directory without an `index.html` file will actually show the directory contents. This enables anyone to browse any file that may be accessible from the web server—including backup versions, temporary files, and hidden or personal directories. Removing the `Indexes` option blocks open directories and returns an error. If a specific directory should be open, then I can open it on an as-needed basis.

- **Enable CGI scripts**—I do a lot of programming, so I like to have CGI scripts enabled. I usually edit the `public_html` section and add `ExecCGI` to the list of options. This way, any executable in any user's `public_html` directory will act as a CGI script. The entire section ends up looking like:

```
<Directory /home/*/public_html>
    AllowOverride FileInfo AuthConfig Limit
    Options MultiViews SymLinksIfOwnerMatch ExecCGI
    <Limit GET POST OPTIONS PROPFIND>
        Order allow,deny
        Allow from all
    </Limit>
    <Limit PUT DELETE PATCH PROPPATCH MKCOL COPY MOVE LOCK UNLOCK>
        Order deny,allow
        Deny from all
    </Limit>
</Directory>
```

You will also need to go down to the `AddHandler` section and uncomment the CGI handler line:

```
AddHandler cgi-script .cgi .sh .pl
```

This handler allows any file that ends with `.cgi`, `.sh`, or `.pl` to be used as a CGI script.

Warning

Enabling CGI scripts is definitely *not* for everyone. There are huge security implications here. If you enable CGI scripts for everyone, then there is a very serious threat of an attacker exploiting a weak script and compromising your system. For public servers that host many different users, I strongly recommend *not* enabling ExecCGI for everyone. But if it is just you on a private server, then this is a very convenient option.

After changing the `/etc/apache/httpd.conf` file, you will need to reload the configuration file.

```
sudo /etc/init.d/apache reload
```

Extending Apache

The basic Apache installation is good for serving web pages and handling basic CGI scripts. However, there are many additional packages that can be added to extend the server's functionality. These additional modules provide functionality that integrates into the web server. The full list of available modules can be found with `apt-cache search libapache-mod`.

Table 12-5 lists some of the available packages and the functionality that they provide. You can install any of them using `apt-get install package`. In some cases, there will be additional configuration steps needed before the modules can be used.

Note For many of these modules, you can install them as an Apache plug-in or statically linked into the web server. For example, mod_perl can be loaded using `libapache-mod-perl` or statically provided by `apache-perl`. From my viewpoint, there is no real reason to have most of these libraries statically linked.

Table 12-5   Additional Apache Packages

Package	Functionality
`libapache-mod-perl`	Adds support for Perl support. You can use `<Perl>...</Perl>` sections in your HTML to execute server-side scripting with Perl.
`libapache-mod-ssl`	Adds SSL support to the Apache server. This enables you to use HTTP or HTTPS. However, you will need to configure your SSL certificates before enabling SSL.
`libapache-mod-php4`	Provides PHP version 4 server-side scripting support. (If you are using Apache 2.x, then install `libapache2-mod-php4` instead.)
`libapache2-mod-php5`	Provides PHP version 5 server-side scripting support for Apache 2.x. Unfortunately, at the time of this writing, `libapache-mod-php5` was not available as a package for the Apache 1.x server. However, the `php5-cgi` package provides similar functionality.
`tomcat5`	This module provides support for Java and JSP web pages. Unlike the other modules, this one requires a large number of dependencies for supporting the Java environment.

Creating Web Pages

After configuring the web server, you will want to create some HTML web pages. At minimum, you will want to replace the default placeholder (as previously shown in Figure 12-1) with your own page—or a blank page. Unless you change it (like I usually do), the default server web pages are located in `/var/www/` and the placeholder is `/var/www/index.html`. Individual users can create a `public_html` directory (`mkdir $HOME/public_html`) and place their personal files in this directory. For example, Bill (my technical reviewer) can use:

```
mkdir /home/bill/public_html
echo "Test page" > /home/bill/public_html/index.html
```

He can then access his test page using `http://localhost/~bill/`.

Tip	If you get an error accessing your page, check the file and directory permissions. Your home directory, `public_html` directory, and every web page need to be accessible by user ww-data or group www-data. This usually means making your home directory at least world-executable (`chmod a+x $HOME`) and the web directory world readable: `find $HOME/public_html -type d -exec chmod 755 '{}' \;` and `chmod -R a+r $HOME/public_html`.

Summary

It does not take much skill to install a basic Ubuntu system and use the out-of-the-box configuration. However, configuring, tuning, optimizing, and securing the system to fit you needs takes serious skills. If you want to safely enable network services, then you'll need to start with a basic system and customize it to your needs. Although these services enable you to provide support for other systems on the network, they also open up your system and provide vectors for attackers. However, these hacks for network services should enable you to run the servers you want and need, without opening you up to too much risk.

Index

A

ACPI (Advanced Configuration and Power Interface), 13
aliases, bash, 42–43
Alternate CD-ROM installation, 6, 10–11
Alt+Tab, switching applications and, 235
anacron, 224–225
Apache, 372–377
application-specific proxy configurations, 339–341
applications
    associating, USB, 93–94
    processes, 205
    switching, 233
        Alt+Tab, 235
        Ctrl+Alt+Tab, 236
        Firefox tabs, 236–237
        Window List, 234–235
        Window Selector, 234–235
    windows
        custom, 238–242
        Devil's Pie, 240–242
        X-Windows, 239–240
APT (Advanced Package Tool), 105
    cache, 116
        cleaning, 311–312
    CD-ROM repositories, 115
    installation and, 117
    packages, removing, 117–119
    repository location, 112
    searches, 116–117
    upgrades and, 120
associating, applications, with USB, 93–94
at, 224
ATI video card, Open GL and, 262
ATM (Asynchronous Transfer Mode), network cards, 68
audio
    file formats, converting, 34–35
    files, modifying, 36
    sox, 34–35

automation, 245–247
Automatix, 123

B

background
    animating desktop, 272–274
    changing, 36–39
    color, 38
    emblems, 57
backups, 84
Bash (Bourne-Again Shell), 41
    aliases, 42–43
    commands, 44
    file completion, 41
    functions, 43–44
boot image, USB drive and, 22–23
boot options
    services-admin and, 71
    sysv-rc-conf and, 71–73
booting
    speeding up boot time, 229–231
    from USB drive, 19–21
browsers
    Konquerer, 146
    Lynx, 146
    Mozilla, 145
buffers, 242–245
buttons, GDM, 51–53

C

caches
    APT, cleaning, 311–312
    Web, erasing, 311
Calc (Open Office), 180
ccd function, 43–44
CD-ROM repositories, APT, 115
clipboards, creating, 244–245
clock, synchronization, 167–168
collaboration, networks
    desktop sharing, 185–187

remote desktops, 183
VNC viewer, 184–185
color, background, 38
configuration
boot options
services-admin and, 71
sysv-rc-conf and, 71–73
dual boot, 7–8
EncFS, 305–307
Evolution accounts, 153 154
Nautilus, 57
network devices, 315–318
RAIDs, 85
wireless networks
drivers, 318, 319
ndiswrapper, 319–322
tools, 322–324
WEP (Wireless Equivalent Privacy), 324
CPUs
multiple, enabling, 73–75
resources, 213
tracking usage, 249–250
cron, 224–225
Ctrl+Alt+Delete, enabling/disabling, 44–45
Ctrl+Alt+Tab, switching applications, 236
CUPS, printer sharing, 78

D
ddcprobe, 256
debugging
EasyUbuntu, 122–123
network
EtherApe, 343–344
Ethereal, 344–345
Snort, 346–347
Tcpdump, 346–347
Wacom tablet, 95–96
X-Windows, 263–264
desktop
background, animating, 272–274
sharing, 185–187
Desktop CD-ROM installation, 6, 8–10
device drivers, 65–66

devices
network, configuration, 315–318
starting, 69–73
Devil's Pie, 240–242
digital cameras, 99–101
directories, SAMBA, sharing with Windows, 173
disk I/O, processes and, 214–215
disk space, processes and, 213
disk usage, tracking, 250–254
distributions
dapper, 106
dapper-backports, 106
dapper-security, 106
dapper-updates, 106
selecting, 3–5
dnotify, 245
downloading, source code, reasons for, 127–128
dpi (fonts), 39
dpkg (Debian Package Manager), 107
drawing tables, enabling, 94–97
drivers
video, changing, 260
wireless networks, 318, 319
drives
backups, 84
mounting systems, 83
upgrading, 81–83
dual boot, configuration, 7–8
DVD, support, 124

E
e-mail
Evolution, account configuration, 153–154
fetchmail, 156–158
FreePOPs, 159–160
Gmail, 154–156
GPG integration, 304–305
LDAP, 160–161
Thunderbird, 162–163
Yahoo!, 158–159
EasyUbuntu
debugging, 122–123
installation, 120–122
Edubuntu, 4

Ekiga, 164–165
emblems (Nautilus), 57–58
    uses, 58
    XML files, 58
emulators
    file sharing, 199
    hardware, 189
    limitations, 190
    Qemu, 192–193
        partitions, 195
        Qemu VM, running, 194
        Qemu VM installation, 193–194
    software, 189
        selecting, 189–191
    virtual disks, 191
    VMware, 196–198
    Xen, 198–200
EncFS
    configuration, 305–307
    encrypting
        CD-ROMs, 308
        directories, 307–308
        networked file systems, 308
        USB drives, 308
    installation, 305–307
    limitations, 309
    maintenance, 307
encfs, 306–307
encrypting file systems
    CD-ROMs, 308
    directories, 307–308
    EncFS
        configuration, 305–307
        installation, 305–307
    networked file systems, 308
    USB drives, 308
erasing Web caches, 311
EtherApe, 343–344
Ethereal, 344–345
Evolution
    accounts, configuration, 153–154
    crashes, 161–162
    fetchmail, 156–157
        FreePOPs and, 159–160
        Gmail, adding, 156
        recovery, 161–162

F
faad package, 124
fetchmail, 156–157
file encryption, GPG, 302–303
file sharing
    emulators and, 199
    NFS
        client, 171
        enabling, 170–173
        server, 172
    SAMBA
        directories, Windows and, 173
        Windows directories, accessing, 175–176
    USB drives, 18–19
file system, installation, full file system, 23–27
Firefox
    browsers, remote, 145
    file configurations, 140–142
    handlers, 144–145
    plug-ins
        adding, 143
        removing, 144
    preferences, 133
        Advanced, 137–139
        Content, 136–137
        Downloads, 137
        General, 134
        Privacy, 134–136
        Tabs, 137
    profiles, 139–140
    search engines, 142–143
    switching tabs, 236–237
firewalls
    IP tables and, 328–331
    tcpwrappers and, 326–327
        enabling, 327–328
        testing configuration, 327
Flash player, 125
flashplugin-nonfree package, 125

flipping screen, 258–259
fonts
 dpi, 39
 large, 39–40
 Nautilus, 60–61
 packages
  gsfonts (Ghostscript fonts), 126
  installing, 126–127
  international fonts, 127
  ttf (TrueType fonts), 126
  Windows fonts, 127
  xfonts, 126
FreePOPs, 159–160
FreshMeat, 105
FTP
 anonymous access, 366–367
 enabling, 365–369
 regular access, 367–369
 VSFTPD, 365–366
full file system, installation, 23–27

G
g++ (Gnu C++), 129
Gaim instant messaging, 163–164
gcc (Gnu C Compiler), 129
GDM (Gnome Desktop Manager)
 background, 37
 menus, adding, 54
 panels, adding, 53
 prompt button, 51–53
 skins, 54–56
 themes, 54–56
general system proxy, 338–339
GIMP (GNU Image Manipulation Program), 66
Gmail
 configuration, 155
 invitations, 155
 retrieving messages, 154
Gnome desktop, 4
 applications, startups, 221–224
GnomeMeeting, 164
Gnu C Compiler (gcc), 129
Gnu C++ (g++), 129

GPG (Gnu Privacy Guard), 296
 e-mail integration, 304–305
 file encryption, 302–303
 keys
  creating, 296–298
  searches, 299
  transferring, 299–300
 signing data, 303
 trust, 300–302
GRUB, 22
gsfonts (Ghostscript fonts), 126
Gstreamer interface, 124
Gtk resources, 239
gxine package, 125

H
hardware emulators, 189

I
I/O bound processes, 209
icons, stretching, 59–60
ifconfig, 69
IMAP (Instant Message Access Protocol), 153
Impress (Open Office), 178–179
init.d, 70
insmod command, 67–68
installation
 APT and, 117
 dual boot configuration, 7–8
 EasyUbuntu, 120–122
 EncFS, 305–307
 file system, full file system, 23–27
 font packages, 126–127
 Mac, 15–16
 minimal system, 13–14
 modules, 67–69
 multimedia support, 124–125
 network, 14–15
  USB drives and, 21–22
 options, 13
 server, 6–9
 source code, 128–129
 SSH server, 147–148
 Synaptic, from CD-ROM or directory, 110–111

web support, 125–126
workstation, 6–9
instant messaging, Gaim, 163–164
international fonts, 127
IPsec
    configuration, 336–338
    enabling, 332
    keys, creating, 333–338

J
Java, enabling, 130–131

K
kernel, parameters, 226
    per user settings, 228–229
    RAM, 226–227
    shared memory, 227–228
keyboard
    layouts, changing, 49
    Macintosh, 47–49
        remapping Alt key, 50–51
        remapping Command key, 50–51
    replacing keys as joke, 51
keycodes, 48
keysyms, 48
killing processes, 208–211
Konquerer browser, 146
Kubuntu, 4

L
lame package, 124
LDAP (Lightweight Directory Access Protocol),
        160–161
libdvdcss2 package, 124
libxvidcore24 package, 124
Live CD, USB drive
    floppy, 23–25
    hard drive, 25–27
login, startup music, 33–36
logs
    rotating, 312–313
    temporary files, clearing, 309–310
LPD, printer sharing, 79–80
lsmod command, 67
Lynx browser, 146

M
Macintosh
    installation, 15–16
    keyboard, 47–49
        remapping Alt key, 50–51
        remapping Command key, 50–51
    mouse, 46–47
main component package repository, 106
make command, 129
memory
    sharing, modifying, 227–228
    video, 216
menus, Nautilus scripting menus, 61–64
Microsoft Exchange, 153
minimal system installation, 13–14
mjpegtools package, 124
modprobe command, 67
modules
    installing, 67–69
    loading, 66–69
    optimization, 69
    removing, 67–69
    viewing, 67
monitors, configuring dual
    two computers
        different desktops, 281–285
        one desktop, 278–281
    two heads, 274–278
mounting systems, 83
mouse
    Macintosh, 46–47
    serial, 88–89
    Xorg.conf, 89
Mozilla browser, 145
MP3, support, 124
MPEG, support, 124
MPEG 4, support, 124
multimedia
    Gstreamer interface, 124
    support, installing, 124–125
    Xine, 125
multiverse component package repository, 106
music, startup, 33–36

N

Nautilus, 56–57
  Actions, installation, 61–62
  commands, custom menu commands, 63–64
  configuration, 57
  emblems, 57–58
  fonts, 60–61
  icons, stretching, 59–60
  menus, scripting menus, 61–64
  templates, 61
ndiswrapper, 319–322
NetMeeting, 164
netstat, 350–352
network
  collaboration, 182–183
    desktop sharing, 185–187
    remote desktops, 183
    VNC viewer, 184–185
  debugging
    EtherApe, 343–344
    Ethereal, 344–345
    Snort, 346–347
    Tcpdump, 346–347
  devices, configuration, 315–318
  firewalls
    IP tables and, 328–331
    tcwrappers, 326–328
  installation, 14–15
    USB drives and, 21–22
  IPsec
    enabling, 332
    key creation, 333–338
  mitigating risks, 356
  monitoring attacks, 357–361
  threats, recognizing, 354–355
  throughput, 217
nfs-common, 170
nfs-kernel-server, 170
NFS (network file system)
  client, 171
  enabling, 170–173
  server, 172
nmap, 352–354

Novel GroupWise, 153
nUbuntu, 4
NVIDIA card, Open GL and, 262–263

O

Ogg Vorbis, support, 124
Open Office
  Calc, 180
  document viewers, 181
  Impress, 178–179
  oobase, 180
  oodraw, 180
  oomath, 180
  oowriter
    limitations, 178
    OpenDocument standard, 177
    PDF files, 176
    security, 177
  presentation viewers, 181
  spreadsheet viewers, 181–182
OpenGL, enabling, 260–263
optimization, modules, 69

P

packages
  APT, removing, 117–119
  dpkg (Debian Package Manager), 107
  faad, 124
  flashplugin-nonfree, 125
  font packages, 126–127
  gxine, 125
  lame, 124
  libdvdcss2, 124
  libxvidcore4, 124
  mjpegtools, 124
  realplayer, 125–126
  repositories
    main component, 106
    multiverse component, 106
    testricted component, 106
    universe component, 106
  RPM (RedHat Package Manager), 107
  source code, installing, 128–129

sox, 124
vorbis-tools, 124
w32codecs, 124
panels, GDM, 53
paper size, printers, 76
parameters, kernel, 226
    per user settings, 228–229
    RAM, 226–227
    shared memory, 227–228
partitions
    Qemu, 195
    VMware, 198
passwords, security and, 290
pinger, 43
plug-ins, Firefox
    adding, 143
    removing, 144
POP (Post Office Protocol) accounts, 153
Postfix, enabling, 369–372
primary clipboard, 242
printers
    HP JetDirect, 77
    IPP (CUPS printer), 77
    LPD (Unix Printer), 77
    paper size, 76
    sharing
        CUPS, 78
        LPD, 79–80
        Windows, 80–81
    SMB (Windows Printer), 77
proc directory, resources and, 212
processes, 205
    CPU, 213
    disk I/O, 214–215
    disk space, 213
    interception, 210
    killing, 208–211
    killing all, 211
    memory usage, 215–216
    network throughput, 217
    resources, 212–217
    running processses, 206–212
    services, 205

startups
    boot scripts, 218
    desktop scripts, 220–221
    devices, 218
    Gnome applications, 221–224
    network services, 218–219
    shell startup scripts, 219–220
    video memory, 216
projects, tracking
    CPU usage, 249–250
    disk usage, 250–254
    quotas, 250–254
    time, 247–249
prompt button, GDM, 51–53
properties, emblems, 57
proxies
    application-specific configurations, 339–341
    general system, 338–339
    SOCKS clients, 341–342
    Tor (The Onion Router), 342

Q
Qemu, 192–193
    partitions, 195
    Qemu VM
        installation, 193–194
        running, 194
quotas, 250
    editing, 252–253
    enabling, 251–252
    reporting, 253–254

R
racoon, 332
RAID (Redundant Array of Inexpensive Disks),
        configuration, 85
RAM, adding, 226–227
RAM disk, configuration, 13
rc directories, 70
RealPlayer, 125–126
realplayer package, 125–126
remapping keyboard, 51
removing, modules, 67–69

repositories
    CD-ROM, 115
        main component, 106
        multiverse component, 106
        restricted component, 106
        Synaptic, changing, 109
        universe component, 106
restricted component package repository, 106
rmmod command, 67–68
root, security and, 290
root disk, alternate, 13
rotating logs, 312–313
RPM (RedHat Package Manager), 107
run levels, 71
running processes, 206–212

S

SAMBA
    directories, sharing with Windows, 173
    file sharing, Windows directories, accessing,
        175–176
sane (Scanner Access Now Easy), 66
scanners, 99–101
schedulers
    at, 224
    anacron, 225
    cron, 224–225
screen, flipping, 258–259
screen resolution
    testing, 258
    xrandr, 257
screensaver
    new, 271–272
    switching, 269–274
scripting
    menus, Nautilus, 61–64
    security and, 290
searches
    APT, 116–117
    Firefox, 142–143
    Synaptic, 109
security
    defaults, 289–291
    GPG (Gnu Privacy Guard), 296

    e-mail integration, 304–305
    file encryption, 302–303
    key creation, 296–298
    key searches, 299
    signing data, 303
    transferring keys, 299–300
    trust, 300–302
network services and, 290
networks
    firewalls, IP tables and, 328–331
    firewalls, tcpwrappers and, 326–328
    IPsec, enabling, 332
    IPsec, key creation, 333–338
passwords and, 290
proxies, general system, 338–339
root and, 290
scripts and, 290
software sources and, 290
Sudo, 292
    options, 294–295
    root, 295
    users, 293–294
VNC viewer, 188–189
wireless networks, WPA (Wi-Fi Protected
    Access), 325–326
xrandr, 258
serial mouse, 88–89
server, installation, 6–9
Server CD-ROM installation, 6, 11–13
servers, netstat and, 351
services
    Apache, 372–377
    FTP, enabling, 365–369
    netstat, 350–352
    nmap, 352–354
    Postfix, 369–372
    running, SSH hardening, 361–365
services-admin, boot options and, 71
sharing
    desktop, 185–187
    memory, modifying, 227–228
    printers
        CUPS, 78
        LPD, 79–80
        Windows, 80–81

skins, GDM, 54–56
Skype, 164
SMP (symmetric multiprocessing), 73–75
SOCKS clients, enabling, 341–342
software emulators, 189
source code
    downloading, reasons for, 127–128
    installing, 128–129
SourceForge, 105
sox, 34–35
    audio files, 36
sox package, 124
SSH (Secure Shell), 146
    ciphers, 153
    Dante server, 150
    debugging connections, 364–365
    keys, 363–364
    ports, opening, 149
    proxies, starting, 149–151
    server, installation, 147–148
    SOCKS server, testing, 151
    SOCKS server proxy, 147
    tunnel, 147
        establishing, 151–152
startup music, changing, 33–36
static USB devices, 91–93
stretching icons, 59–60
Sudo, 292
    options, 294–295
    root, 295
    users, 293–294
switching applications, 233
    Alt+Tab, 235
    Ctrl+Alt+Tab, 236
    Firefox tabs, 236–237
    Window List, 234–235
    Window Selector, 234–235
Synaptic
    installation, from CD-ROM or directory,
        110–111
    repositories, changing, 109
    searches, 109
    starting, 108
    updates, 111–112
synchronization, clock, 167–168

SYSLINUX, 22
sysv-rc-conf, boot options and, 71–73

T
telco, 43
templates, Nautilus, 61
temporary files, clearing, 309–310
themes, GDM, 54–56
thumb drives. See USB drives
Thunderbird mail, 162–163
TiVo, 97
Tor (The Onion Router), 342
touch pad, support, 89–90
tracking projects
    CPU usage, 249–250
    disk usage, 250–254
    quotas, 250–254
    time, 247–249
ttf (TrueType fonts), 126
TV cards, tuning, 97–99

U
Ubuntu Dapper Drake 6.06 LTS, CD-ROM
        options, 6–7
universe component package repository, 106
update-flashplugin command, 125
updates, Synaptic, 111–112
upgrades, 29–31
    APT and, 120
    drives, 81–83
USB drives
    associating applications, 93–94
    boot image and, 22–23
    booting from, 19–21
        configuring, 20–21
        variations, 27–29
    configuration, 90–94
    file sharing, 18–19
    formatting, 17–18
    hard drives, 19
    large, 19
    network installation and, 21–22
    small, 19
    static devices, 91–93

V

video
    drivers, changing, 260
    memory, 216
    support, 124
virtual disks, 191
virtualizers, 190
VMware, 196–198
VNC
    emulation and, 192
    VM and, 192
VNC viewer, 184–185
    security, 188–189
VoIP, 164–165
vorbis-tools package, 124

W

Wacom tablet
    debugging, 95–96
    tuning, 96–97
w32codecs package, 124
web, support, installing, 125–126
Web caches, erasing, 311
webcams, 99–101
WengoPhone, 164
WEP (Wireless Equivalent Privacy), 324
Window List, switching applications, 234–235
Window Selector, switching applications, 234–235
Windows
    fonts, 127
    printer sharing, 80–81
windows
    applications, Devil's Pie, 240–242
    custom, 238–242
        X-Windows, 239–240
    X-Windows, 239–240
wireless networks
    configuration
        drivers, 318, 319
        ndiswrapper, 319–322

        tools, 322–324
        WEP (Wireless Equivalent Privacy), 324
    security, WPA (Wi-Fi Protected Access), 325–326
Workplace Switcher, 237
    Workspace Switcher
        Ctrl+Alt+Arrows, 237
        preferences, 237–238
workstation, installation, 6–9
WPA (Wi-Fi Protected Access), 325–326

X

X11 graphic library, 130
X-Windows
    custom windows, 239–240
    debugging, 263–264
    keycodes, 48
    keysyms, 48
xawtv, 99
xclip, 243
Xen, 198–200
xfonts, 126
Xine, 125
xmodmap command, 51
Xorg.conf, mouse, 89
xrandr, 257
    security and, 258
    uses for, 259–260
xresprobe, 256
xscreensaver, 269
Xubuntu, 4
xvidtune, 265–267

Y

Yahoo!
    fetchyahoo, 158
    YPOPs, 158

Z

zlib library, 130
zombies, 209